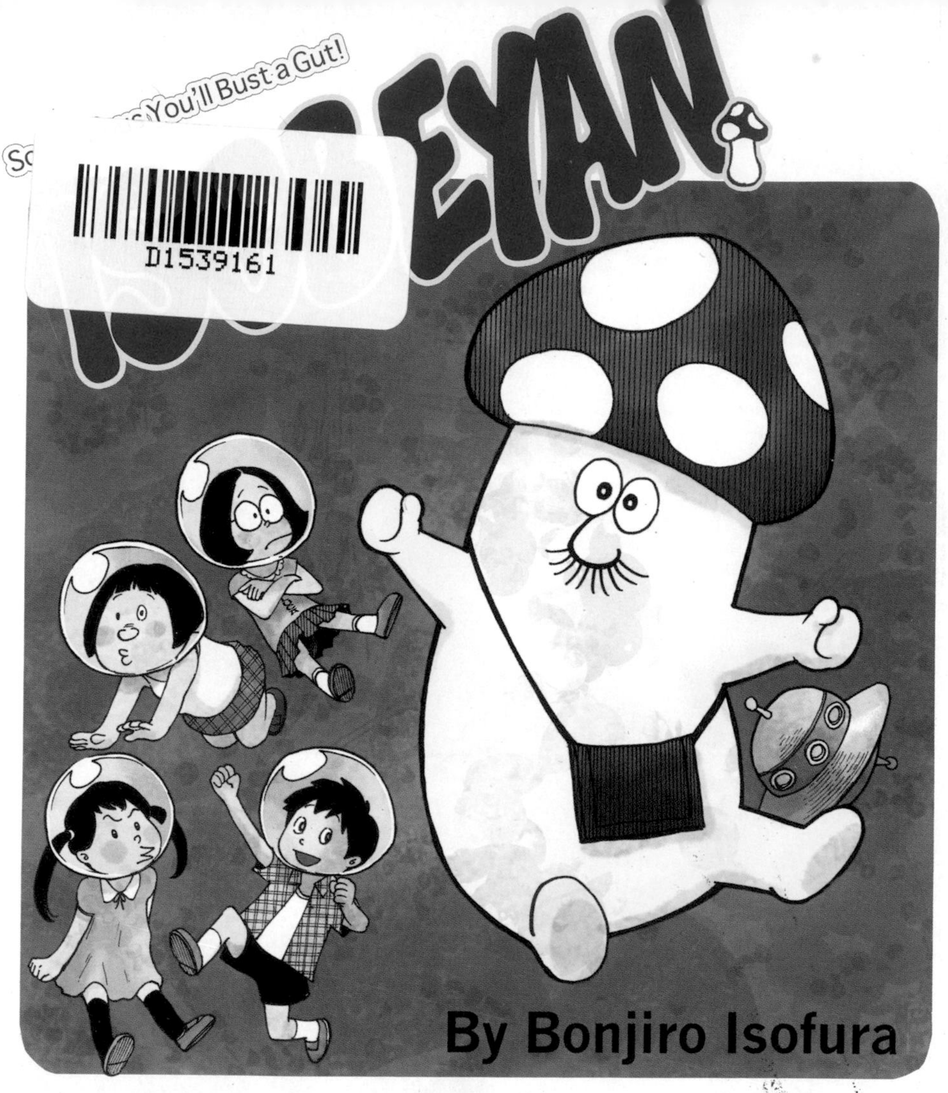
You'll Bust a Gut!
By Bonjiro Isofura

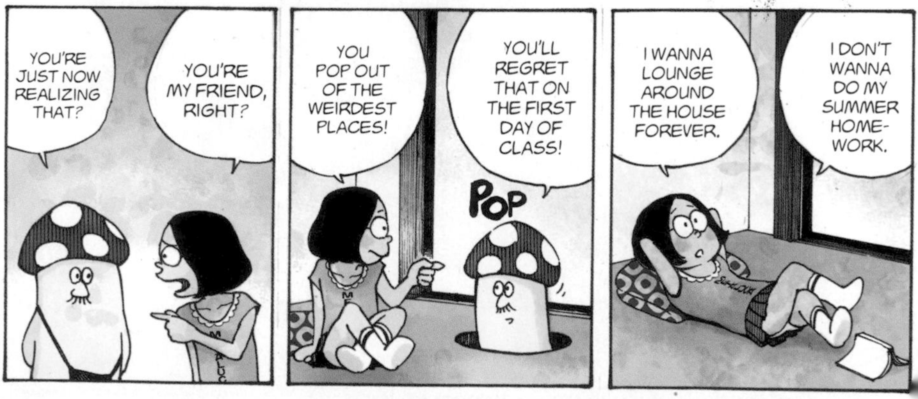
I DON'T WANNA DO MY SUMMER HOME-WORK.
I WANNA LOUNGE AROUND THE HOUSE FOREVER.
YOU'LL REGRET THAT ON THE FIRST DAY OF CLASS!
POP
YOU POP OUT OF THE WEIRDEST PLACES!
YOU'RE MY FRIEND, RIGHT?
YOU'RE JUST NOW REALIZING THAT?

●Chapter 52: Brain Bulb?!●

☆ My mom and dad and I all laugh together as we read Isobeyan. (Shunsuke Motegi, Saitama Prefecture)

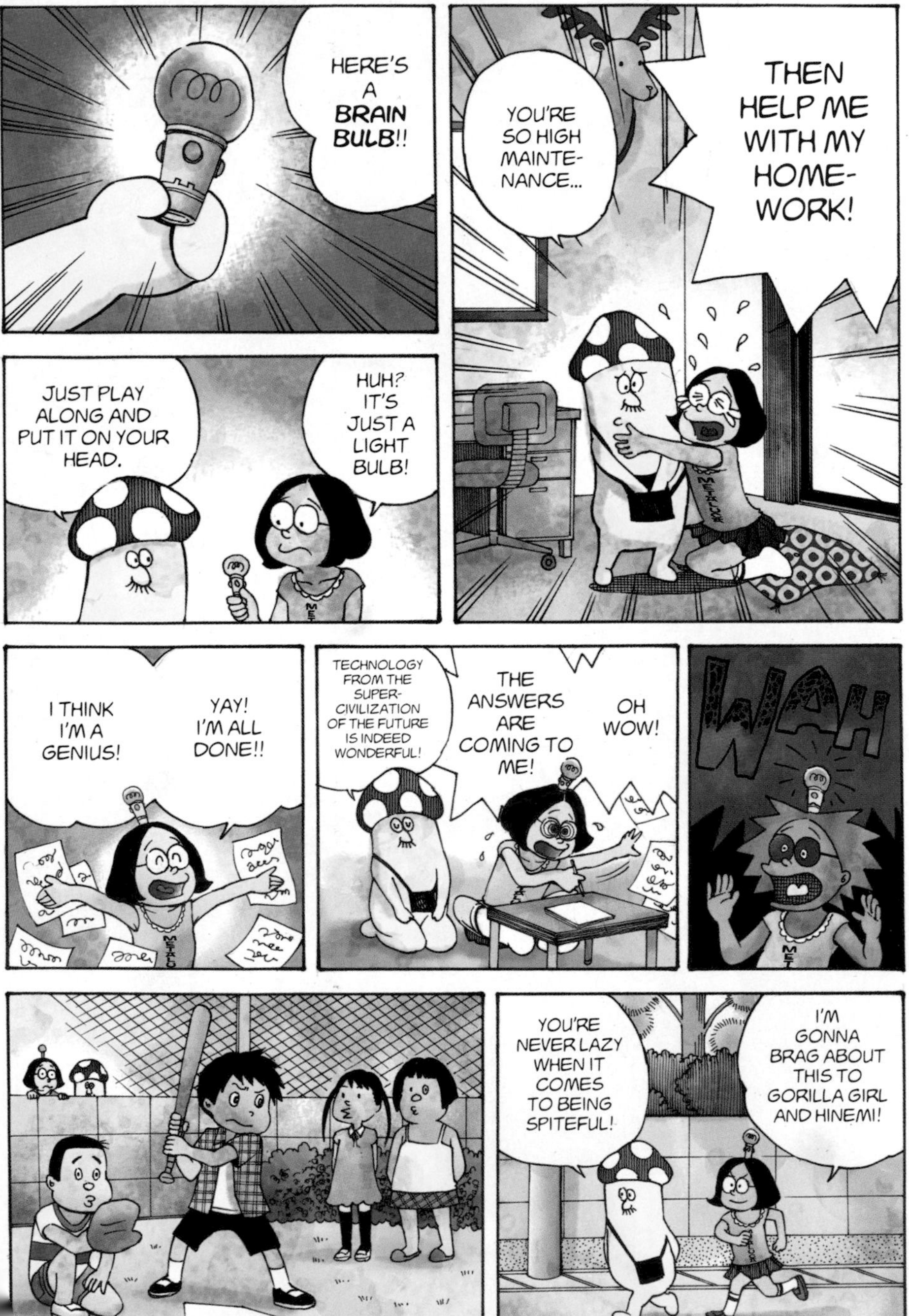
THEN HELP ME WITH MY HOME-WORK!
YOU'RE SO HIGH MAINTE-NANCE...
HERE'S A **BRAIN BULB**!!
HUH? IT'S JUST A LIGHT BULB!
JUST PLAY ALONG AND PUT IT ON YOUR HEAD.
WAH
OH WOW!
THE ANSWERS ARE COMING TO ME!
TECHNOLOGY FROM THE SUPER-CIVILIZATION OF THE FUTURE IS INDEED WONDERFUL!
YAY! I'M ALL DONE!!
I THINK I'M A GENIUS!
I'M GONNA BRAG ABOUT THIS TO GORILLA GIRL AND HINEMI!
YOU'RE NEVER LAZY WHEN IT COMES TO BEING SPITEFUL!

SUPER-POPULAR MASTERPIECE COMEDY **ISOBEYAN**

☆ Bonjiro Isofura, the creator of *Isobeyan*, is waiting for your letters. So send 'em in!

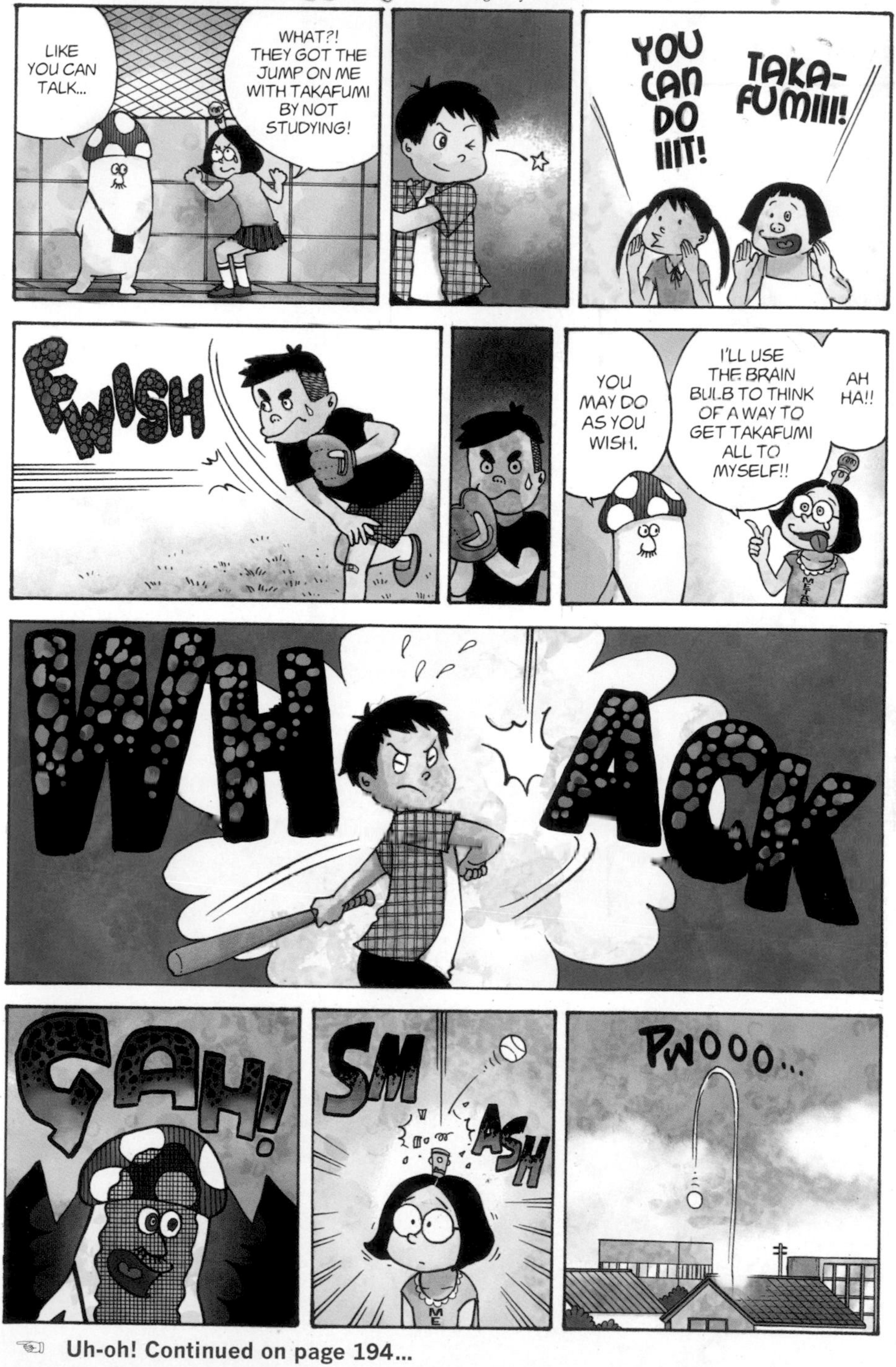
TAKA-FUMIIII!
YOU CAN DO IIIT!
WHAT?! THEY GOT THE JUMP ON ME WITH TAKAFUMI BY NOT STUDYING!
LIKE YOU CAN TALK...
AH HA!!
I'LL USE THE BRAIN BULB TO THINK OF A WAY TO GET TAKAFUMI ALL TO MYSELF!!
YOU MAY DO AS YOU WISH.
FWISH
WHACK
PWOOO...
SMASH
GAH!

Uh-oh! Continued on page 194...

DEAD DEAD DEMON'S DEDE DEDE DESTRUCTION

1

Chapter 1	005
Chapter 2	043
Chapter 3	067
Chapter 4	087
Chapter 5	105
Chapter 6	123
Extra	141
Chapter 7	157
Chapter 8	175

CHAPTER 1

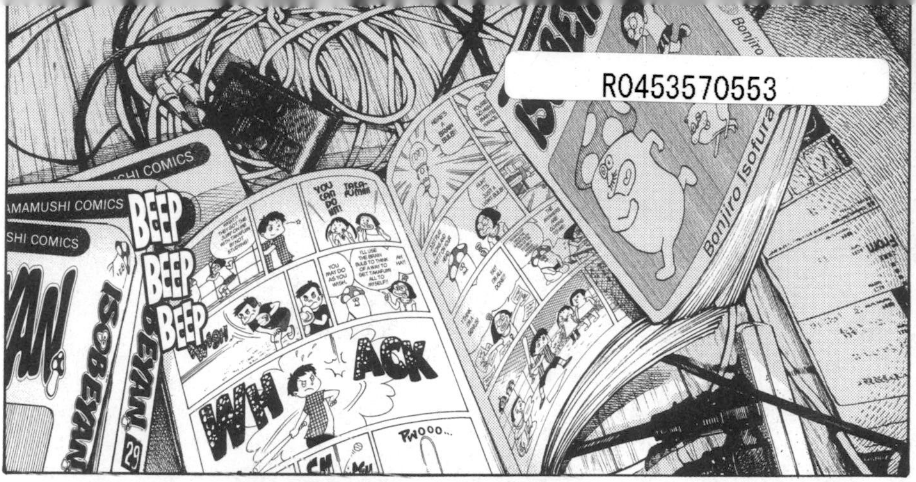
BEEP
BEEP
BEEP
WH ACK
Bonjiro Isofura

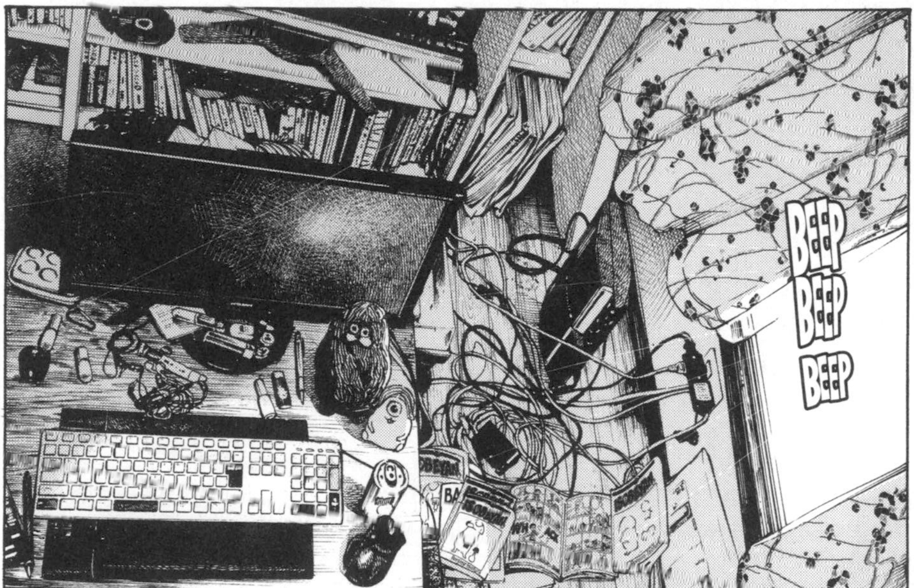
BEEP
BEEP
BEEP

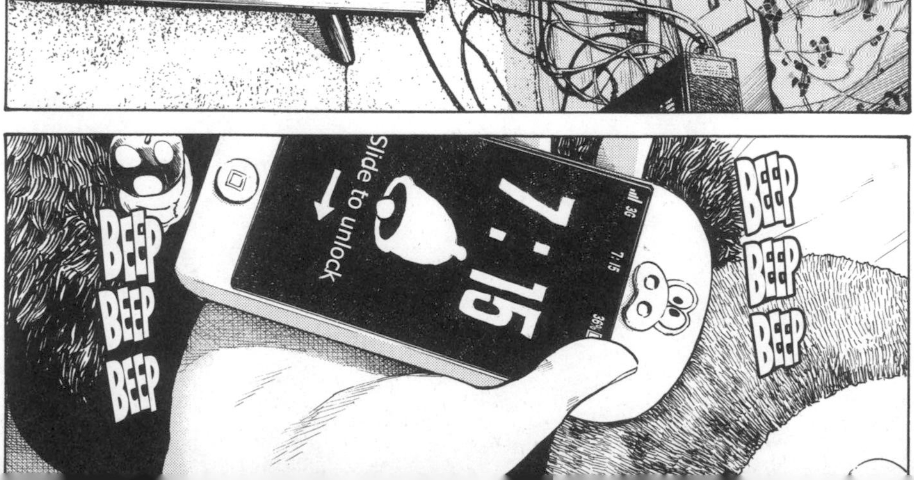
BEEP
BEEP
BEEP
7:15
Slide to unlock
BEEP
BEEP
BEEP

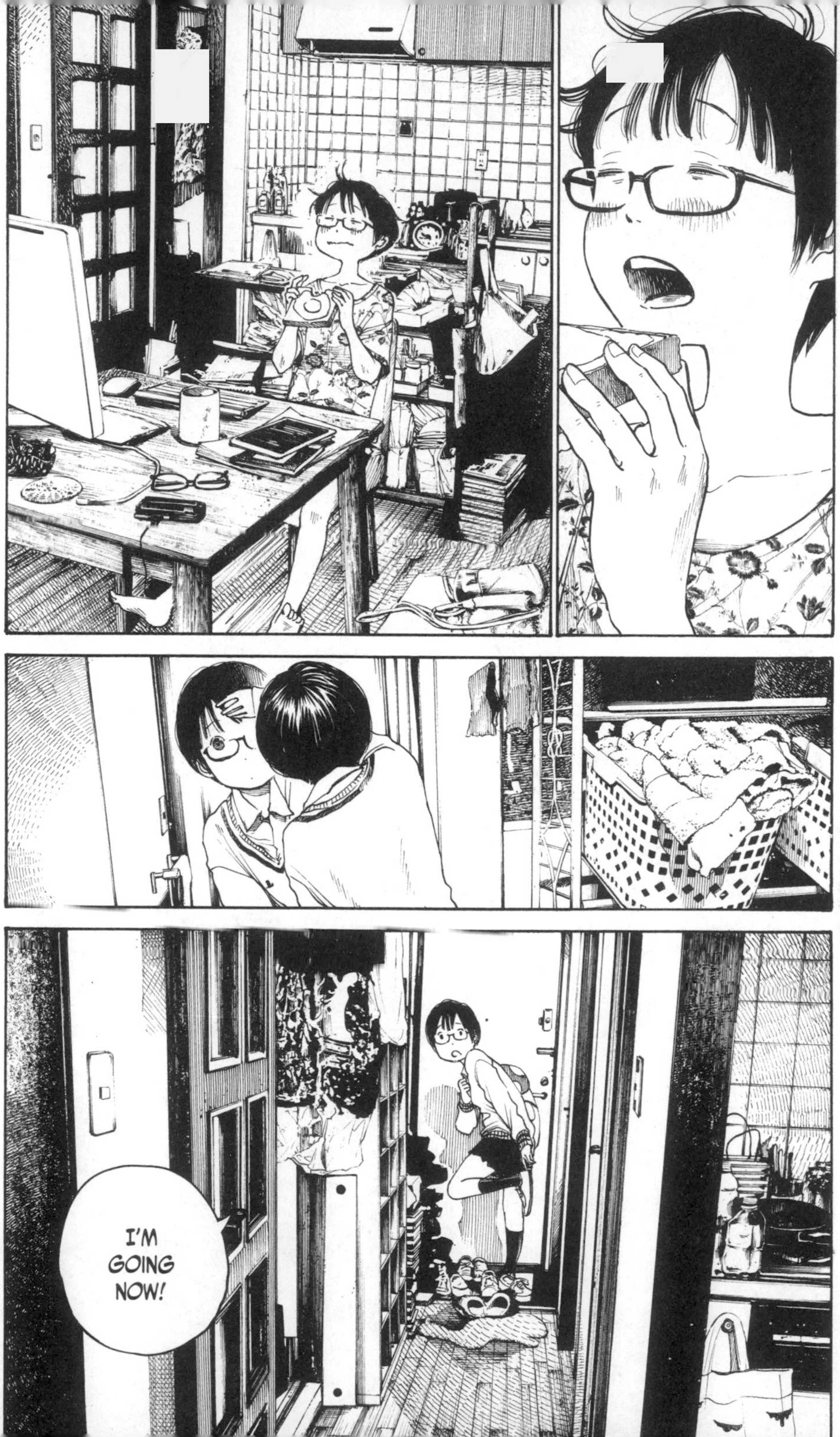
I'M GOING NOW!

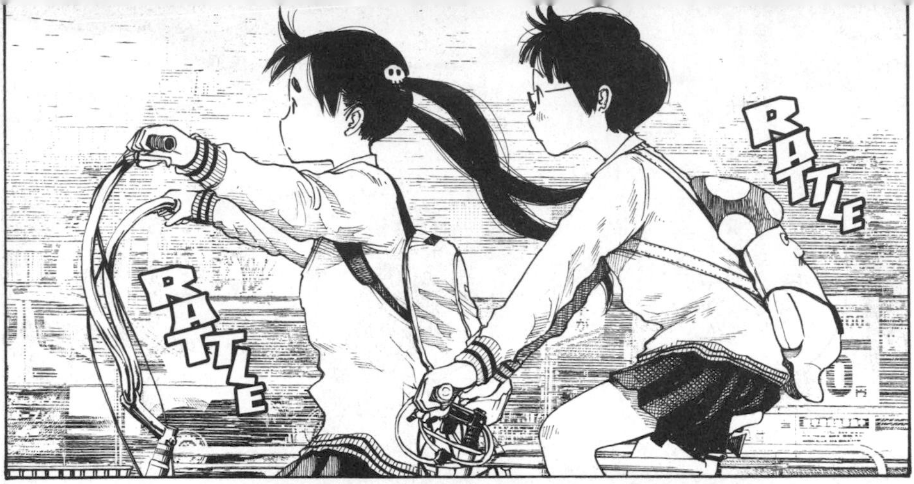
RATTLE
RATTLE

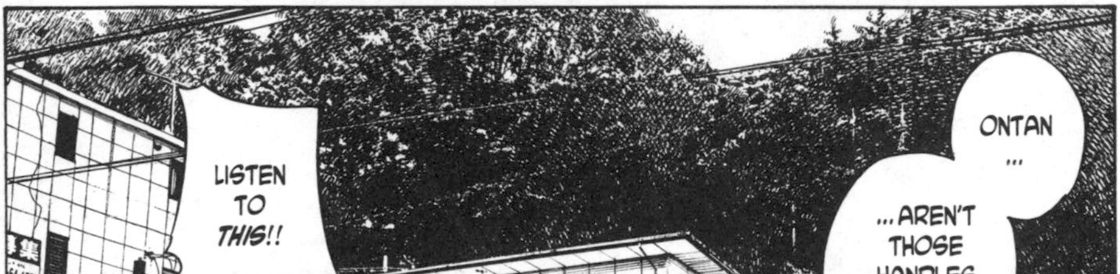
ONTAN ...
...AREN'T THOSE HANDLES HARD TO USE?
LISTEN TO *THIS!!*
I READ IT ON THE INTERNET YESTERDAY!!
RATTLE
RATTLE
RATTLE
有料駐車場
有料駐車場

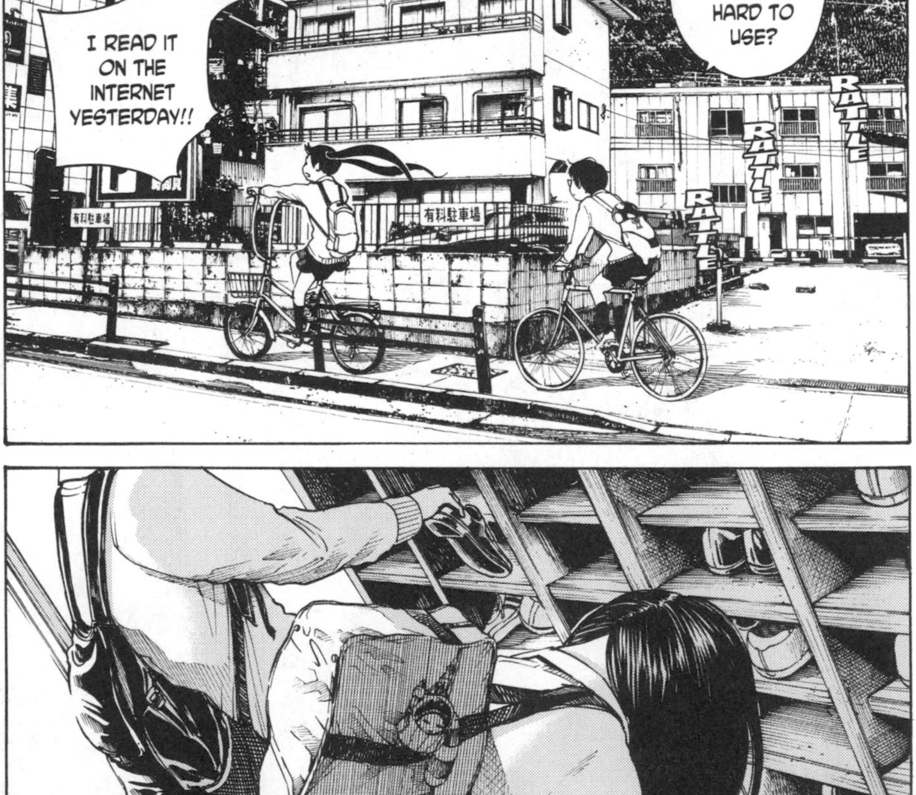

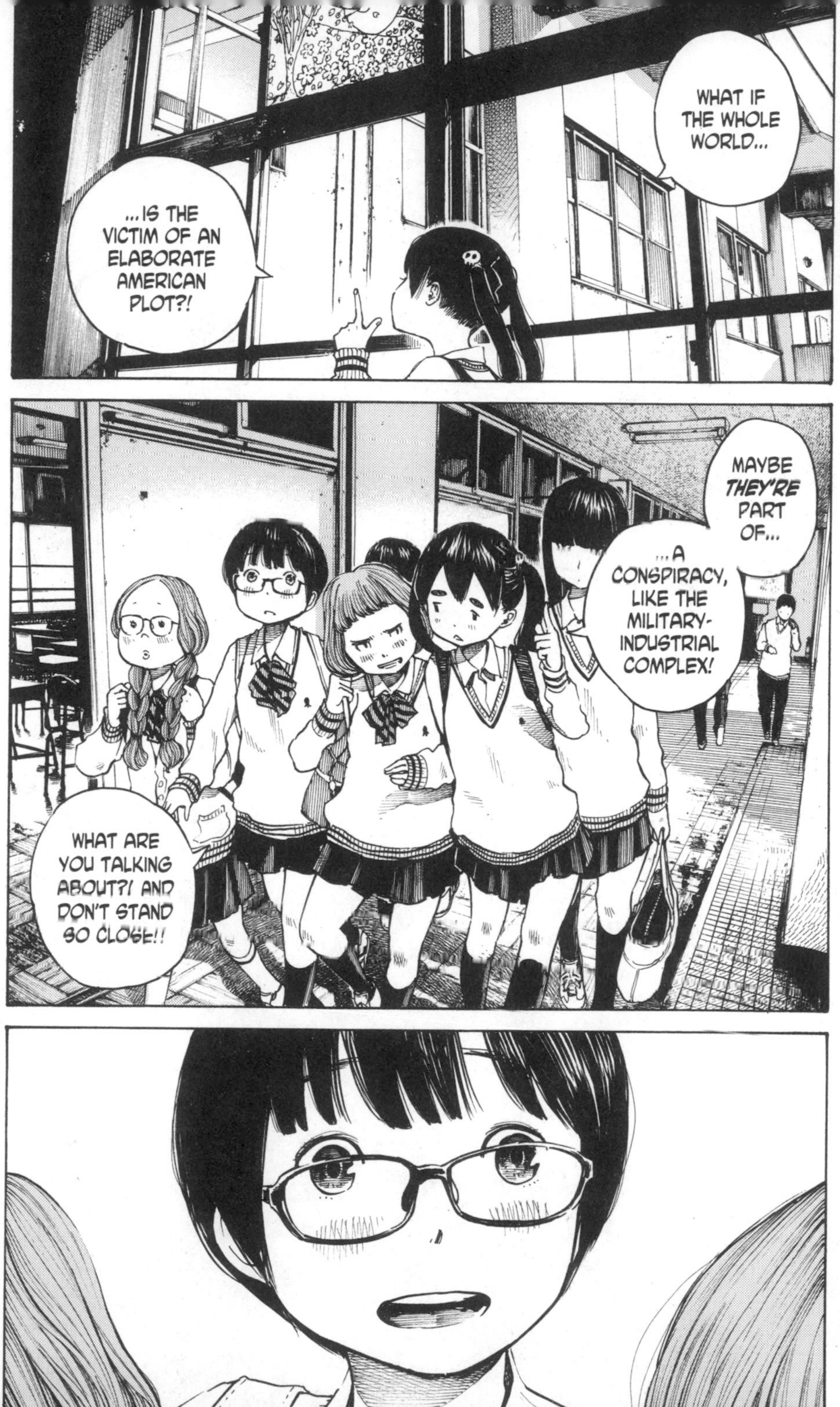
WHAT IF THE WHOLE WORLD...
...IS THE VICTIM OF AN ELABORATE AMERICAN PLOT?!
MAYBE *THEY'RE* PART OF...
...A CONSPIRACY, LIKE THE MILITARY-INDUSTRIAL COMPLEX!
WHAT ARE YOU TALKING ABOUT?! AND DON'T STAND SO CLOSE!!

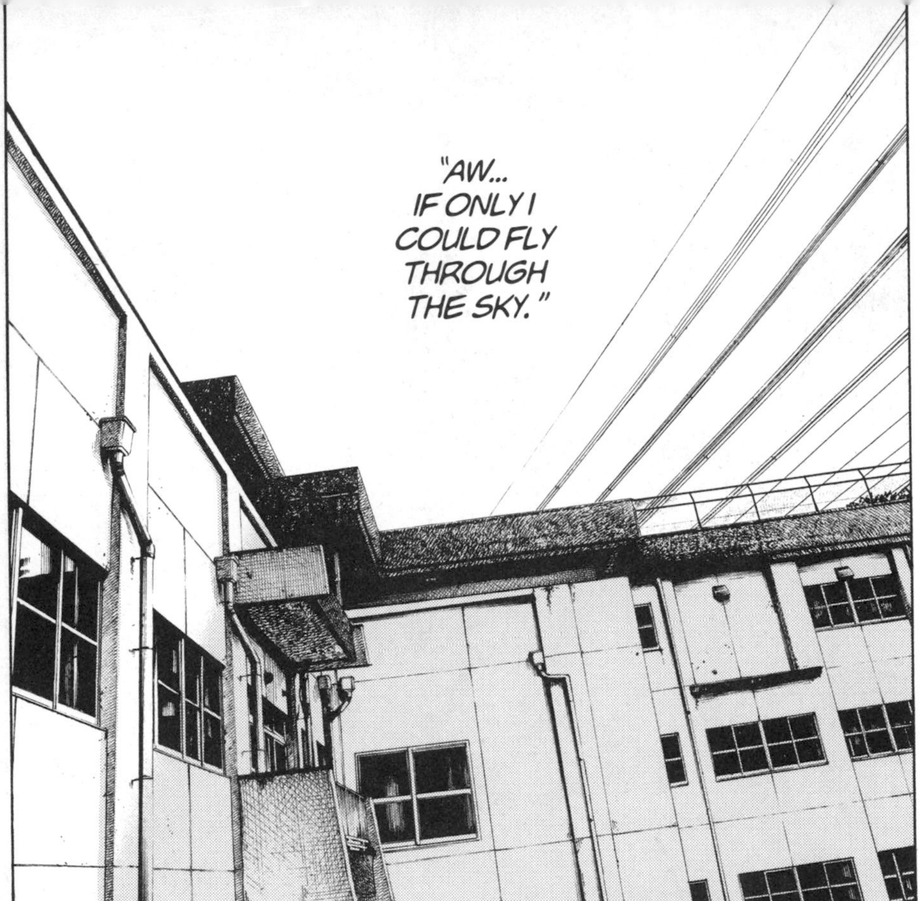
"AW... IF ONLY I COULD FLY THROUGH THE SKY."

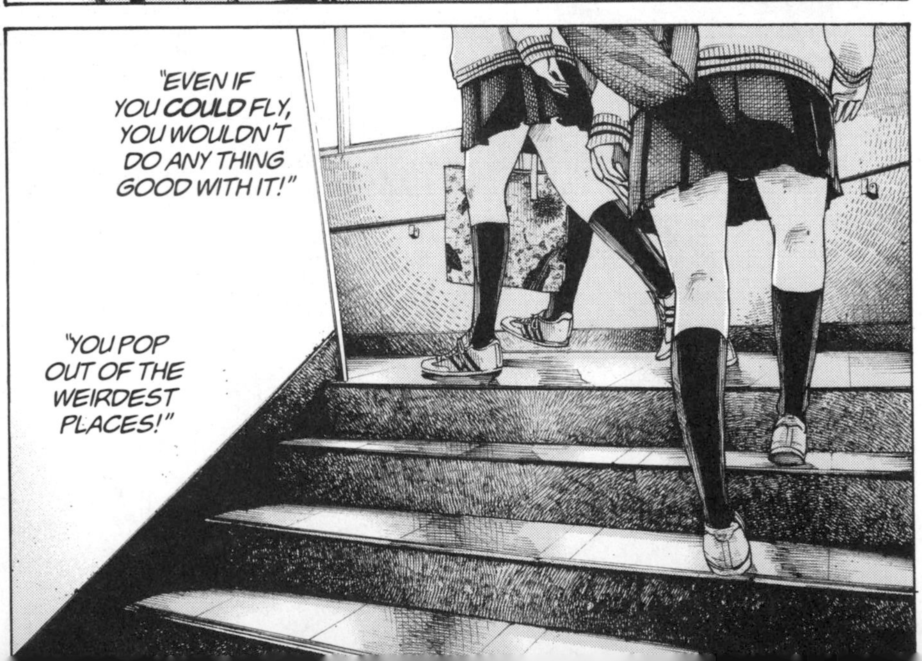
"EVEN IF YOU **COULD** FLY, YOU WOULDN'T DO ANY THING GOOD WITH IT!"
"YOU POP OUT OF THE WEIRDEST PLACES!"

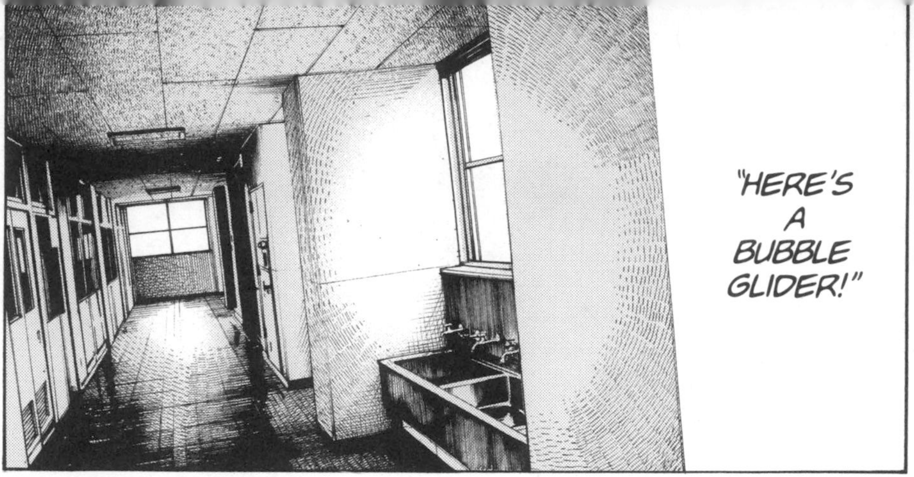
"HERE'S A BUBBLE GLIDER!"

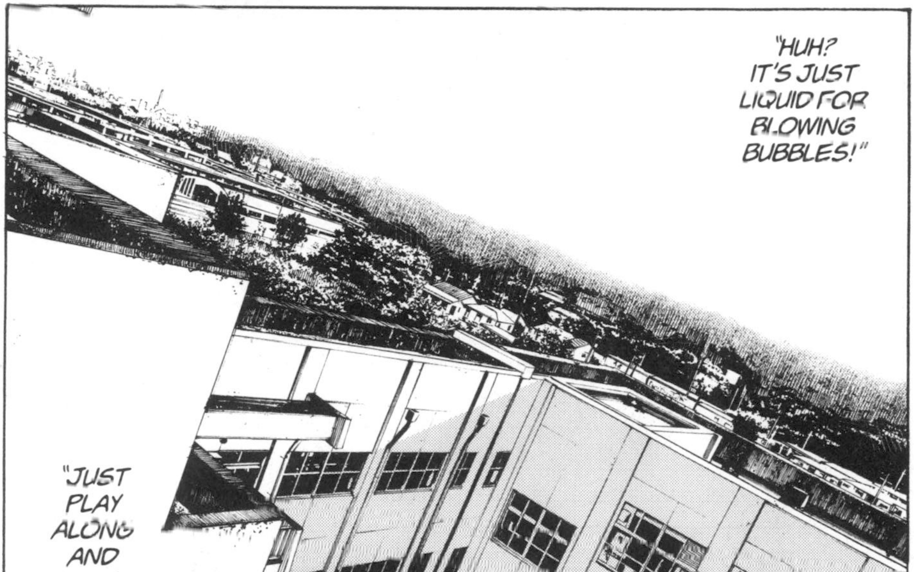
"HUH? IT'S JUST LIQUID FOR BLOWING BUBBLES!"
"JUST PLAY ALONG AND BLOW A BUBBLE."

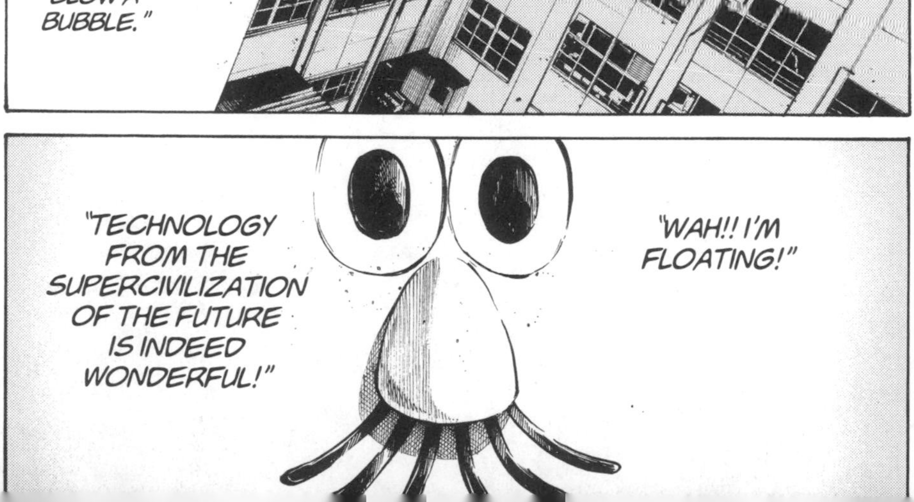
"WAH!! I'M FLOATING!"
"TECHNOLOGY FROM THE SUPERCIVILIZATION OF THE FUTURE IS INDEED WONDERFUL!"

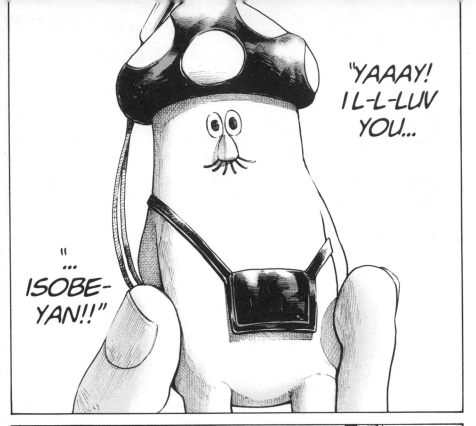

"YAAAY! I L-L-LUV YOU...

"...ISOBE-YAN!!"

HEY...

KADODE KOYAMA!!

GASP!

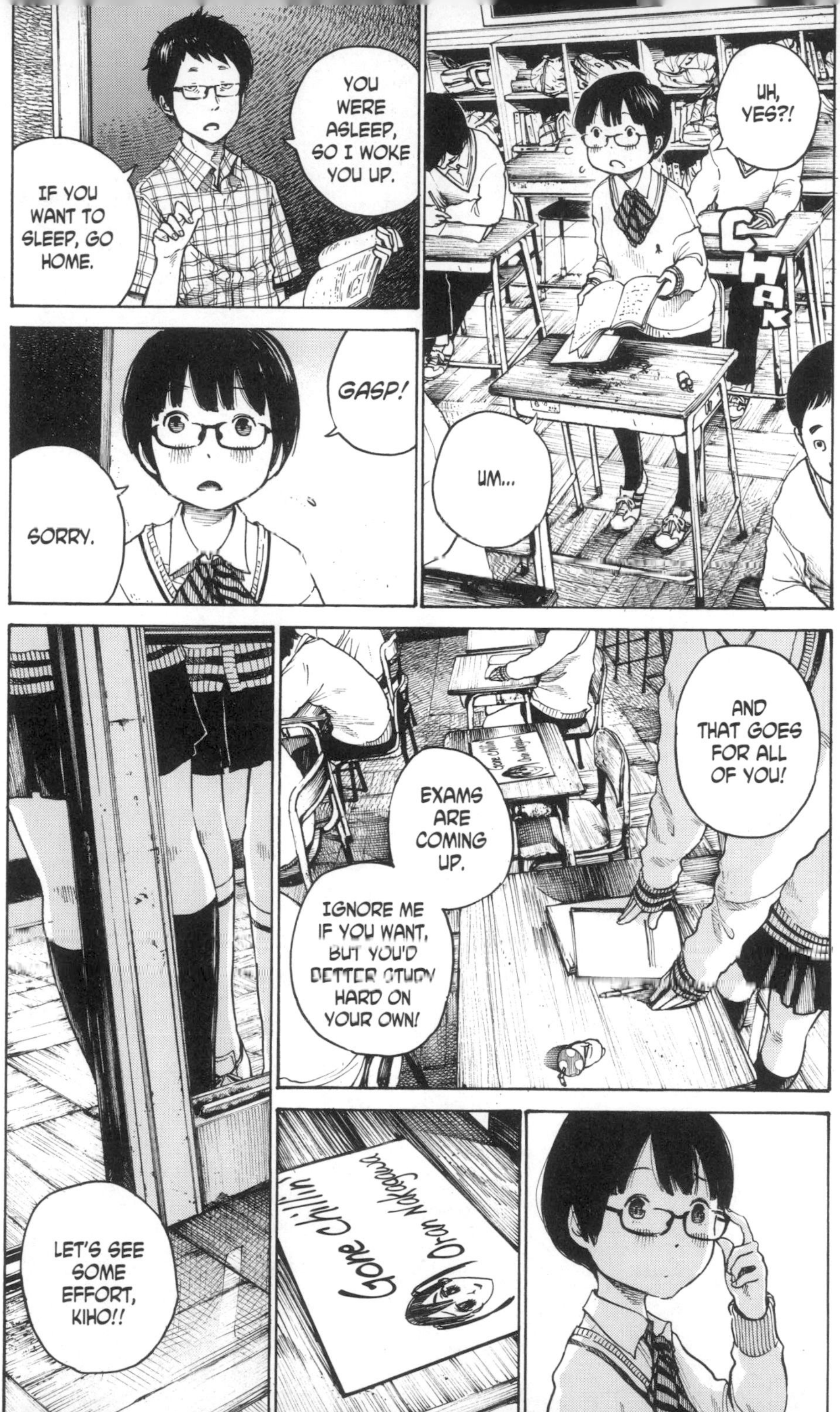
UH, YES?!
CHAK
UM...
YOU WERE ASLEEP, SO I WOKE YOU UP.
IF YOU WANT TO SLEEP, GO HOME.
GASP!
SORRY.
AND THAT GOES FOR ALL OF YOU!
EXAMS ARE COMING UP.
IGNORE ME IF YOU WANT, BUT YOU'D BETTER STUDY HARD ON YOUR OWN!
Gone Chillin'
Oran Nakagawa
LET'S SEE SOME EFFORT, KIHO!!

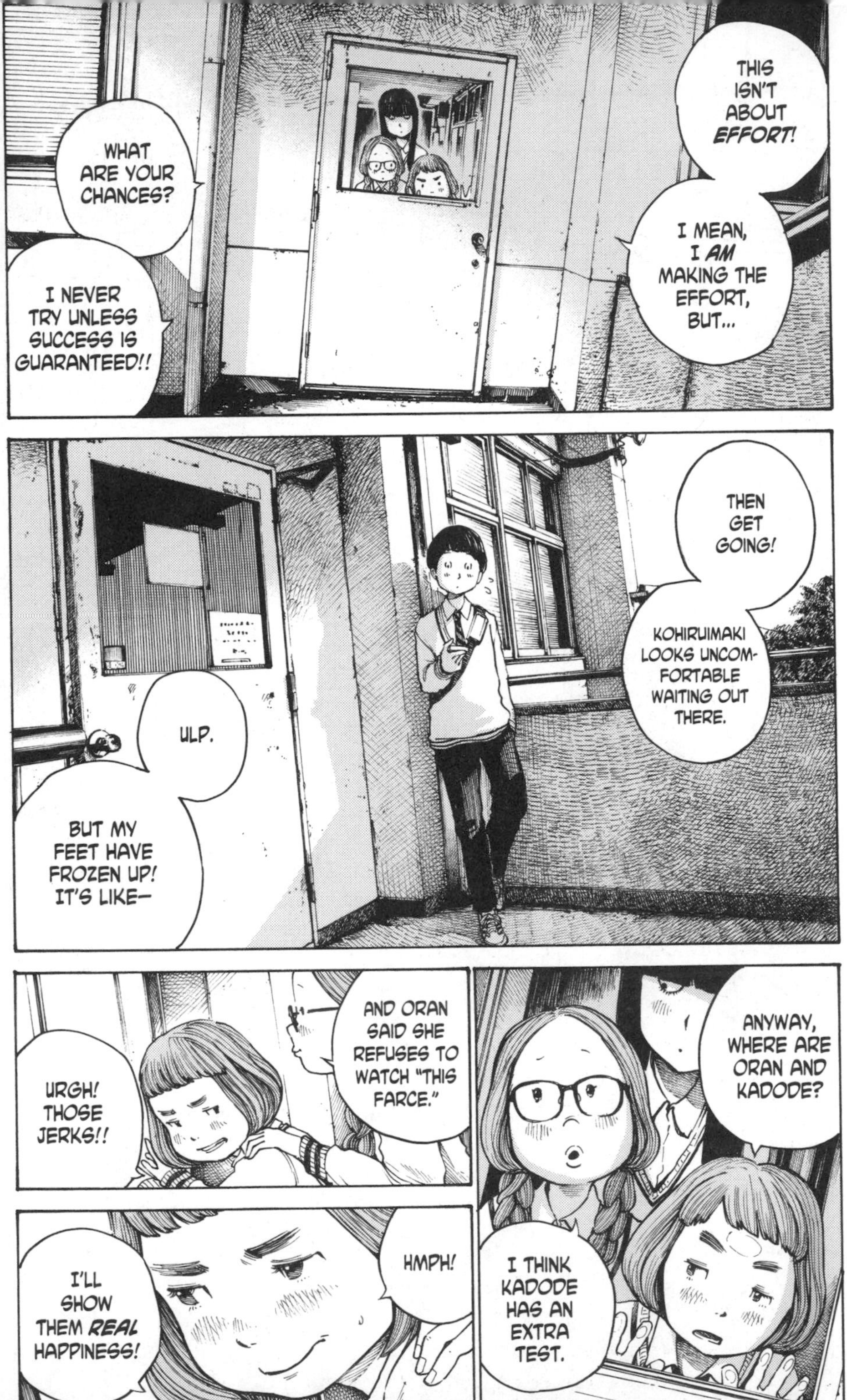
THIS ISN'T ABOUT *EFFORT*!
I MEAN, I *AM* MAKING THE EFFORT, BUT...
WHAT ARE YOUR CHANCES?
I NEVER TRY UNLESS SUCCESS IS GUARANTEED!!
THEN GET GOING!
KOHIRUIMAKI LOOKS UNCOM-FORTABLE WAITING OUT THERE.
ULP.
BUT MY FEET HAVE FROZEN UP! IT'S LIKE—
ANYWAY, WHERE ARE ORAN AND KADODE?
I THINK KADODE HAS AN EXTRA TEST.
AND ORAN SAID SHE REFUSES TO WATCH "THIS FARCE."
URGH! THOSE JERKS!!
HMPH!
I'LL SHOW THEM *REAL* HAPPINESS!

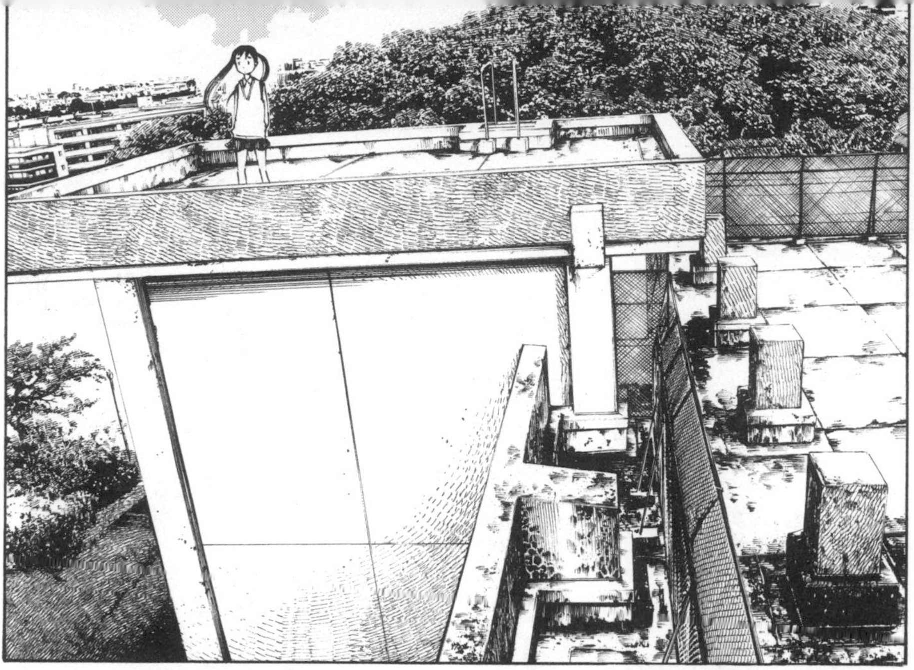
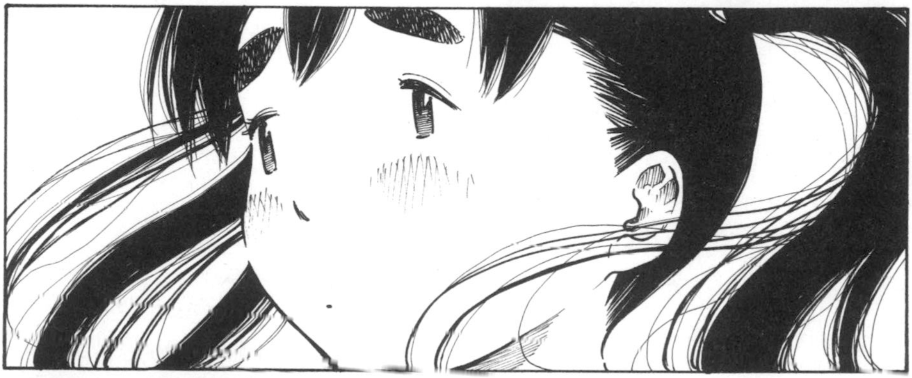
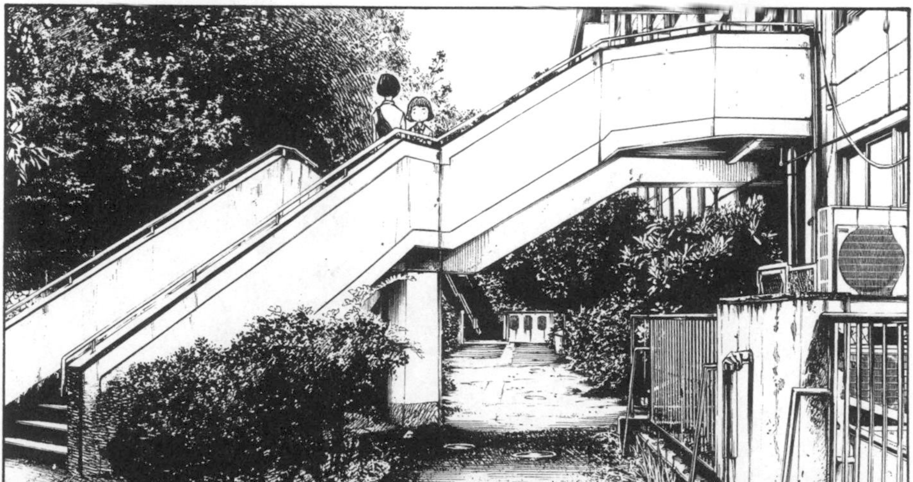

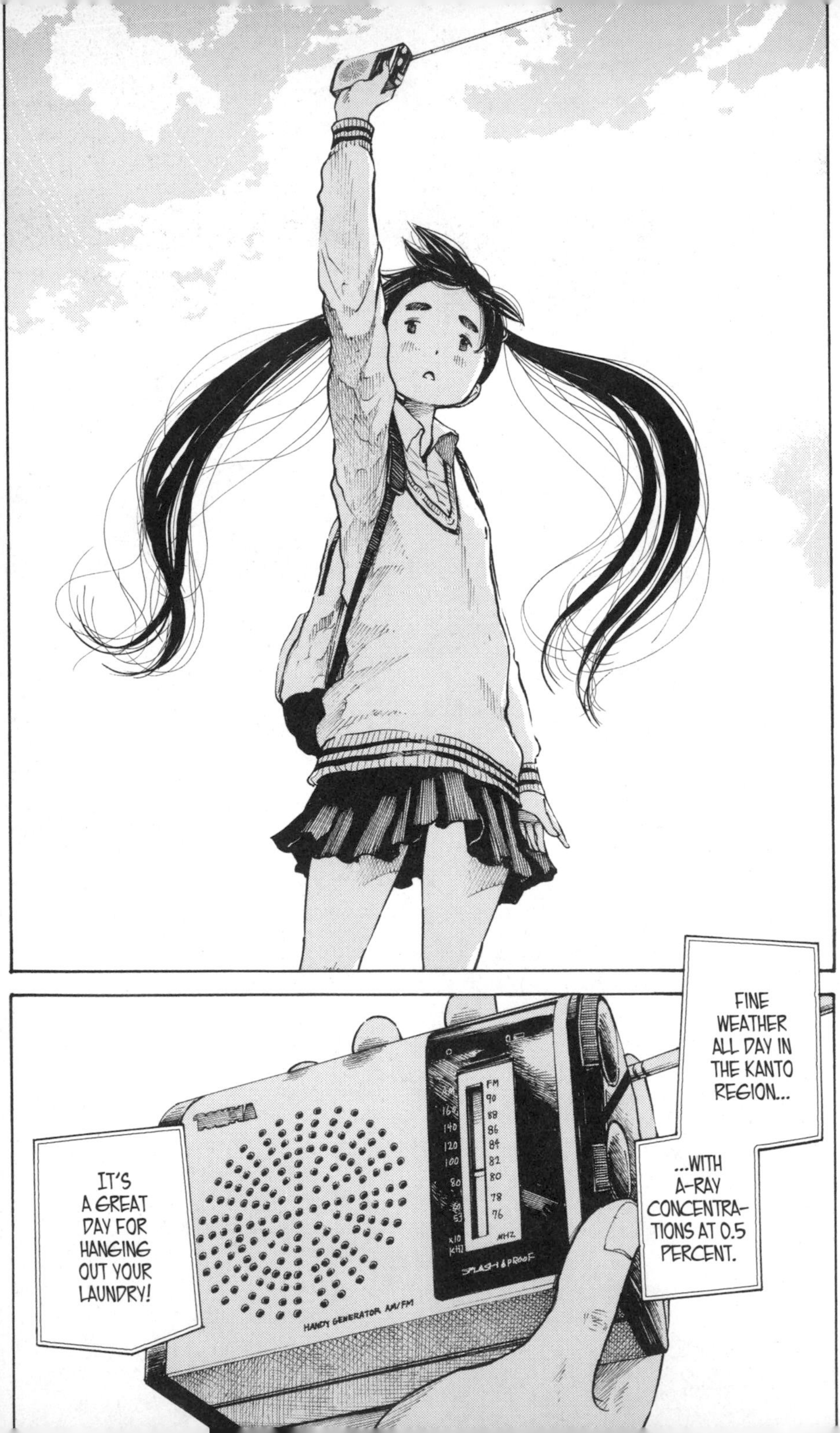
FINE WEATHER ALL DAY IN THE KANTO REGION...
...WITH A-RAY CONCENTRATIONS AT 0.5 PERCENT.
IT'S A GREAT DAY FOR HANGING OUT YOUR LAUNDRY!
HANDY GENERATOR AM/FM
SPLASH PROOF

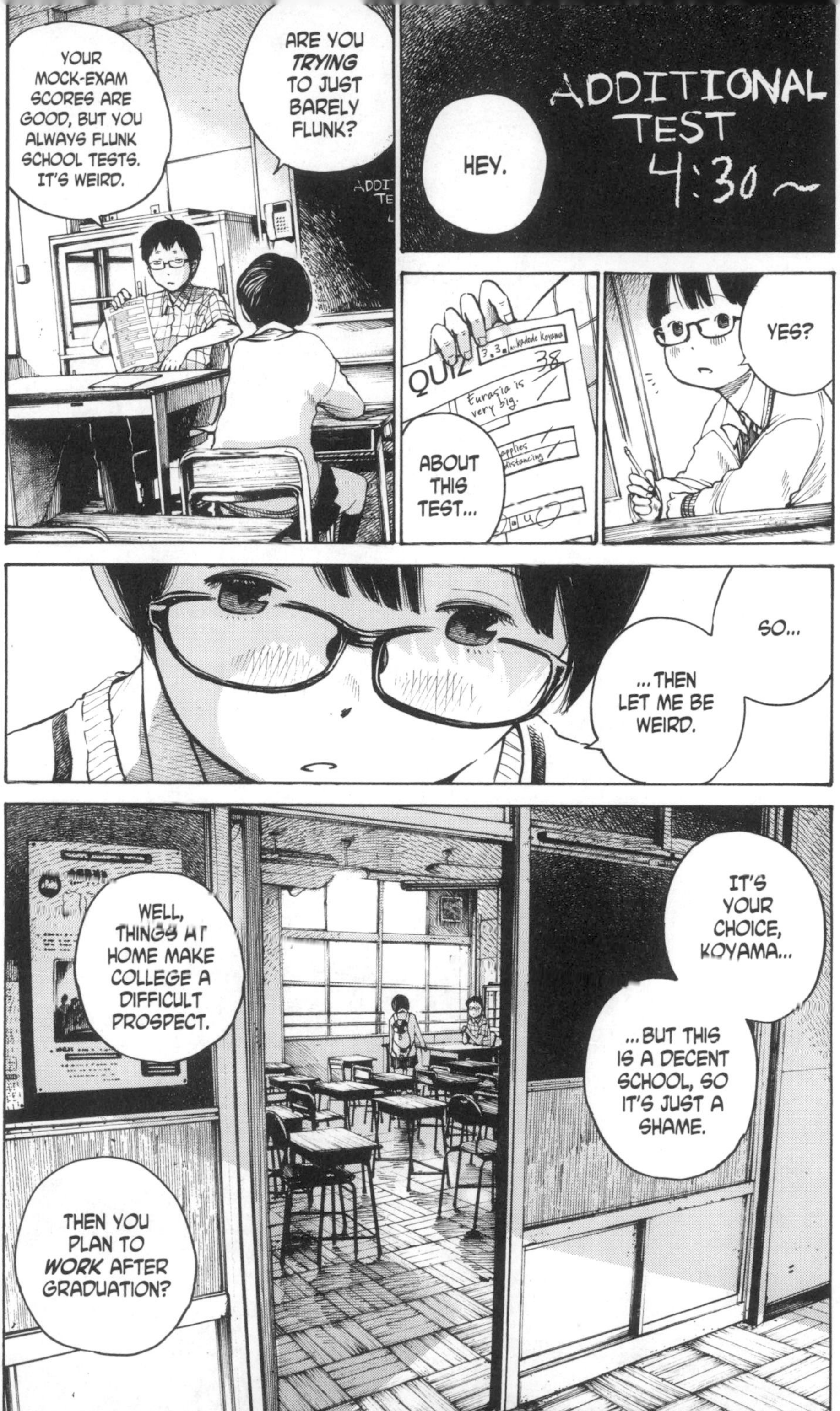
ADDITIONAL TEST 4:30 ~
HEY.
YES?
QUIZ
Kadode Koyama
38
Eurasia is very big.
ABOUT THIS TEST...
YOUR MOCK-EXAM SCORES ARE GOOD, BUT YOU ALWAYS FLUNK SCHOOL TESTS. IT'S WEIRD.
ARE YOU *TRYING* TO JUST BARELY FLUNK?
SO...
...THEN LET ME BE WEIRD.
IT'S YOUR CHOICE, KOYAMA...
...BUT THIS IS A DECENT SCHOOL, SO IT'S JUST A SHAME.
WELL, THINGS AT HOME MAKE COLLEGE A DIFFICULT PROSPECT.
THEN YOU PLAN TO *WORK* AFTER GRADUATION?

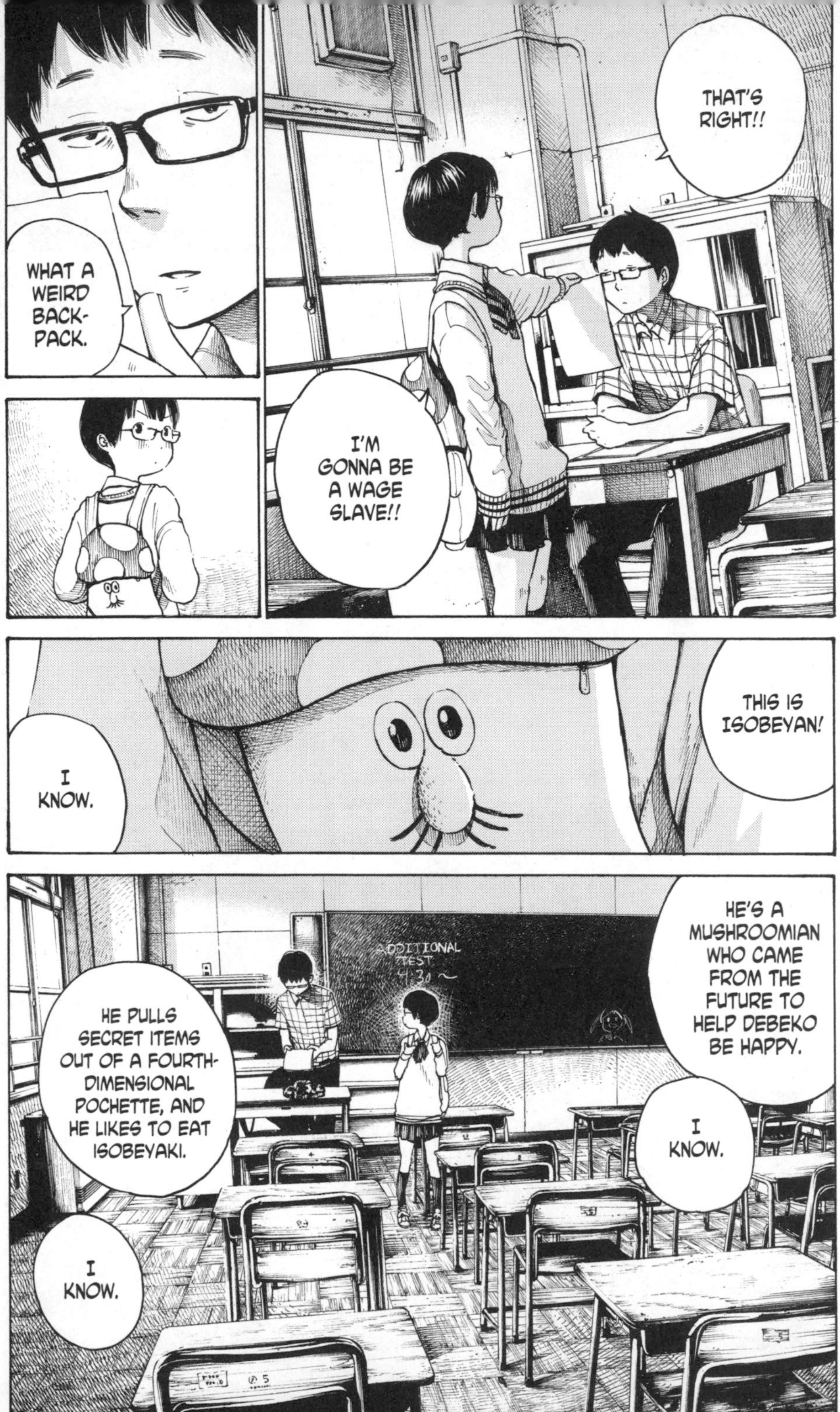

THAT'S RIGHT!!
I'M GONNA BE A WAGE SLAVE!!
WHAT A WEIRD BACK-PACK.
THIS IS ISOBEYAN!
I KNOW.
HE'S A MUSHROOMIAN WHO CAME FROM THE FUTURE TO HELP DEBEKO BE HAPPY.
I KNOW.
HE PULLS SECRET ITEMS OUT OF A FOURTH-DIMENSIONAL POCHETTE, AND HE LIKES TO EAT ISOBEYAKI.
I KNOW.
ADDITIONAL TEST 4:30 ~

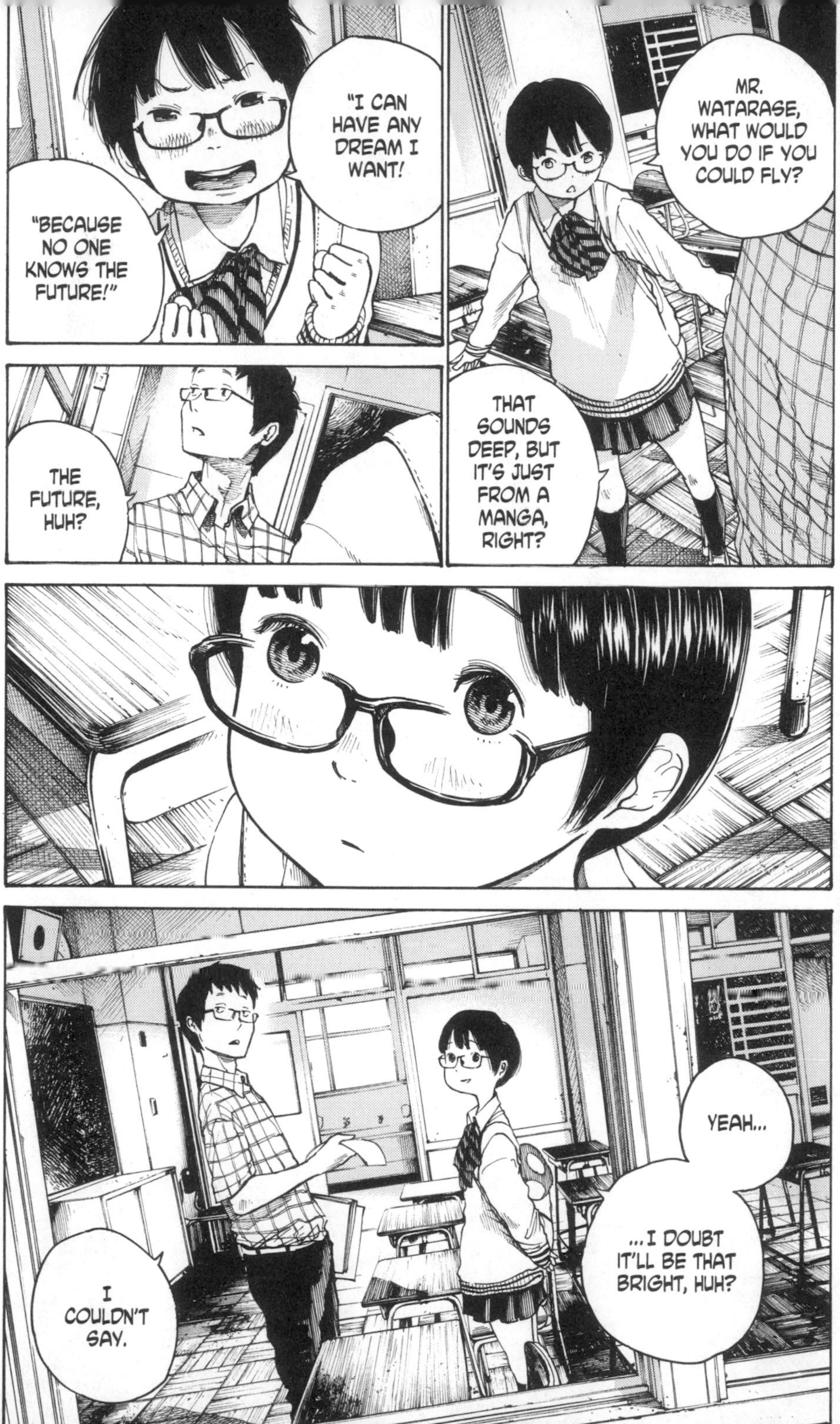
MR. WATARASE, WHAT WOULD YOU DO IF YOU COULD FLY?
THAT SOUNDS DEEP, BUT IT'S JUST FROM A MANGA, RIGHT?
"I CAN HAVE ANY DREAM I WANT!
"BECAUSE NO ONE KNOWS THE FUTURE!"
THE FUTURE, HUH?
YEAH...
...I DOUBT IT'LL BE THAT BRIGHT, HUH?
I COULDN'T SAY.

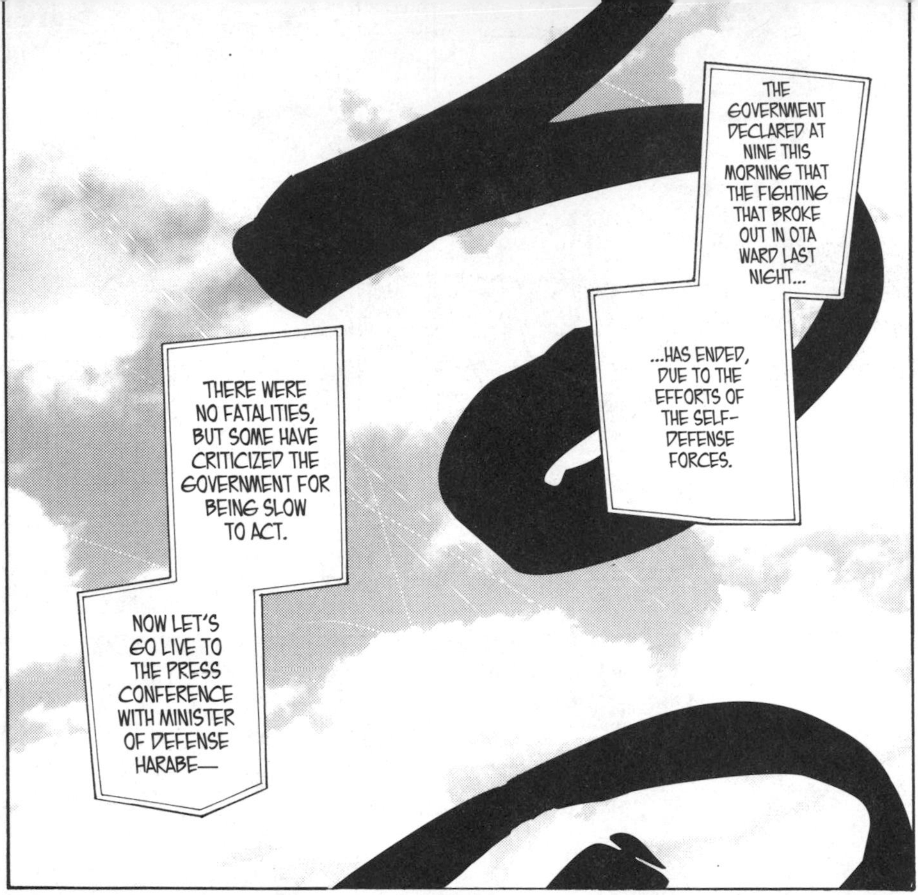
THE GOVERNMENT DECLARED AT NINE THIS MORNING THAT THE FIGHTING THAT BROKE OUT IN OTA WARD LAST NIGHT...
...HAS ENDED, DUE TO THE EFFORTS OF THE SELF-DEFENSE FORCES.
THERE WERE NO FATALITIES, BUT SOME HAVE CRITICIZED THE GOVERNMENT FOR BEING SLOW TO ACT.
NOW LET'S GO LIVE TO THE PRESS CONFERENCE WITH MINISTER OF DEFENSE HARABE—
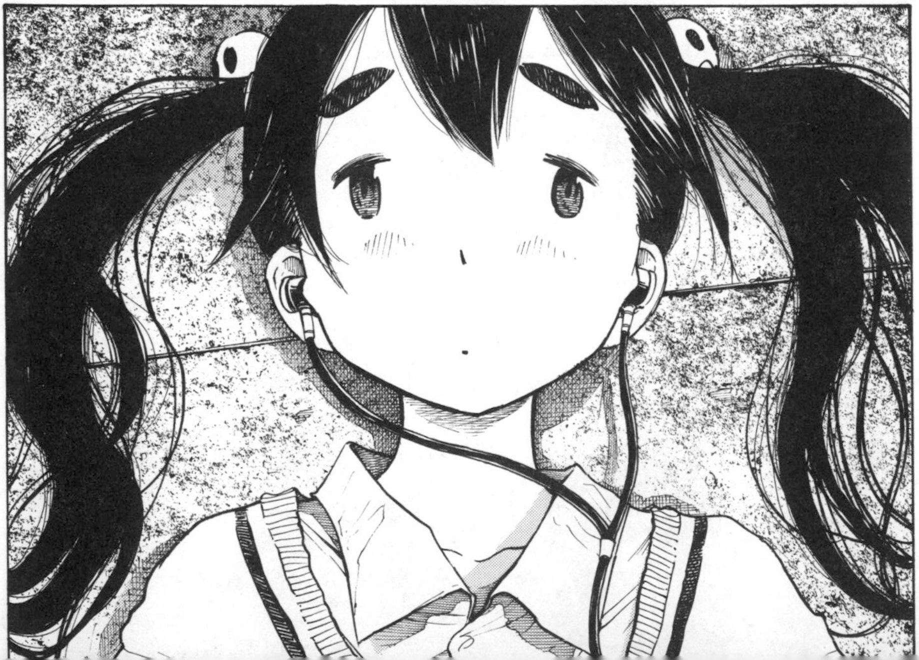

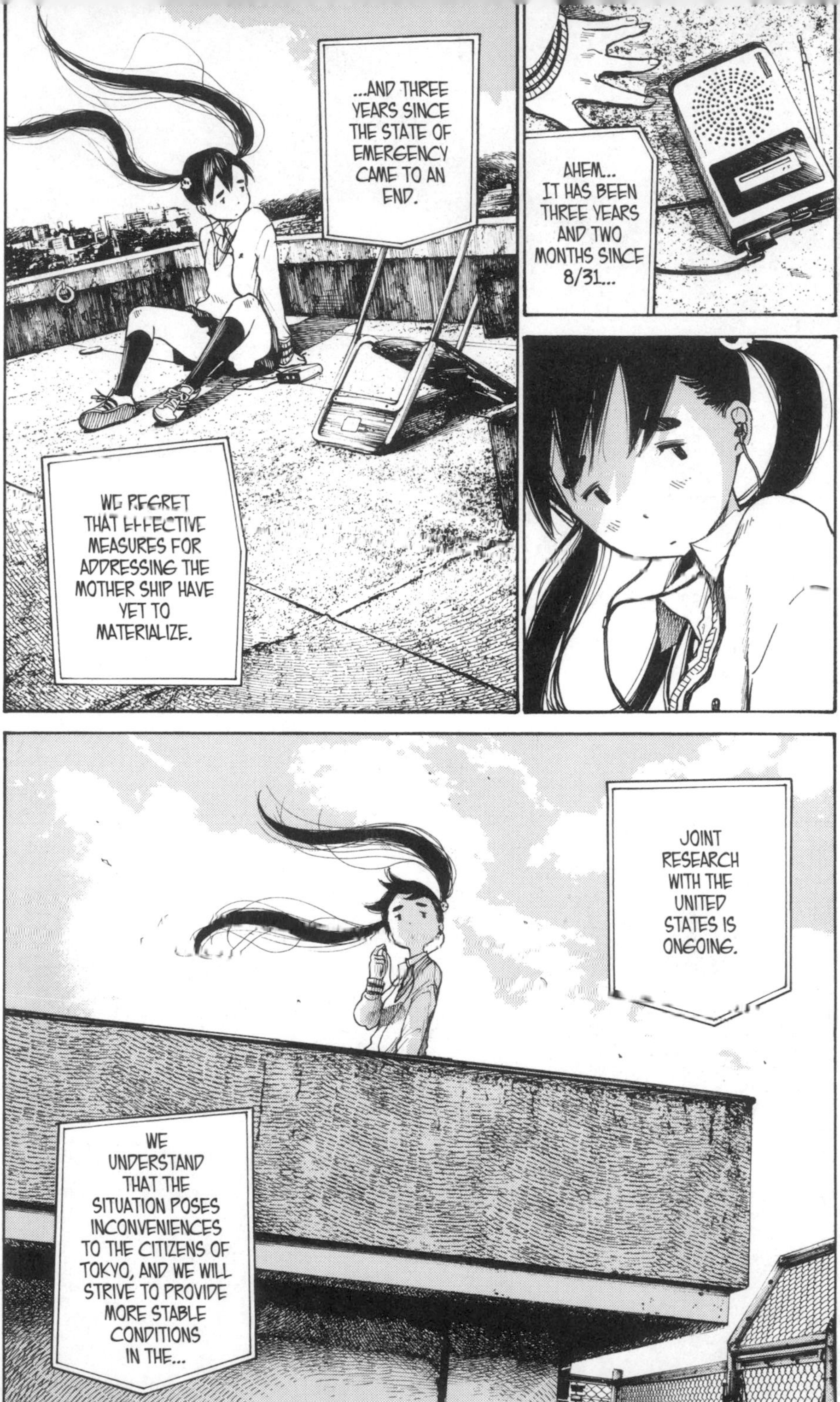
AHEM... IT HAS BEEN THREE YEARS AND TWO MONTHS SINCE 8/31...
...AND THREE YEARS SINCE THE STATE OF EMERGENCY CAME TO AN END.
WE REGRET THAT EFFECTIVE MEASURES FOR ADDRESSING THE MOTHER SHIP HAVE YET TO MATERIALIZE.
JOINT RESEARCH WITH THE UNITED STATES IS ONGOING.
WE UNDERSTAND THAT THE SITUATION POSES INCONVENIENCES TO THE CITIZENS OF TOKYO, AND WE WILL STRIVE TO PROVIDE MORE STABLE CONDITIONS IN THE...

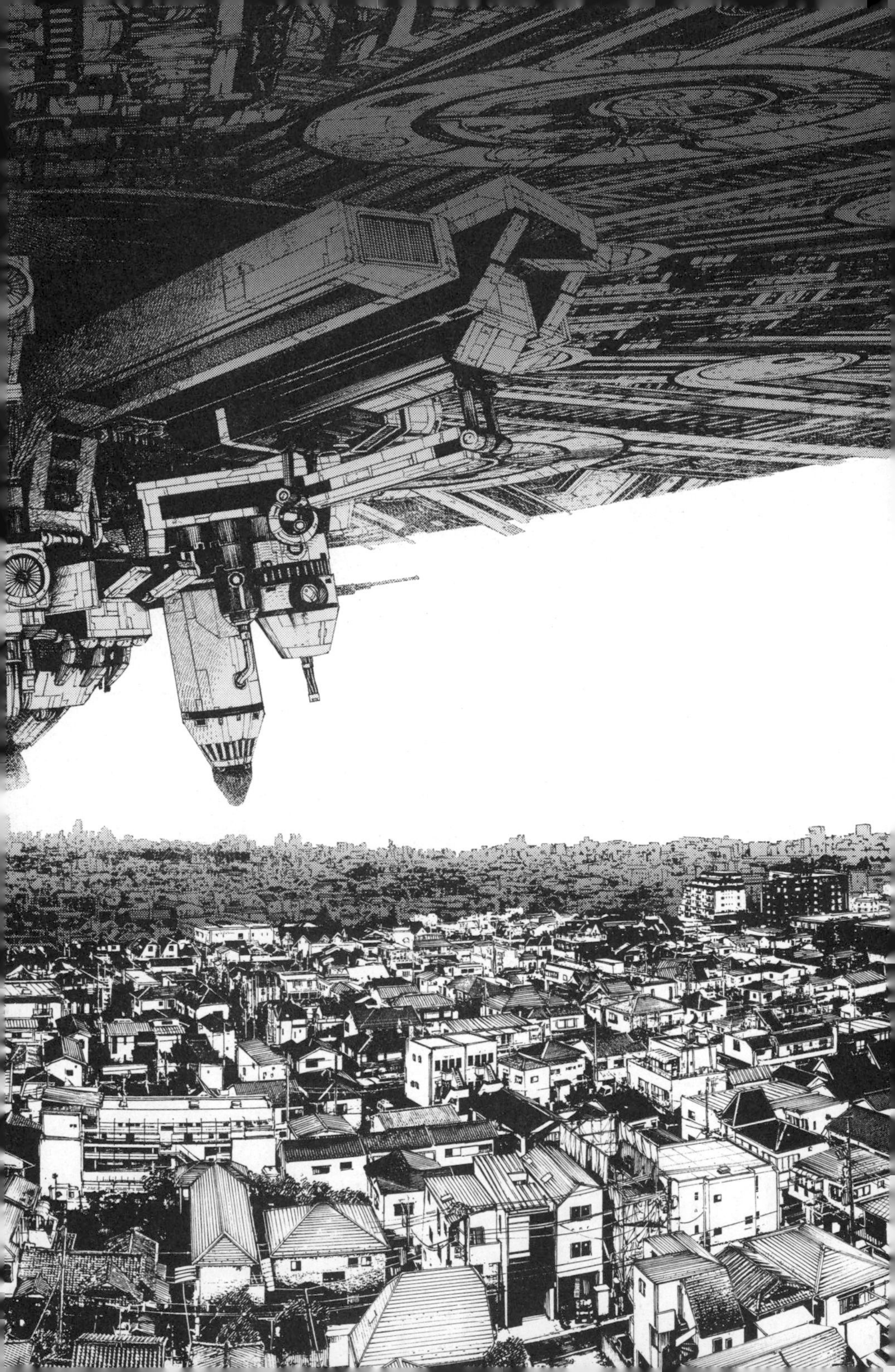

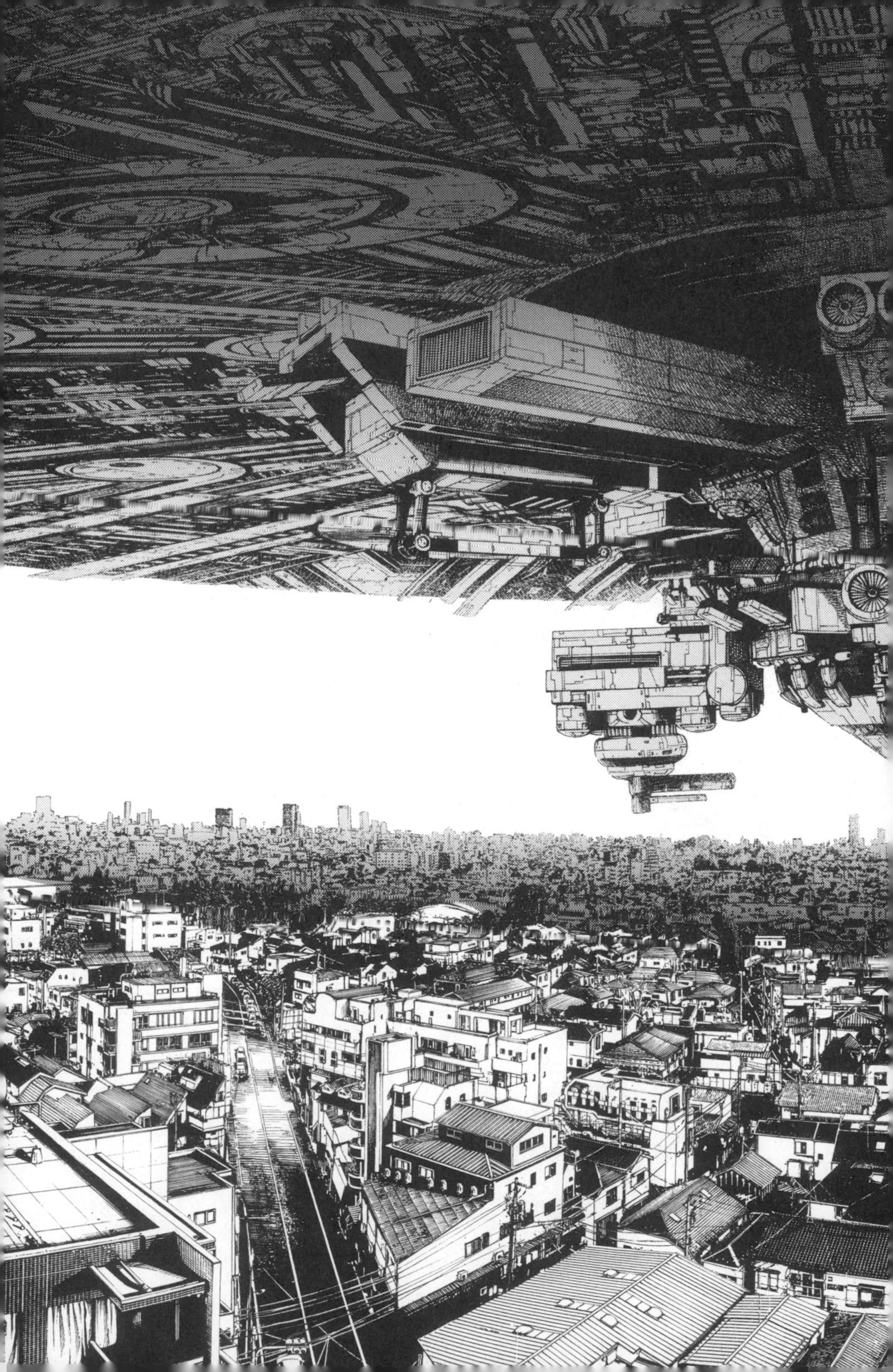

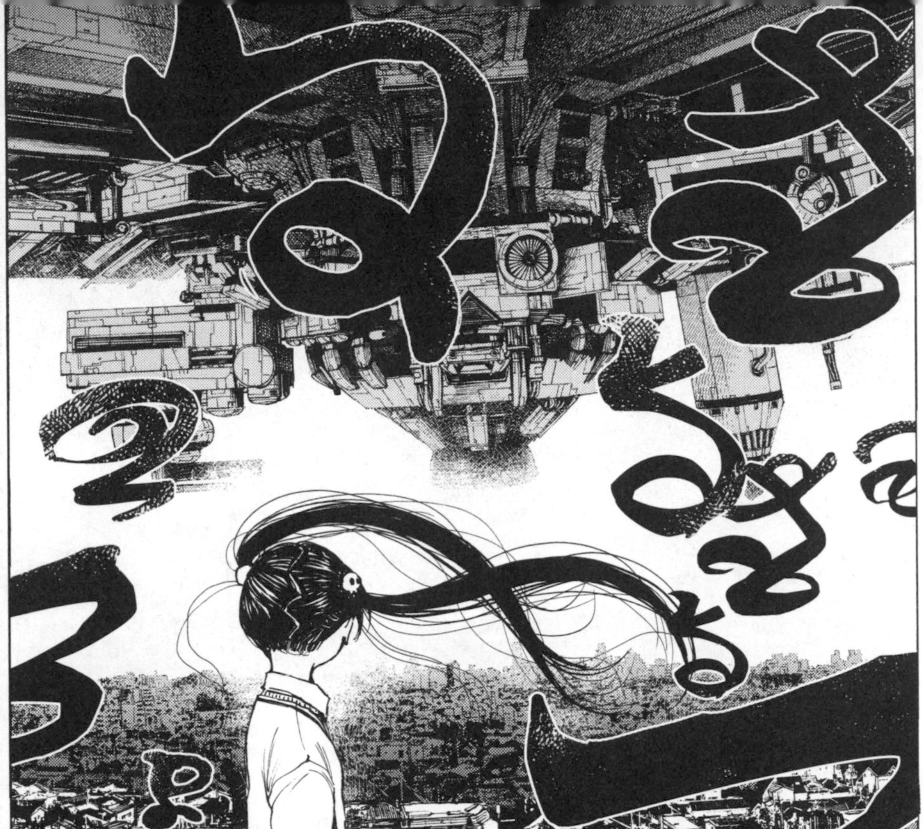

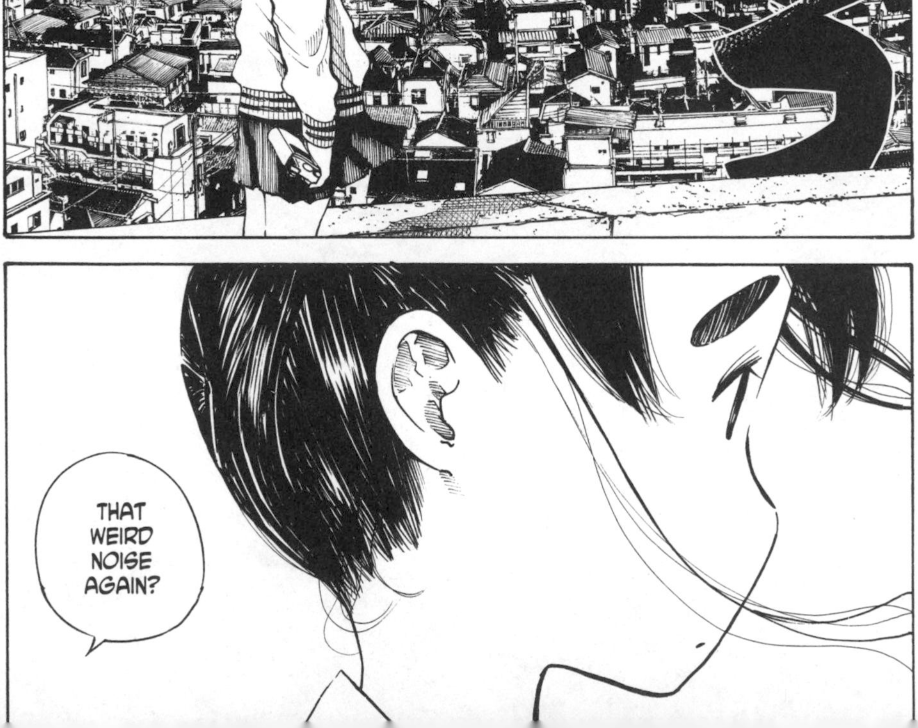
THAT WEIRD NOISE AGAIN?

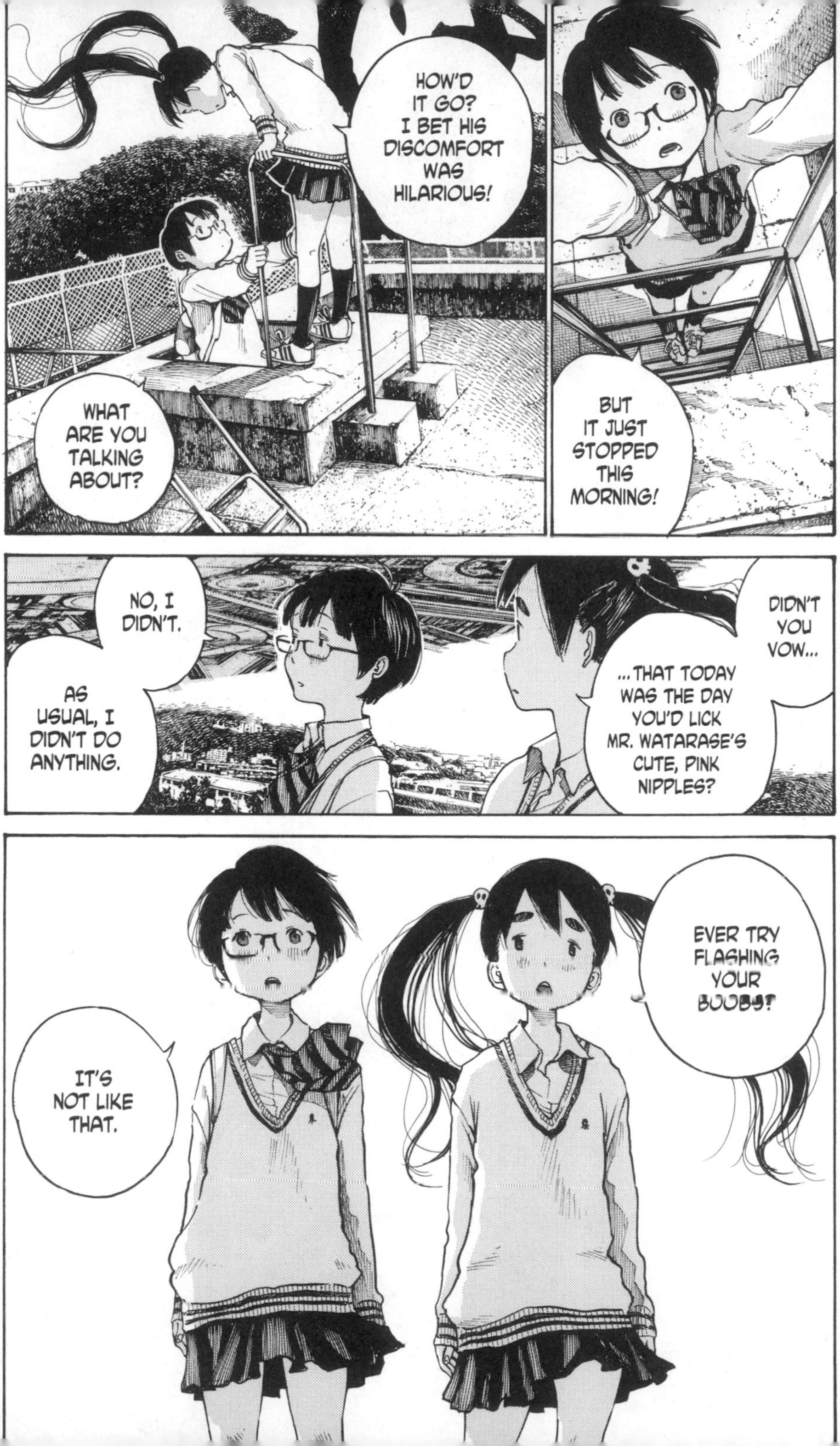
BUT IT JUST STOPPED THIS MORNING!
HOW'D IT GO? I BET HIS DISCOMFORT WAS HILARIOUS!
WHAT ARE YOU TALKING ABOUT?
DIDN'T YOU VOW...
...THAT TODAY WAS THE DAY YOU'D LICK MR. WATARASE'S CUTE, PINK NIPPLES?
NO, I DIDN'T.
AS USUAL, I DIDN'T DO ANYTHING.
EVER TRY FLASHING YOUR BOOBS?
IT'S NOT LIKE THAT.

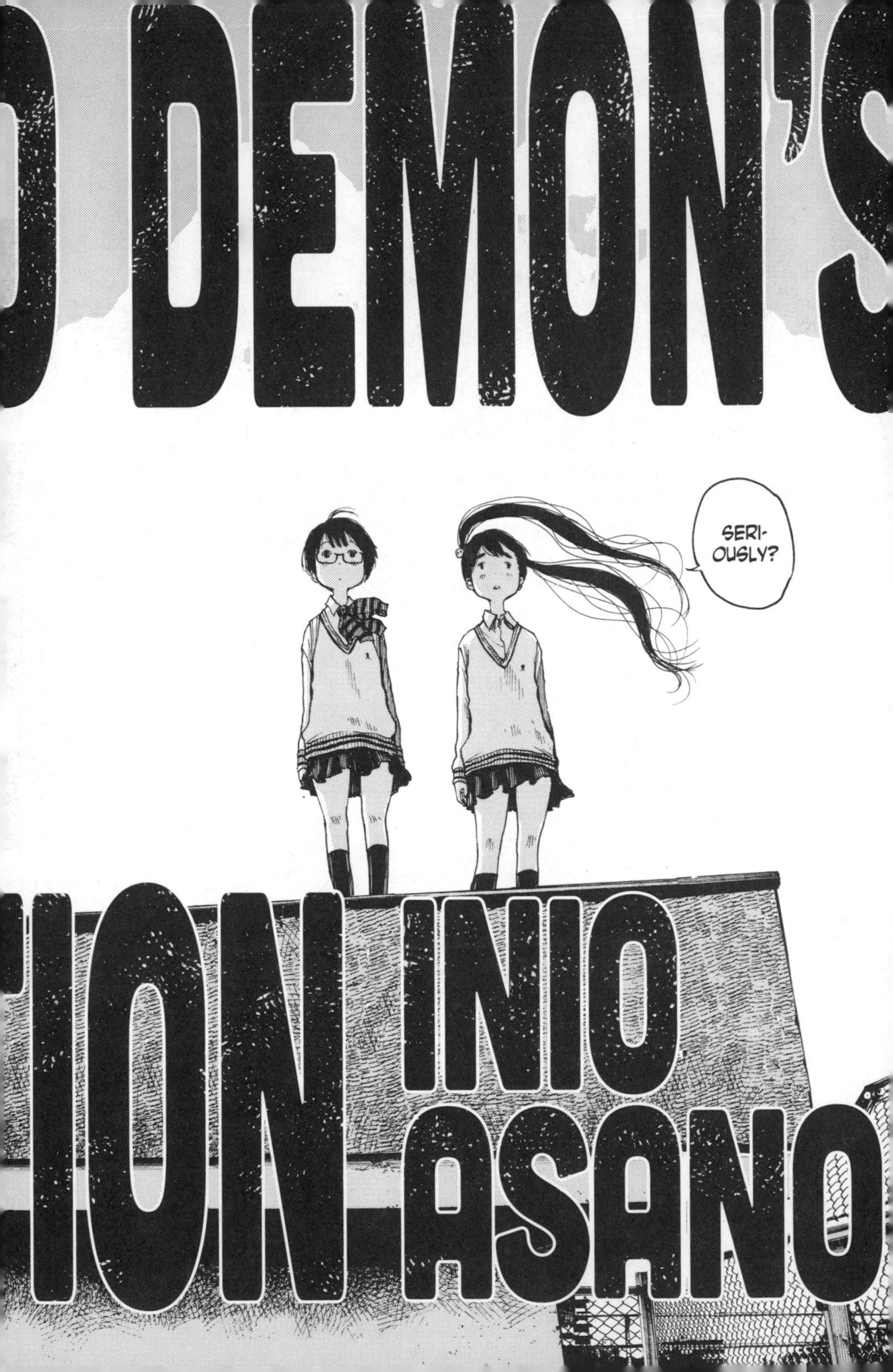
DEMON'S
SERI-
OUSLY?
TION
INIO
ASANO

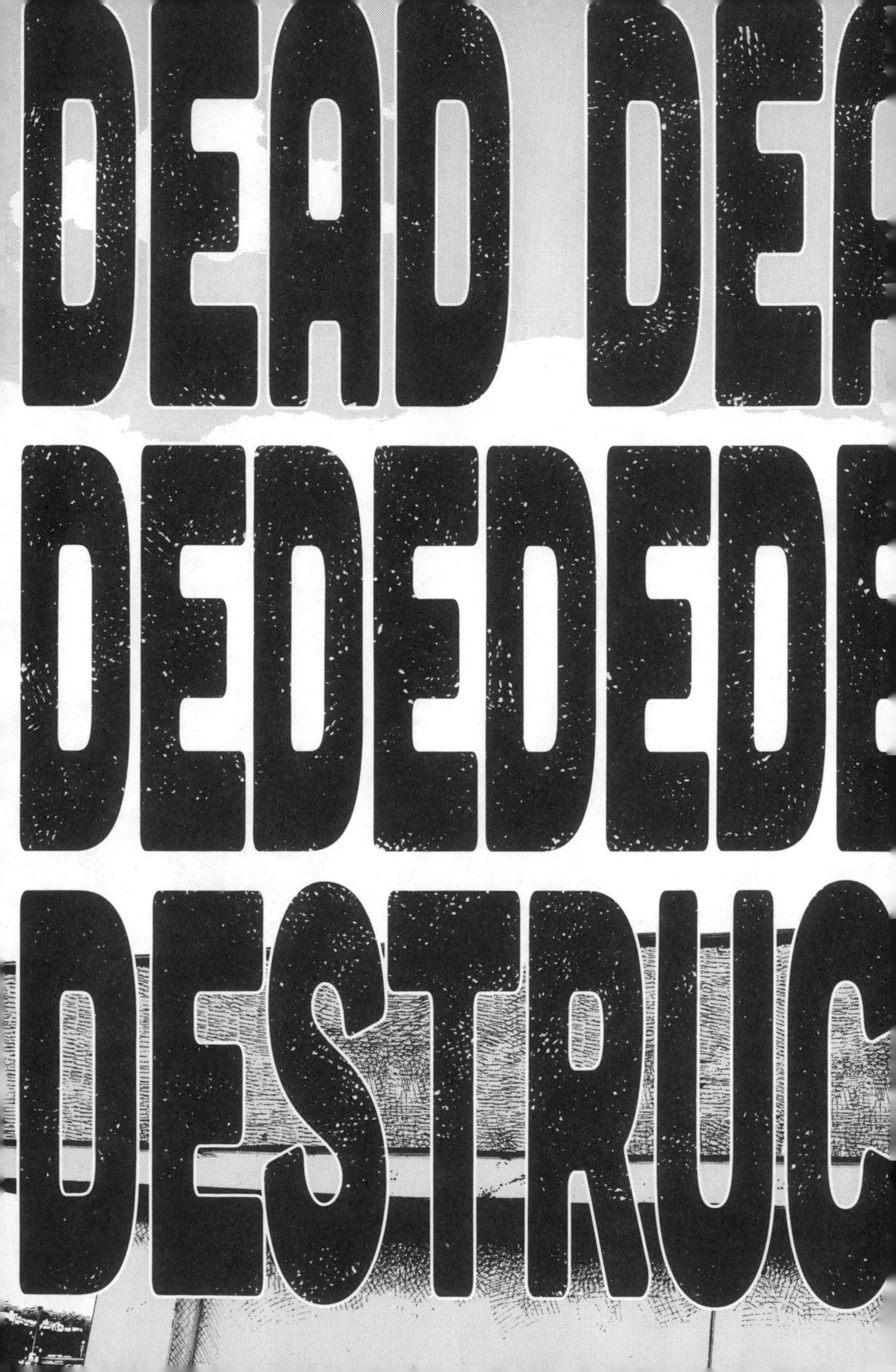
DEAD DEA
DEDEDEDE
DESTRUC

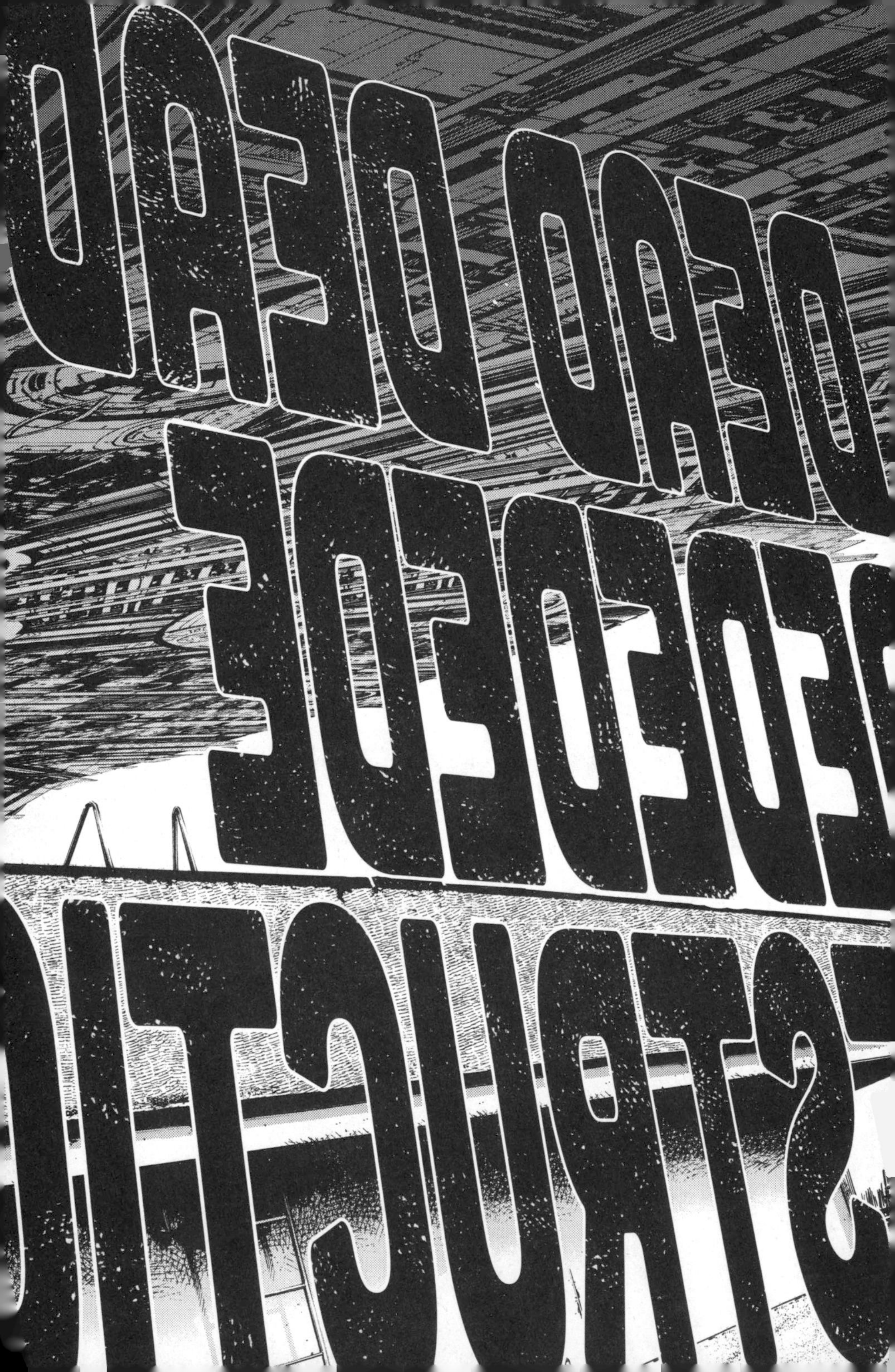

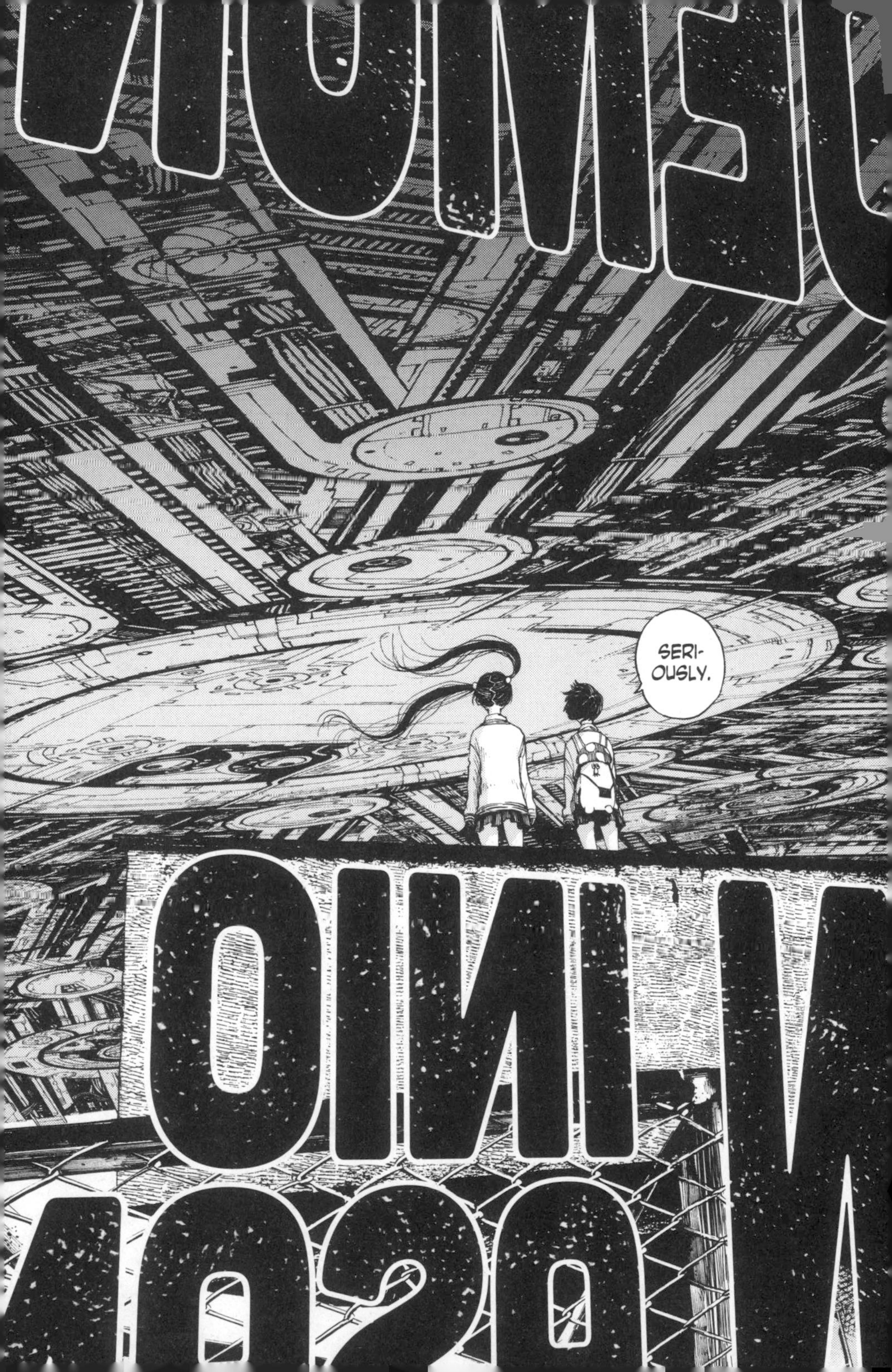
SERI-OUSLY.

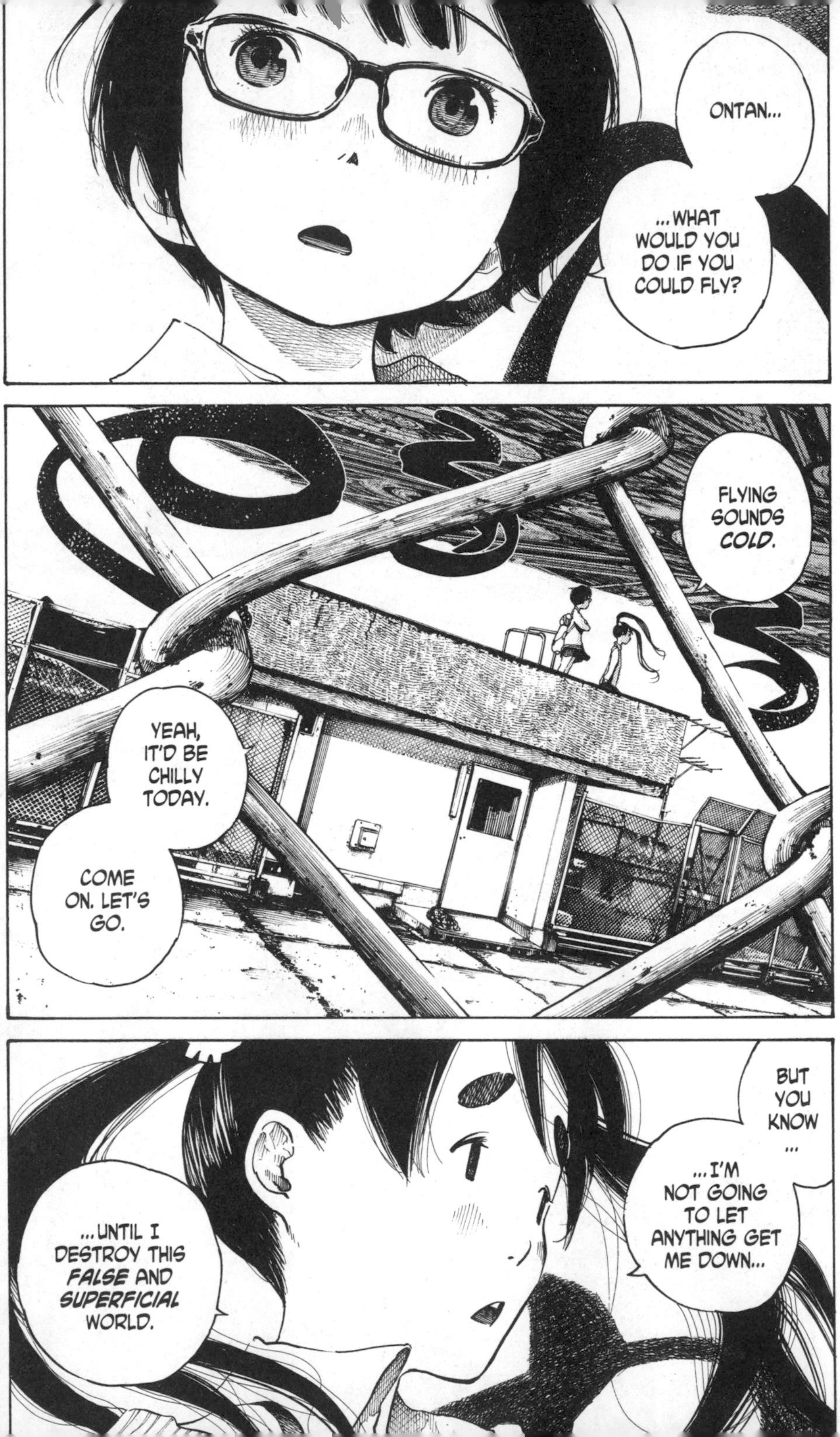
ONTAN...
...WHAT WOULD YOU DO IF YOU COULD FLY?
FLYING SOUNDS *COLD*.
YEAH, IT'D BE CHILLY TODAY.
COME ON. LET'S GO.
BUT YOU KNOW...
...I'M NOT GOING TO LET ANYTHING GET ME DOWN...
...UNTIL I DESTROY THIS *FALSE* AND *SUPERFICIAL* WORLD.

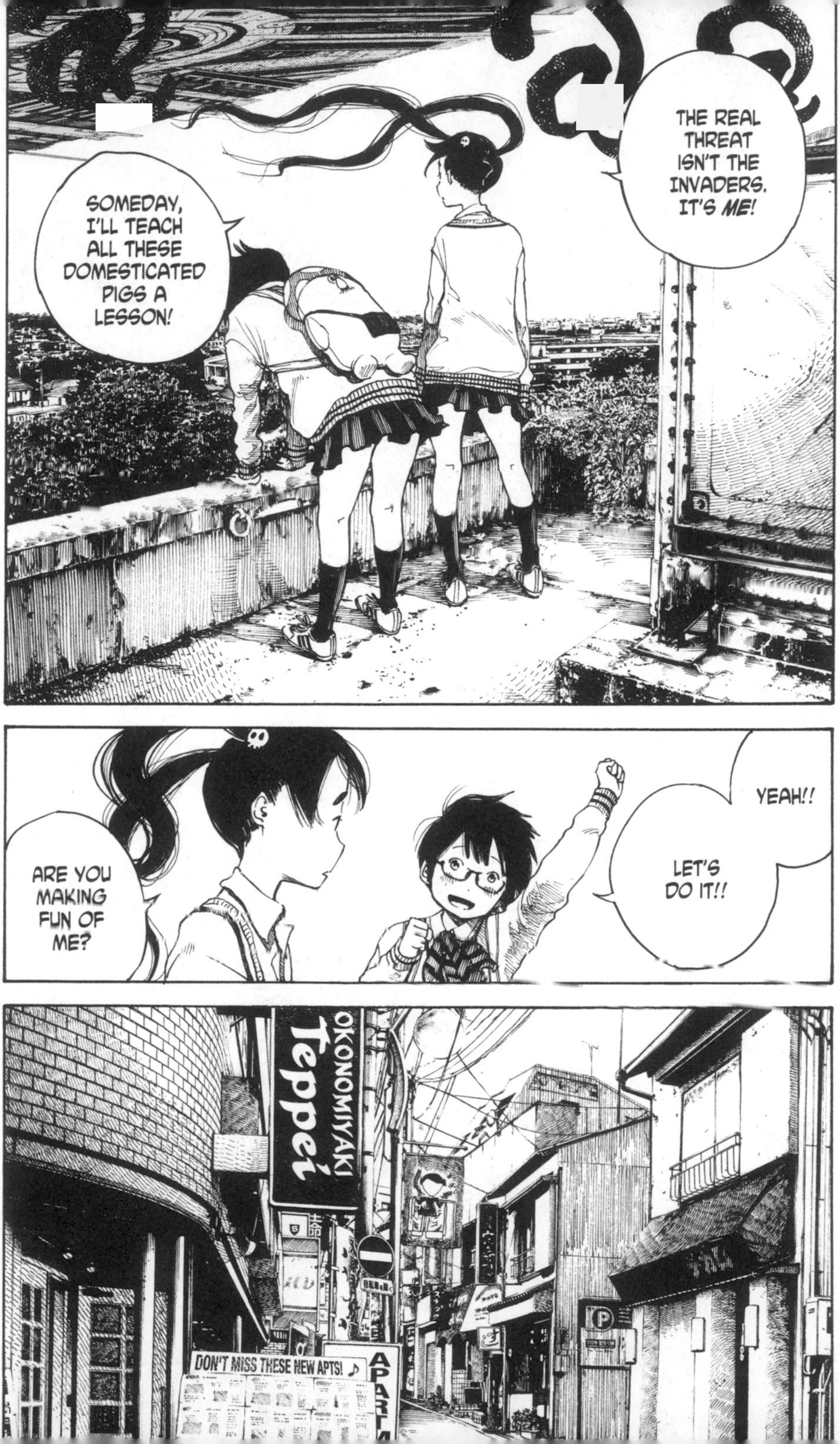
THE REAL THREAT ISN'T THE INVADERS. IT'S *ME!*
SOMEDAY, I'LL TEACH ALL THESE DOMESTICATED PIGS A LESSON!
YEAH!! LET'S DO IT!!
ARE YOU MAKING FUN OF ME?
OKONOMIYAKI Teppei
DON'T MISS THESE NEW APTS! ♪

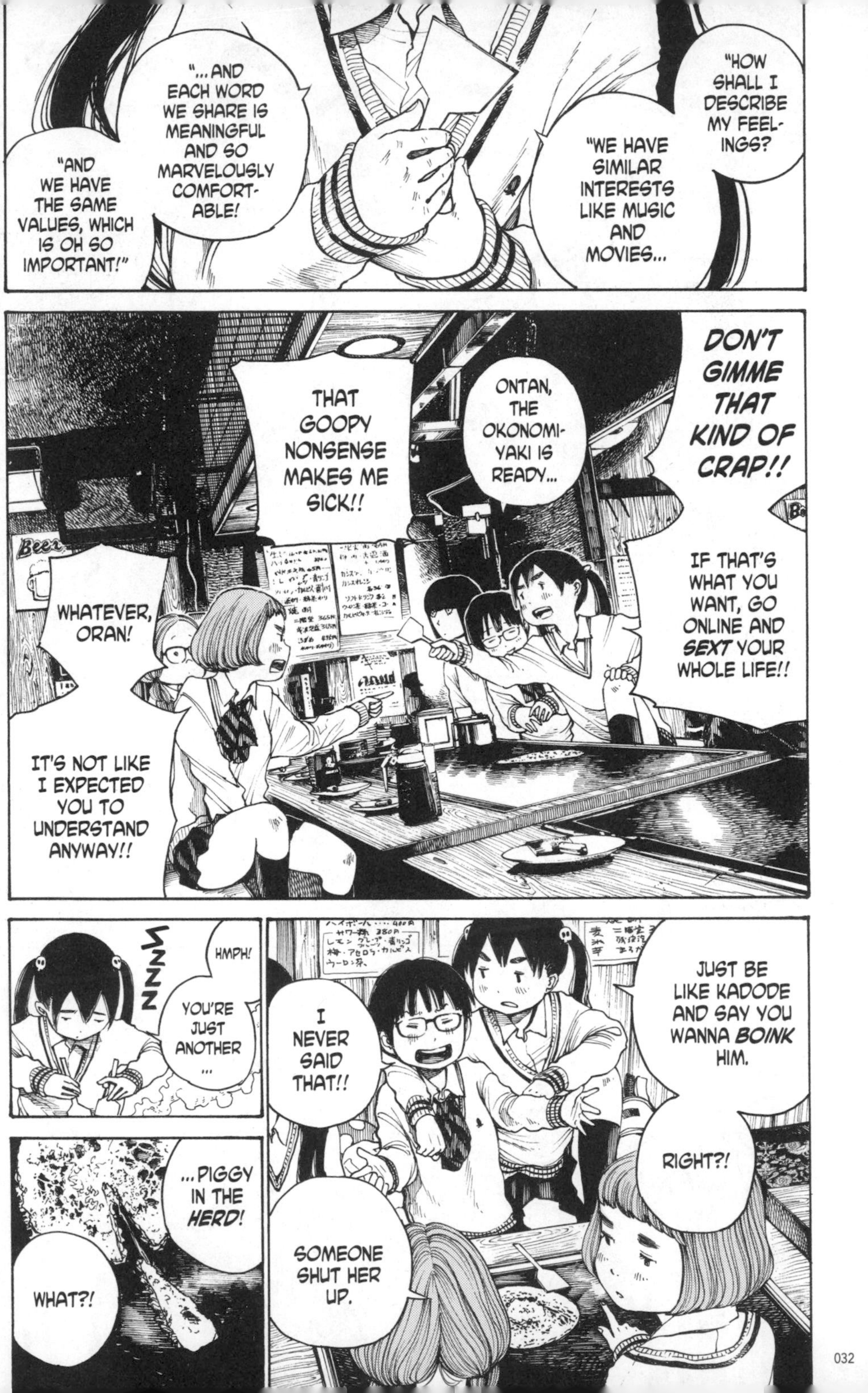
"HOW SHALL I DESCRIBE MY FEEL-INGS?
"WE HAVE SIMILAR INTERESTS LIKE MUSIC AND MOVIES...
"...AND EACH WORD WE SHARE IS MEANINGFUL AND SO MARVELOUSLY COMFORT-ABLE!
"AND WE HAVE THE SAME VALUES, WHICH IS OH SO IMPORTANT!"
DON'T GIMME THAT KIND OF CRAP!!
IF THAT'S WHAT YOU WANT, GO ONLINE AND *SEXT* YOUR WHOLE LIFE!!
ONTAN, THE OKONOMI-YAKI IS READY...
THAT GOOPY NONSENSE MAKES ME SICK!!
WHATEVER, ORAN!
IT'S NOT LIKE I EXPECTED YOU TO UNDERSTAND ANYWAY!!
JUST BE LIKE KADODE AND SAY YOU WANNA *BOINK* HIM.
RIGHT?!
I NEVER SAID THAT!!
SOMEONE SHUT HER UP.
HMPH!
YOU'RE JUST ANOTHER ...
...PIGGY IN THE *HERD*!
WHAT?!

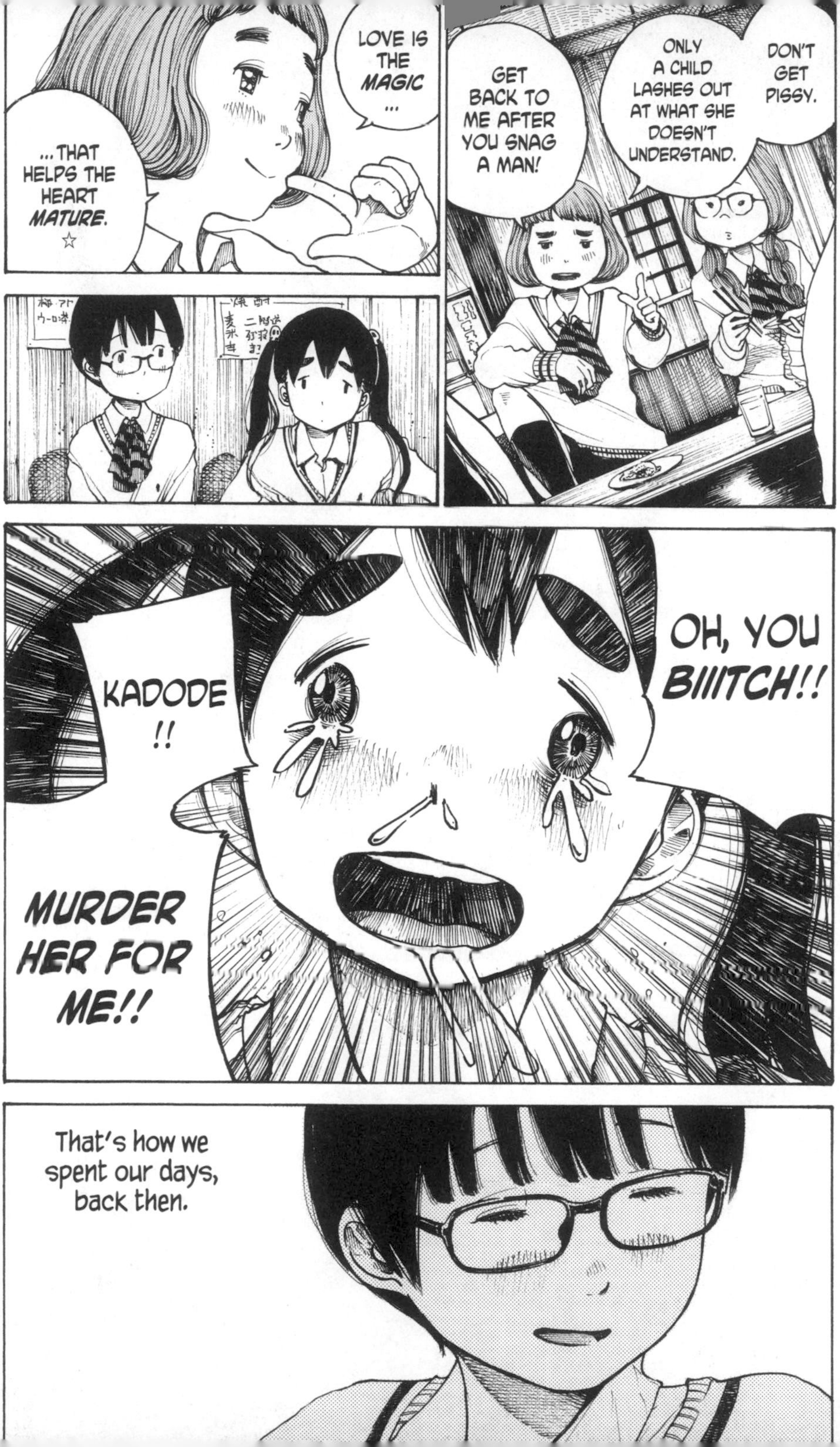
DON'T GET PISSY.
ONLY A CHILD LASHES OUT AT WHAT SHE DOESN'T UNDERSTAND.
GET BACK TO ME AFTER YOU SNAG A MAN!
LOVE IS THE MAGIC ...
...THAT HELPS THE HEART MATURE. ☆
OH, YOU BIIITCH!!
KADODE !!
MURDER HER FOR ME!!
That's how we spent our days, back then.

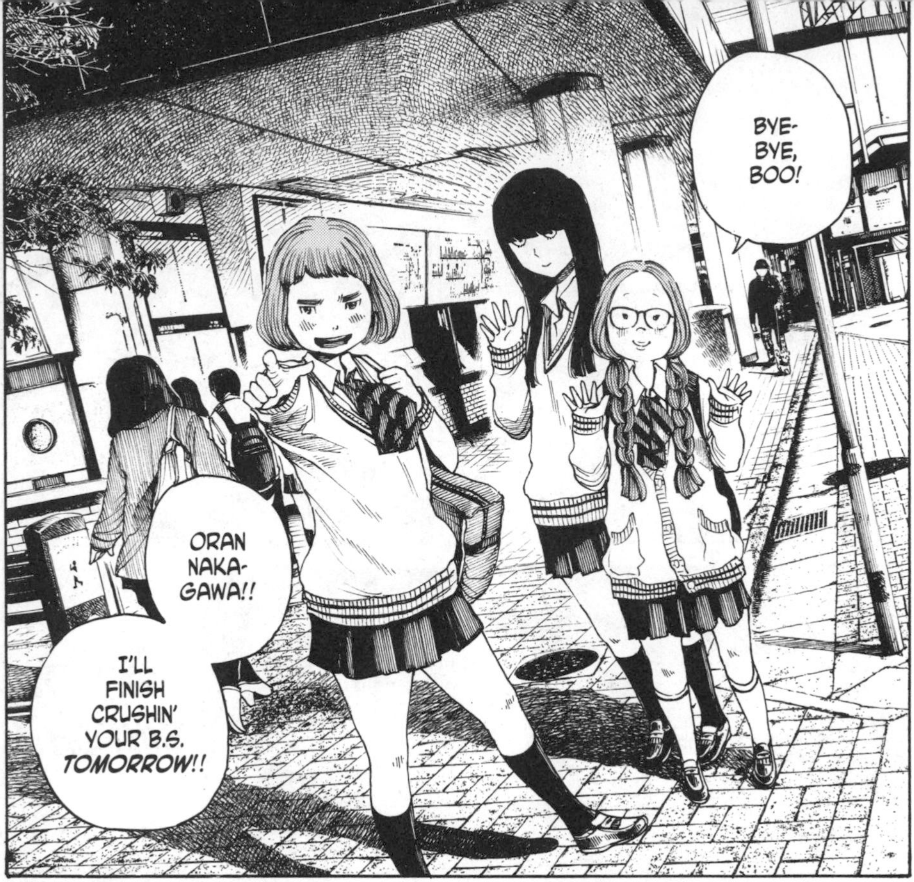
BYE-BYE, BOO!
ORAN NAKAGAWA!!
I'LL FINISH CRUSHIN' YOUR B.S. *TOMORROW*!!

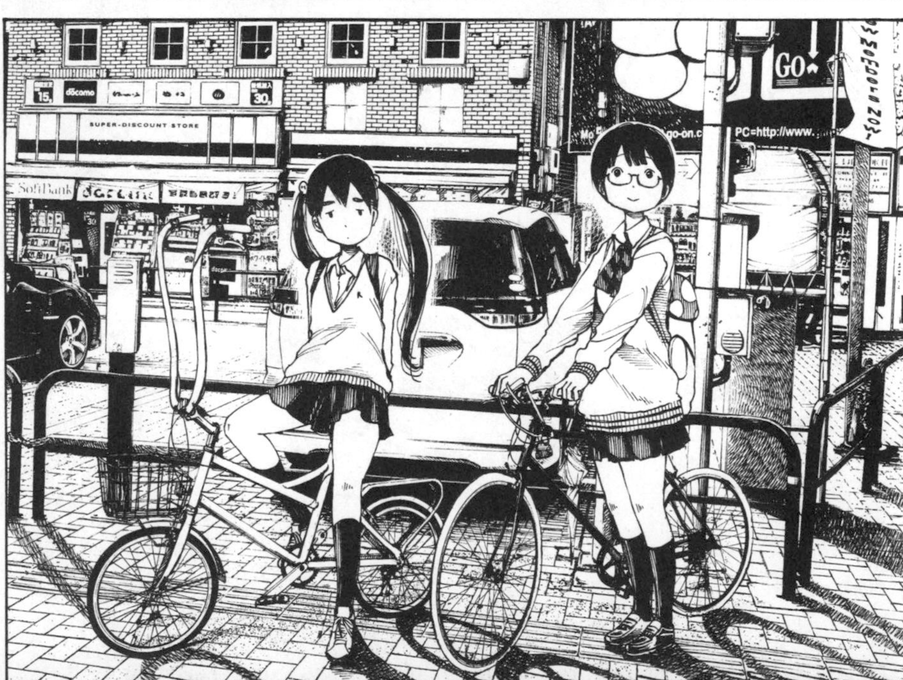
docomo
SUPER-DISCOUNT STORE
SoftBank
Go
PC=http://www.

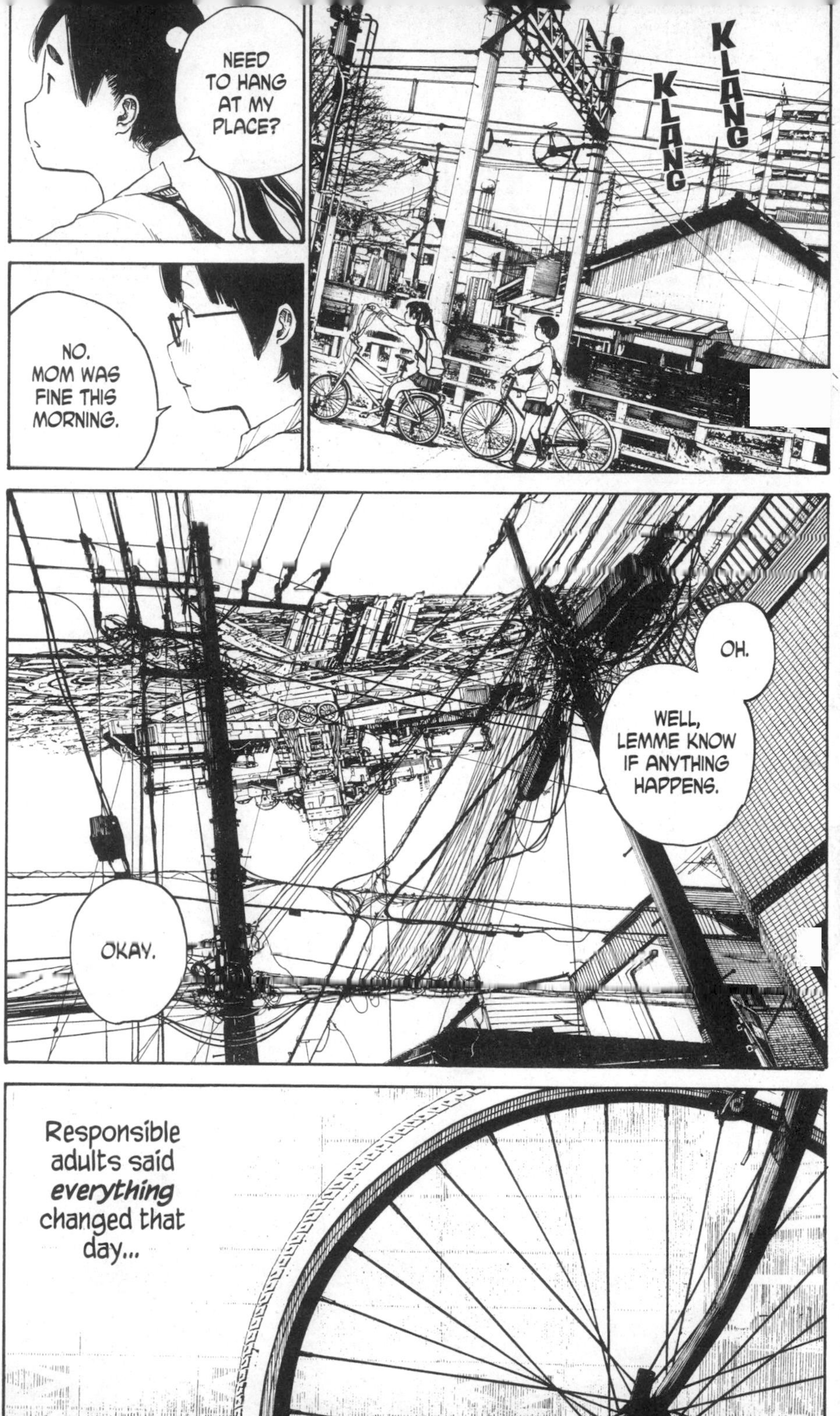
KLANG
KLANG
NEED TO HANG AT MY PLACE?
NO. MOM WAS FINE THIS MORNING.
OH.
WELL, LEMME KNOW IF ANYTHING HAPPENS.
OKAY.
Responsible adults said *everything* changed that day...

SKSSH

YESTERDAY'S BATTLE CASUALTIES	YESTERDAY'S TRAFFIC ACCIDENTS
DEAD 0	DEAD 0
INJURED 122	INJURED 5

...but back then, I was never entirely satisfied with how everything seemed to stay the same.

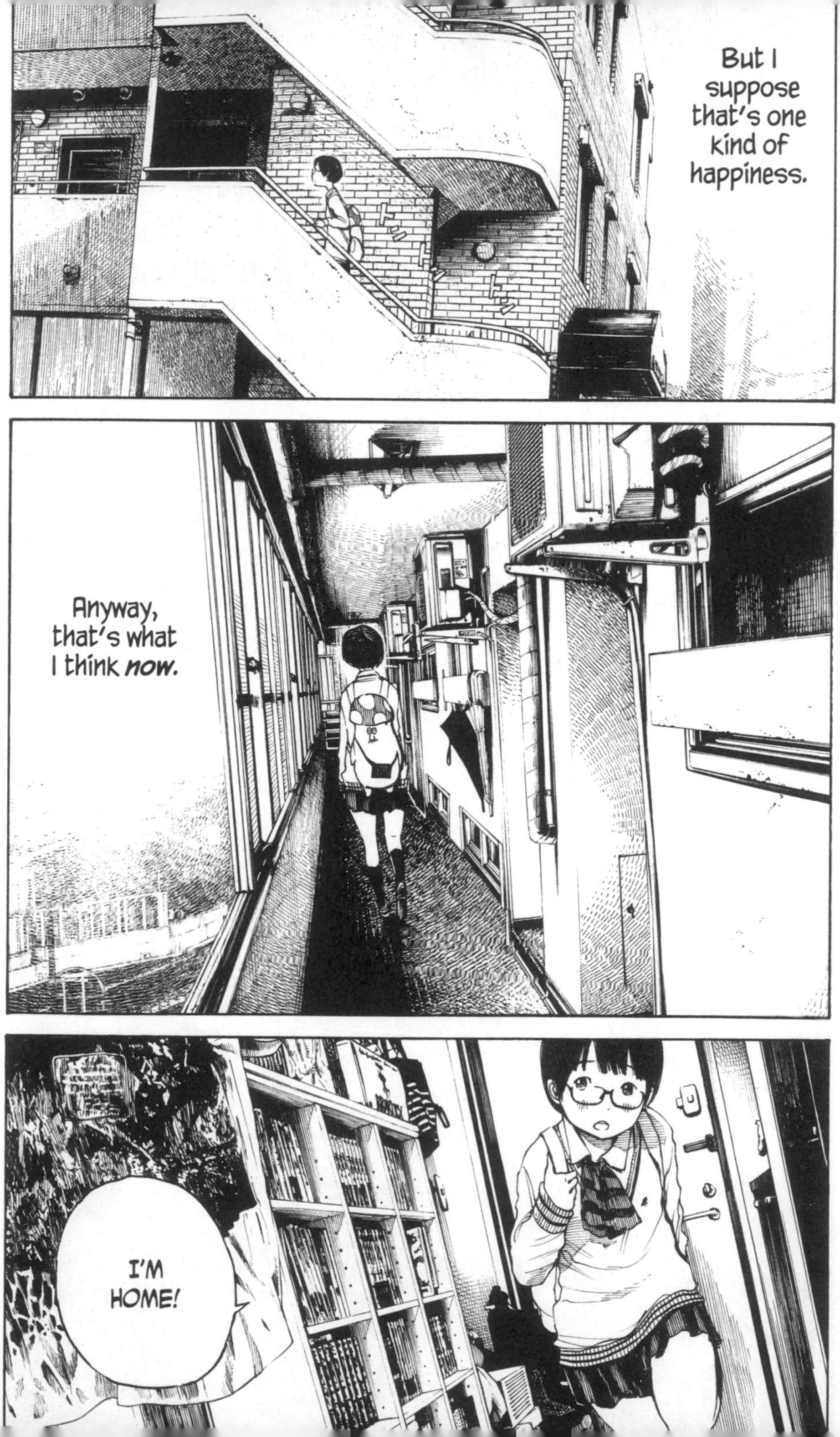
But I suppose that's one kind of happiness.
Anyway, that's what I think *now*.
I'M HOME!

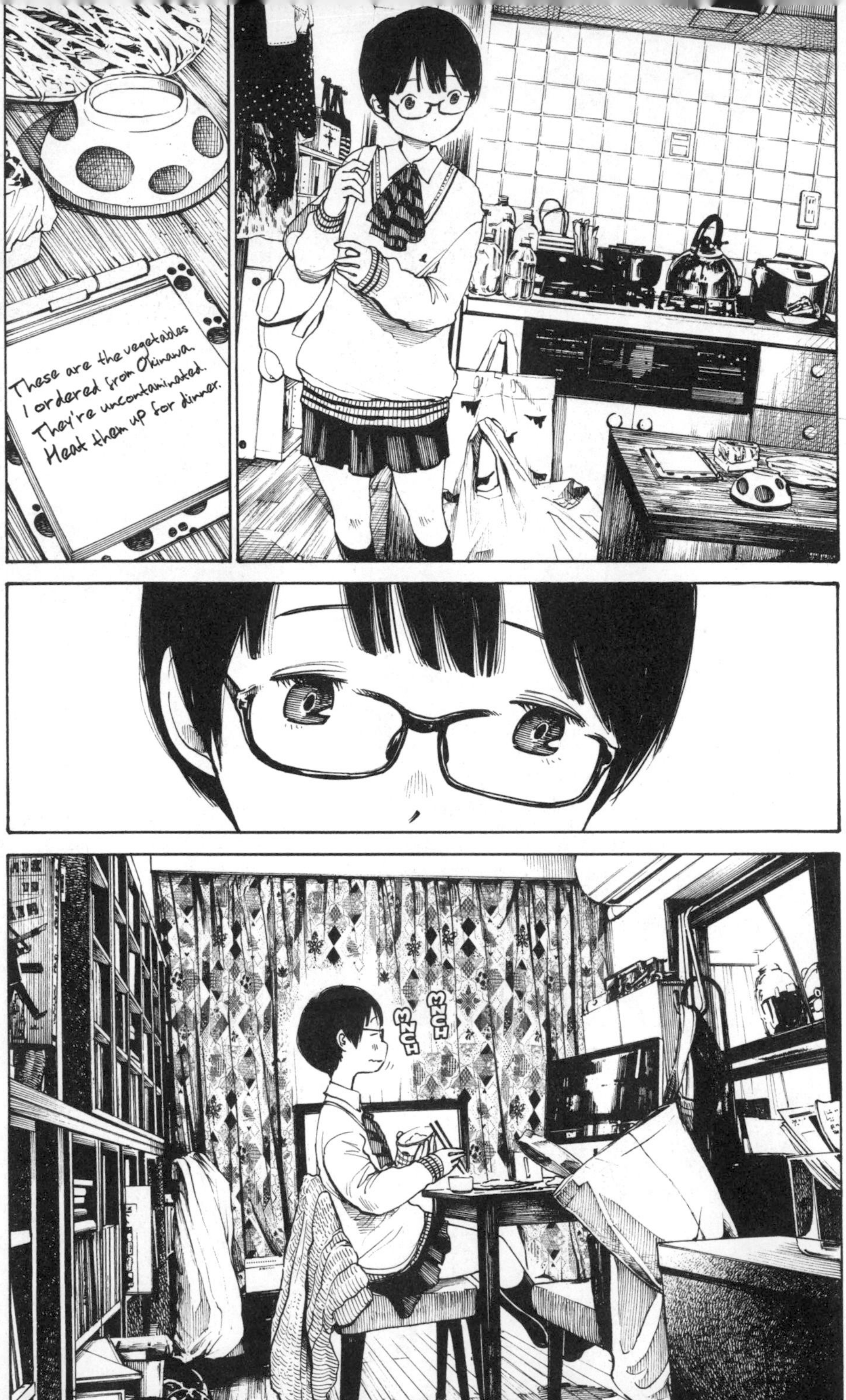
These are the vegetables
I ordered from Okinawa.
They're uncontaminated.
Heat them up for dinner.
MNCH
MNCH

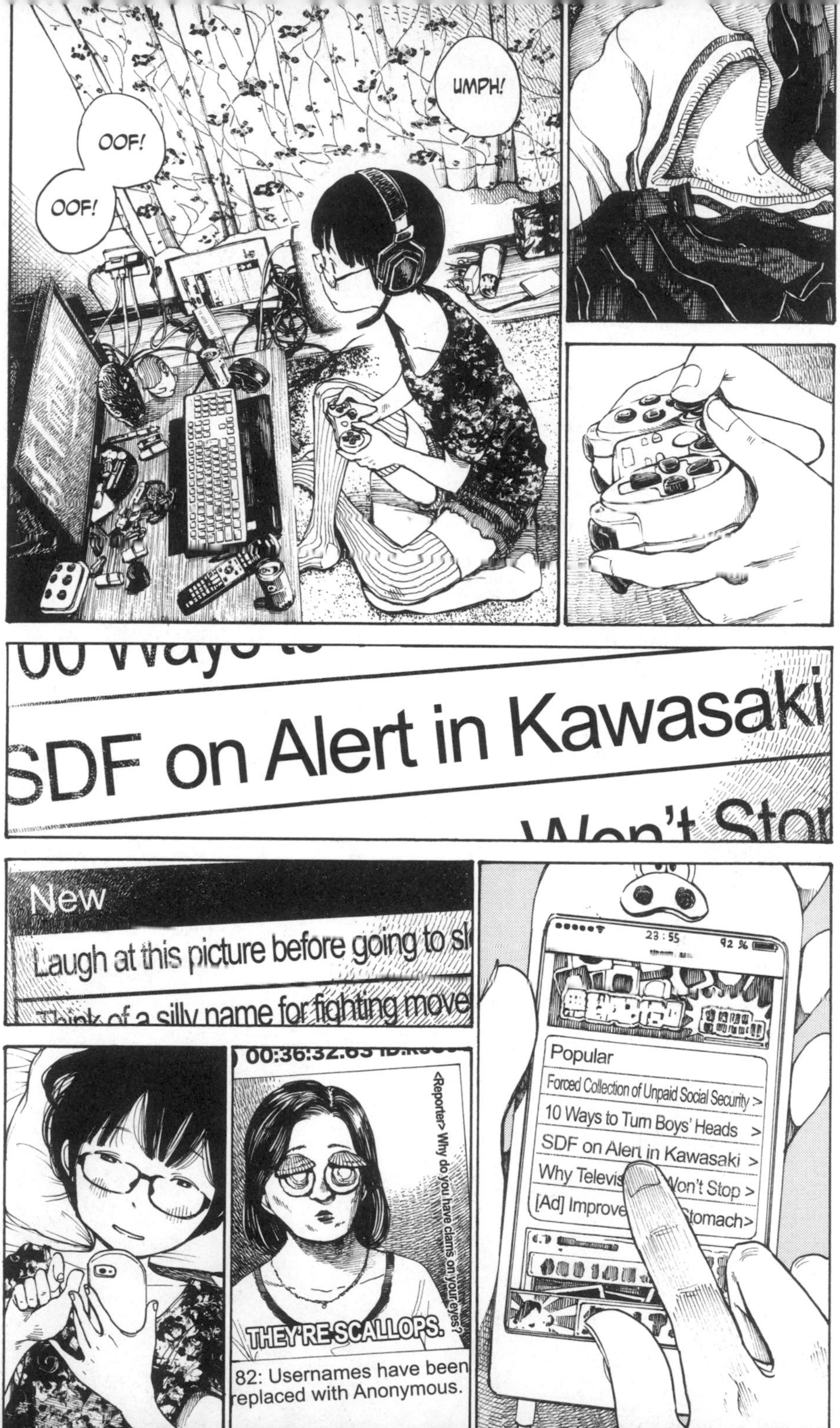

UMPH!
OOF!
OOF!
SDF on Alert in Kawasaki
23:55
92 %
Popular
Forced Collection of Unpaid Social Security >
10 Ways to Turn Boys' Heads >
SDF on Alert in Kawasaki >
Why Televis Won't Stop >
[Ad] Improve Stomach>
New
Laugh at this picture before going to sl
00:36:32.63
<Reporter> Why do you have clams on your eyes?
THEY'RE SCALLOPS.
82: Usernames have been replaced with Anonymous.

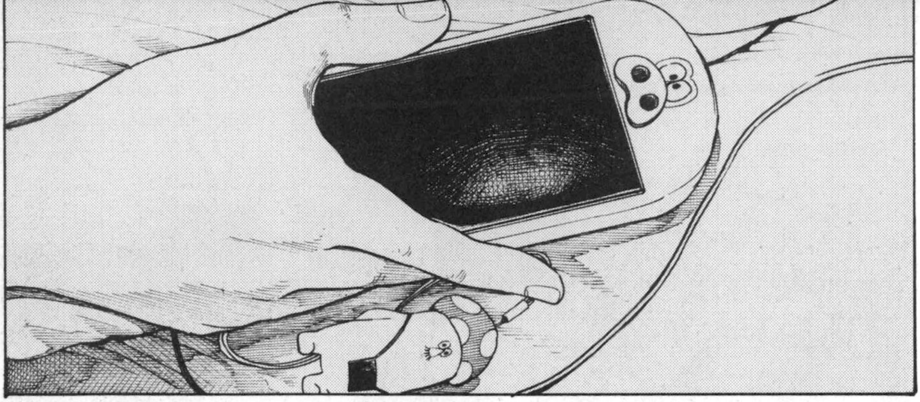
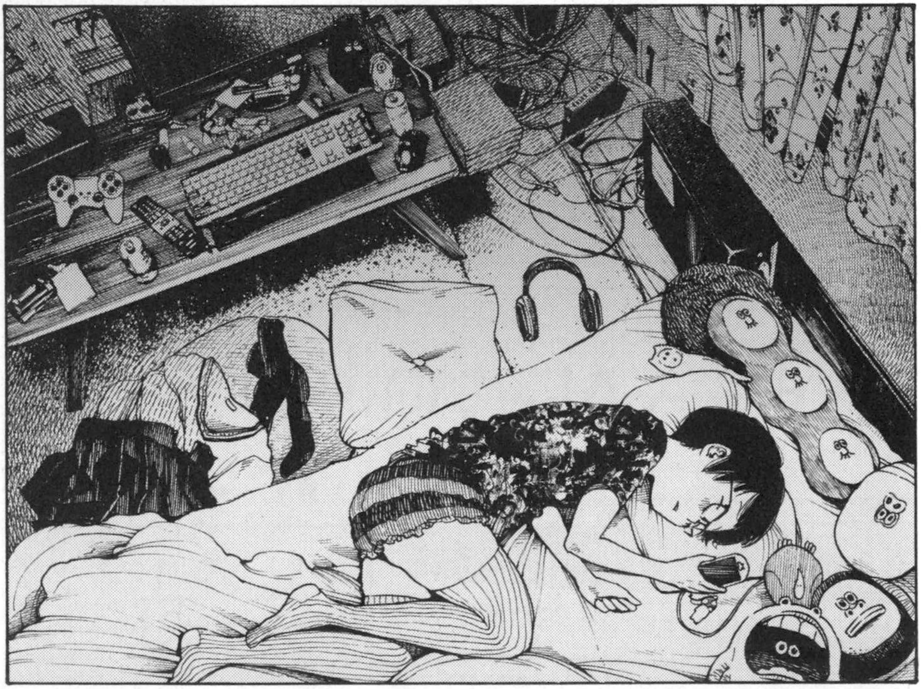
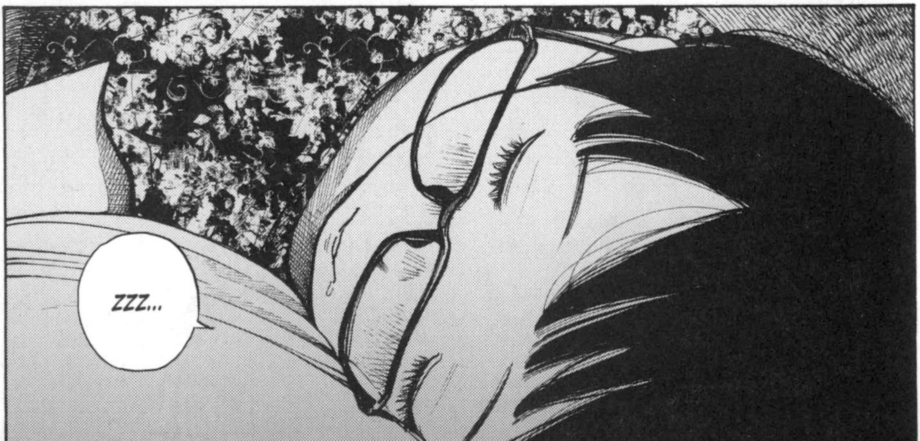
ZZZ...

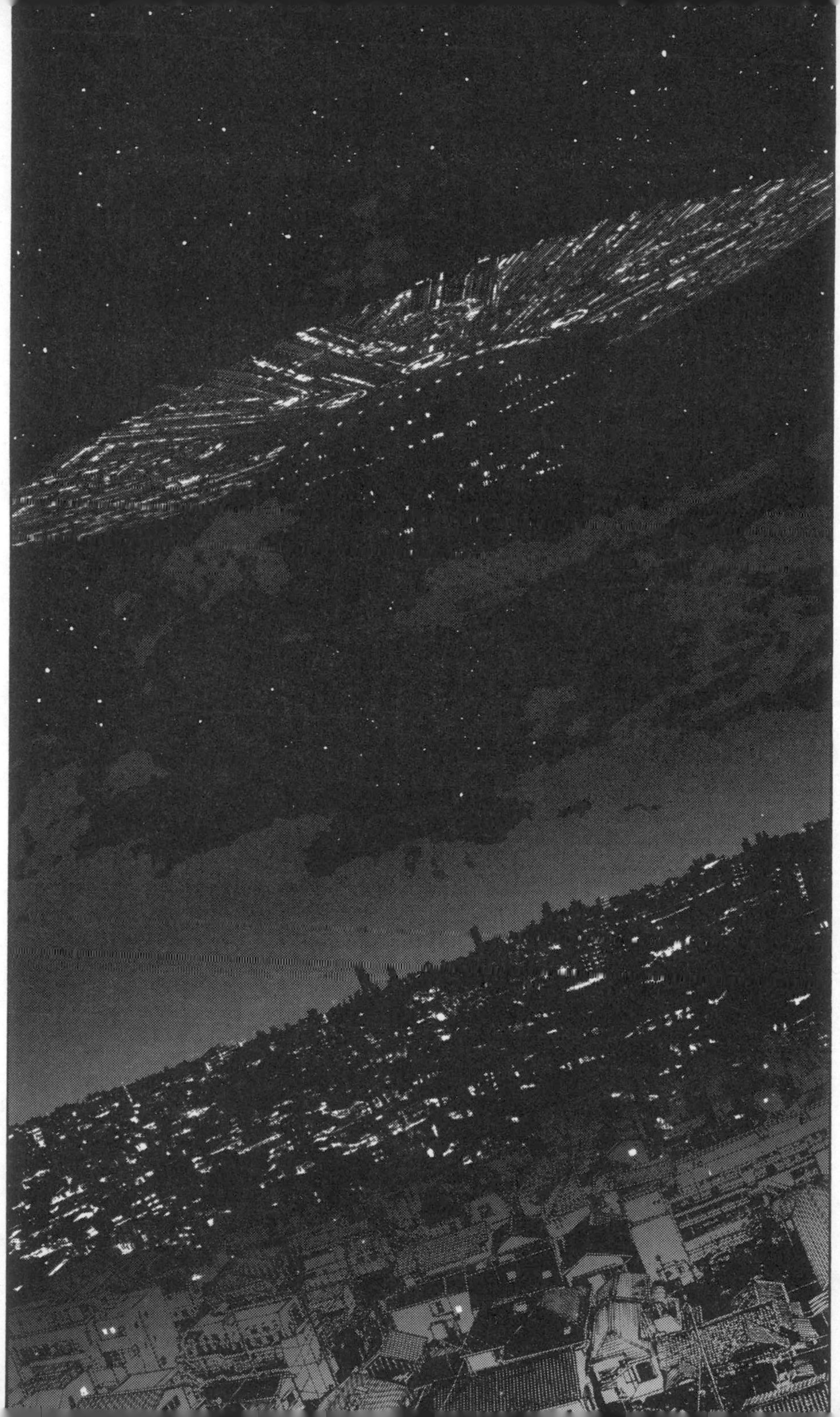

DEDE
DEDE

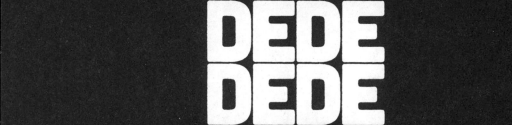

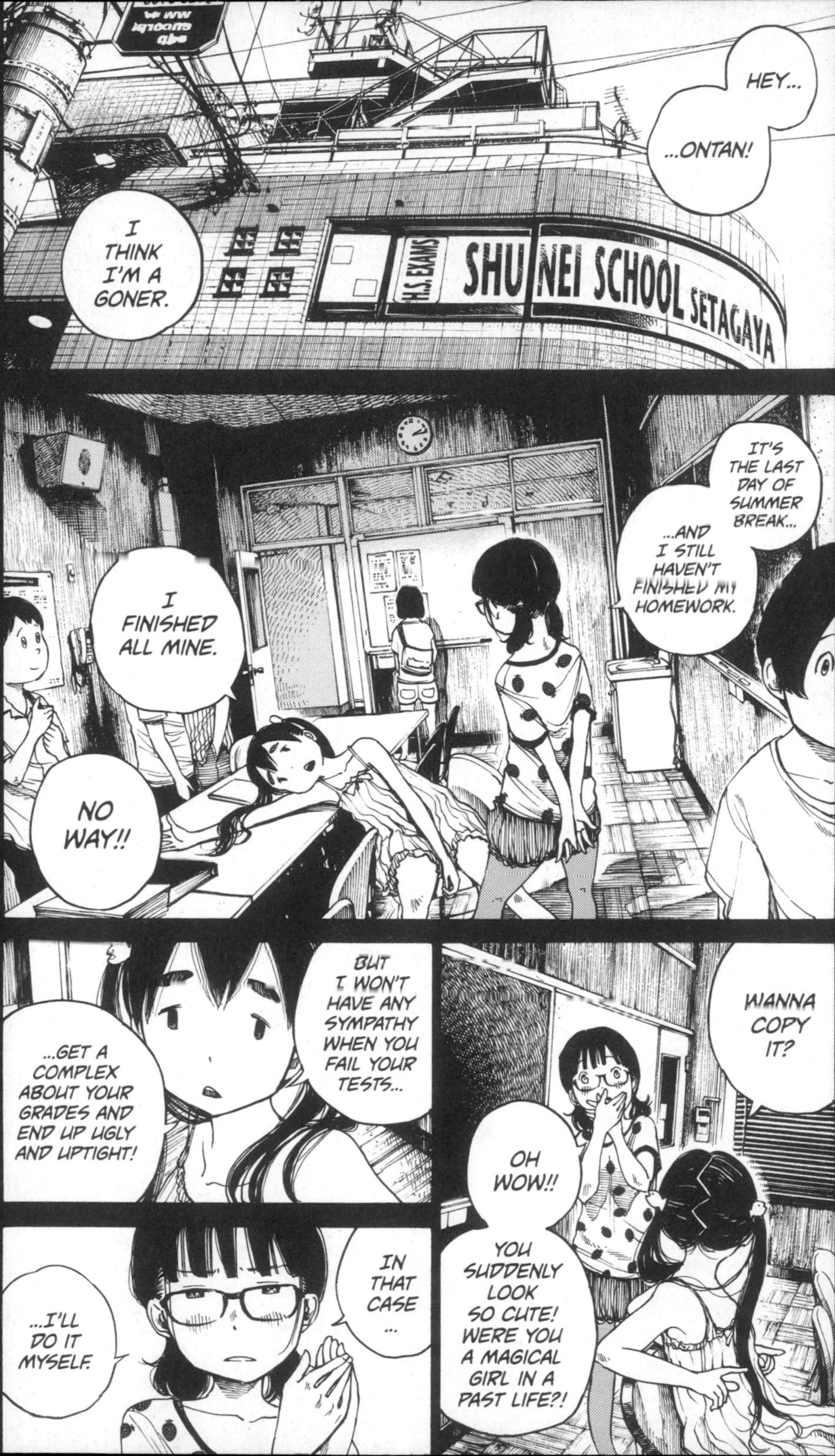
HEY...
...ONTAN!
I THINK I'M A GONER.
H.S. EXAMS
SHU NEI SCHOOL SETAGAYA
IT'S THE LAST DAY OF SUMMER BREAK...
...AND I STILL HAVEN'T FINISHED MY HOMEWORK.
I FINISHED ALL MINE.
NO WAY!!
WANNA COPY IT?
OH WOW!!
YOU SUDDENLY LOOK SO CUTE! WERE YOU A MAGICAL GIRL IN A PAST LIFE?!
BUT I WON'T HAVE ANY SYMPATHY WHEN YOU FAIL YOUR TESTS...
...GET A COMPLEX ABOUT YOUR GRADES AND END UP UGLY AND UPTIGHT!
IN THAT CASE...
...I'LL DO IT MYSELF.

CHAPTER 2

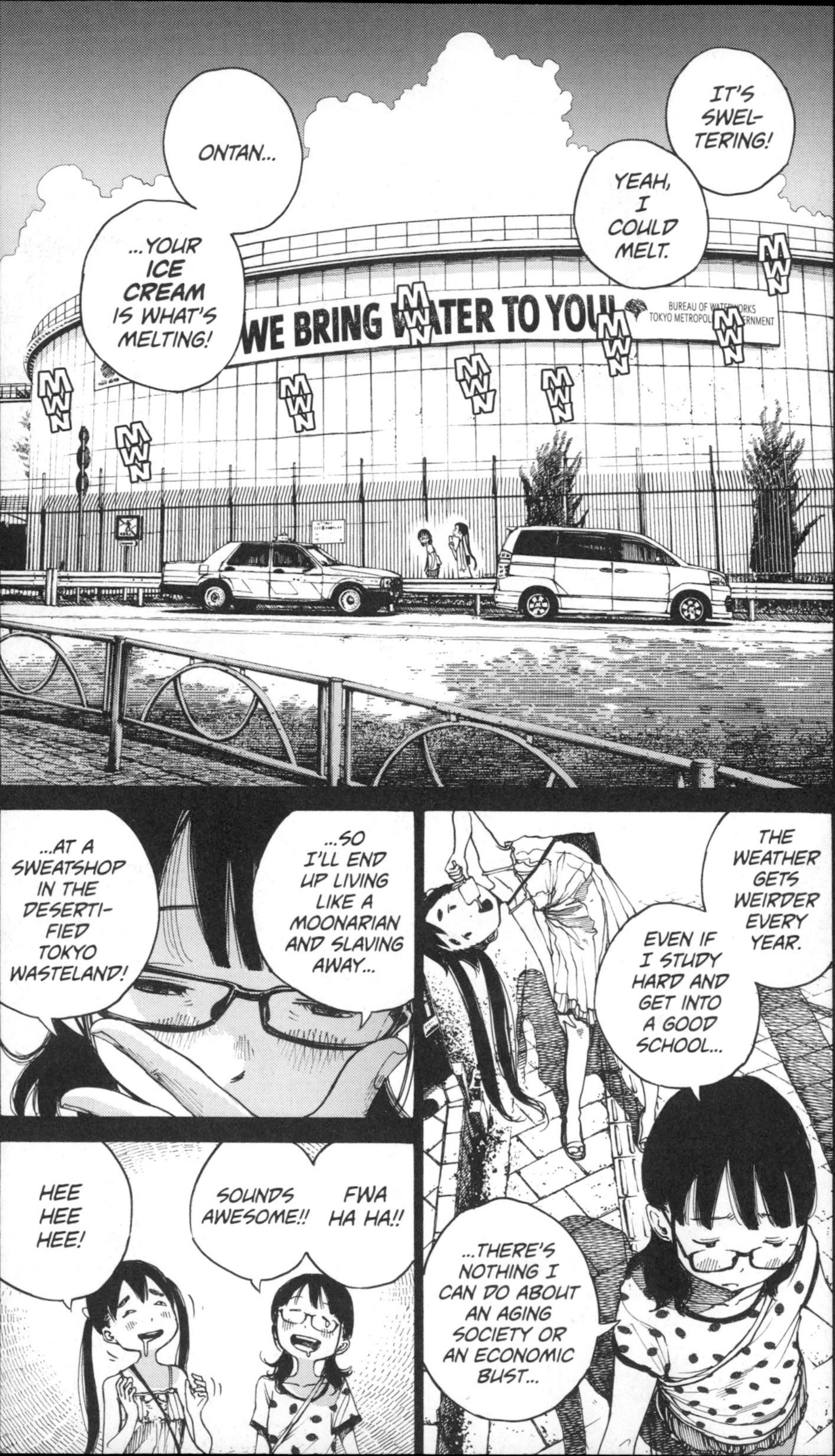
IT'S SWELTERING!
YEAH, I COULD MELT.
ONTAN...
...YOUR ICE CREAM IS WHAT'S MELTING!
MWN
THE WEATHER GETS WEIRDER EVERY YEAR.
EVEN IF I STUDY HARD AND GET INTO A GOOD SCHOOL...
...THERE'S NOTHING I CAN DO ABOUT AN AGING SOCIETY OR AN ECONOMIC BUST...
...SO I'LL END UP LIVING LIKE A MOONARIAN AND SLAVING AWAY...
...AT A SWEATSHOP IN THE DESERTIFIED TOKYO WASTELAND!
FWA HA HA!!
SOUNDS AWESOME!!
HEE HEE HEE!

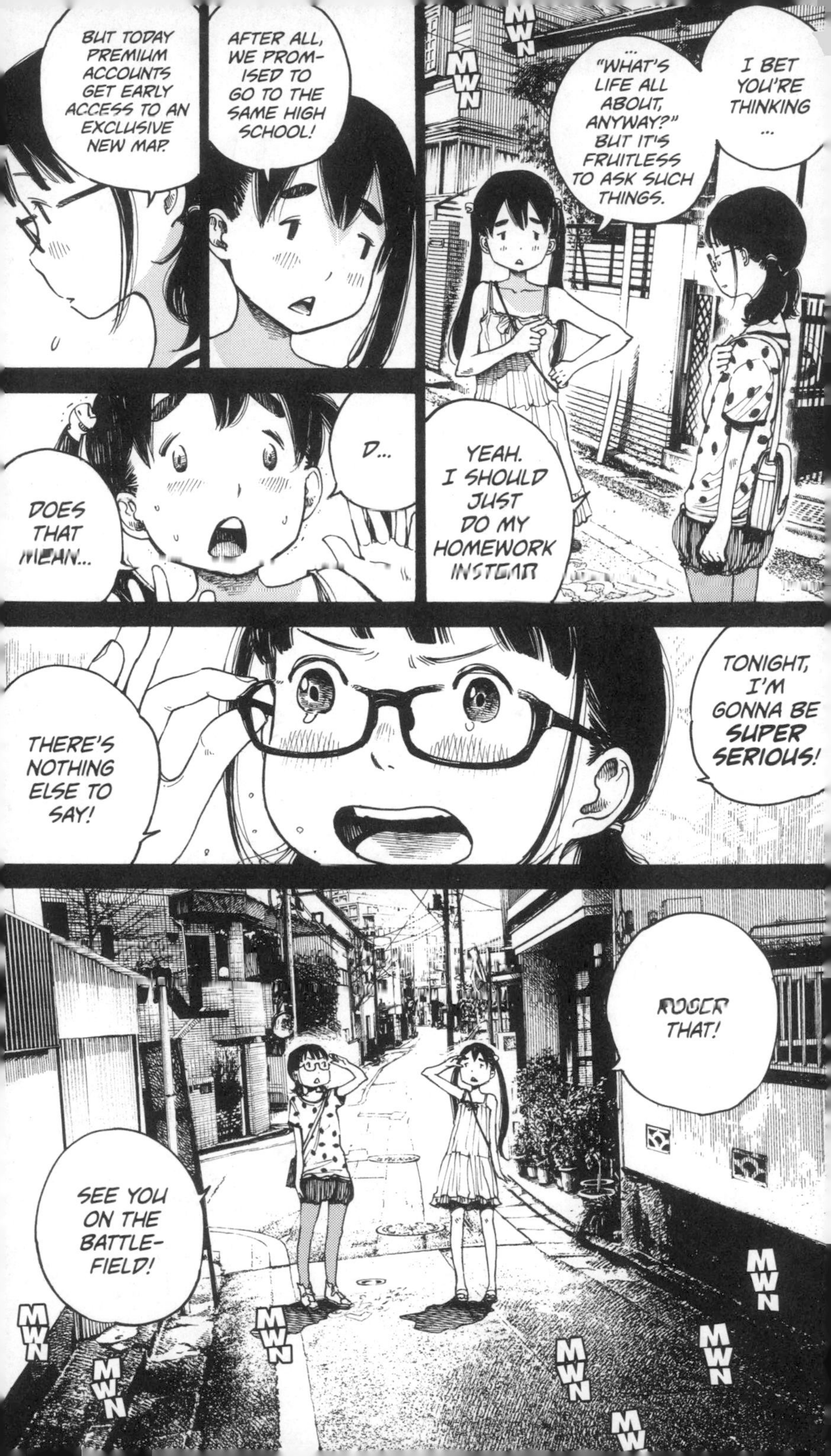
MWN
MWN
I BET YOU'RE THINKING ...
... "WHAT'S LIFE ALL ABOUT, ANYWAY?" BUT IT'S FRUITLESS TO ASK SUCH THINGS.
YEAH. I SHOULD JUST DO MY HOMEWORK INSTEAD
AFTER ALL, WE PROMISED TO GO TO THE SAME HIGH SCHOOL!
BUT TODAY PREMIUM ACCOUNTS GET EARLY ACCESS TO AN EXCLUSIVE NEW MAP.
D...
DOES THAT MEAN...
TONIGHT, I'M GONNA BE SUPER SERIOUS!
THERE'S NOTHING ELSE TO SAY!
ROGER THAT!
SEE YOU ON THE BATTLE-FIELD!
MWN
MWN
MWN
MWN
MWN
MWN
MW

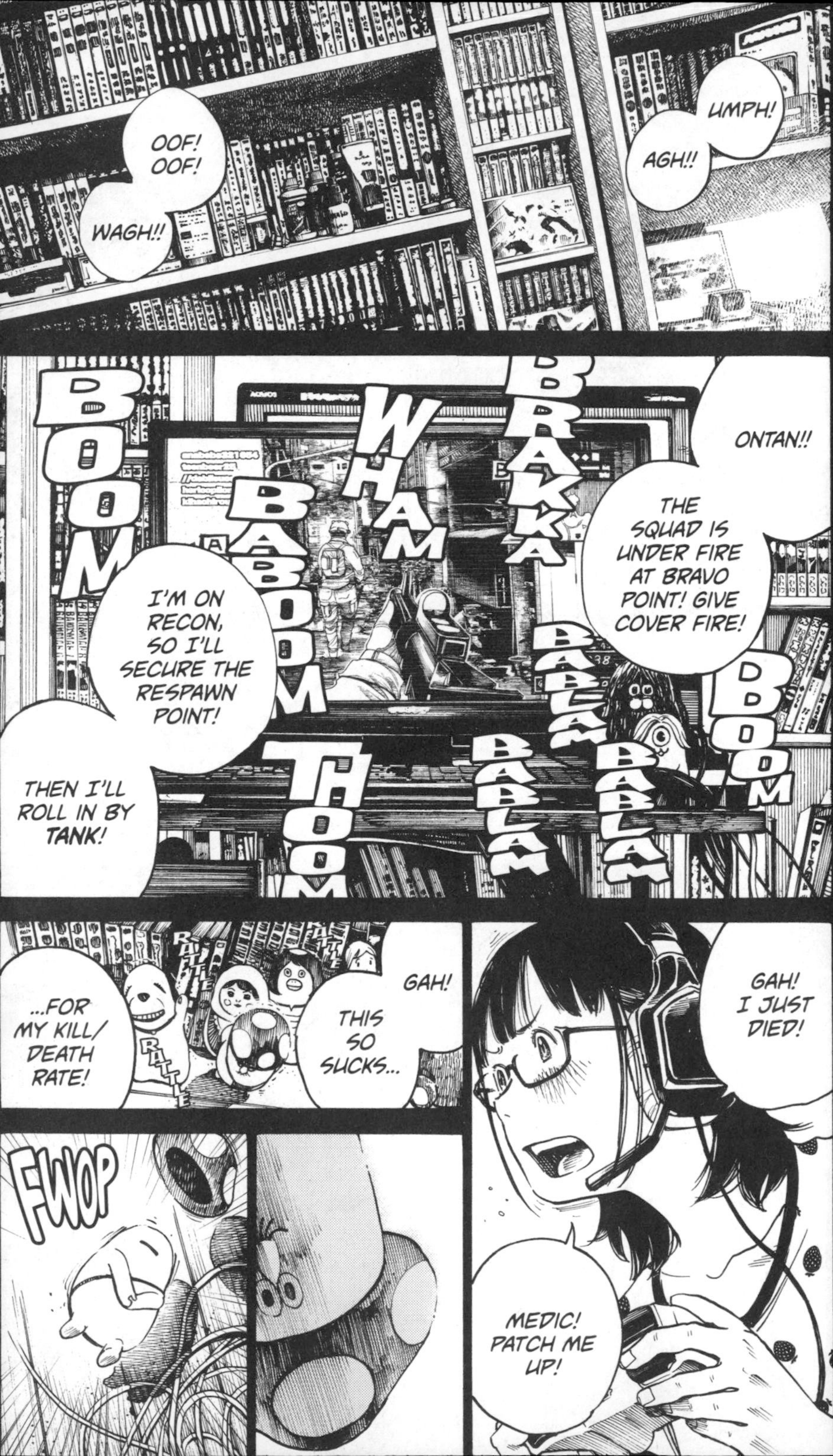
UMPH!
AGH!!
OOF! OOF!
WAGH!!
ONTAN!!
THE SQUAD IS UNDER FIRE AT BRAVO POINT! GIVE COVER FIRE!
BOOM
BRAKA
BABLAM BABLAM
BABLAM
WHAM
BABOOM
BOOM
I'M ON RECON, SO I'LL SECURE THE RESPAWN POINT!
THEN I'LL ROLL IN BY TANK!
THOOM
GAH! I JUST DIED!
RATTLE
RATTLE
GAH!
THIS SO SUCKS...
...FOR MY KILL/ DEATH RATE!
RATTLE
MEDIC! PATCH ME UP!
FWOP

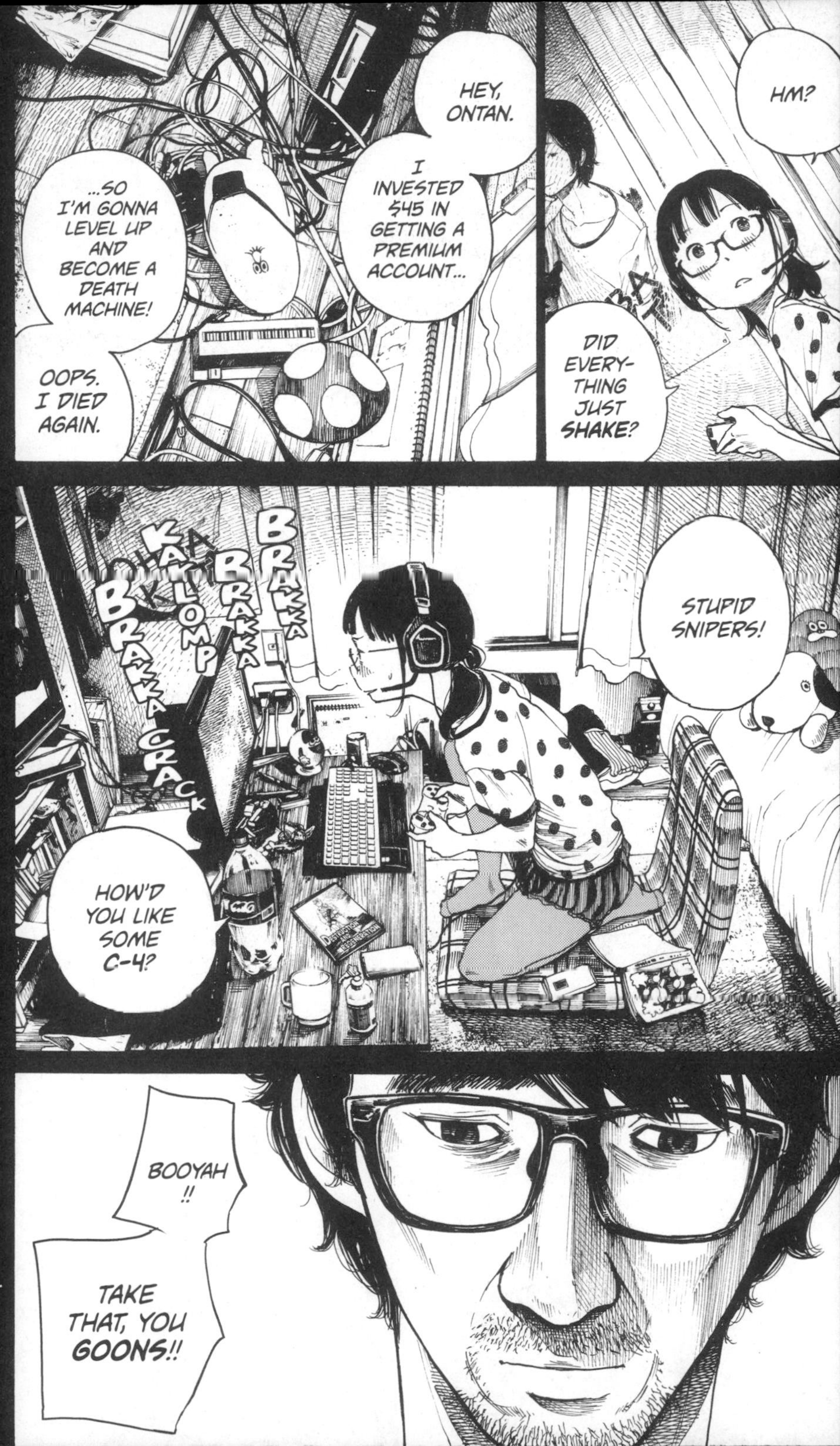
HM?
DID EVERYTHING JUST SHAKE?
HEY, ONTAN.
I INVESTED $45 IN GETTING A PREMIUM ACCOUNT...
...SO I'M GONNA LEVEL UP AND BECOME A DEATH MACHINE!
OOPS. I DIED AGAIN.
STUPID SNIPERS!
BRAKKA
BRAKKA
KA-KLOMP
BRAKKA CRACK
HOW'D YOU LIKE SOME C-4?
BOOYAH!!
TAKE THAT, YOU GOONS!!

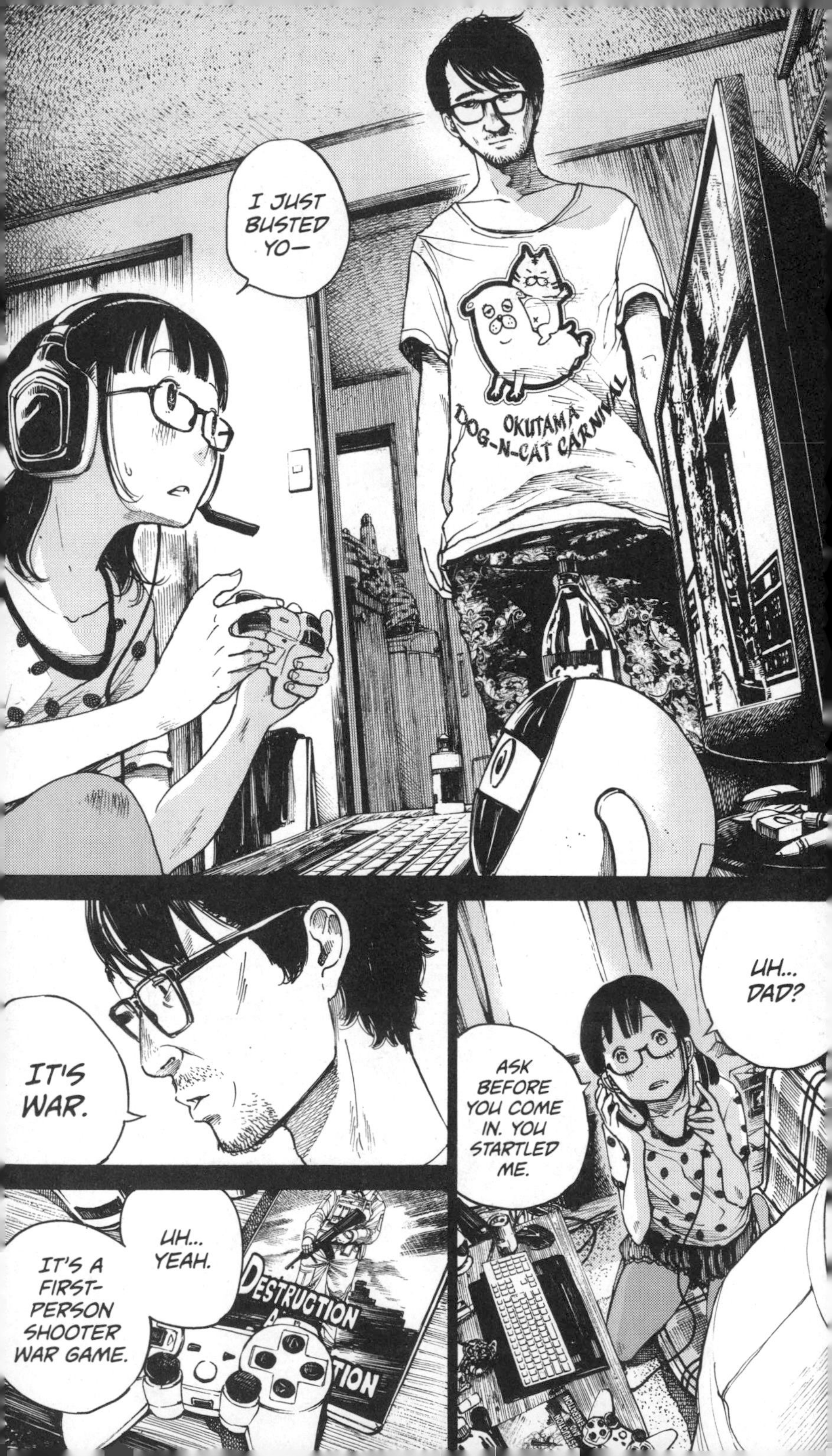
I JUST BUSTED YO—
OKUTAMA DOG-N-CAT CARNIVAL
UH... DAD?
ASK BEFORE YOU COME IN. YOU STARTLED ME.
IT'S WAR.
UH... YEAH.
IT'S A FIRST-PERSON SHOOTER WAR GAME.
DESTRUCTION

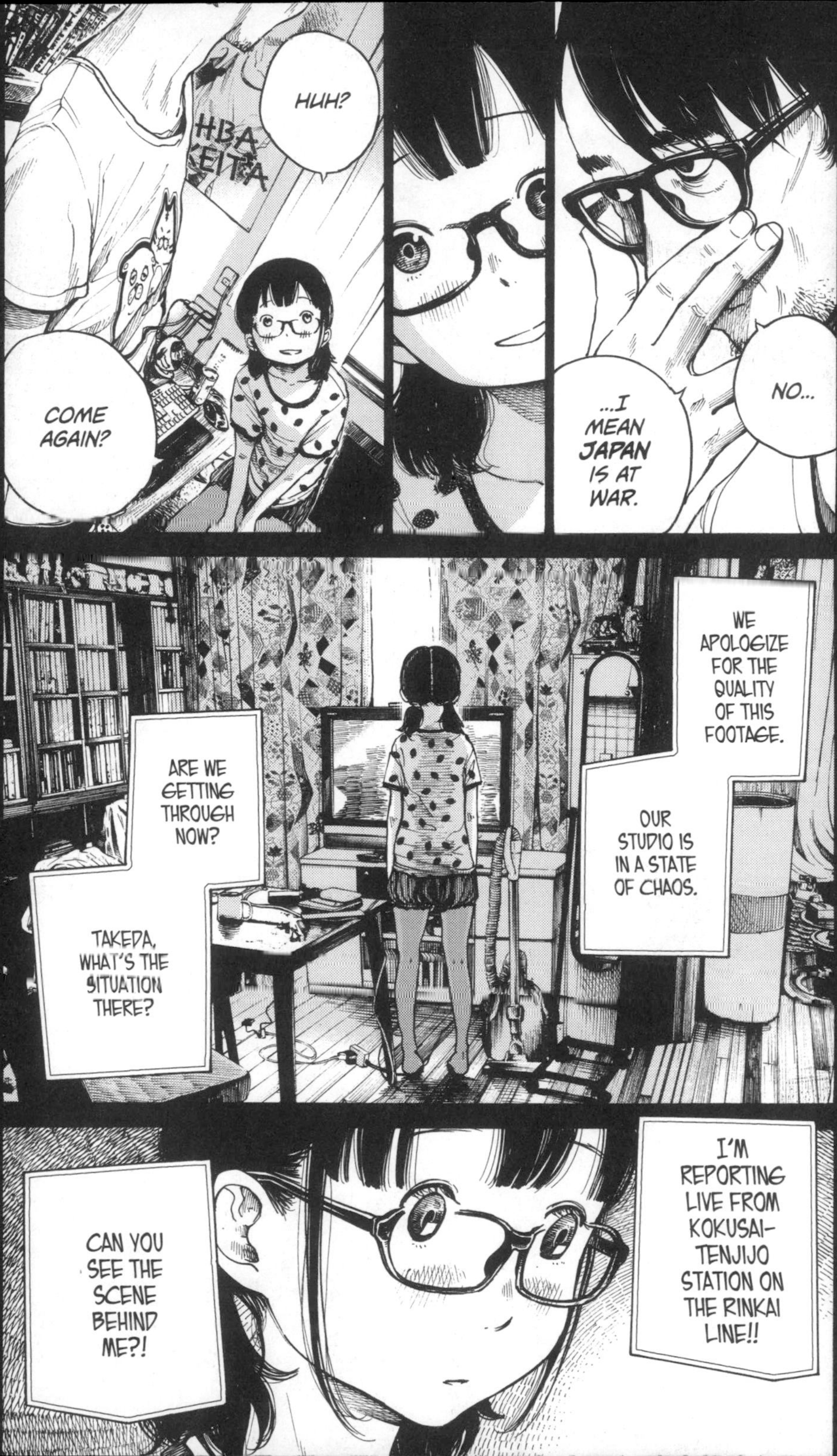
NO...
...I MEAN JAPAN IS AT WAR.
HUH?
COME AGAIN?
WE APOLOGIZE FOR THE QUALITY OF THIS FOOTAGE.
OUR STUDIO IS IN A STATE OF CHAOS.
ARE WE GETTING THROUGH NOW?
TAKEDA, WHAT'S THE SITUATION THERE?
I'M REPORTING LIVE FROM KOKUSAI-TENJIJO STATION ON THE RINKAI LINE!!
CAN YOU SEE THE SCENE BEHIND ME?!

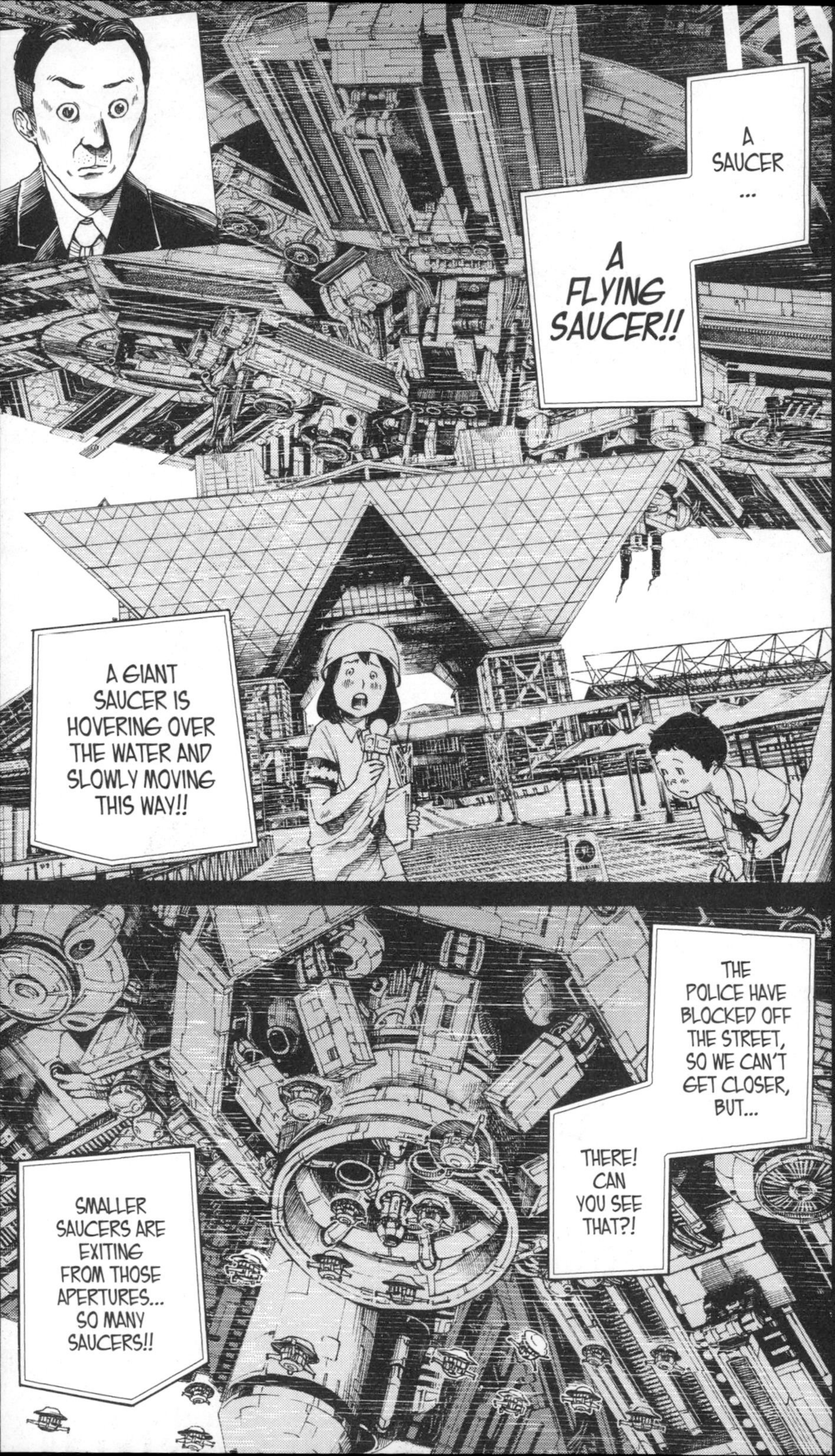
A SAUCER ...
A FLYING SAUCER!!
A GIANT SAUCER IS HOVERING OVER THE WATER AND SLOWLY MOVING THIS WAY!!
THE POLICE HAVE BLOCKED OFF THE STREET, SO WE CAN'T GET CLOSER, BUT...
THERE! CAN YOU SEE THAT?!
SMALLER SAUCERS ARE EXITING FROM THOSE APERTURES... SO MANY SAUCERS!!

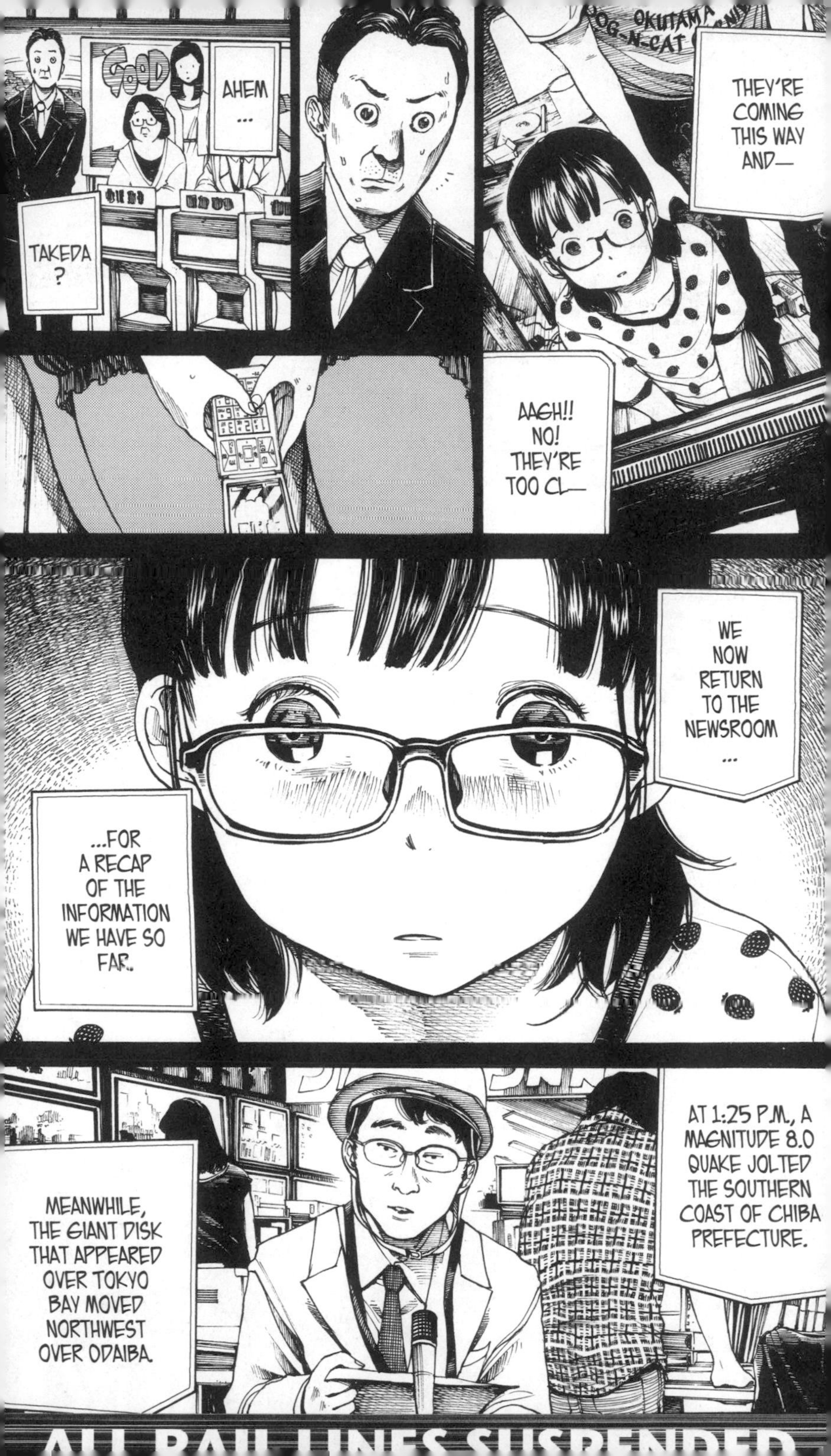
OKUTAMA
THEY'RE COMING THIS WAY AND—
GOOD
AHEM ...
TAKEDA ?
AAGH!! NO! THEY'RE TOO CL—
WE NOW RETURN TO THE NEWSROOM ...
...FOR A RECAP OF THE INFORMATION WE HAVE SO FAR..
AT 1:25 P.M., A MAGNITUDE 8.0 QUAKE JOLTED THE SOUTHERN COAST OF CHIBA PREFECTURE.
MEANWHILE, THE GIANT DISK THAT APPEARED OVER TOKYO BAY MOVED NORTHWEST OVER ODAIBA.

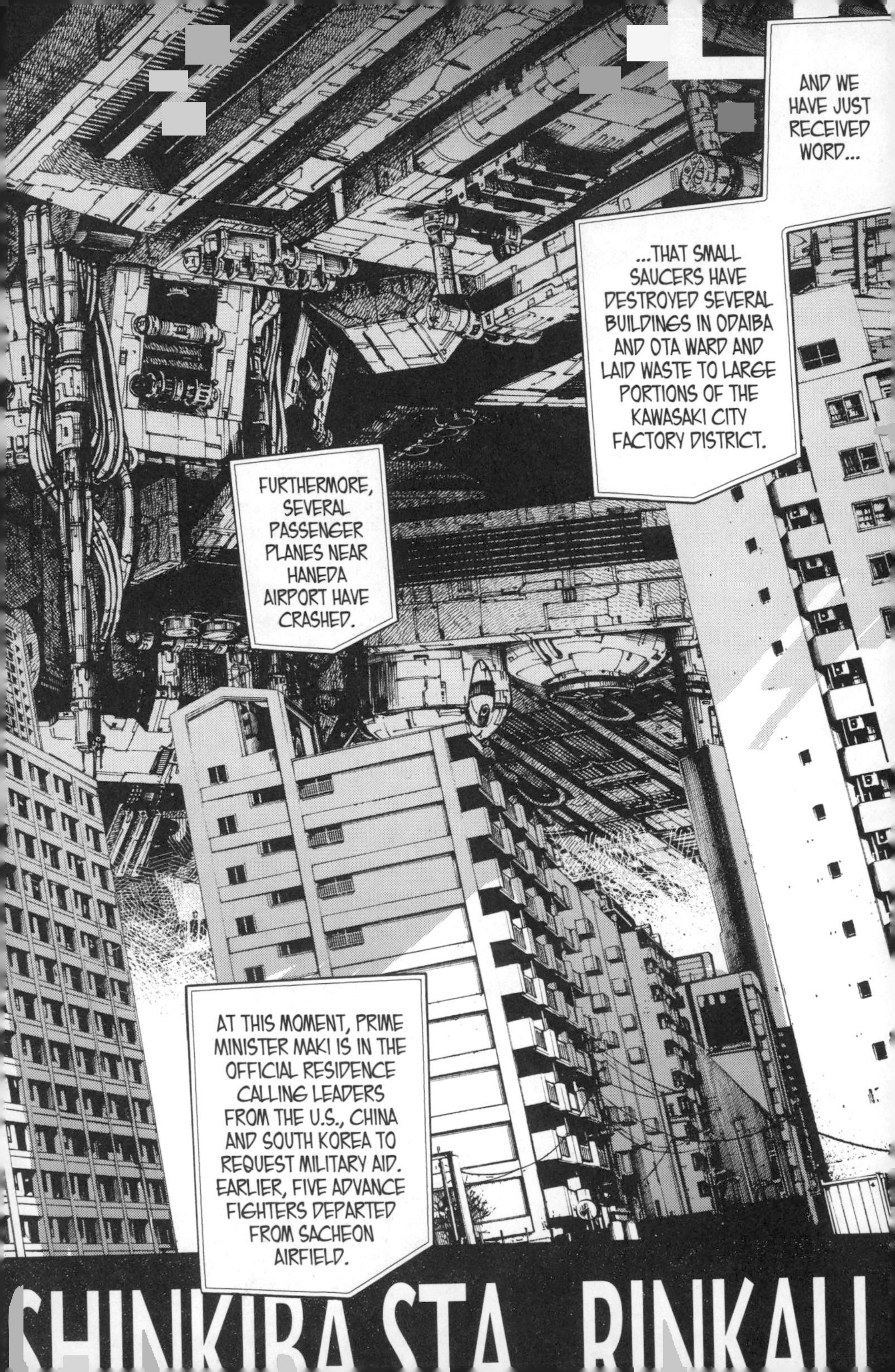
AND WE HAVE JUST RECEIVED WORD...
...THAT SMALL SAUCERS HAVE DESTROYED SEVERAL BUILDINGS IN ODAIBA AND OTA WARD AND LAID WASTE TO LARGE PORTIONS OF THE KAWASAKI CITY FACTORY DISTRICT.
FURTHERMORE, SEVERAL PASSENGER PLANES NEAR HANEDA AIRPORT HAVE CRASHED.
AT THIS MOMENT, PRIME MINISTER MAKI IS IN THE OFFICIAL RESIDENCE CALLING LEADERS FROM THE U.S., CHINA AND SOUTH KOREA TO REQUEST MILITARY AID. EARLIER, FIVE ADVANCE FIGHTERS DEPARTED FROM SACHEON AIRFIELD.

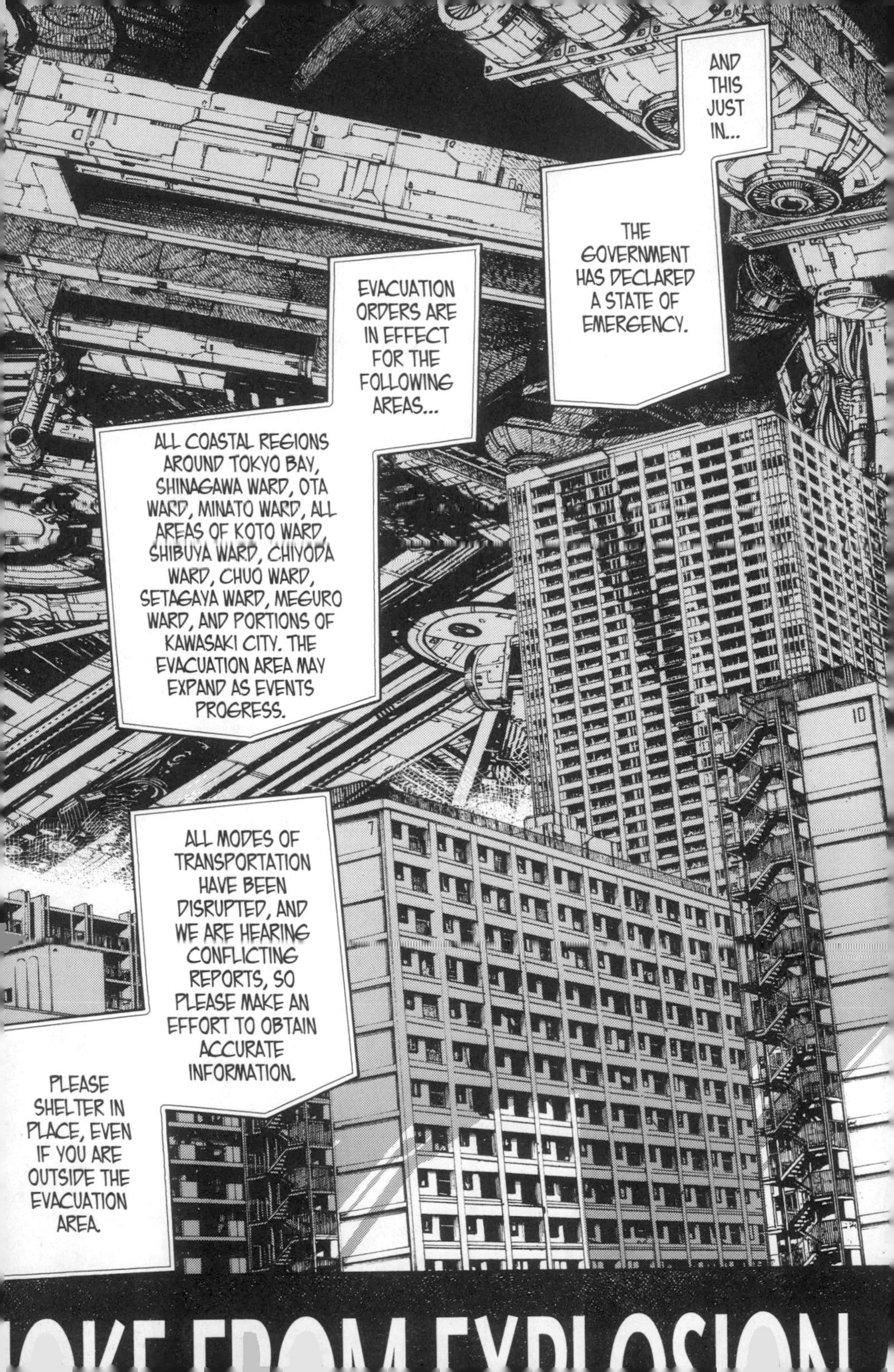
AND THIS JUST IN...
THE GOVERNMENT HAS DECLARED A STATE OF EMERGENCY.
EVACUATION ORDERS ARE IN EFFECT FOR THE FOLLOWING AREAS...
ALL COASTAL REGIONS AROUND TOKYO BAY, SHINAGAWA WARD, OTA WARD, MINATO WARD, ALL AREAS OF KOTO WARD, SHIBUYA WARD, CHIYODA WARD, CHUO WARD, SETAGAYA WARD, MEGURO WARD, AND PORTIONS OF KAWASAKI CITY. THE EVACUATION AREA MAY EXPAND AS EVENTS PROGRESS.
ALL MODES OF TRANSPORTATION HAVE BEEN DISRUPTED, AND WE ARE HEARING CONFLICTING REPORTS, SO PLEASE MAKE AN EFFORT TO OBTAIN ACCURATE INFORMATION.
PLEASE SHELTER IN PLACE, EVEN IF YOU ARE OUTSIDE THE EVACUATION AREA.
10
7
OKE FROM EXPLOSION

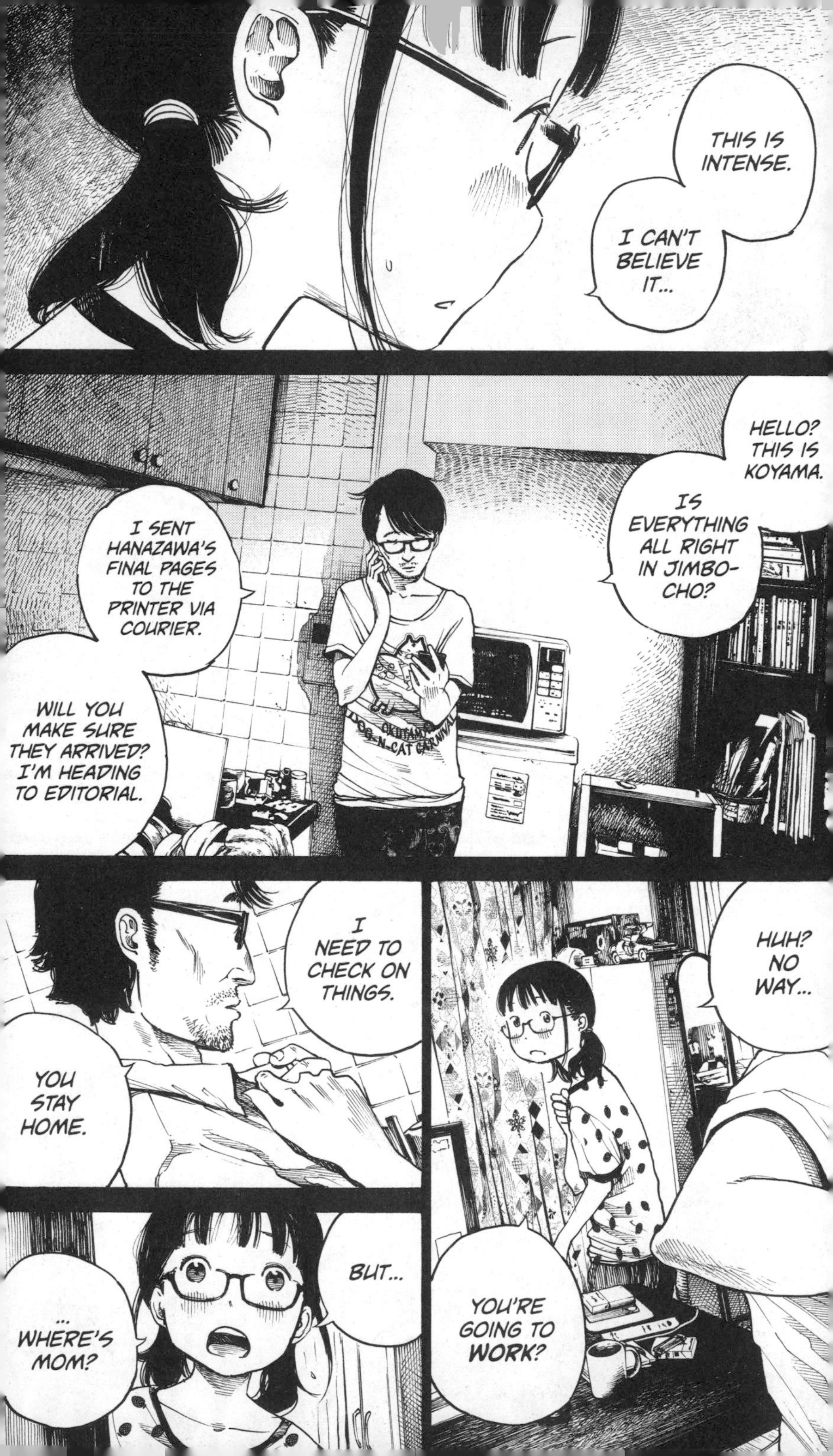
THIS IS INTENSE.
I CAN'T BELIEVE IT...
HELLO? THIS IS KOYAMA.
IS EVERYTHING ALL RIGHT IN JIMBO-CHO?
I SENT HANAZAWA'S FINAL PAGES TO THE PRINTER VIA COURIER.
WILL YOU MAKE SURE THEY ARRIVED? I'M HEADING TO EDITORIAL.
HUH? NO WAY...
YOU'RE GOING TO WORK?
I NEED TO CHECK ON THINGS.
YOU STAY HOME.
BUT...
...WHERE'S MOM?

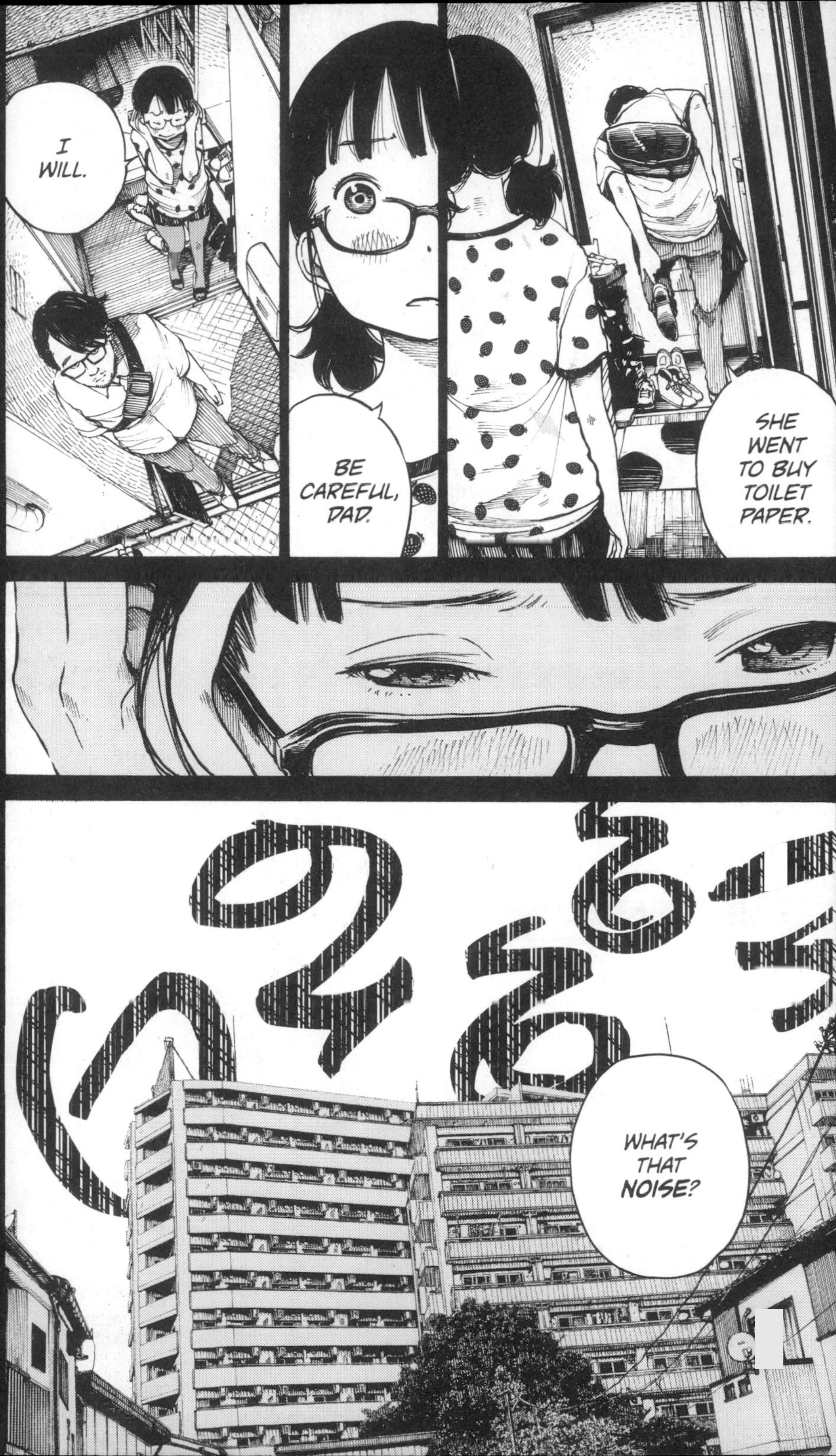
SHE WENT TO BUY TOILET PAPER.
BE CAREFUL, DAD.
I WILL.
WHAT'S THAT NOISE?

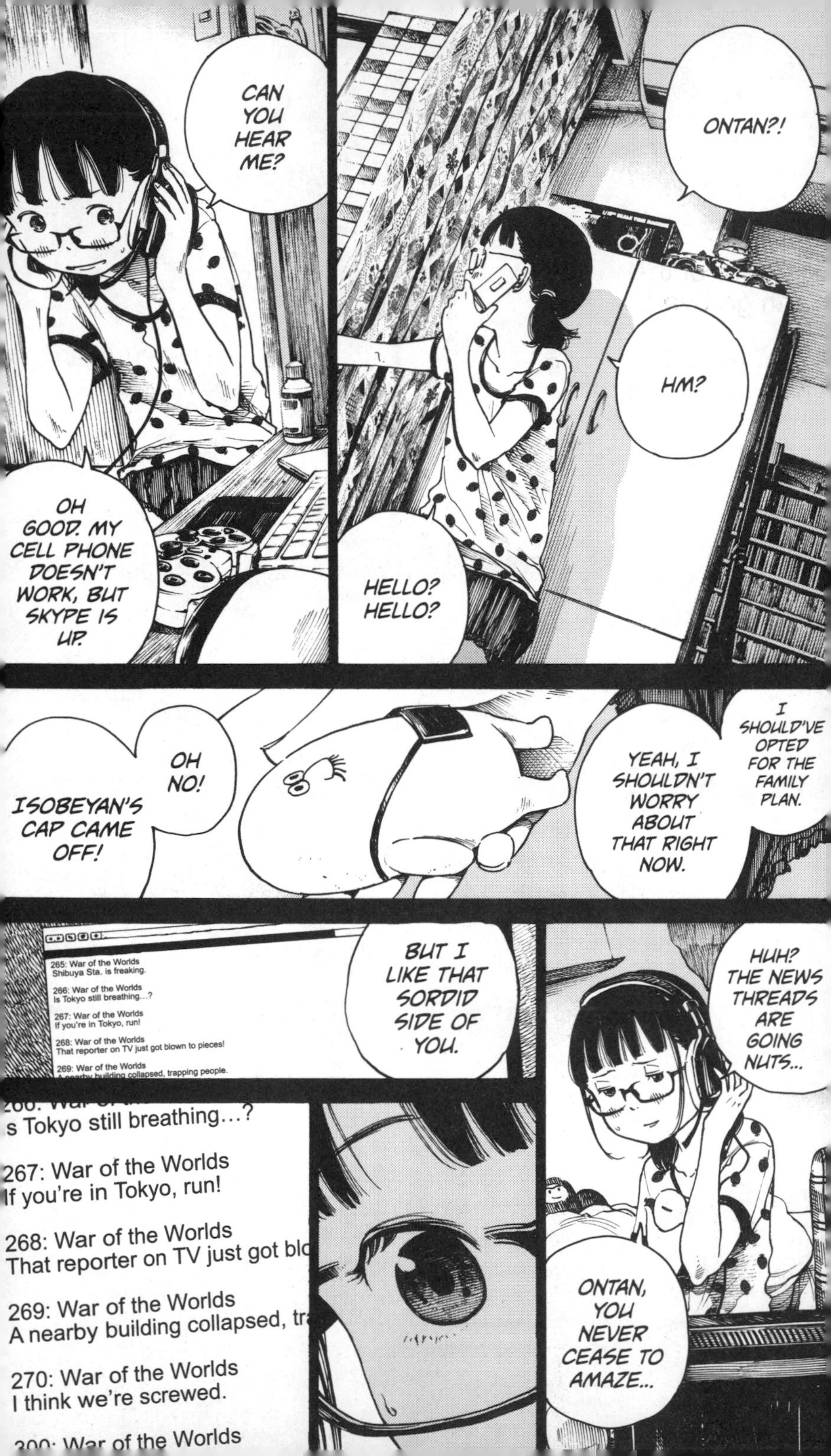
ONTAN?!
HM?
HELLO? HELLO?
CAN YOU HEAR ME?
OH GOOD. MY CELL PHONE DOESN'T WORK, BUT SKYPE IS UP.
I SHOULD'VE OPTED FOR THE FAMILY PLAN.
YEAH, I SHOULDN'T WORRY ABOUT THAT RIGHT NOW.
OH NO!
ISOBEYAN'S CAP CAME OFF!
BUT I LIKE THAT SORDID SIDE OF YOU.
265: War of the Worlds
Shibuya Sta. is freaking.
266: War of the Worlds
Is Tokyo still breathing…?
267: War of the Worlds
If you're in Tokyo, run!
268: War of the Worlds
That reporter on TV just got blown to pieces!
269: War of the Worlds
HUH? THE NEWS THREADS ARE GOING NUTS...
s Tokyo still breathing…?
267: War of the Worlds
If you're in Tokyo, run!
268: War of the Worlds
That reporter on TV just got bl
269: War of the Worlds
A nearby building collapsed, tr
270: War of the Worlds
I think we're screwed.
300: War of the Worlds
ONTAN, YOU NEVER CEASE TO AMAZE...

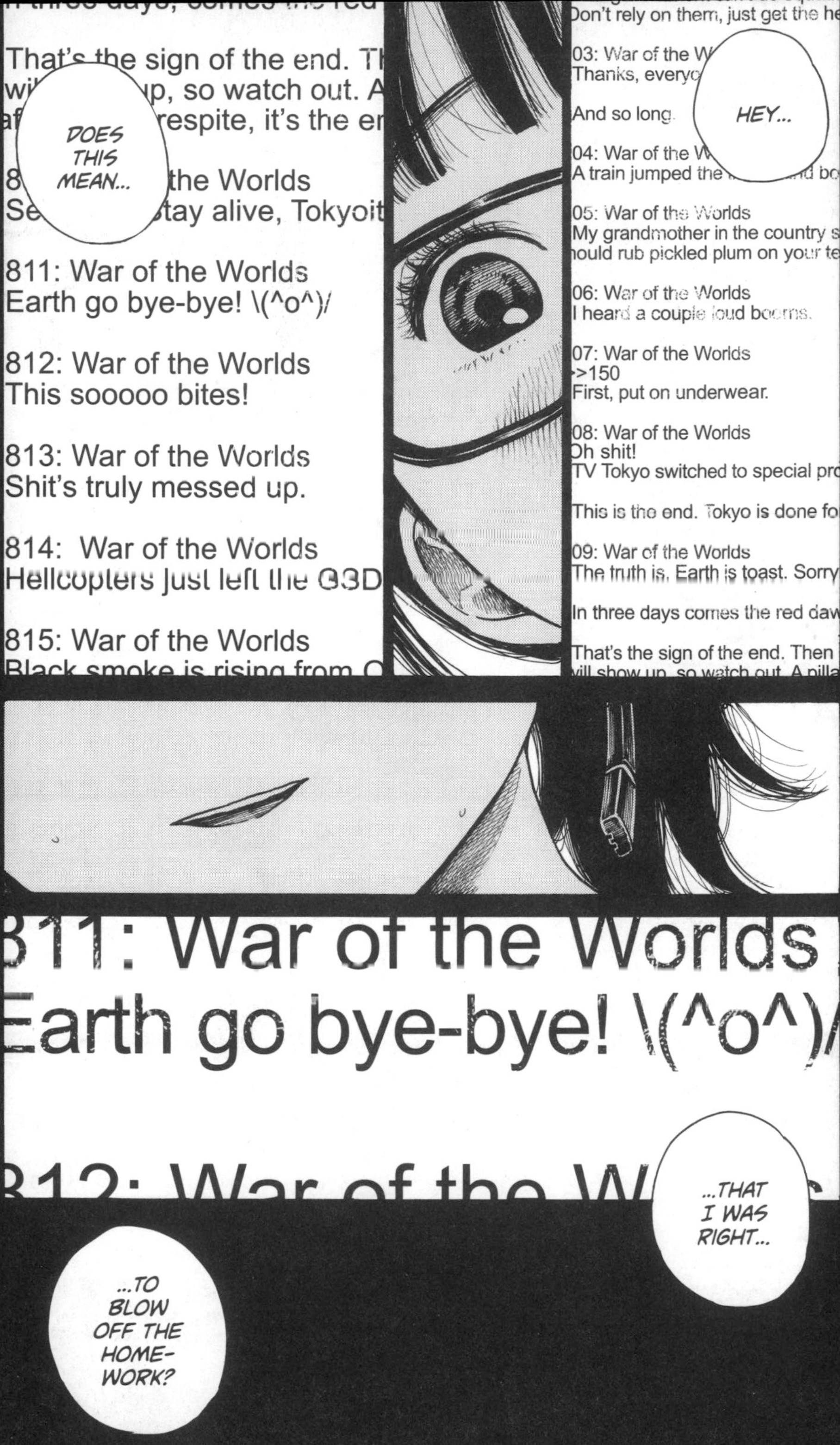

Don't rely on them, just get the
03: War of the W
Thanks, everyo
And so long.
HEY...
04: War of the W
A train jumped the
05: War of the Worlds
My grandmother in the country
ould rub pickled plum on your
06: War of the Worlds
I heard a couple loud booms.
07: War of the Worlds
>150
First, put on underwear.
08: War of the Worlds
Oh shit!
TV Tokyo switched to special pr
This is the end. Tokyo is done fo
09: War of the Worlds
The truth is, Earth is toast. Sorry
In three days comes the red daw
That's the sign of the end. Then
That's the sign of the end. Th
p, so watch out. A
respite, it's the e
DOES THIS MEAN...
the Worlds
stay alive, Tokyoit
811: War of the Worlds
Earth go bye-bye! \(^o^)/
812: War of the Worlds
This sooooo bites!
813: War of the Worlds
Shit's truly messed up.
814: War of the Worlds
Helicopters just left the
815: War of the Worlds
811: War of the Worlds
Earth go bye-bye! \(^o^)/
...THAT I WAS RIGHT...
...TO BLOW OFF THE HOME-WORK?

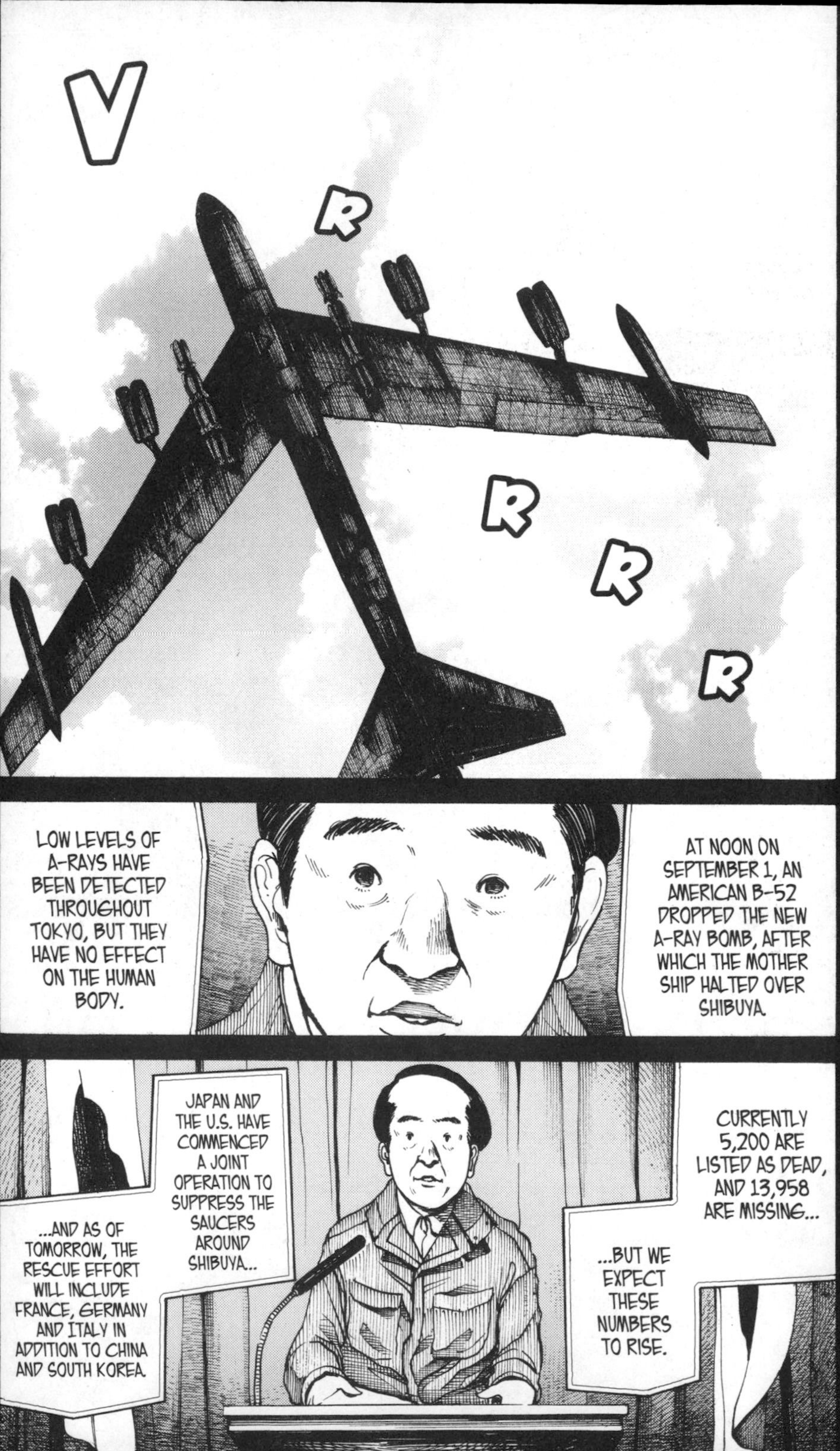
VRRRR
AT NOON ON SEPTEMBER 1, AN AMERICAN B-52 DROPPED THE NEW A-RAY BOMB, AFTER WHICH THE MOTHER SHIP HALTED OVER SHIBUYA.
LOW LEVELS OF A-RAYS HAVE BEEN DETECTED THROUGHOUT TOKYO, BUT THEY HAVE NO EFFECT ON THE HUMAN BODY.
CURRENTLY 5,200 ARE LISTED AS DEAD, AND 13,958 ARE MISSING...
...BUT WE EXPECT THESE NUMBERS TO RISE.
JAPAN AND THE U.S. HAVE COMMENCED A JOINT OPERATION TO SUPPRESS THE SAUCERS AROUND SHIBUYA...
...AND AS OF TOMORROW, THE RESCUE EFFORT WILL INCLUDE FRANCE, GERMANY AND ITALY IN ADDITION TO CHINA AND SOUTH KOREA.

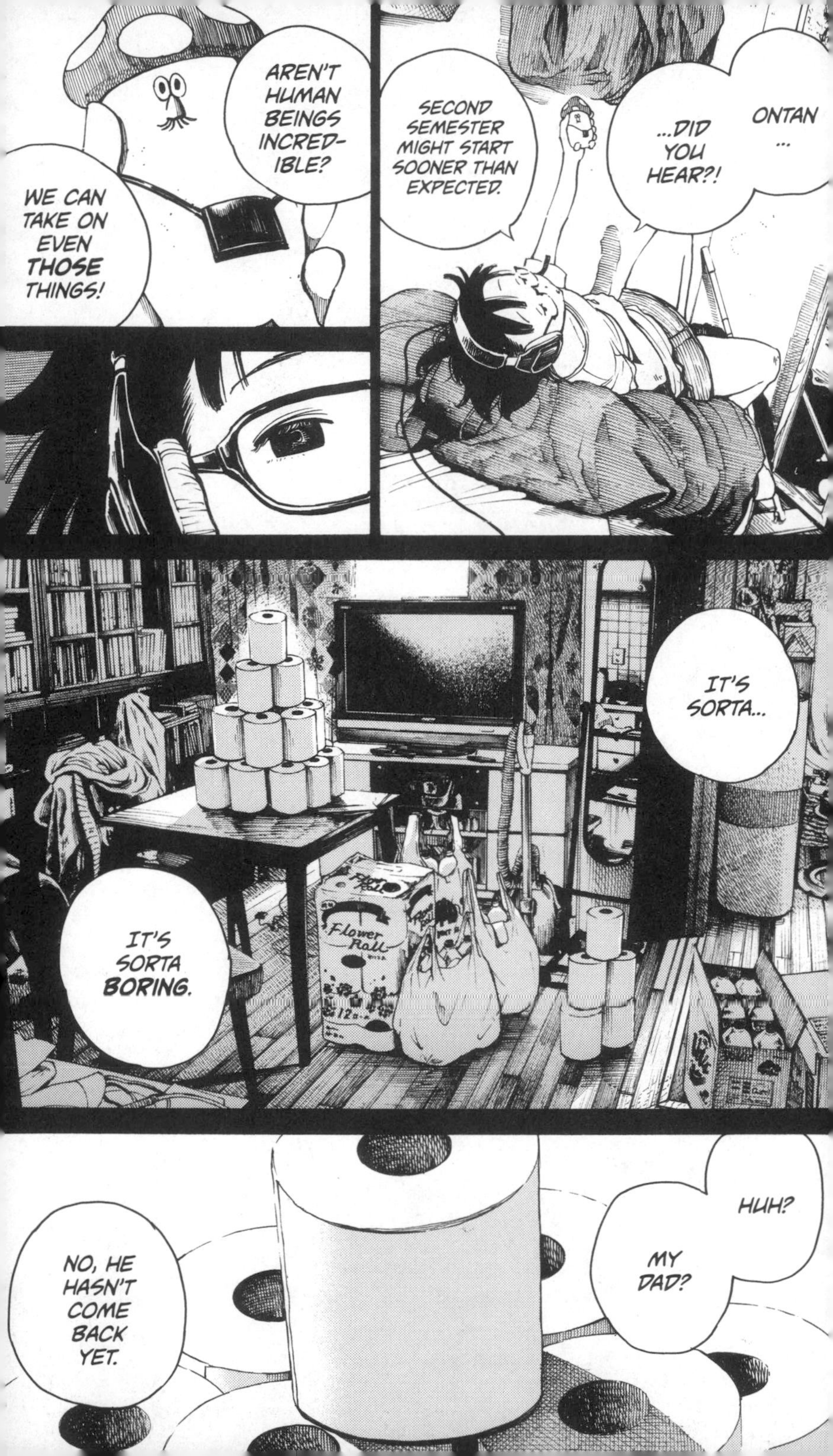
ONTAN ...
...DID YOU HEAR?!
SECOND SEMESTER MIGHT START SOONER THAN EXPECTED.
AREN'T HUMAN BEINGS INCREDIBLE?
WE CAN TAKE ON EVEN THOSE THINGS!
IT'S SORTA...
IT'S SORTA BORING.
HUH?
MY DAD?
NO, HE HASN'T COME BACK YET.

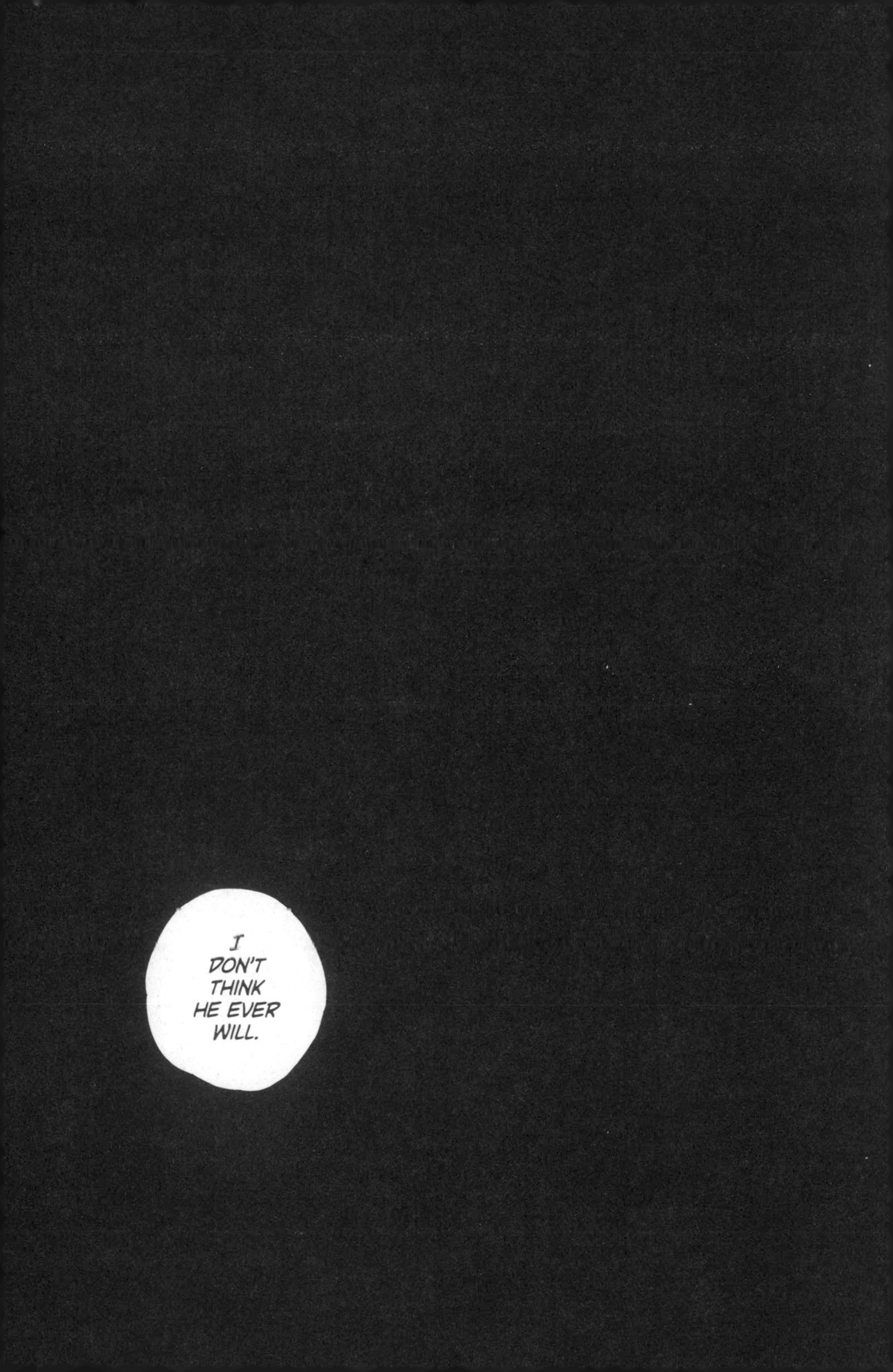
I DON'T THINK HE EVER WILL.

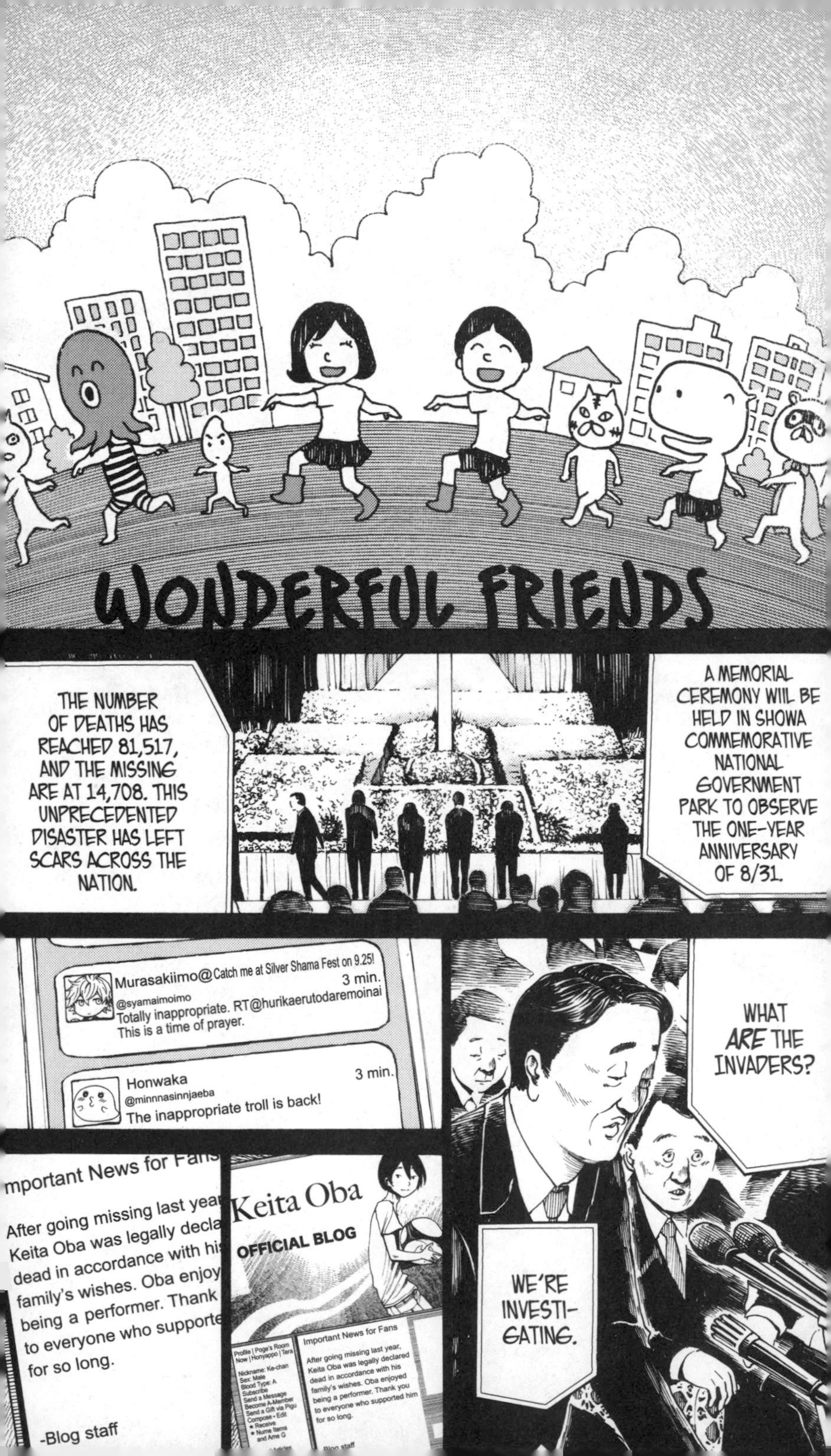
WONDERFUL FRIENDS
A MEMORIAL CEREMONY WILL BE HELD IN SHOWA COMMEMORATIVE NATIONAL GOVERNMENT PARK TO OBSERVE THE ONE-YEAR ANNIVERSARY OF 8/31.
THE NUMBER OF DEATHS HAS REACHED 81,517, AND THE MISSING ARE AT 14,708. THIS UNPRECEDENTED DISASTER HAS LEFT SCARS ACROSS THE NATION.
WHAT ARE THE INVADERS?
WE'RE INVESTI-GATING.
Murasakiimo@Catch me at Silver Shama Fest on 9.25!
3 min.
@syamaimoimo
Totally inappropriate. RT@hurikaerutodaremoinai
This is a time of prayer.
Honwaka
3 min.
@minnnasinnjaeba
The inappropriate troll is back!
mportant News for Fan
After going missing last yea
Keita Oba was legally decla
dead in accordance with hi
family's wishes. Oba enjoy
being a performer. Thank
to everyone who support
for so long.
-Blog staff
Keita Oba
OFFICIAL BLOG
Profile | Poge's Room
Now | Honyappo | Tera
Nickname: Ke-chan
Sex: Male
Blood Type: A
Subscribe
Send a Message
Become A-Member
Send a Gift via Pigu
Compose • Edit
★ Receive
★ Nume Items
and Ame G
Important News for Fans
After going missing last year, Keita Oba was legally declared dead in accordance with his family's wishes. Oba enjoyed being a performer. Thank you to everyone who supported him for so long.

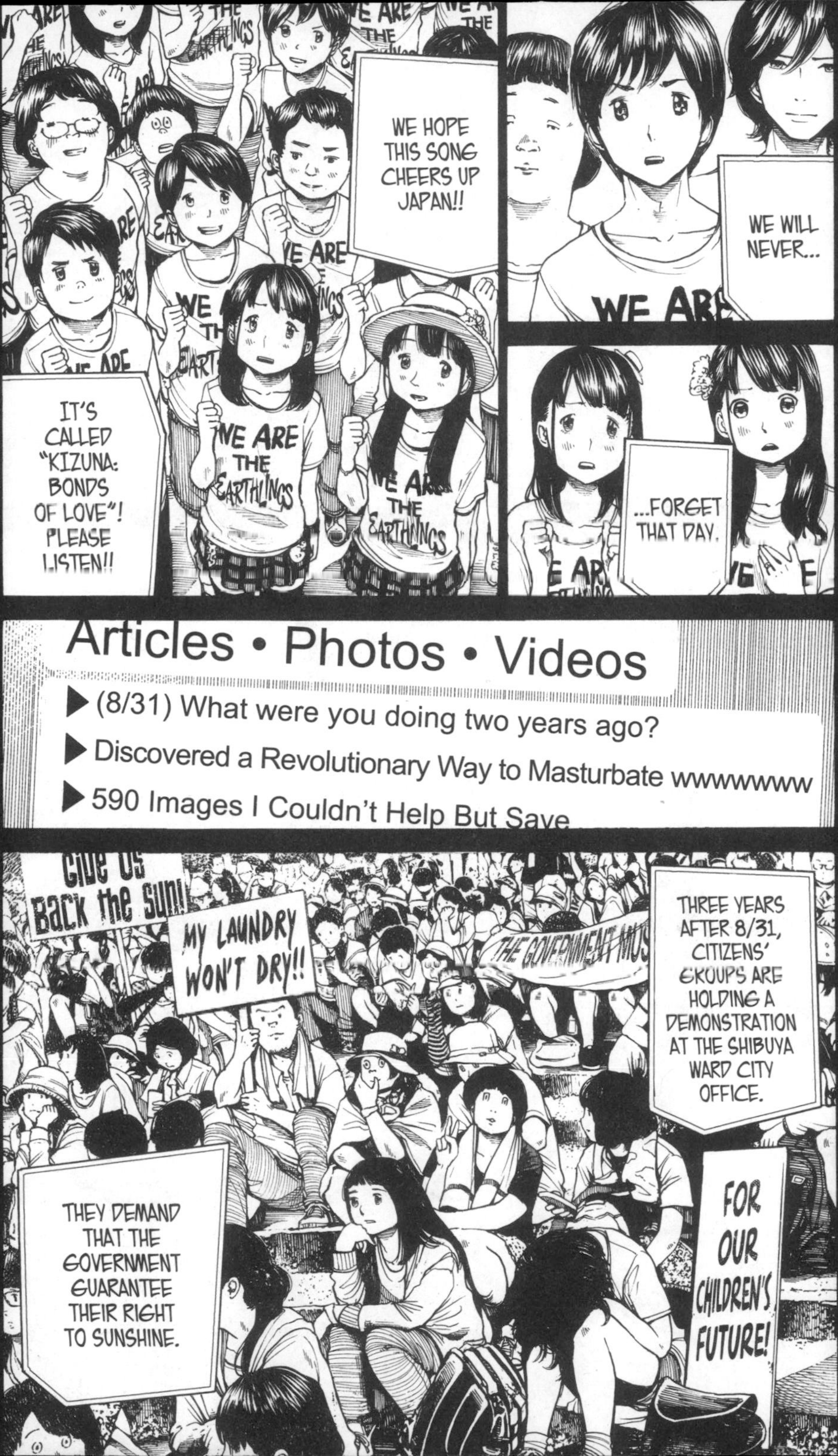
WE WILL NEVER...
...FORGET THAT DAY.
WE HOPE THIS SONG CHEERS UP JAPAN!!
IT'S CALLED "KIZUNA: BONDS OF LOVE"! PLEASE LISTEN!!
Articles • Photos • Videos
▶ (8/31) What were you doing two years ago?
▶ Discovered a Revolutionary Way to Masturbate wwwwwww
▶ 590 Images I Couldn't Help But Save
THREE YEARS AFTER 8/31, CITIZENS' GROUPS ARE HOLDING A DEMONSTRATION AT THE SHIBUYA WARD CITY OFFICE.
MY LAUNDRY WON'T DRY!!
Give Us Back the Sun!
FOR OUR CHILDREN'S FUTURE!
THEY DEMAND THAT THE GOVERNMENT GUARANTEE THEIR RIGHT TO SUNSHINE.

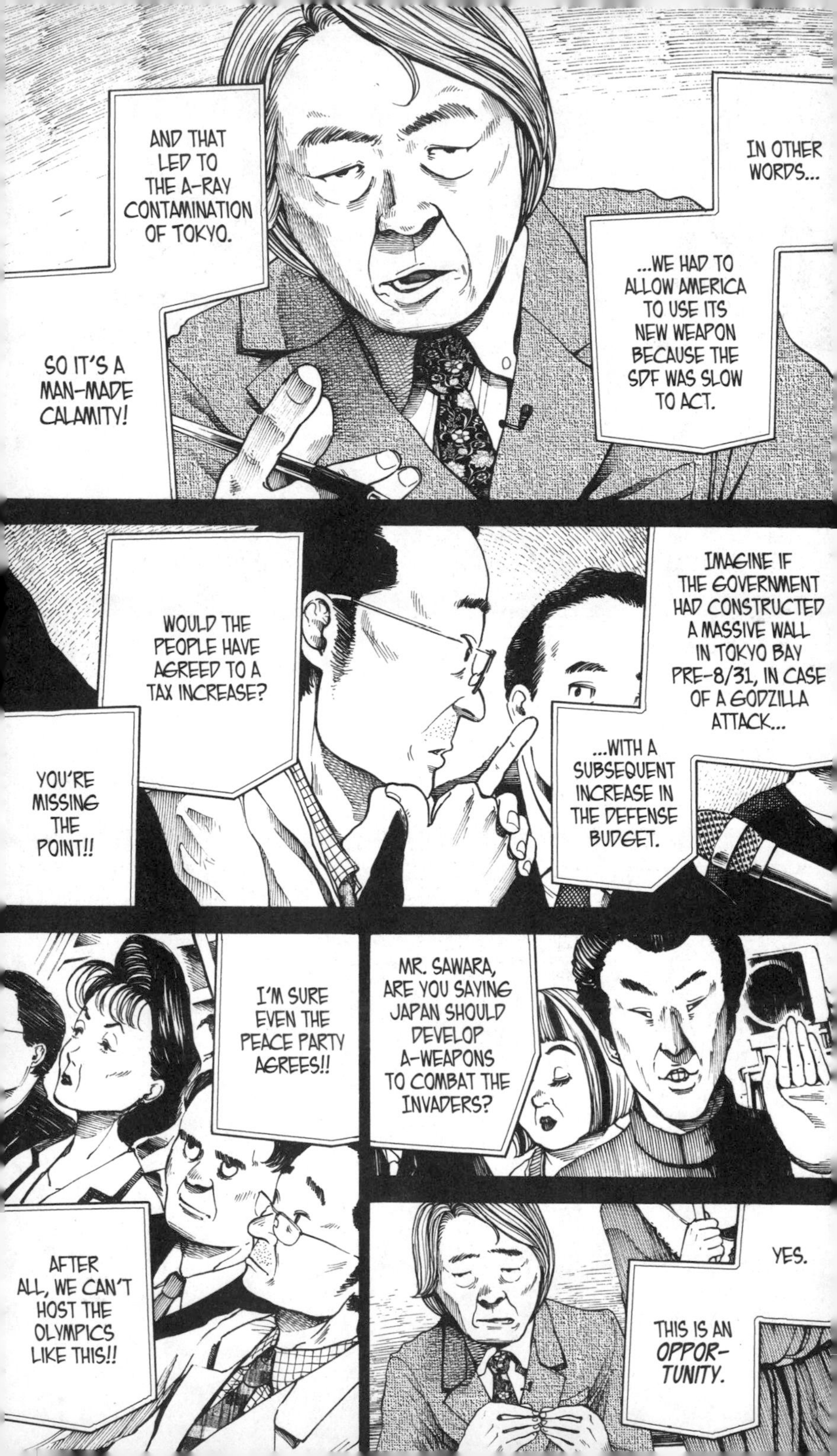
IN OTHER WORDS...
...WE HAD TO ALLOW AMERICA TO USE ITS NEW WEAPON BECAUSE THE SDF WAS SLOW TO ACT.
AND THAT LED TO THE A-RAY CONTAMINATION OF TOKYO.
SO IT'S A MAN-MADE CALAMITY!
IMAGINE IF THE GOVERNMENT HAD CONSTRUCTED A MASSIVE WALL IN TOKYO BAY PRE-8/31, IN CASE OF A GODZILLA ATTACK...
...WITH A SUBSEQUENT INCREASE IN THE DEFENSE BUDGET.
WOULD THE PEOPLE HAVE AGREED TO A TAX INCREASE?
YOU'RE MISSING THE POINT!!
MR. SAWARA, ARE YOU SAYING JAPAN SHOULD DEVELOP A-WEAPONS TO COMBAT THE INVADERS?
YES.
THIS IS AN *OPPOR-TUNITY*.
I'M SURE EVEN THE PEACE PARTY AGREES!!
AFTER ALL, WE CAN'T HOST THE OLYMPICS LIKE THIS!!

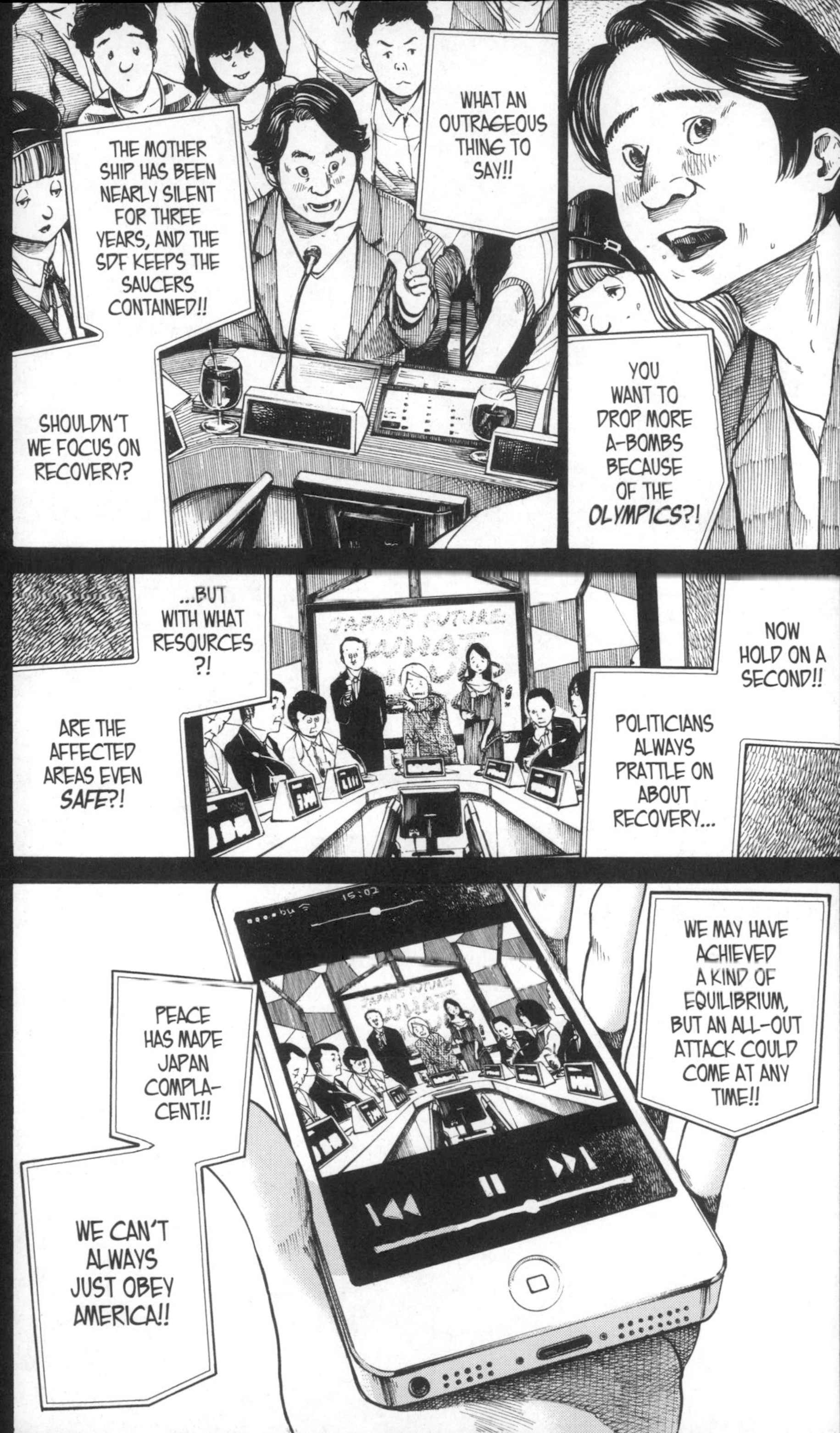
YOU WANT TO DROP MORE A-BOMBS BECAUSE OF THE *OLYMPICS*?!
WHAT AN OUTRAGEOUS THING TO SAY!!
THE MOTHER SHIP HAS BEEN NEARLY SILENT FOR THREE YEARS, AND THE SDF KEEPS THE SAUCERS CONTAINED!!
SHOULDN'T WE FOCUS ON RECOVERY?
NOW HOLD ON A SECOND!!
POLITICIANS ALWAYS PRATTLE ON ABOUT RECOVERY...
...BUT WITH WHAT RESOURCES ?!
ARE THE AFFECTED AREAS EVEN *SAFE*?!
WE MAY HAVE ACHIEVED A KIND OF EQUILIBRIUM, BUT AN ALL-OUT ATTACK COULD COME AT ANY TIME!!
PEACE HAS MADE JAPAN COMPLA-CENT!!
WE CAN'T ALWAYS JUST OBEY AMERICA!!

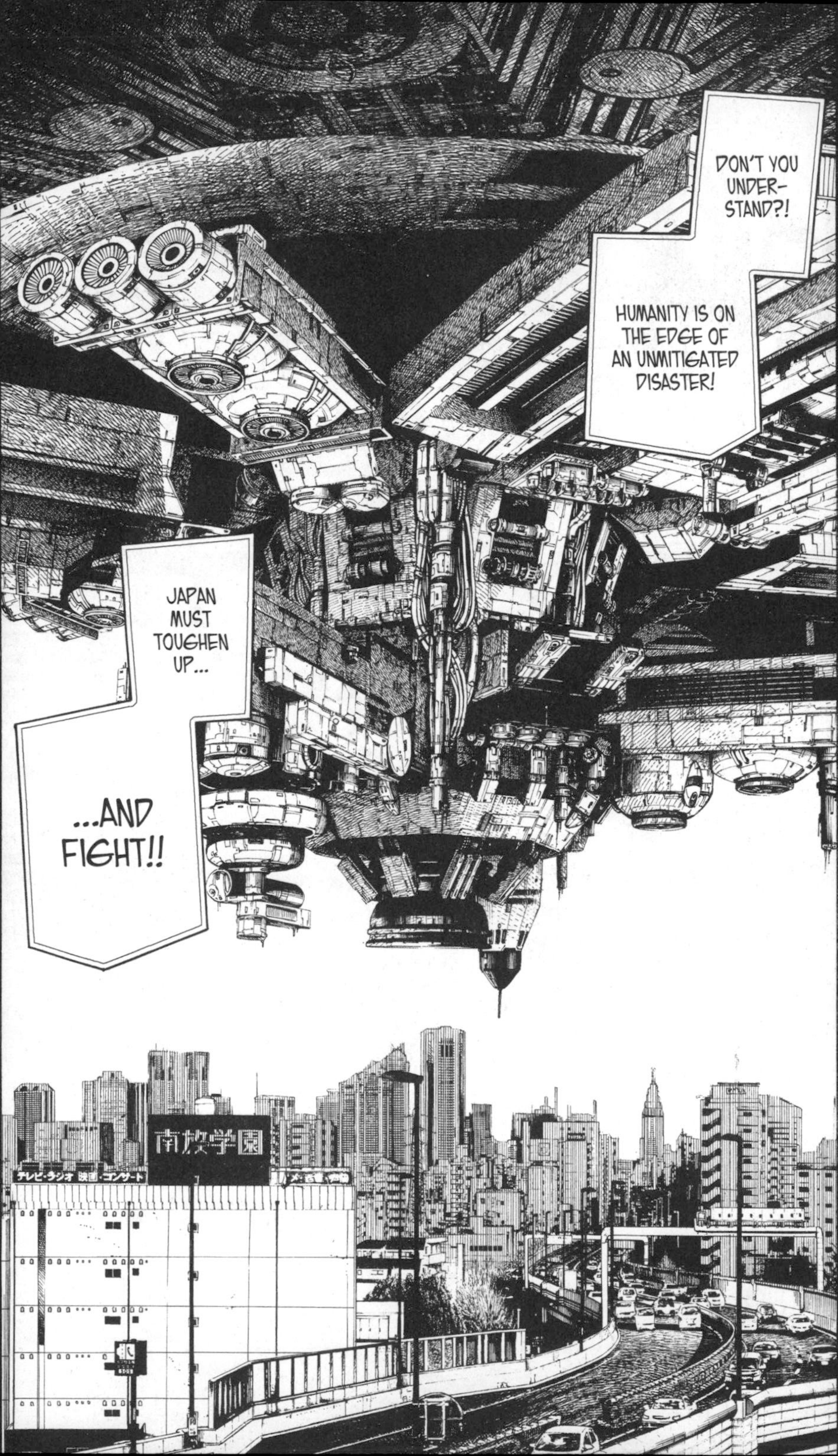
DON'T YOU UNDER-STAND?!
HUMANITY IS ON THE EDGE OF AN UNMITIGATED DISASTER!
JAPAN MUST TOUGHEN UP...
...AND FIGHT!!

DEAD DEAD DEMON'S DEDEDEDE DESTRUCTION

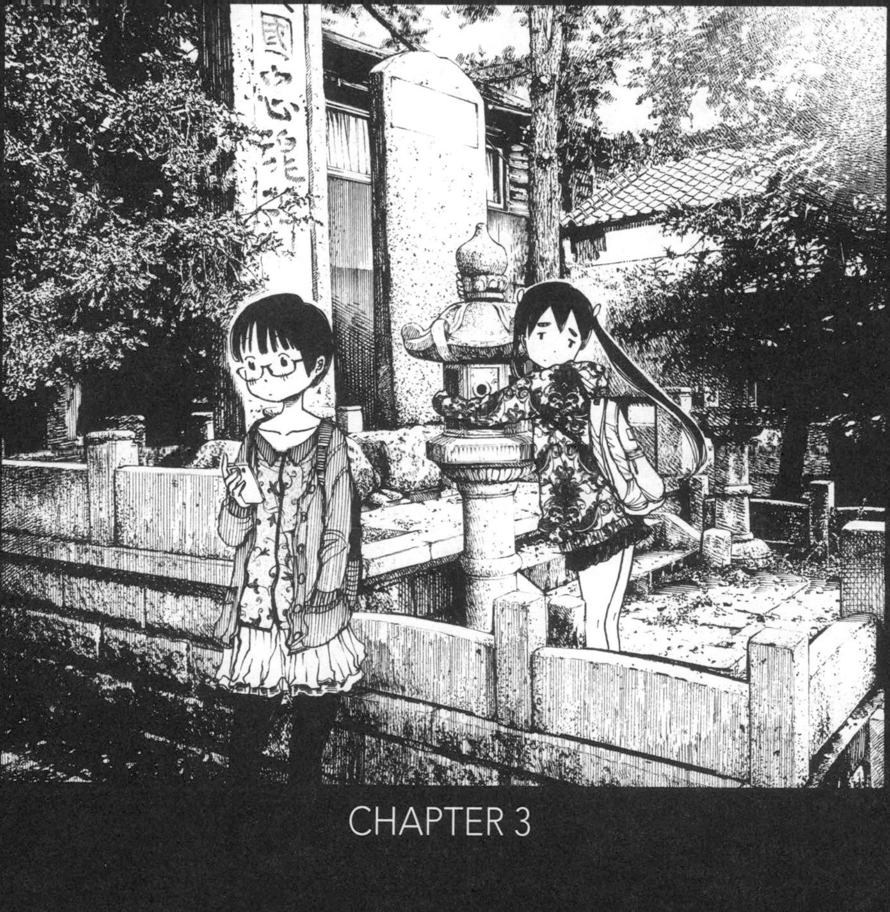

CHAPTER 3

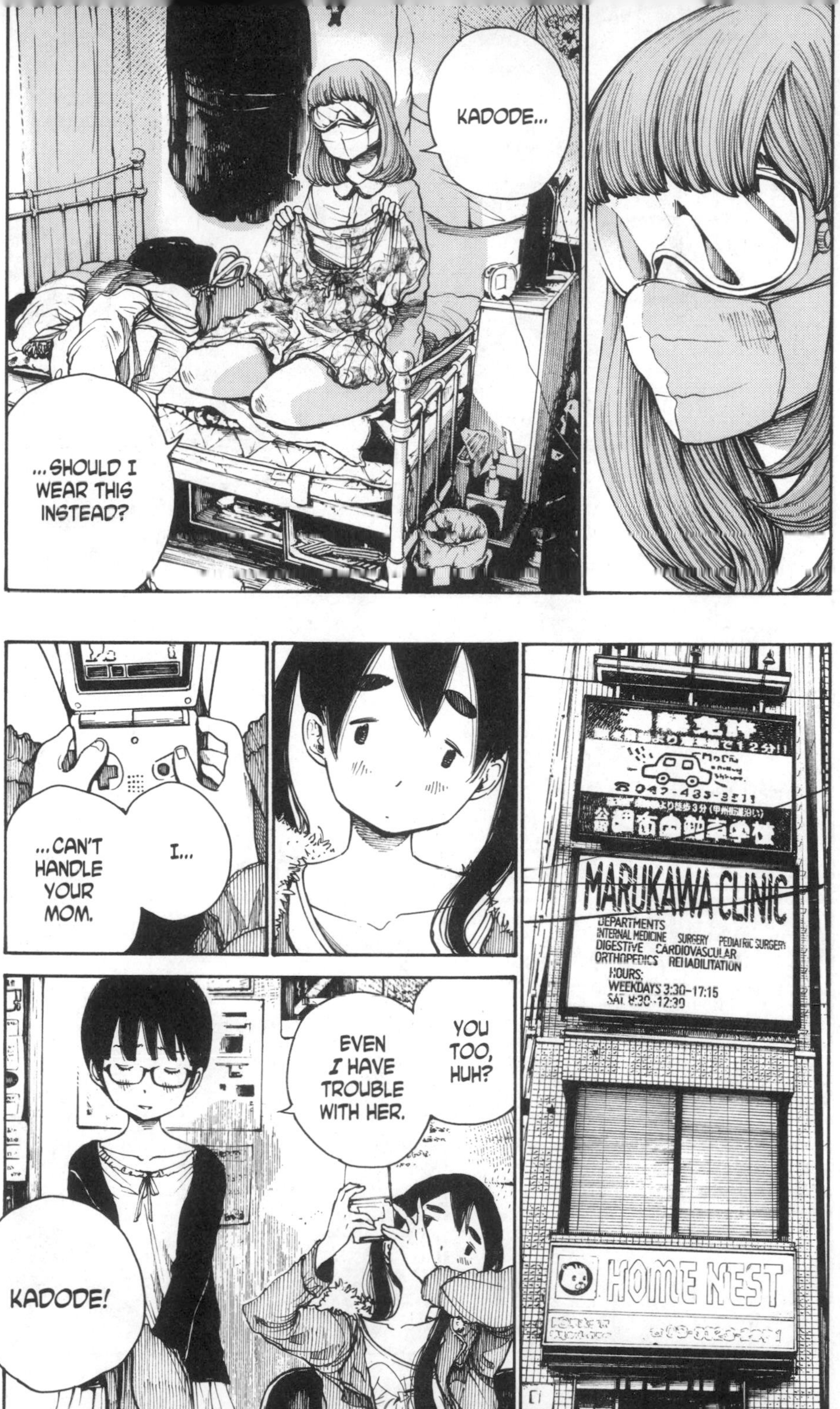
KADODE...
...SHOULD I WEAR THIS INSTEAD?
MARUKAWA CLINIC
DEPARTMENTS
INTERNAL MEDICINE SURGERY PEDIATRIC SURGERY
DIGESTIVE CARDIOVASCULAR
ORTHOPEDICS REHABILITATION
HOURS:
WEEKDAYS 8:30–17:15
SAT 8:30–12:30
HOME NEST
I...
...CAN'T HANDLE YOUR MOM.
YOU TOO, HUH?
EVEN *I* HAVE TROUBLE WITH HER.
KADODE!

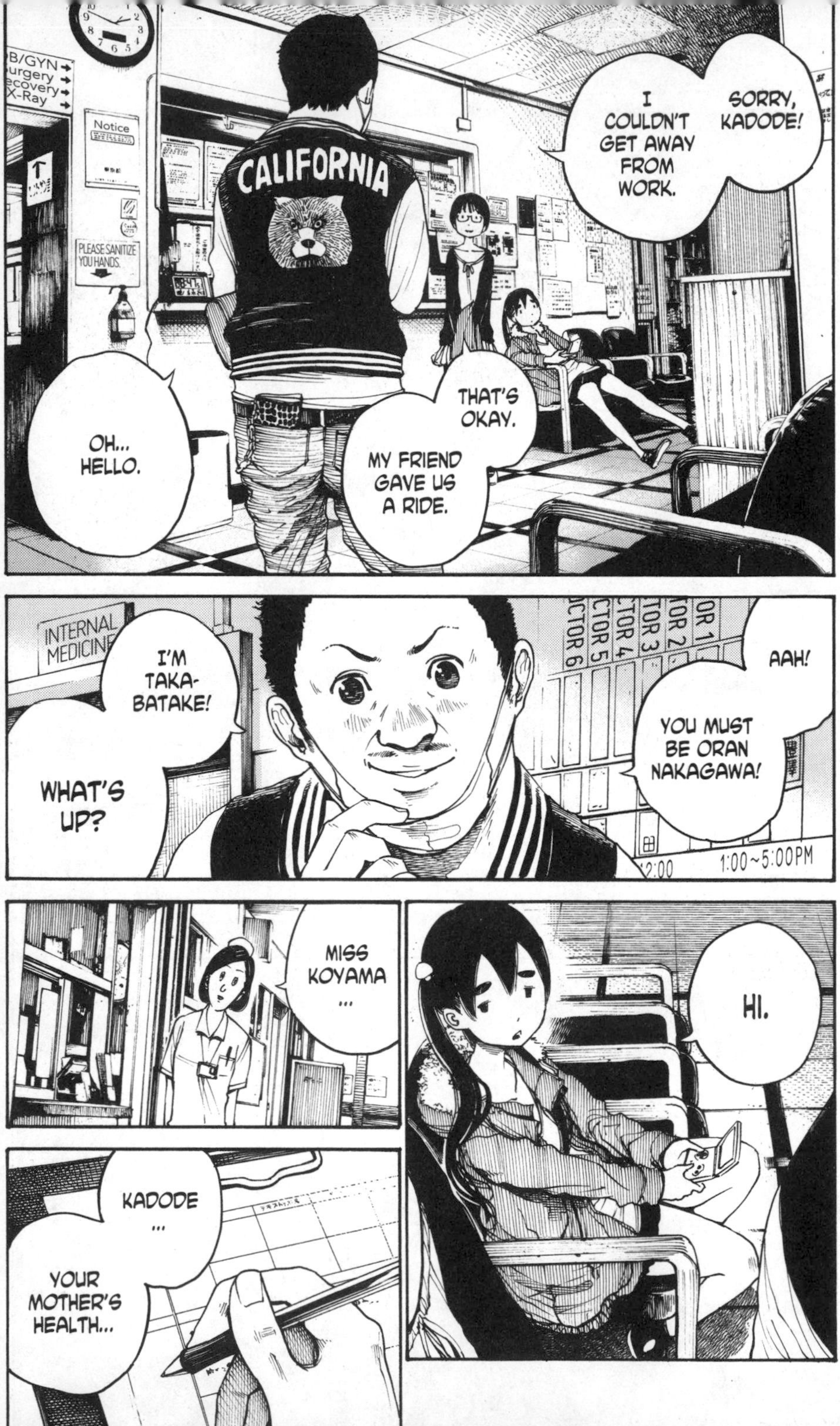
B/GYN
urgery
ecovery
X-Ray
Notice
PLEASE SANITIZE YOU HANDS.
CALIFORNIA
SORRY, KADODE! I COULDN'T GET AWAY FROM WORK.
THAT'S OKAY. MY FRIEND GAVE US A RIDE.
OH... HELLO.
AAH! YOU MUST BE ORAN NAKAGAWA!
I'M TAKA-BATAKE! WHAT'S UP?
INTERNAL MEDICINE
1:00~5:00PM
HI.
MISS KOYAMA ...
KADODE ... YOUR MOTHER'S HEALTH...

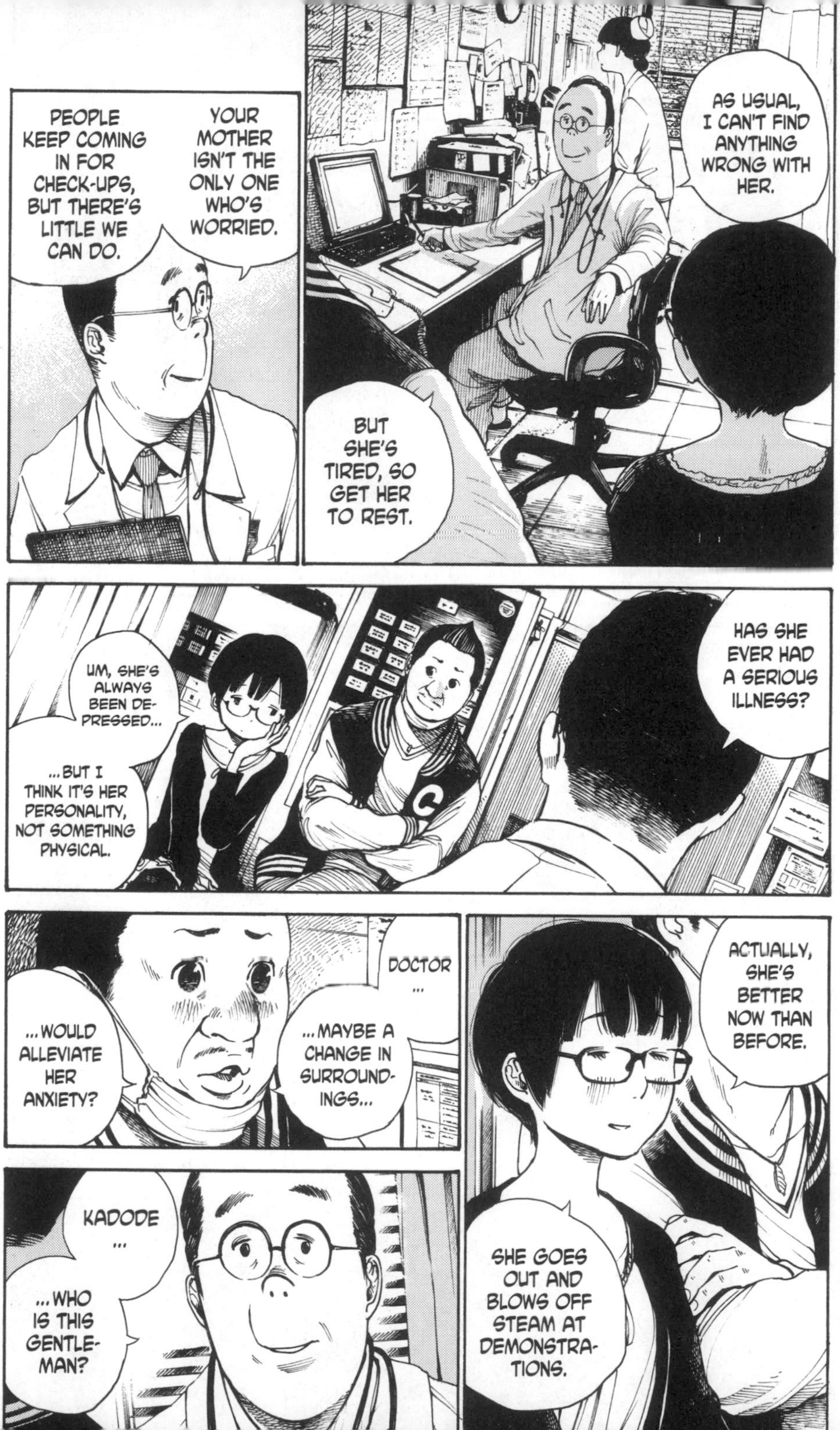
AS USUAL, I CAN'T FIND ANYTHING WRONG WITH HER.
BUT SHE'S TIRED, SO GET HER TO REST.
YOUR MOTHER ISN'T THE ONLY ONE WHO'S WORRIED.
PEOPLE KEEP COMING IN FOR CHECK-UPS, BUT THERE'S LITTLE WE CAN DO.
HAS SHE EVER HAD A SERIOUS ILLNESS?
UM, SHE'S ALWAYS BEEN DE-PRESSED...
...BUT I THINK IT'S HER PERSONALITY, NOT SOMETHING PHYSICAL.
ACTUALLY, SHE'S BETTER NOW THAN BEFORE.
SHE GOES OUT AND BLOWS OFF STEAM AT DEMONSTRA-TIONS.
DOCTOR ...
...MAYBE A CHANGE IN SURROUND-INGS...
...WOULD ALLEVIATE HER ANXIETY?
KADODE ...
...WHO IS THIS GENTLE-MAN?

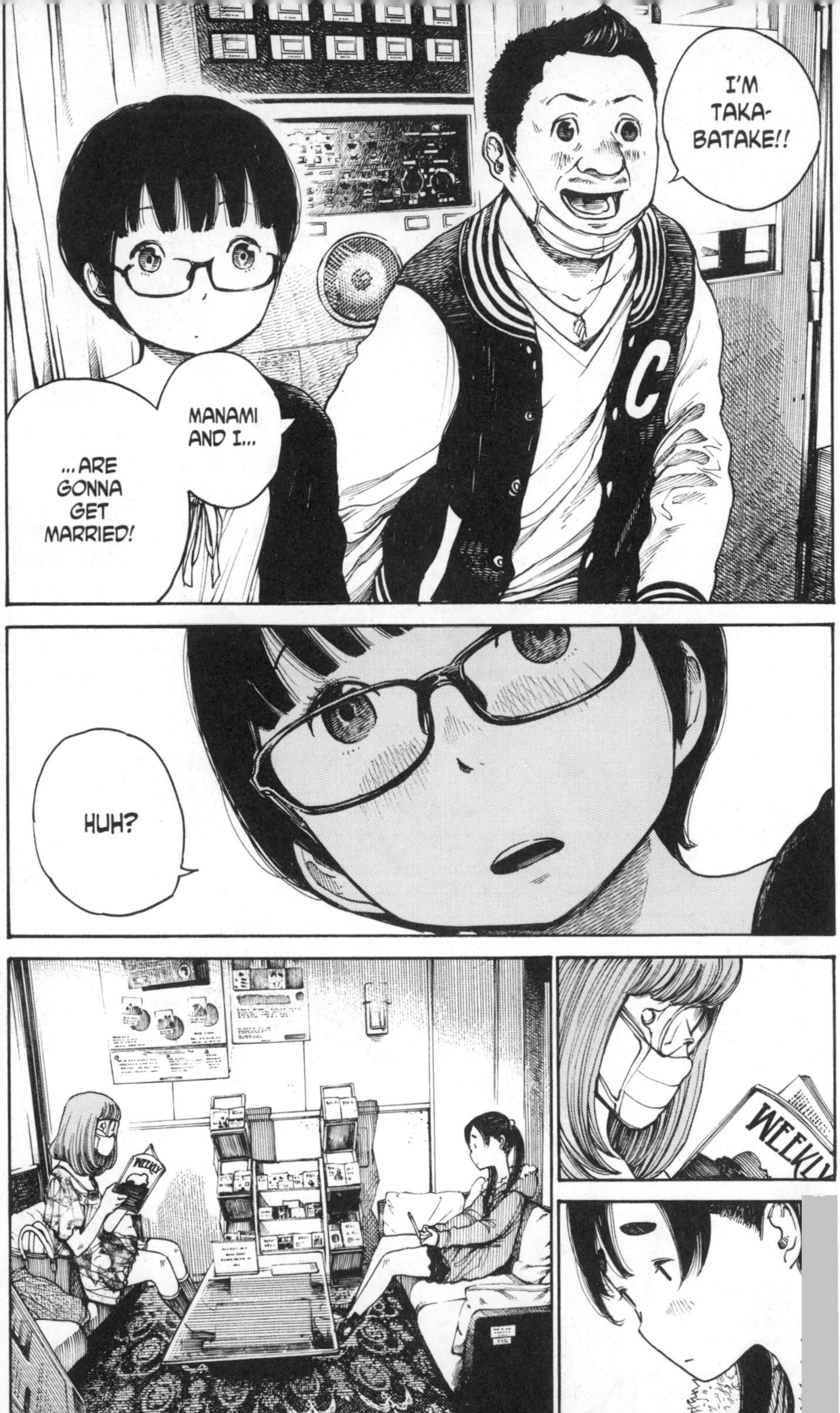
I'M TAKA-BATAKE!!
MANAMI AND I...
...ARE GONNA GET MARRIED!
HUH?
WEEKLY

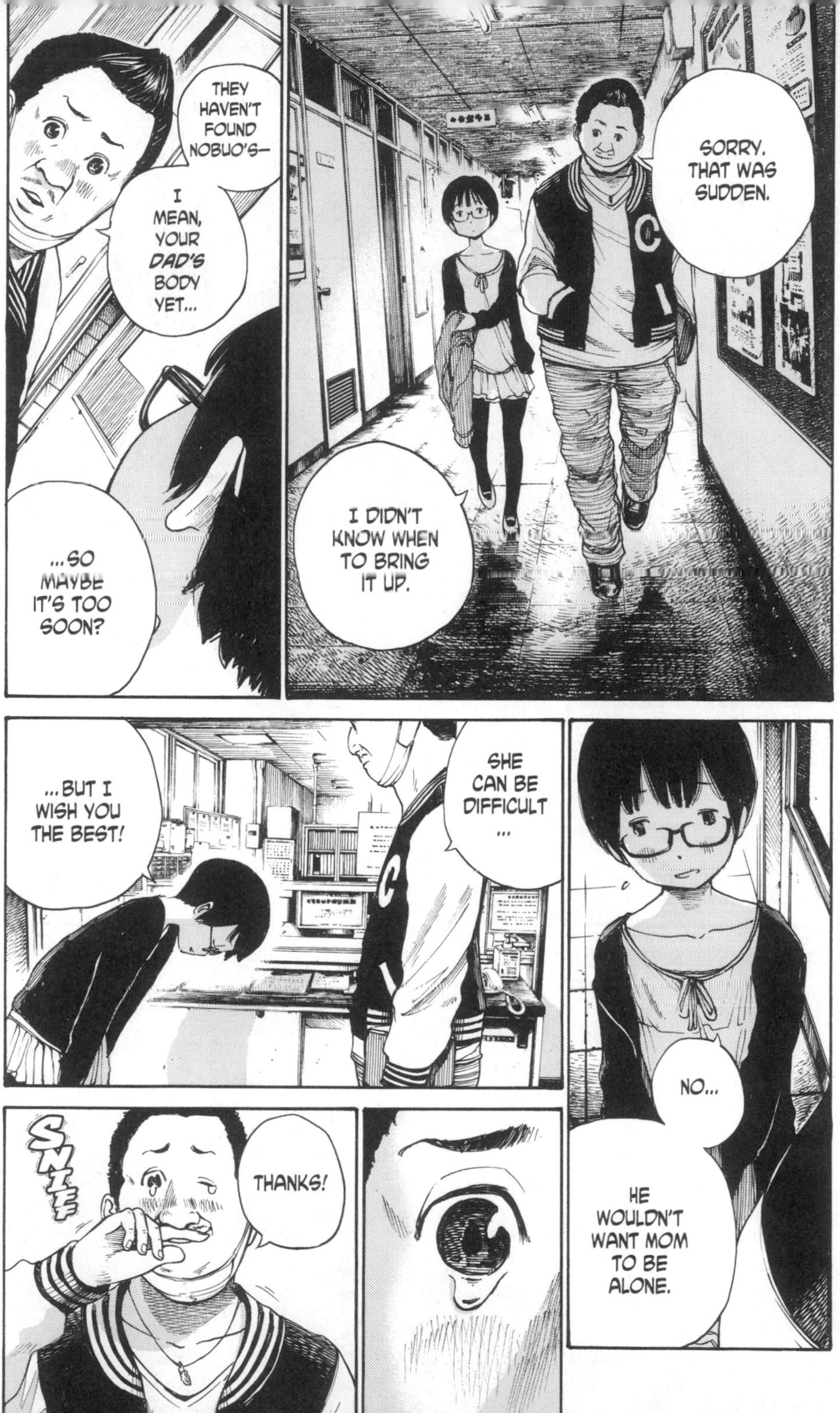
SORRY. THAT WAS SUDDEN.
I DIDN'T KNOW WHEN TO BRING IT UP.
THEY HAVEN'T FOUND NOBUO'S—
I MEAN, YOUR *DAD'S* BODY YET...
...SO MAYBE IT'S TOO SOON?
SHE CAN BE DIFFICULT ...
...BUT I WISH YOU THE BEST!
NO...
HE WOULDN'T WANT MOM TO BE ALONE.
THANKS!
SNIFF

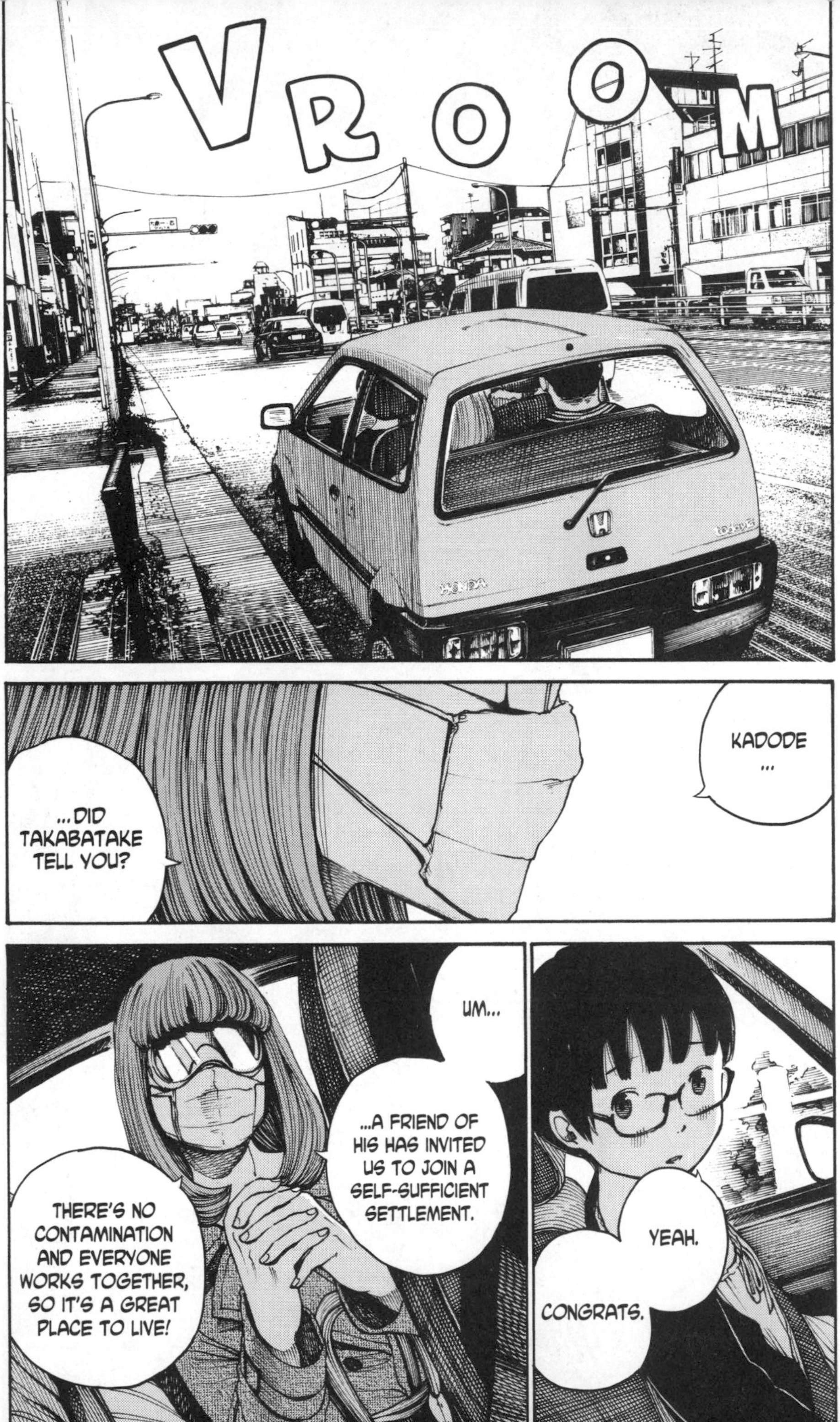
VROOM
KADODE ...
...DID TAKABATAKE TELL YOU?
YEAH.
CONGRATS.
UM...
...A FRIEND OF HIS HAS INVITED US TO JOIN A SELF-SUFFICIENT SETTLEMENT.
THERE'S NO CONTAMINATION AND EVERYONE WORKS TOGETHER, SO IT'S A GREAT PLACE TO LIVE!

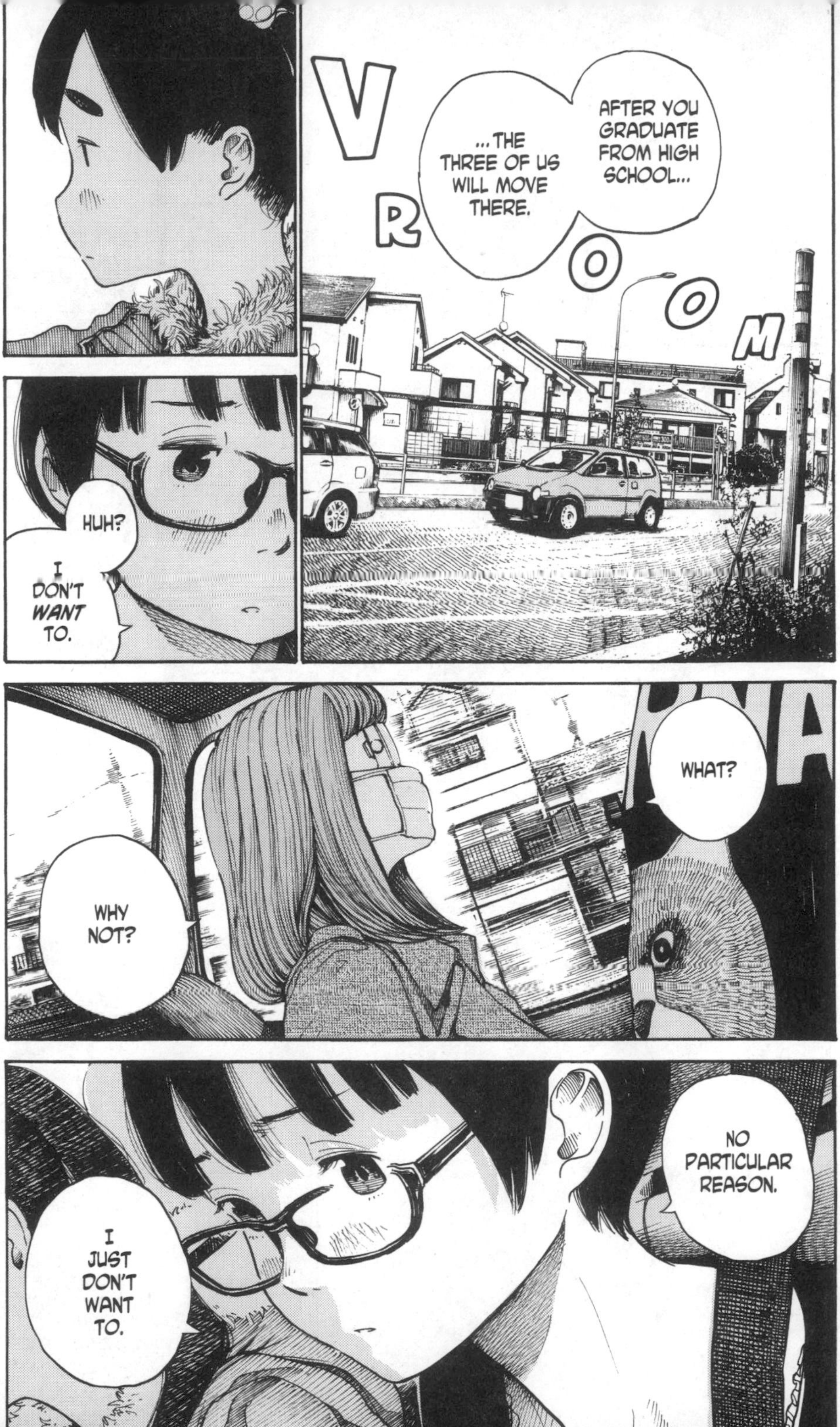
AFTER YOU GRADUATE FROM HIGH SCHOOL...
...THE THREE OF US WILL MOVE THERE.
VROOM
HUH?
I DON'T *WANT* TO.
WHAT?
WHY NOT?
NO PARTICULAR REASON.
I JUST DON'T WANT TO.

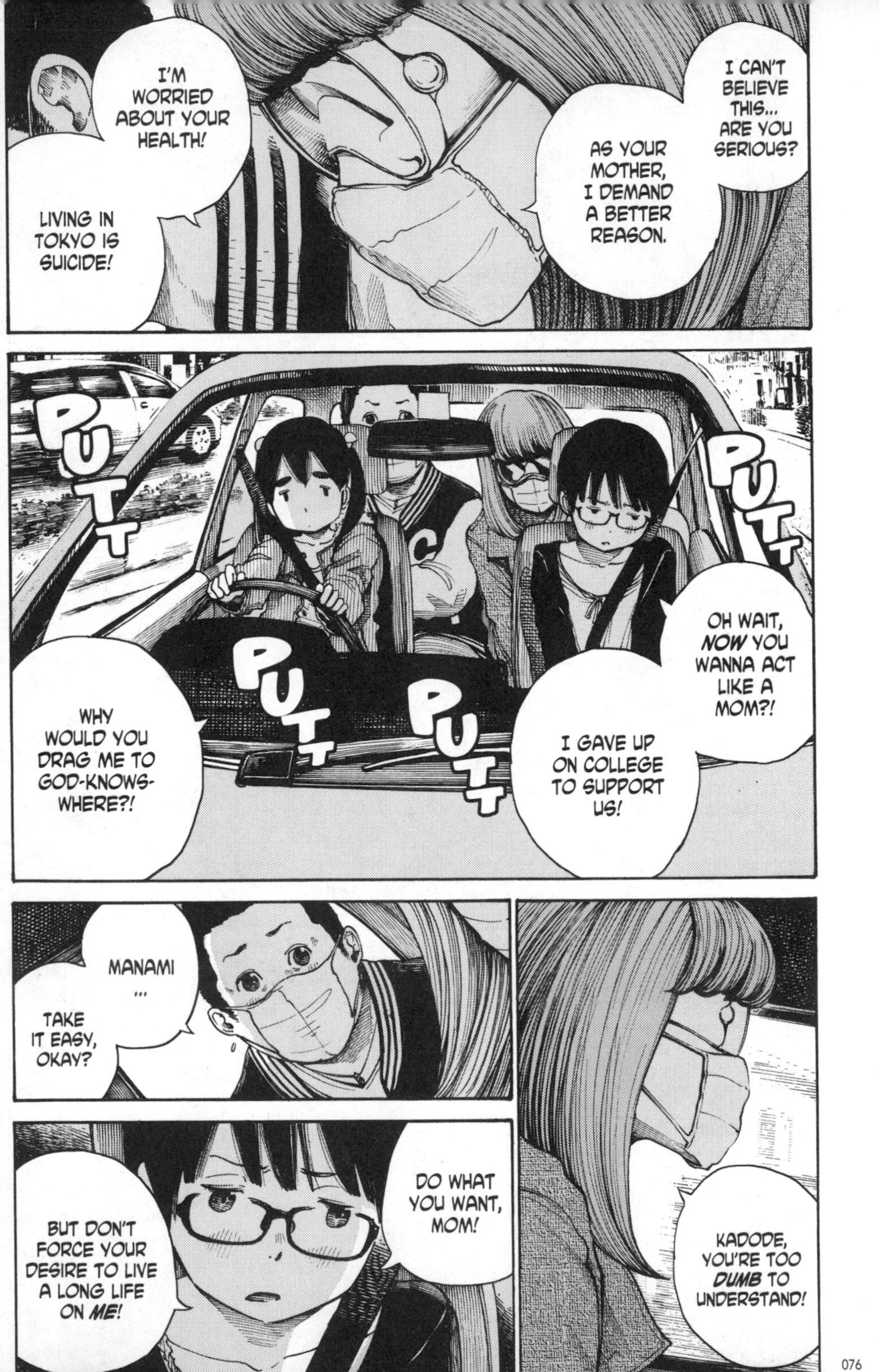
I CAN'T BELIEVE THIS... ARE YOU SERIOUS?
AS YOUR MOTHER, I DEMAND A BETTER REASON.
I'M WORRIED ABOUT YOUR HEALTH!
LIVING IN TOKYO IS SUICIDE!
PUTT
PUTT
OH WAIT, *NOW* YOU WANNA ACT LIKE A MOM?!
I GAVE UP ON COLLEGE TO SUPPORT US!
WHY WOULD YOU DRAG ME TO GOD-KNOWS-WHERE?!
PUTT
PUTT
KADODE, YOU'RE TOO *DUMB* TO UNDERSTAND!
MANAMI ...
TAKE IT EASY, OKAY?
DO WHAT YOU WANT, MOM!
BUT DON'T FORCE YOUR DESIRE TO LIVE A LONG LIFE ON *ME*!

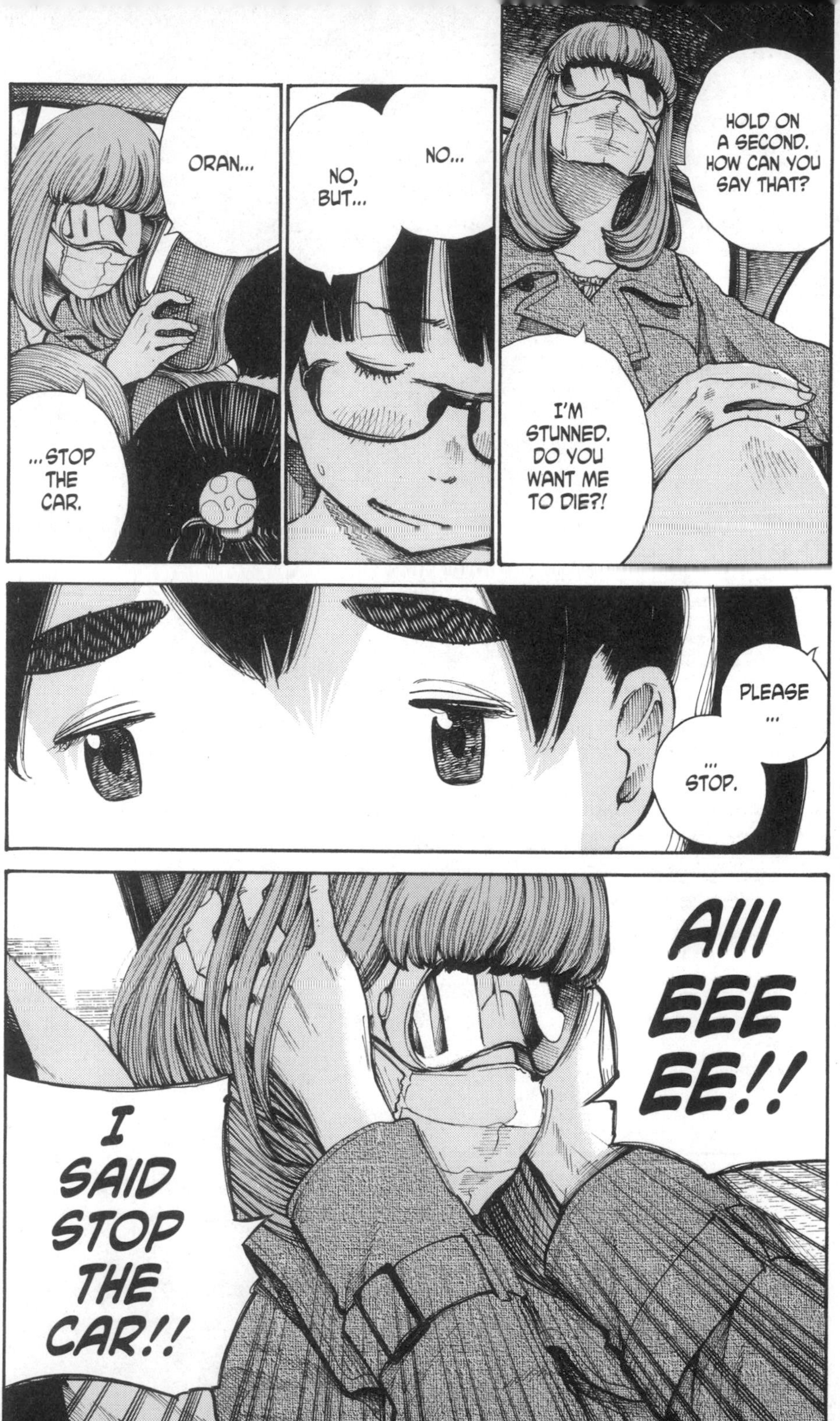
HOLD ON A SECOND. HOW CAN YOU SAY THAT?
I'M STUNNED. DO YOU WANT ME TO DIE?!
NO...
NO, BUT...
ORAN...
...STOP THE CAR.
PLEASE ...
... STOP.
AIII EEE EE!!
I SAID STOP THE CAR!!

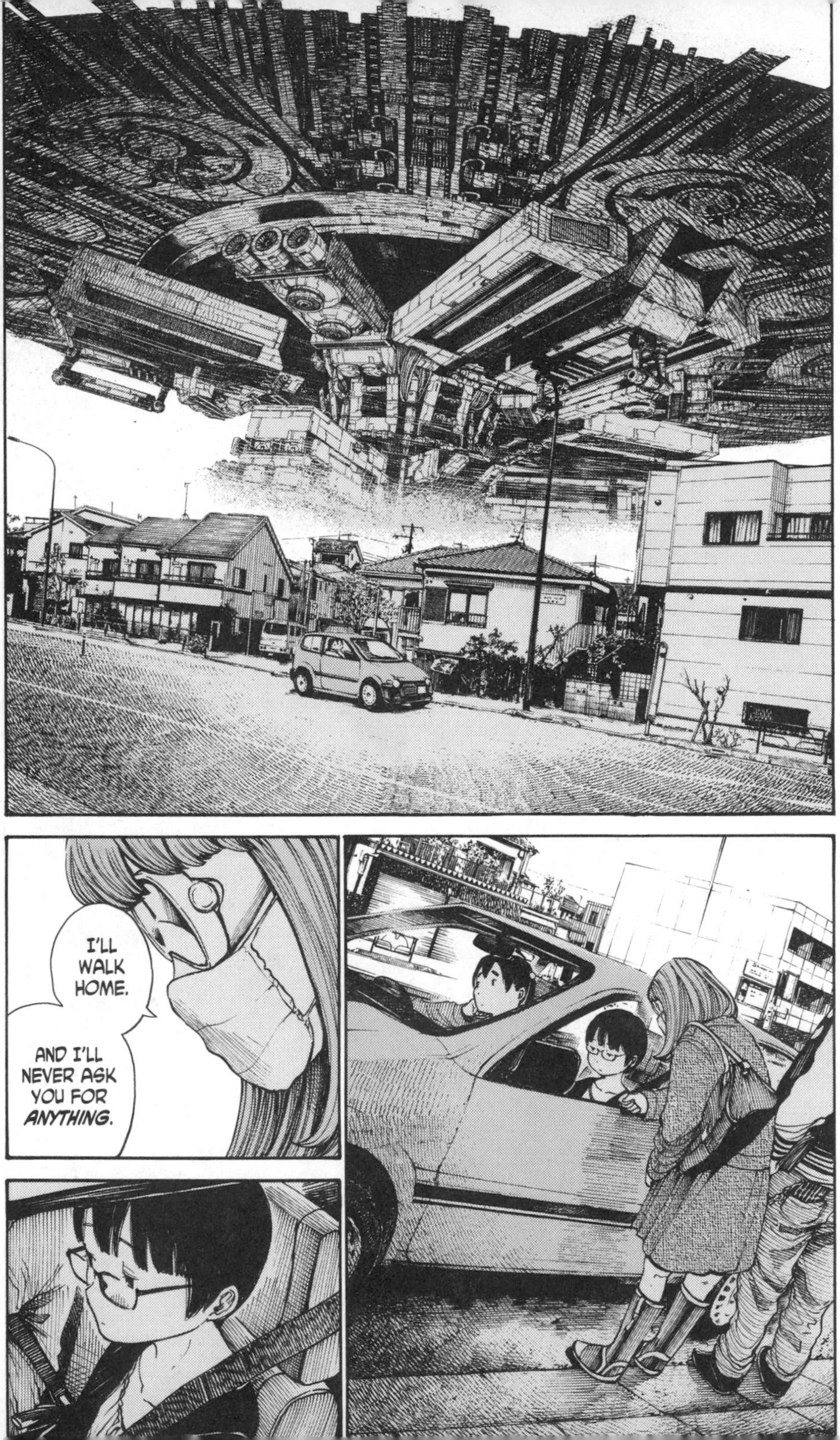
I'LL WALK HOME.
AND I'LL NEVER ASK YOU FOR *ANYTHING*.

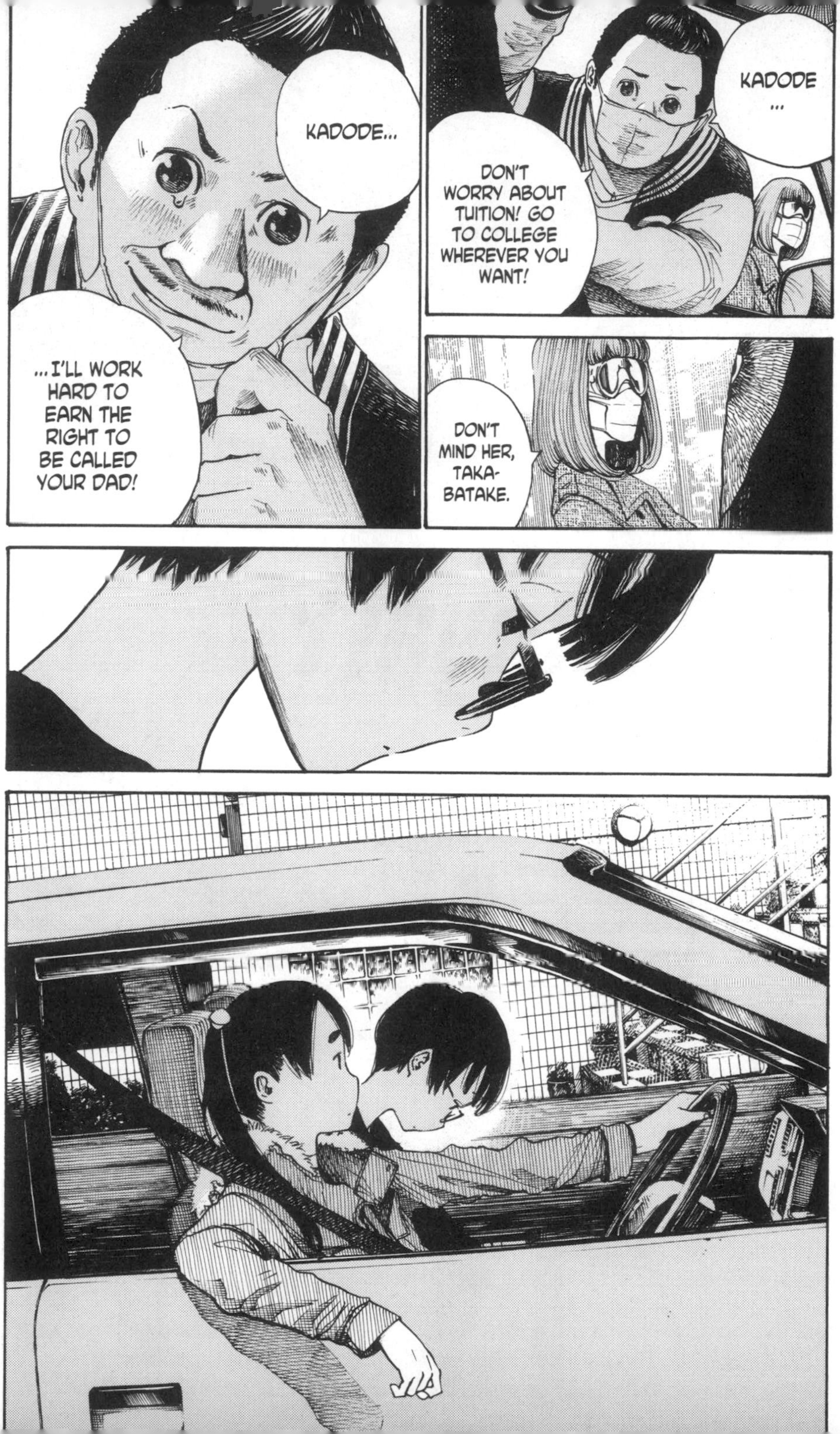
KADODE ...
DON'T WORRY ABOUT TUITION! GO TO COLLEGE WHEREVER YOU WANT!
DON'T MIND HER, TAKA-BATAKE.
KADODE...
...I'LL WORK HARD TO EARN THE RIGHT TO BE CALLED YOUR DAD!

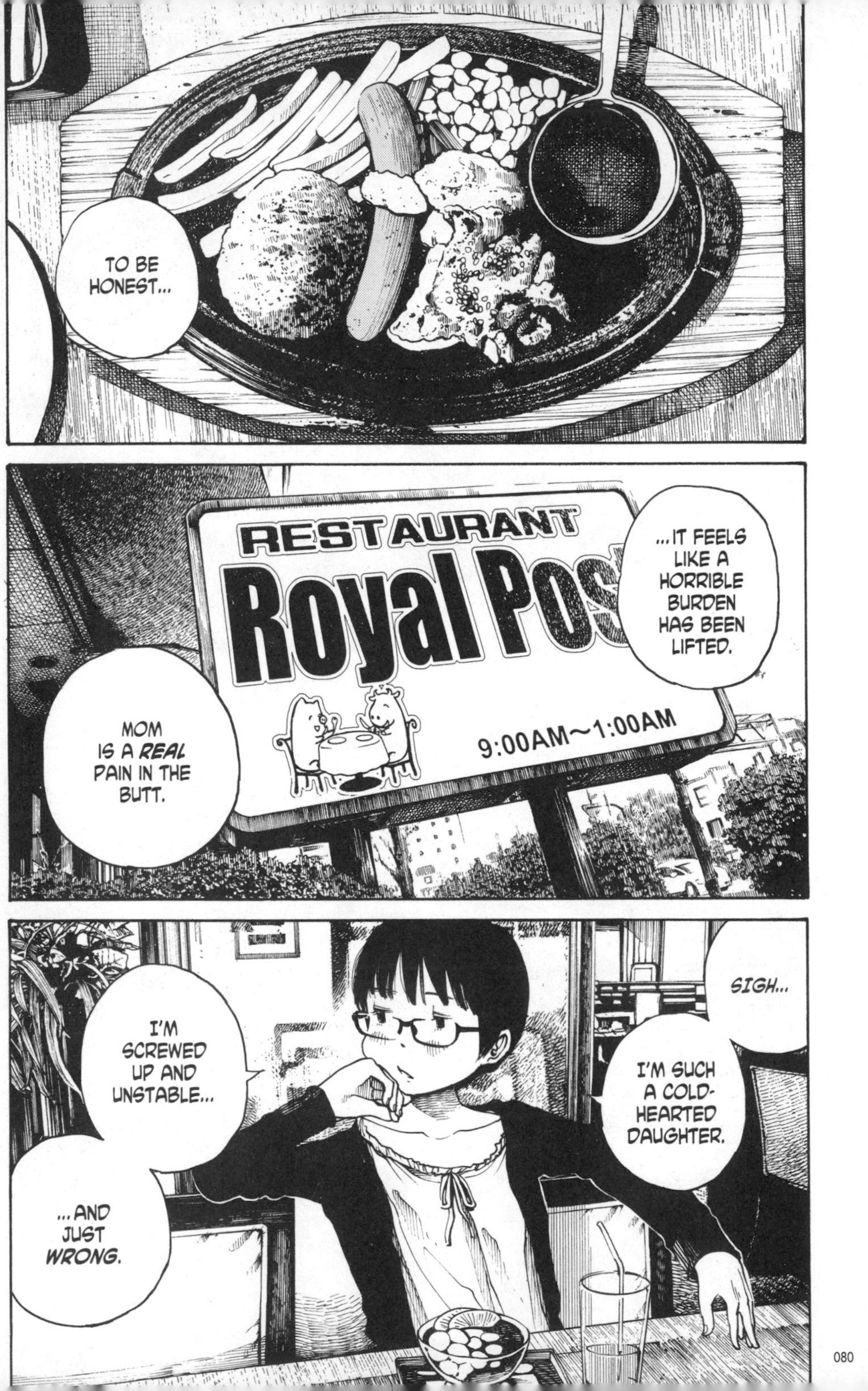
TO BE HONEST...
RESTAURANT
Royal Pos
9:00AM~1:00AM
...IT FEELS LIKE A HORRIBLE BURDEN HAS BEEN LIFTED.
MOM IS A *REAL* PAIN IN THE BUTT.
SIGH...
I'M SUCH A COLD-HEARTED DAUGHTER.
I'M SCREWED UP AND UNSTABLE...
...AND JUST **WRONG**.

LET'S EAT!

MY TREAT!

OH WELL.

SORRY IT GOT WEIRD THERE FOR A SECOND.

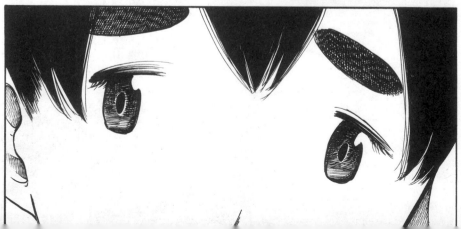

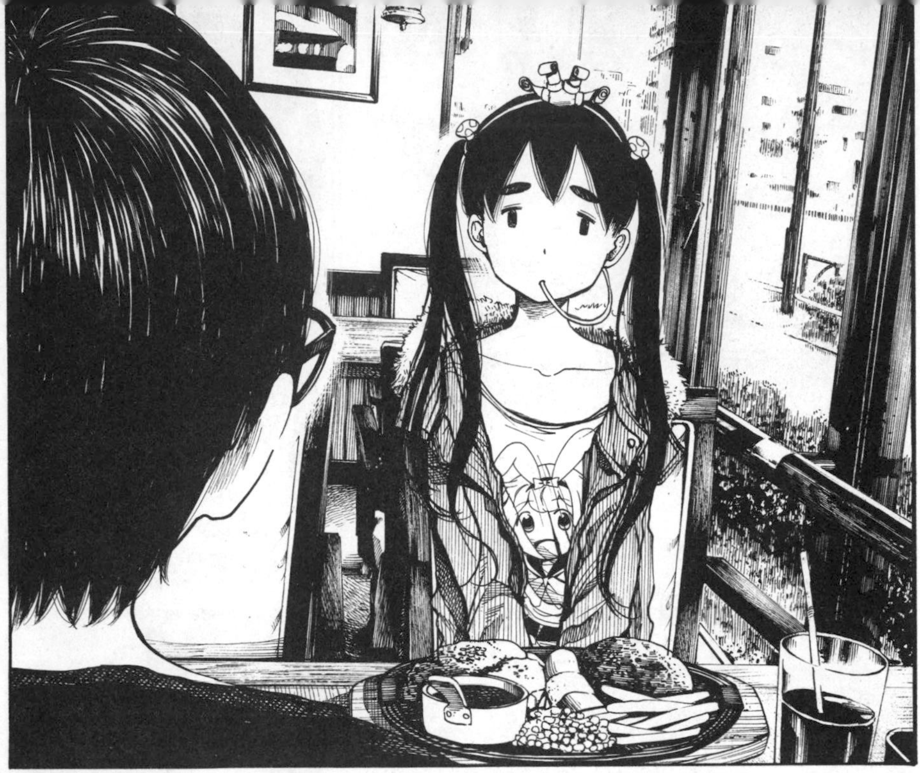

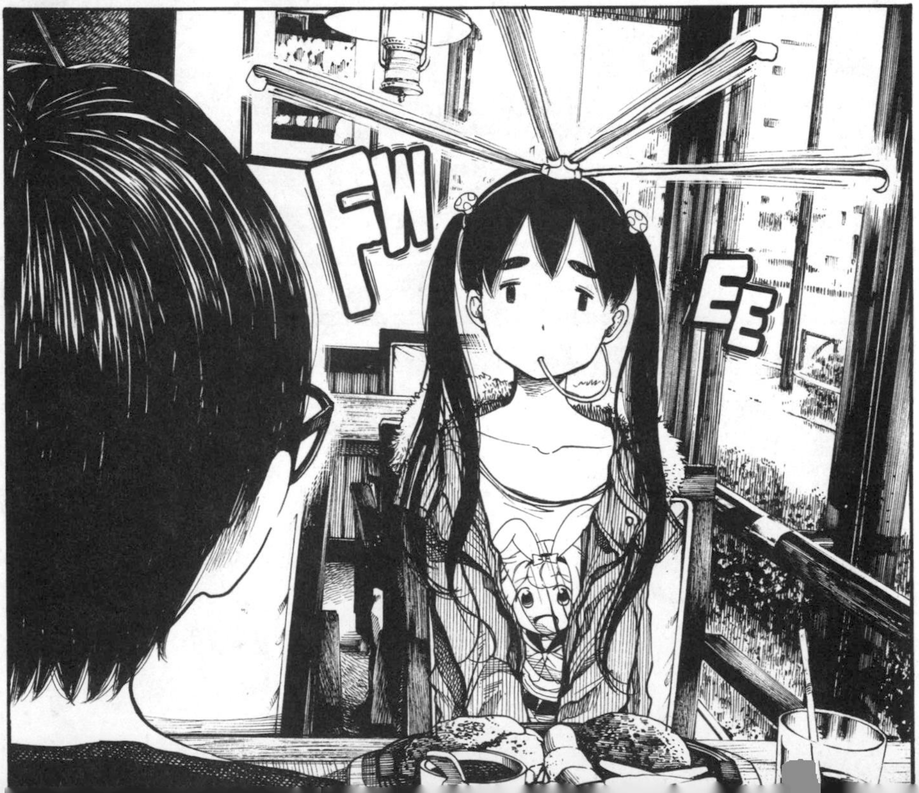
FW
EE

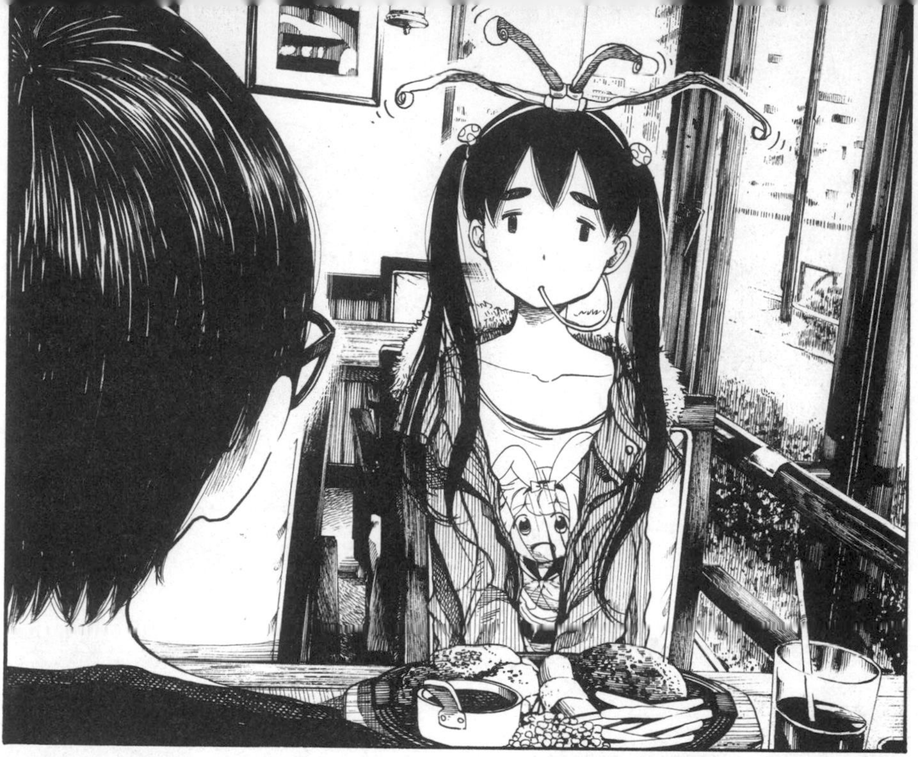

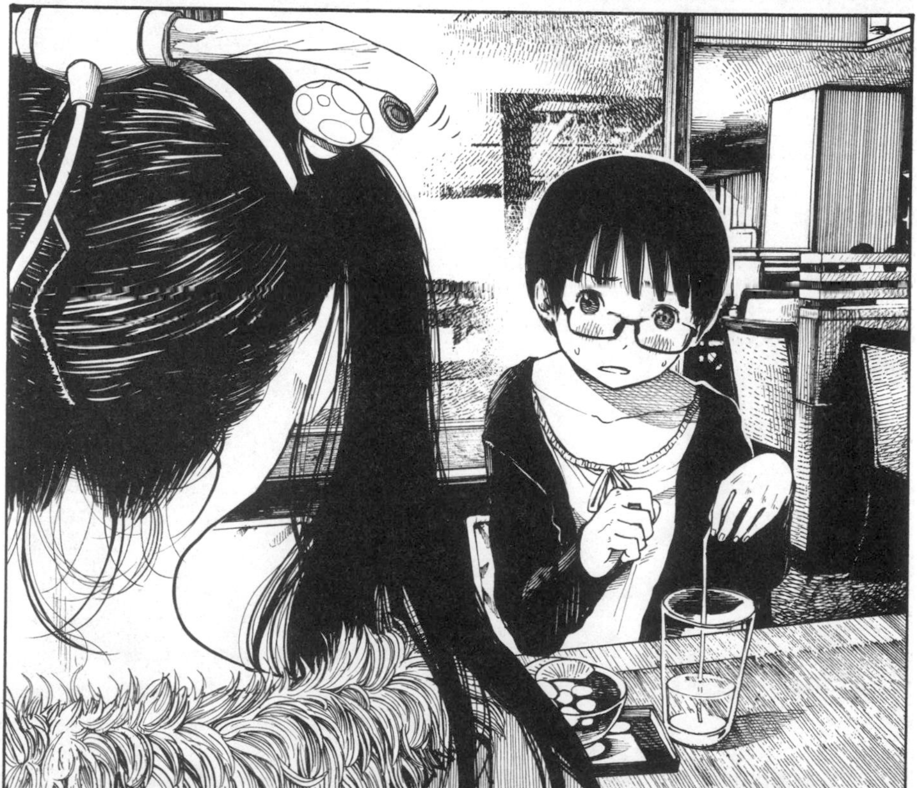

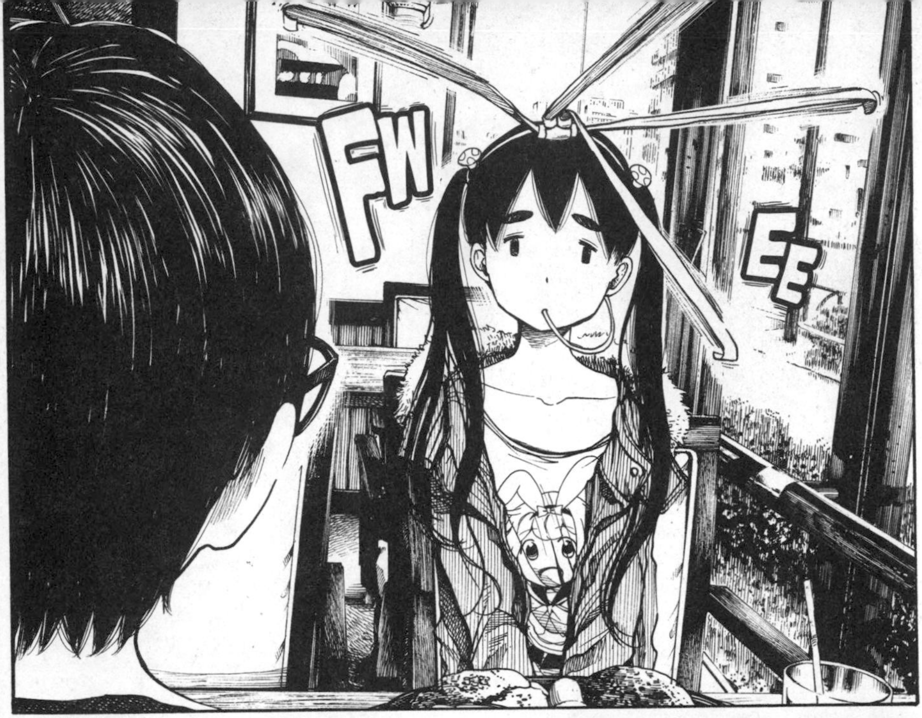
FW
EE

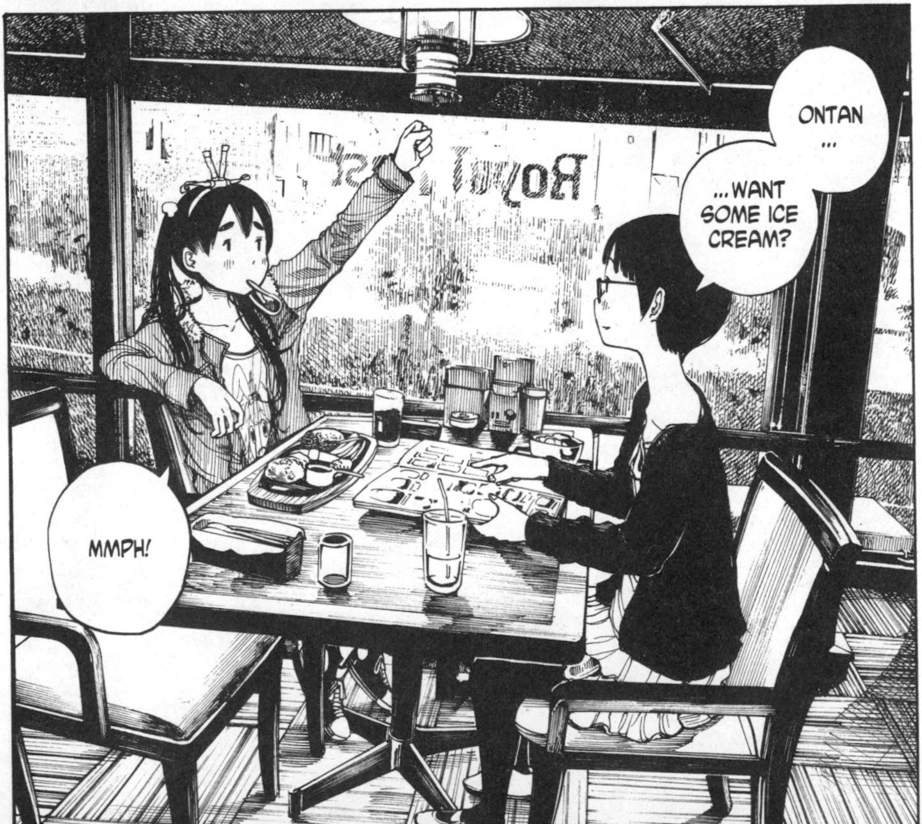
ONTAN ...
...WANT SOME ICE CREAM?
MMPH!

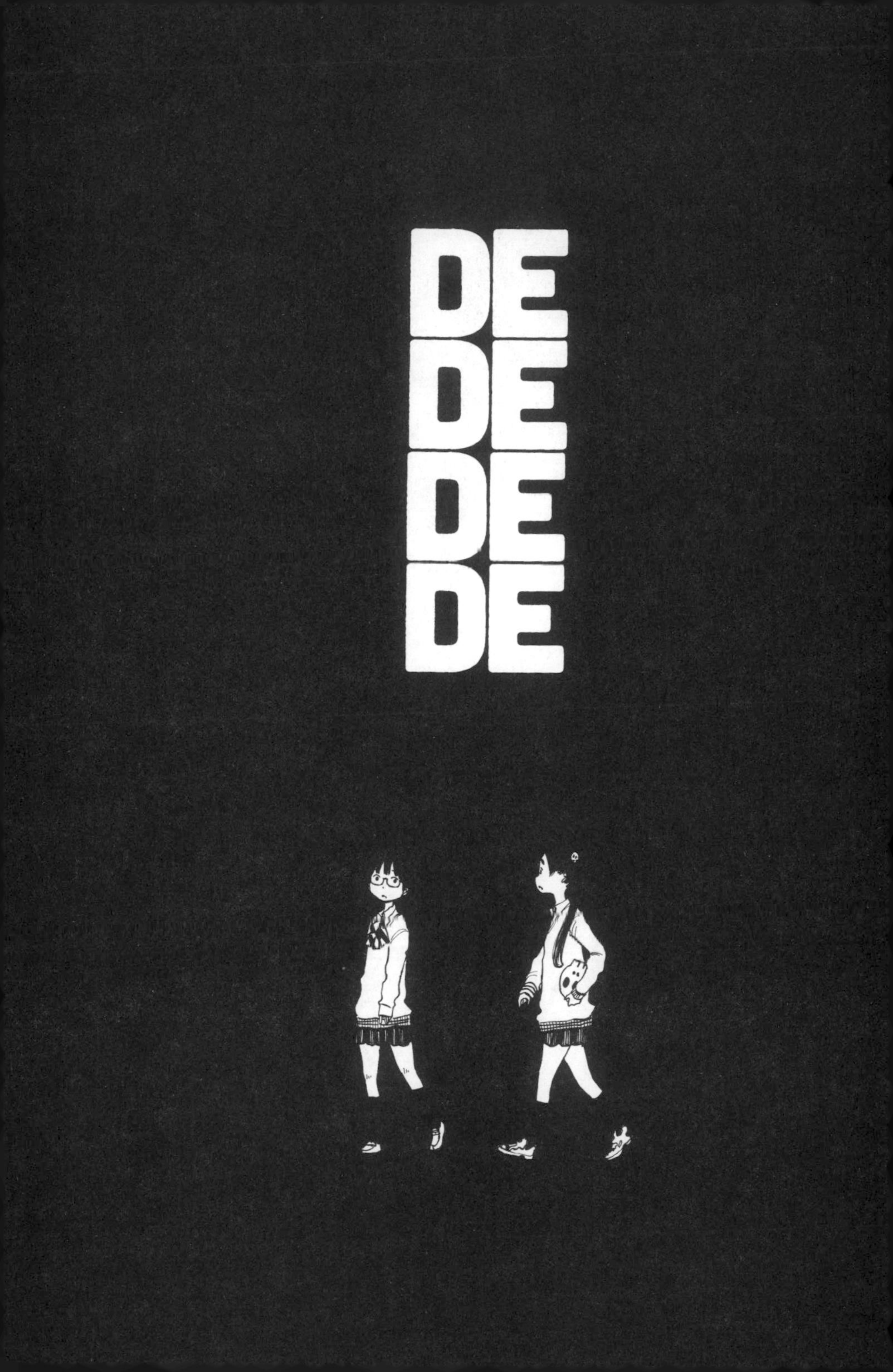
DE
DE
DE
DE

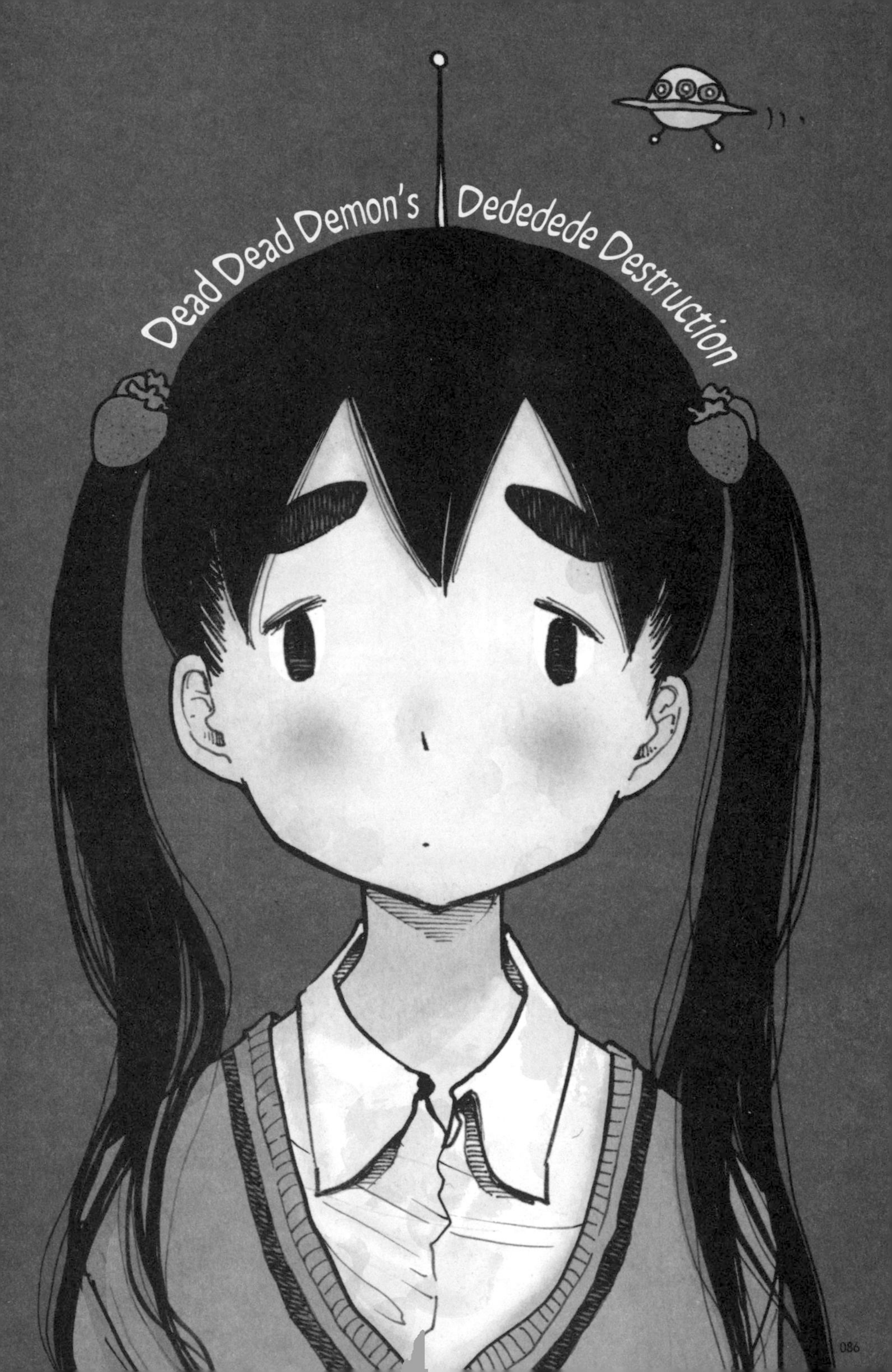
Dead Dead Demon's Dededede Destruction

CHAPTER 4

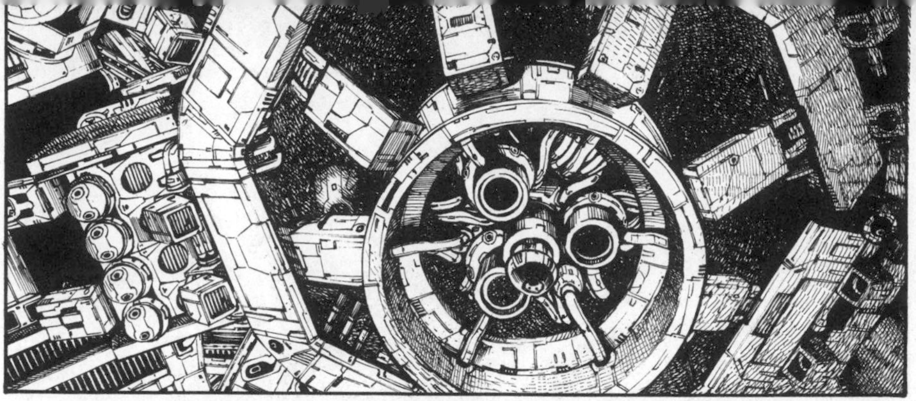

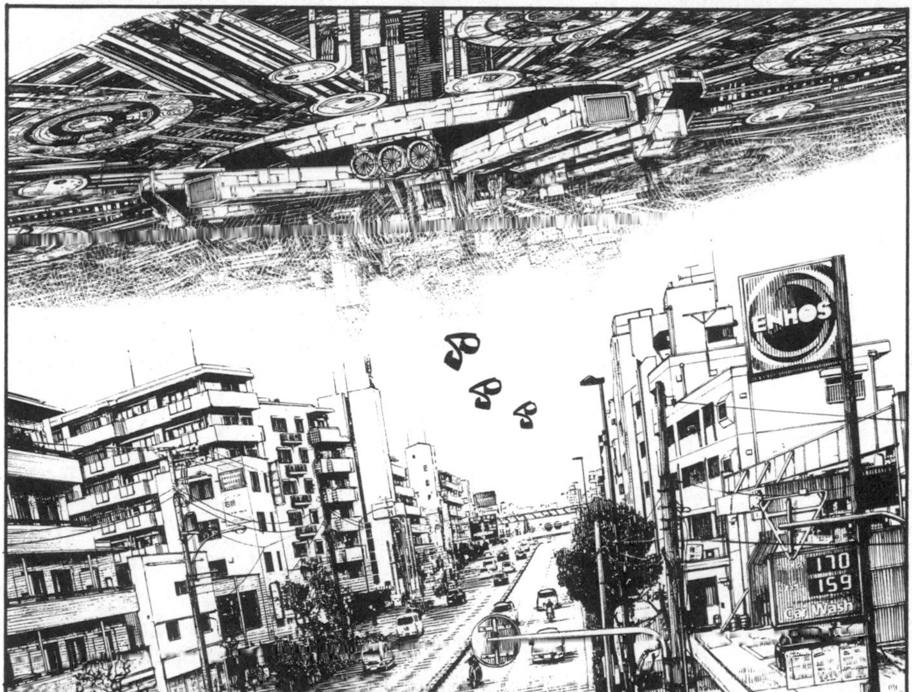
ENHOS
170
159
Car Wash

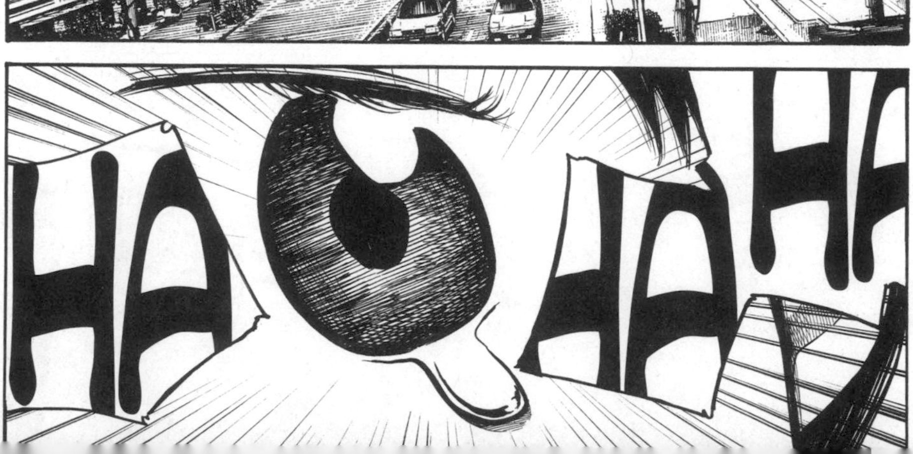
HA HAHA

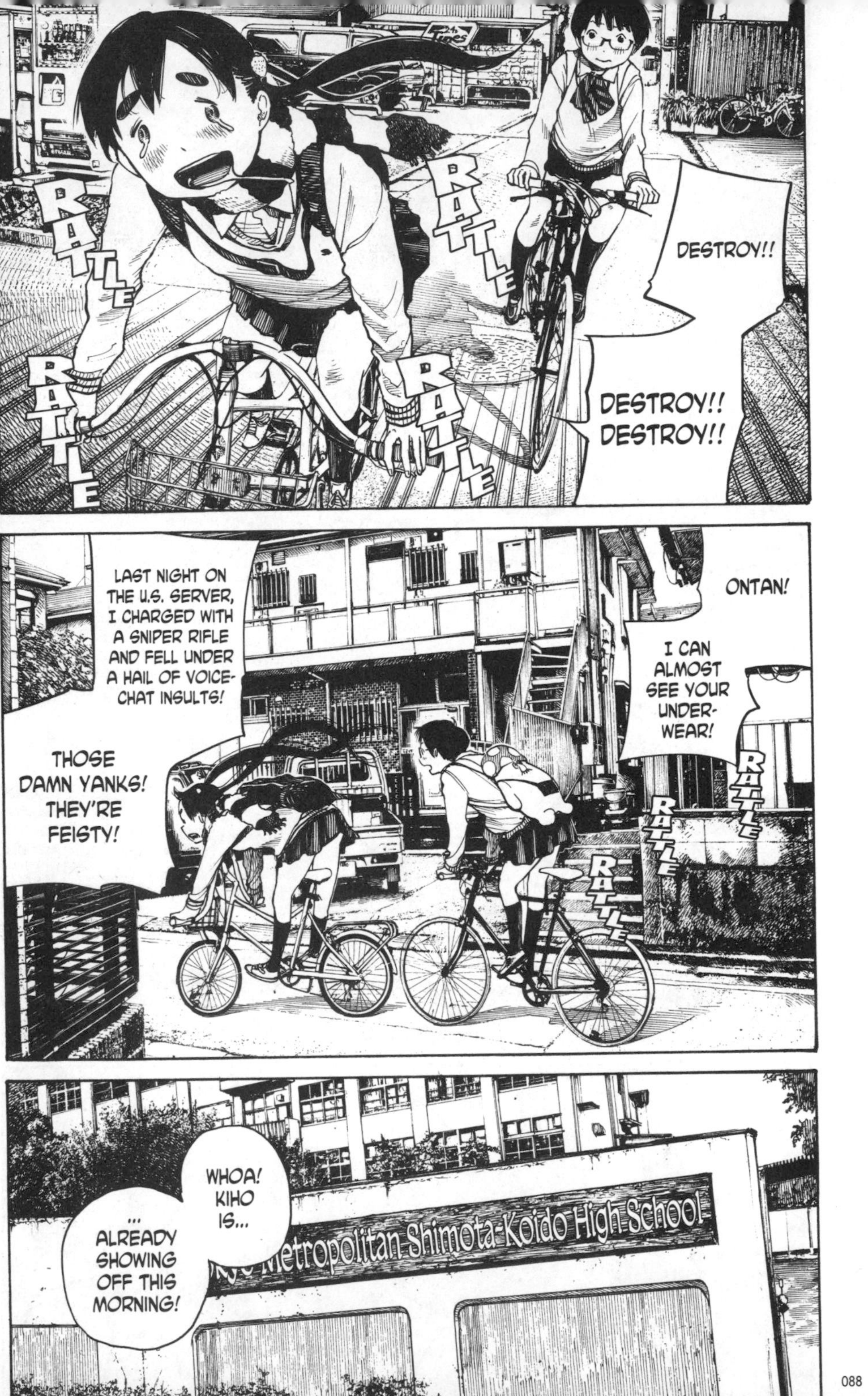
DESTROY!!
RATTLE
RATTLE
RATTLE
RATTLE
DESTROY!! DESTROY!!
ONTAN!
I CAN ALMOST SEE YOUR UNDER-WEAR!
RATTLE
RATTLE
RATTLE
LAST NIGHT ON THE U.S. SERVER, I CHARGED WITH A SNIPER RIFLE AND FELL UNDER A HAIL OF VOICE-CHAT INSULTS!
THOSE DAMN YANKS! THEY'RE FEISTY!
Metropolitan Shimota-Koido High School
WHOA! KIHO IS...
...ALREADY SHOWING OFF THIS MORNING!

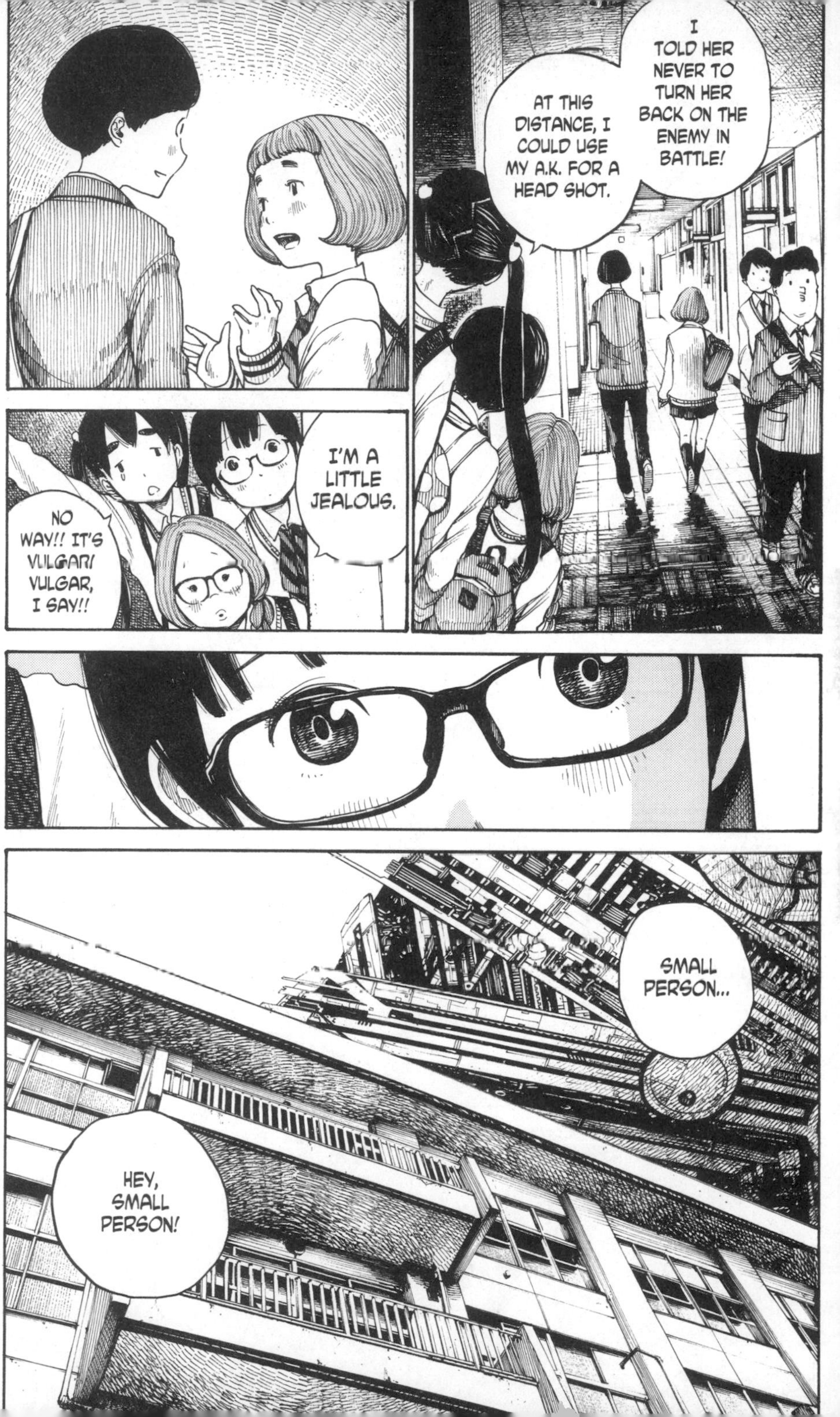
I TOLD HER NEVER TO TURN HER BACK ON THE ENEMY IN BATTLE!
AT THIS DISTANCE, I COULD USE MY A.K. FOR A HEAD SHOT.
I'M A LITTLE JEALOUS.
NO WAY!! IT'S VULGAR! VULGAR, I SAY!!
SMALL PERSON...
HEY, SMALL PERSON!

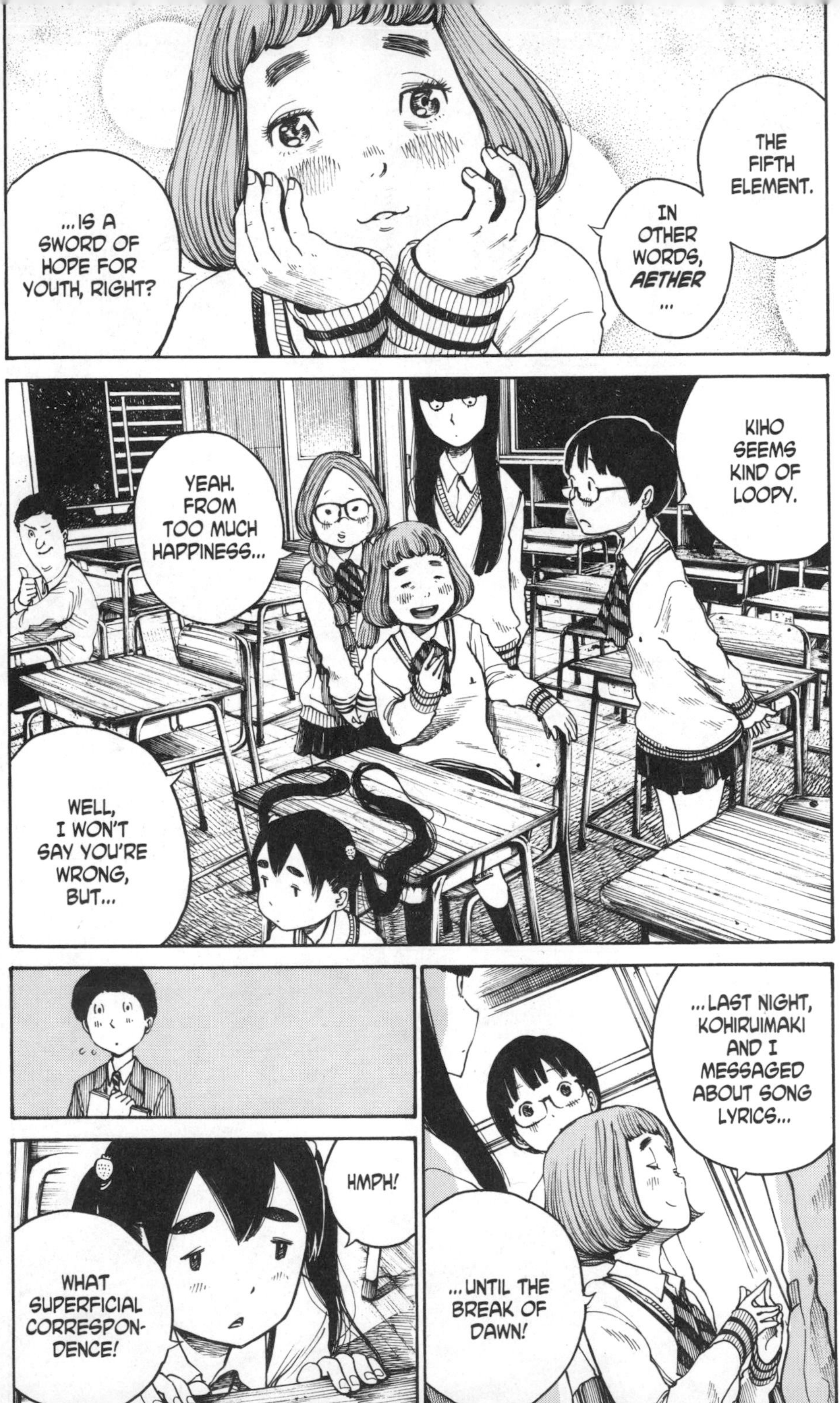
THE FIFTH ELEMENT.
IN OTHER WORDS, *AETHER* ...
...IS A SWORD OF HOPE FOR YOUTH, RIGHT?
KIHO SEEMS KIND OF LOOPY.
YEAH. FROM TOO MUCH HAPPINESS...
WELL, I WON'T SAY YOU'RE WRONG, BUT...
...LAST NIGHT, KOHIRUIMAKI AND I MESSAGED ABOUT SONG LYRICS...
...UNTIL THE BREAK OF DAWN!
HMPH!
WHAT SUPERFICIAL CORRESPON-DENCE!

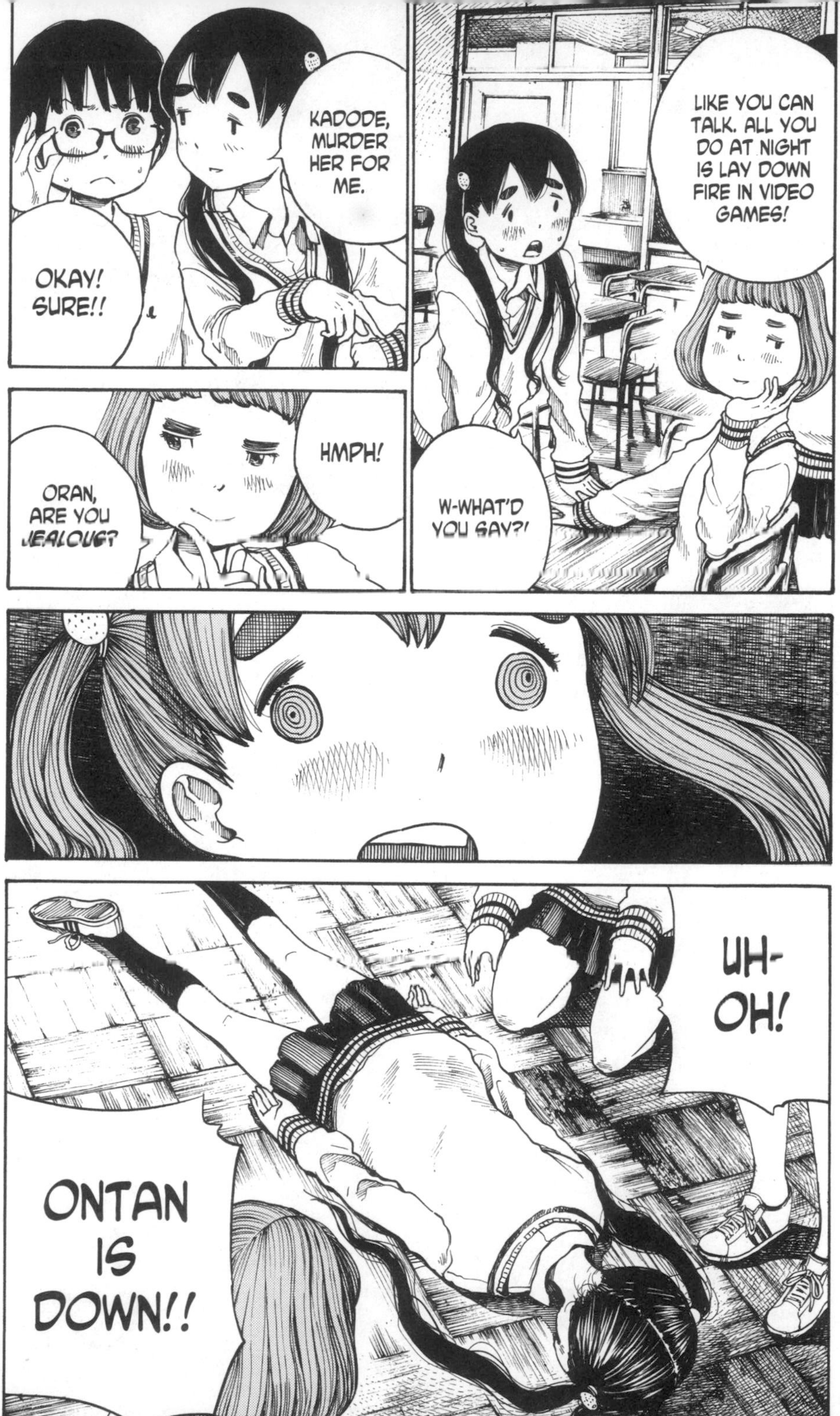
LIKE YOU CAN TALK. ALL YOU DO AT NIGHT IS LAY DOWN FIRE IN VIDEO GAMES!
W-WHAT'D YOU SAY?!
KADODE, MURDER HER FOR ME.
OKAY! SURE!!
HMPH!
ORAN, ARE YOU *JEALOUS*?
UH-OH!
ONTAN IS DOWN!!

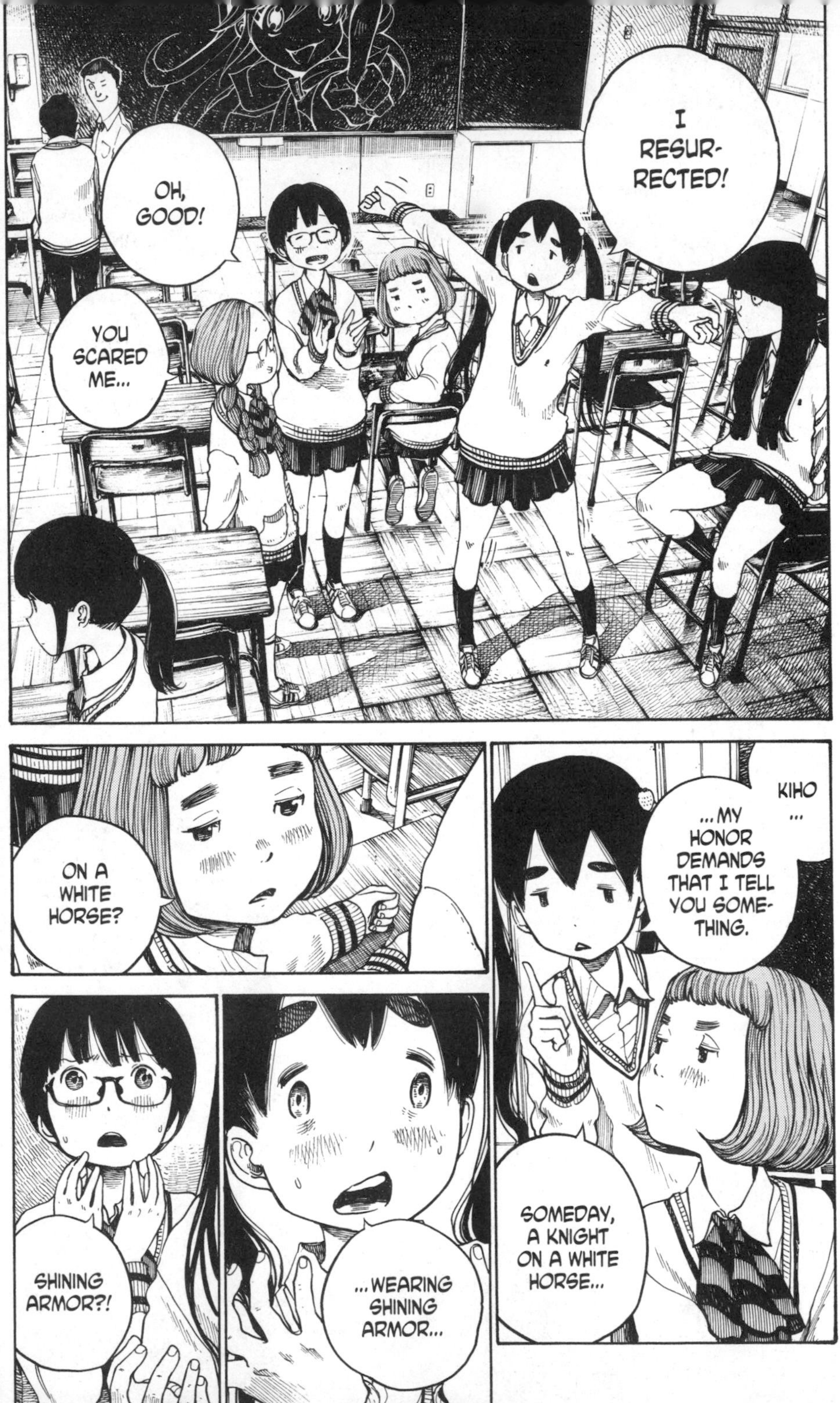
I RESURRECTED!
OH, GOOD!
YOU SCARED ME...
KIHO ...
...MY HONOR DEMANDS THAT I TELL YOU SOMETHING.
SOMEDAY, A KNIGHT ON A WHITE HORSE...
ON A WHITE HORSE?
...WEARING SHINING ARMOR...
SHINING ARMOR?!

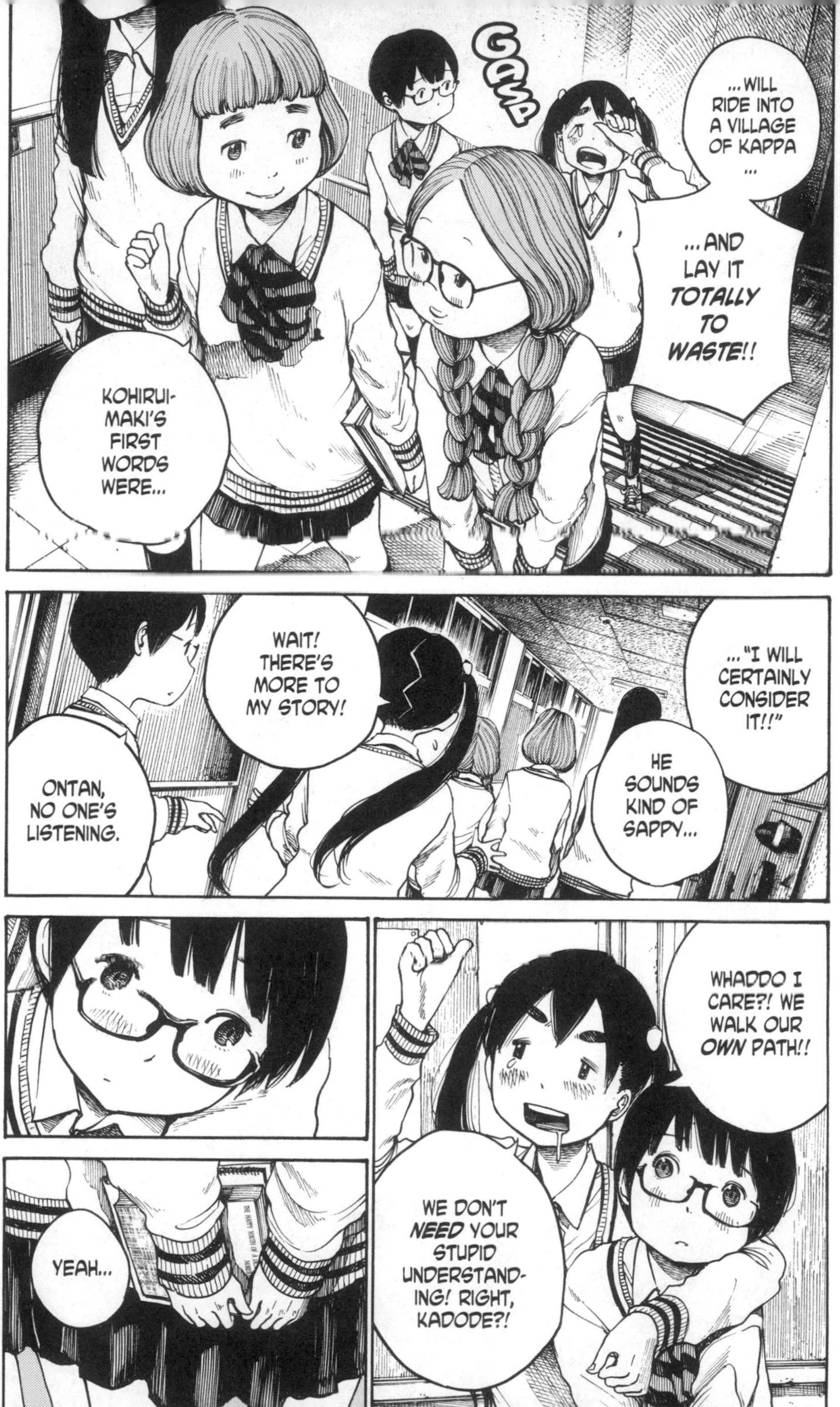
...WILL RIDE INTO A VILLAGE OF KAPPA ...
GAMP
...AND LAY IT *TOTALLY* TO *WASTE*!!
KOHIRUI-MAKI'S FIRST WORDS WERE...
..."I WILL CERTAINLY CONSIDER IT!!"
HE SOUNDS KIND OF SAPPY...
WAIT! THERE'S MORE TO MY STORY!
ONTAN, NO ONE'S LISTENING.
WHADDO I CARE?! WE WALK OUR *OWN* PATH!!
WE DON'T ***NEED*** YOUR STUPID UNDERSTAND-ING! RIGHT, KADODE?!
YEAH...

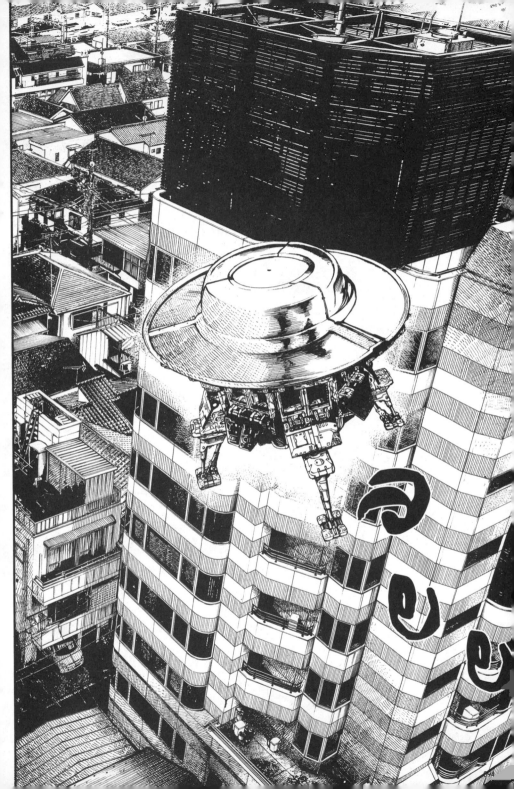

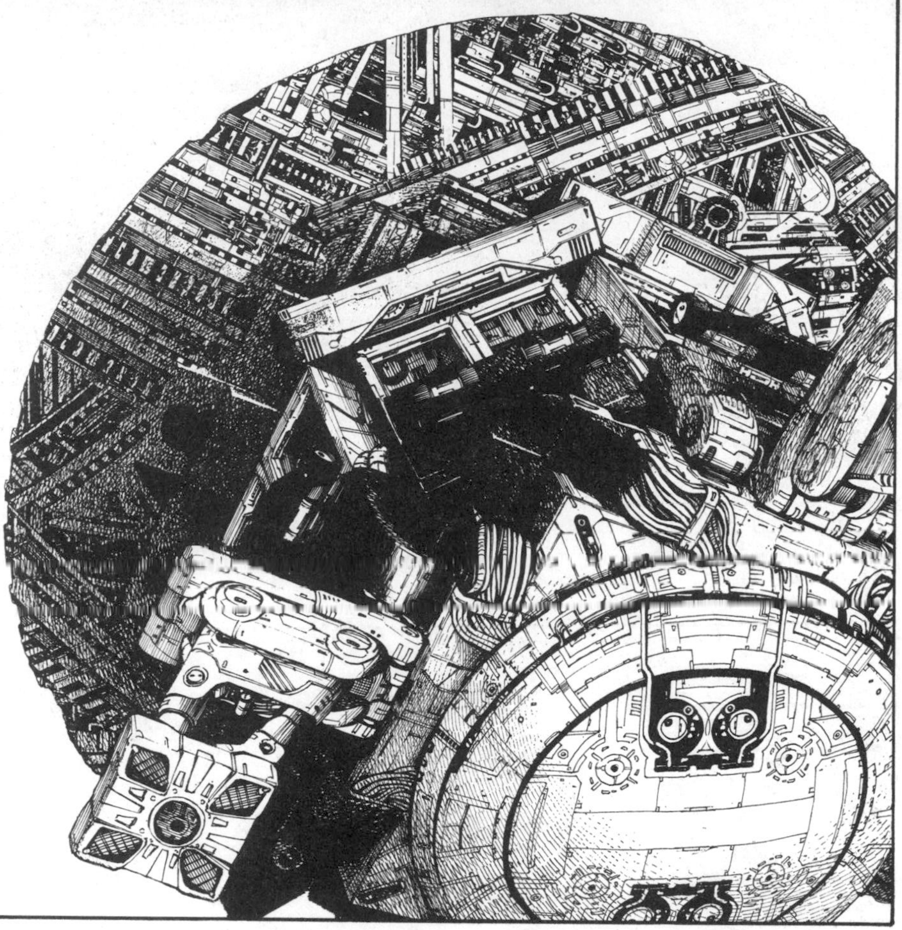

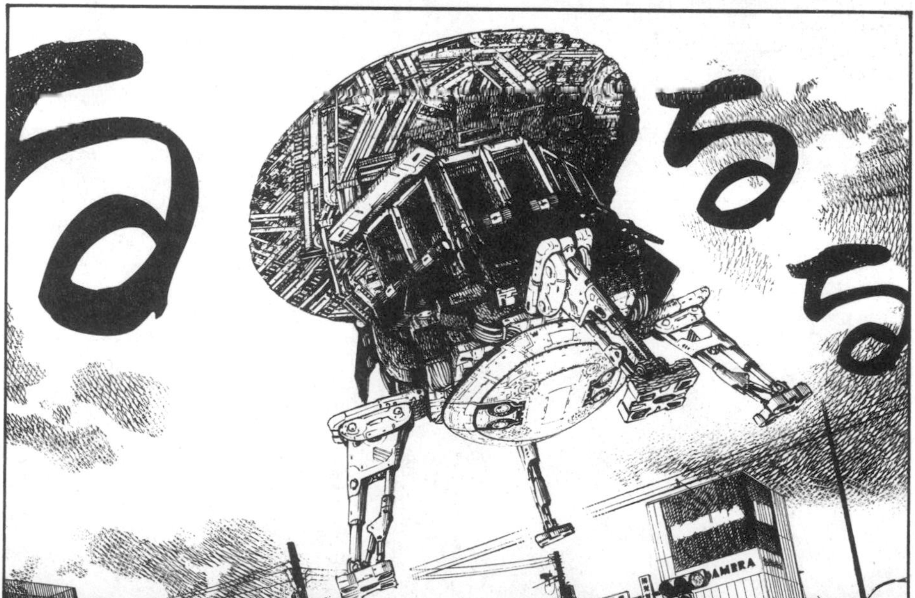
るる
る

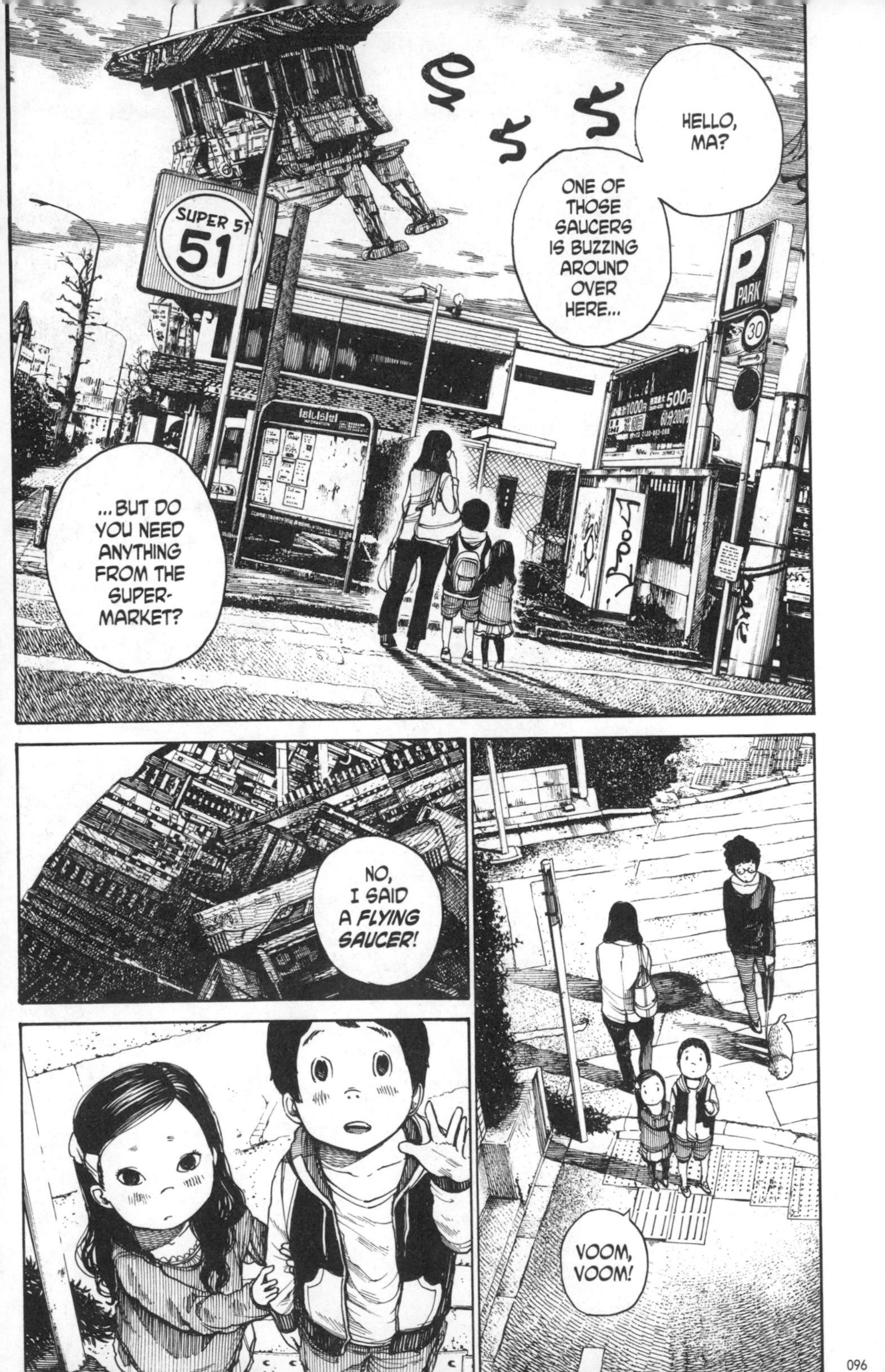
HELLO, MA?
ONE OF THOSE SAUCERS IS BUZZING AROUND OVER HERE...
SUPER 51
51
P
PARK
30
...BUT DO YOU NEED ANYTHING FROM THE SUPER-MARKET?
VOOM, VOOM!
NO, I SAID A *FLYING SAUCER*!

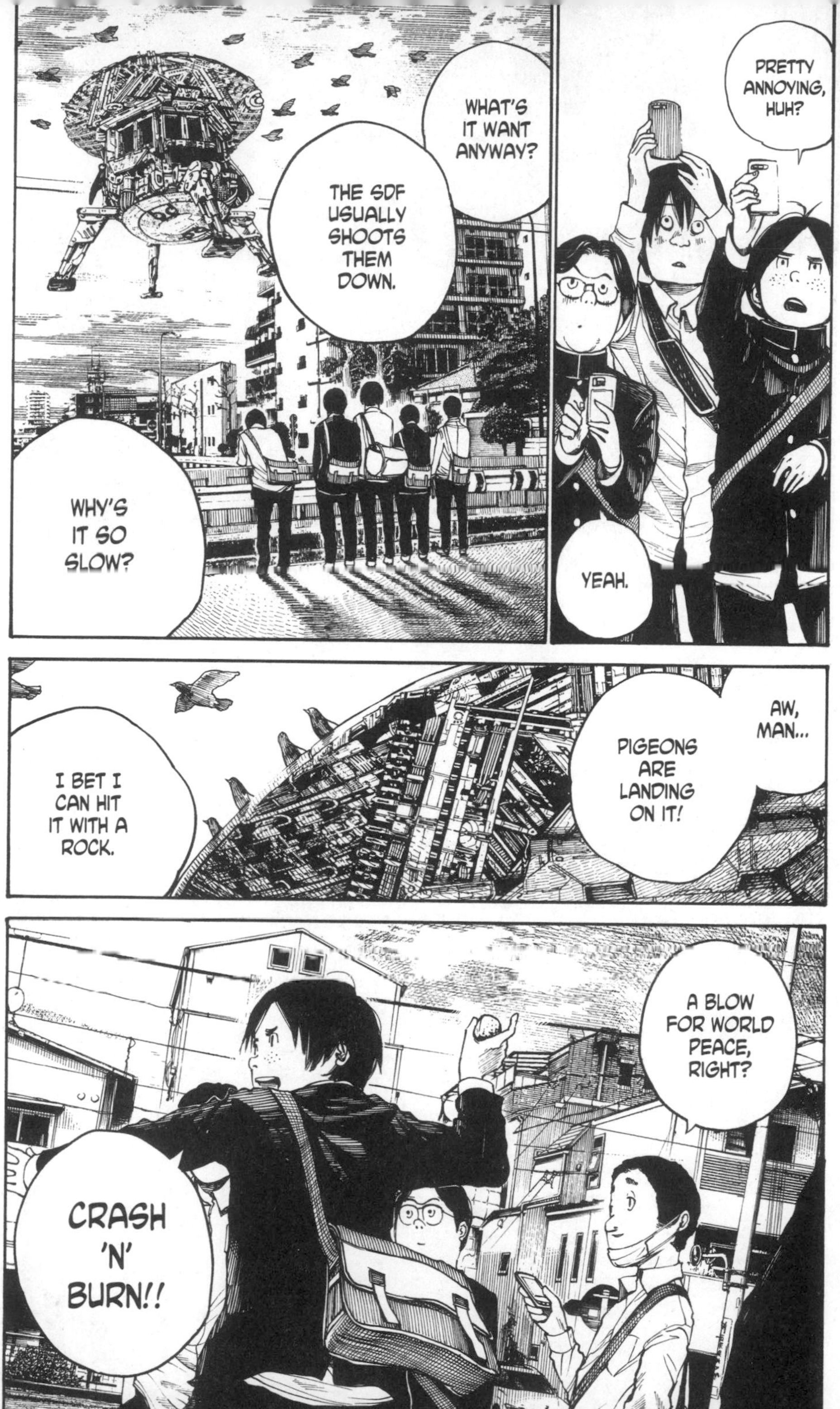
PRETTY ANNOYING, HUH?
YEAH.
WHAT'S IT WANT ANYWAY?
THE SDF USUALLY SHOOTS THEM DOWN.
WHY'S IT SO SLOW?
AW, MAN...
PIGEONS ARE LANDING ON IT!
I BET I CAN HIT IT WITH A ROCK.
A BLOW FOR WORLD PEACE, RIGHT?
CRASH 'N' BURN!!

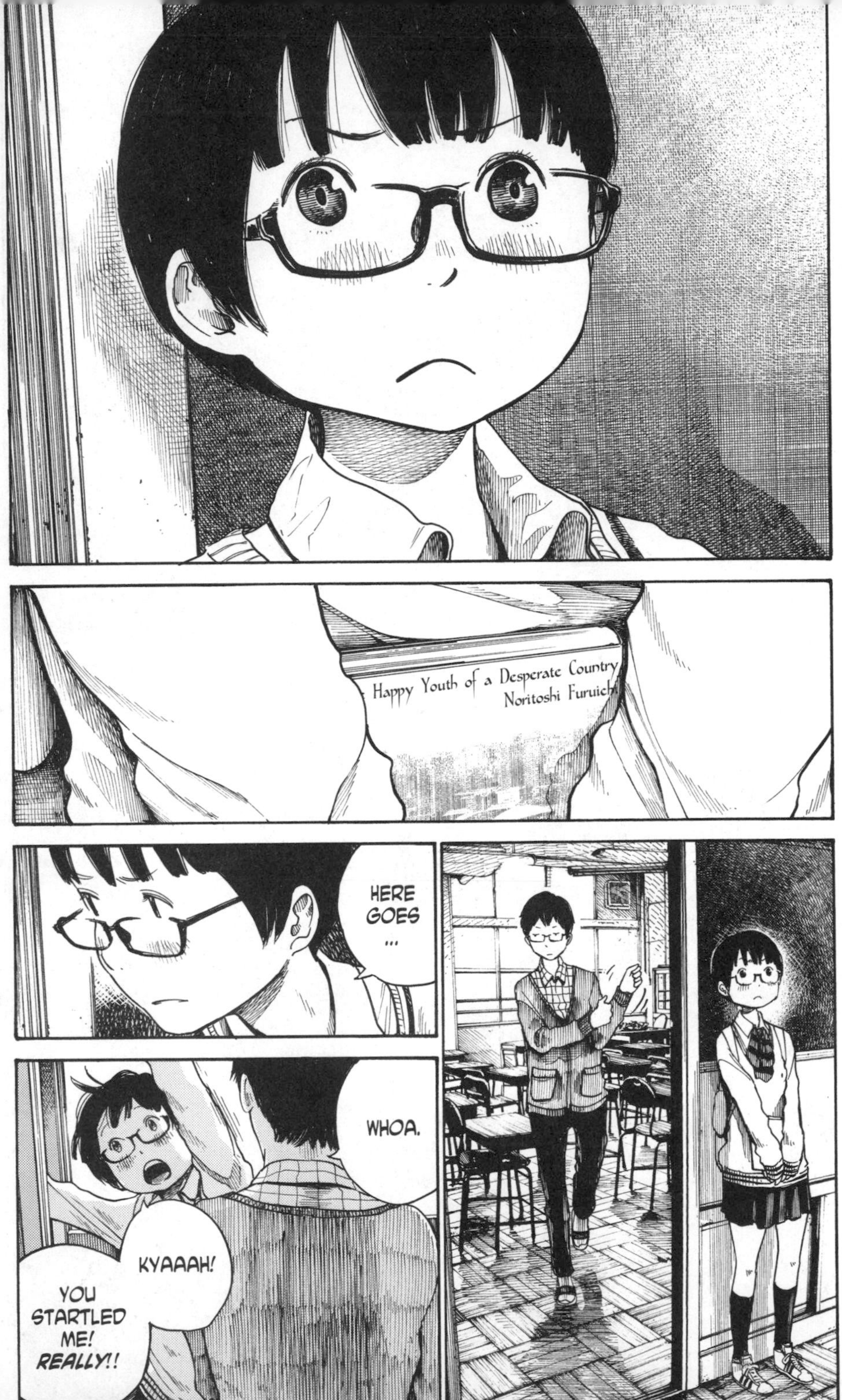
Happy Youth of a Desperate Country
Noritoshi Furuichi
HERE GOES ...
WHOA.
KYAAAH!
YOU STARTLED ME! *REALLY!!*

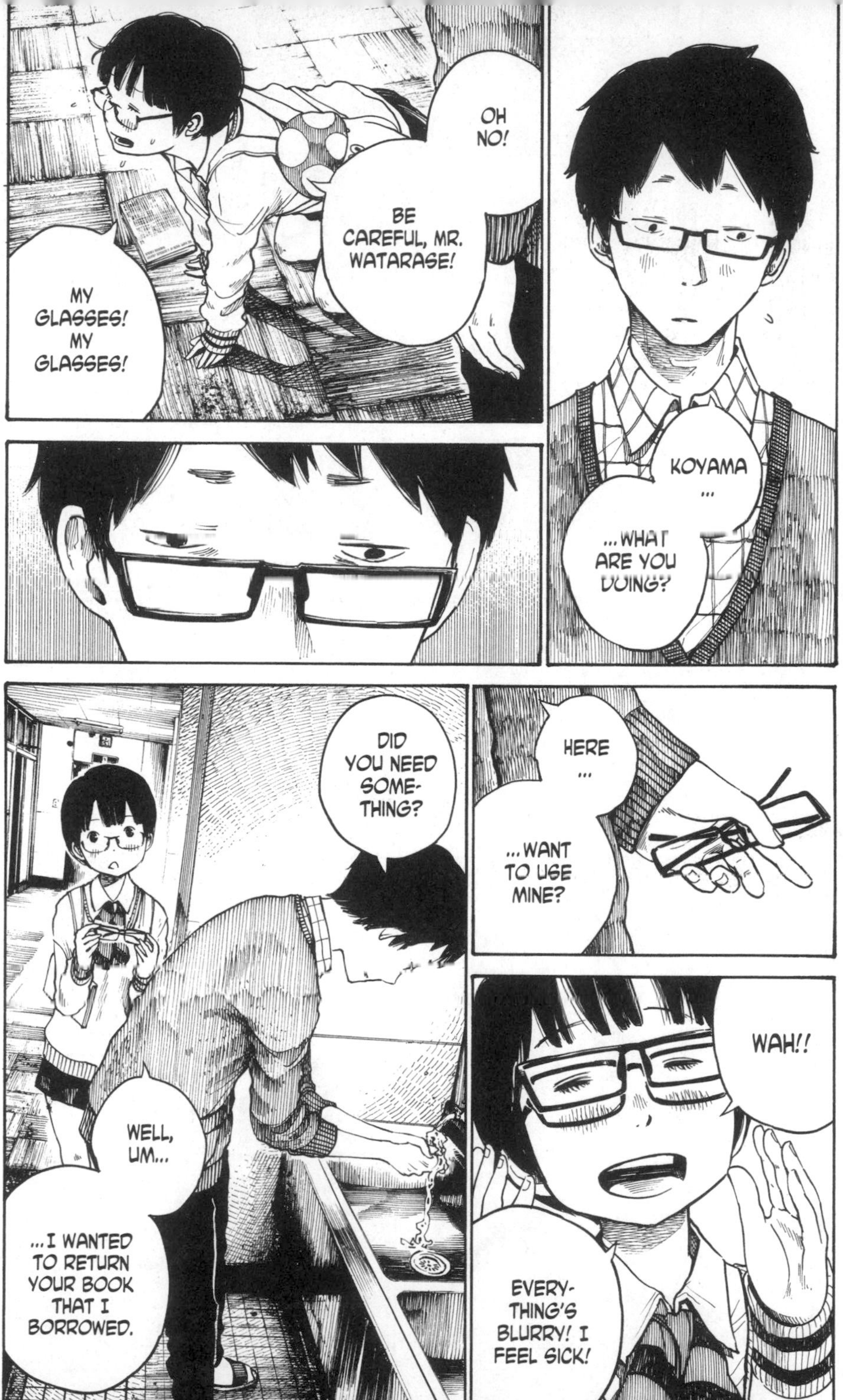

KOYAMA ...
...WHAT ARE YOU DOING?
OH NO!
BE CAREFUL, MR. WATARASE!
MY GLASSES! MY GLASSES!
HERE ...
...WANT TO USE MINE?
WAH!!
EVERY-THING'S BLURRY! I FEEL SICK!
DID YOU NEED SOME-THING?
WELL, UM...
...I WANTED TO RETURN YOUR BOOK THAT I BORROWED.

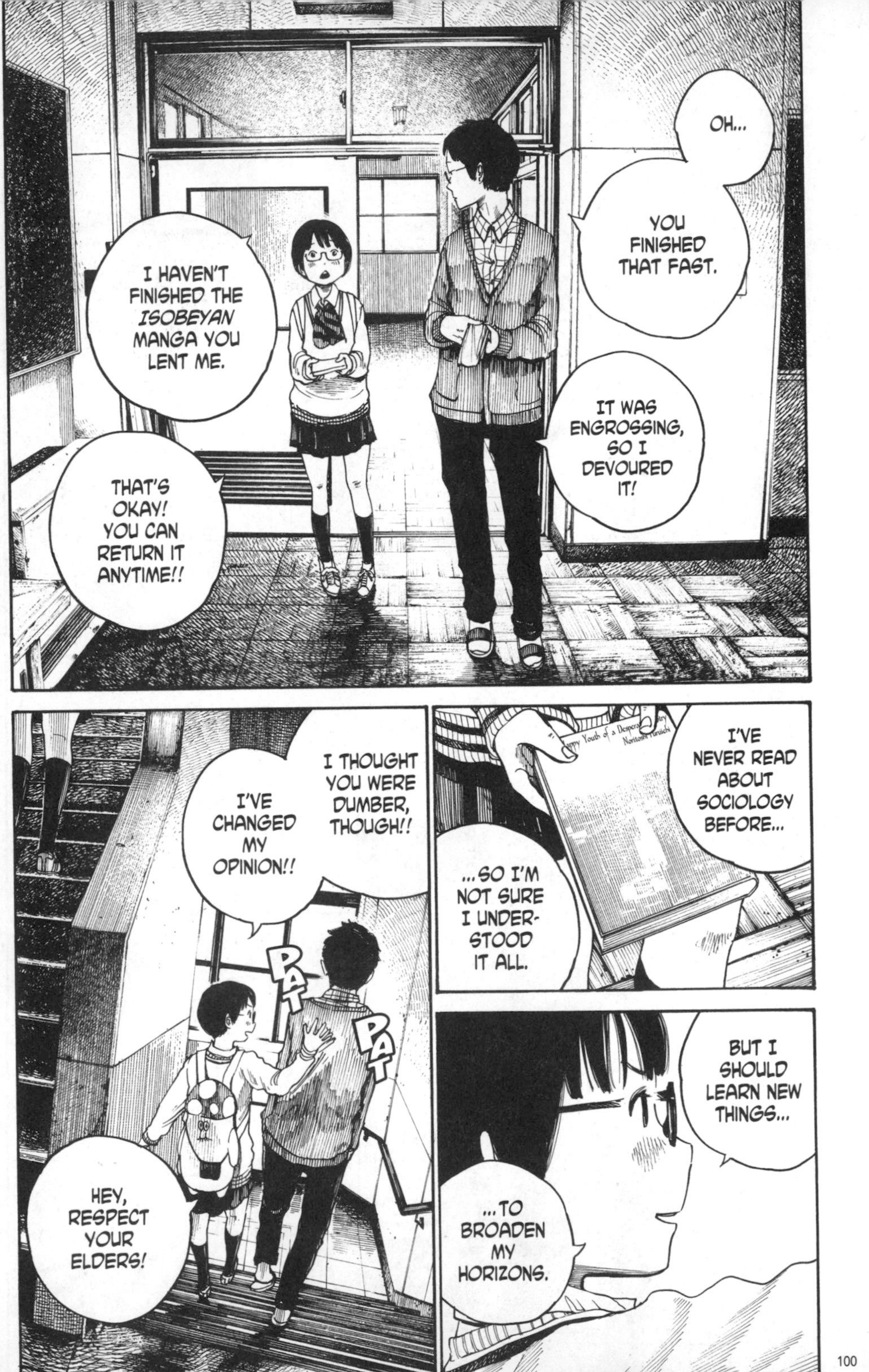
OH...
YOU FINISHED THAT FAST.
IT WAS ENGROSSING, SO I DEVOURED IT!
I HAVEN'T FINISHED THE *ISOBEYAN* MANGA YOU LENT ME.
THAT'S OKAY! YOU CAN RETURN IT ANYTIME!!
I'VE NEVER READ ABOUT SOCIOLOGY BEFORE...
...SO I'M NOT SURE I UNDER-STOOD IT ALL.
BUT I SHOULD LEARN NEW THINGS...
...TO BROADEN MY HORIZONS.
I THOUGHT YOU WERE DUMBER, THOUGH!!
I'VE CHANGED MY OPINION!!
PAT
PAT
HEY, RESPECT YOUR ELDERS!

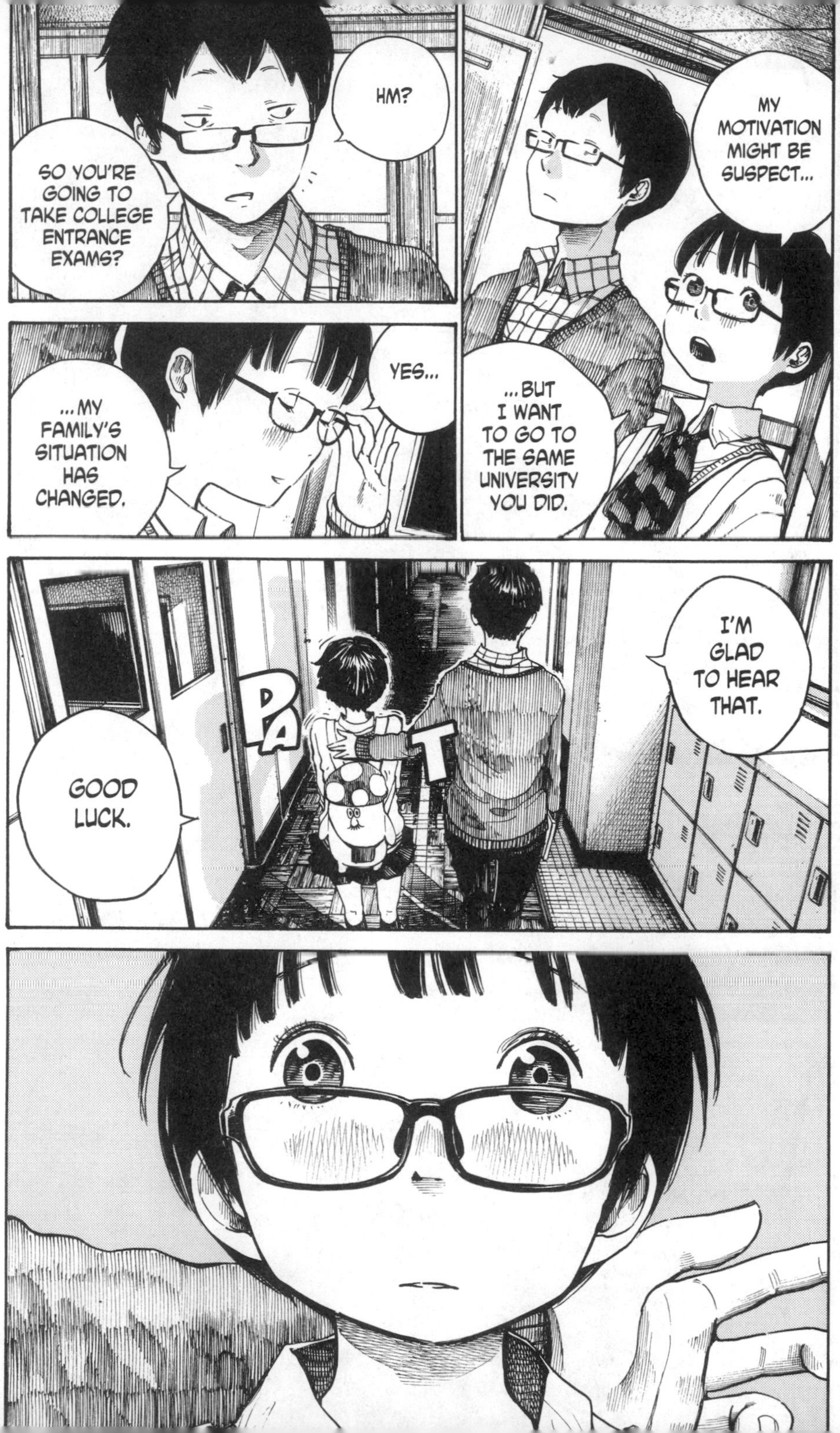
HM?
SO YOU'RE GOING TO TAKE COLLEGE ENTRANCE EXAMS?
YES...
...MY FAMILY'S SITUATION HAS CHANGED.
MY MOTIVATION MIGHT BE SUSPECT...
...BUT I WANT TO GO TO THE SAME UNIVERSITY YOU DID.
I'M GLAD TO HEAR THAT.
PAT
GOOD LUCK.

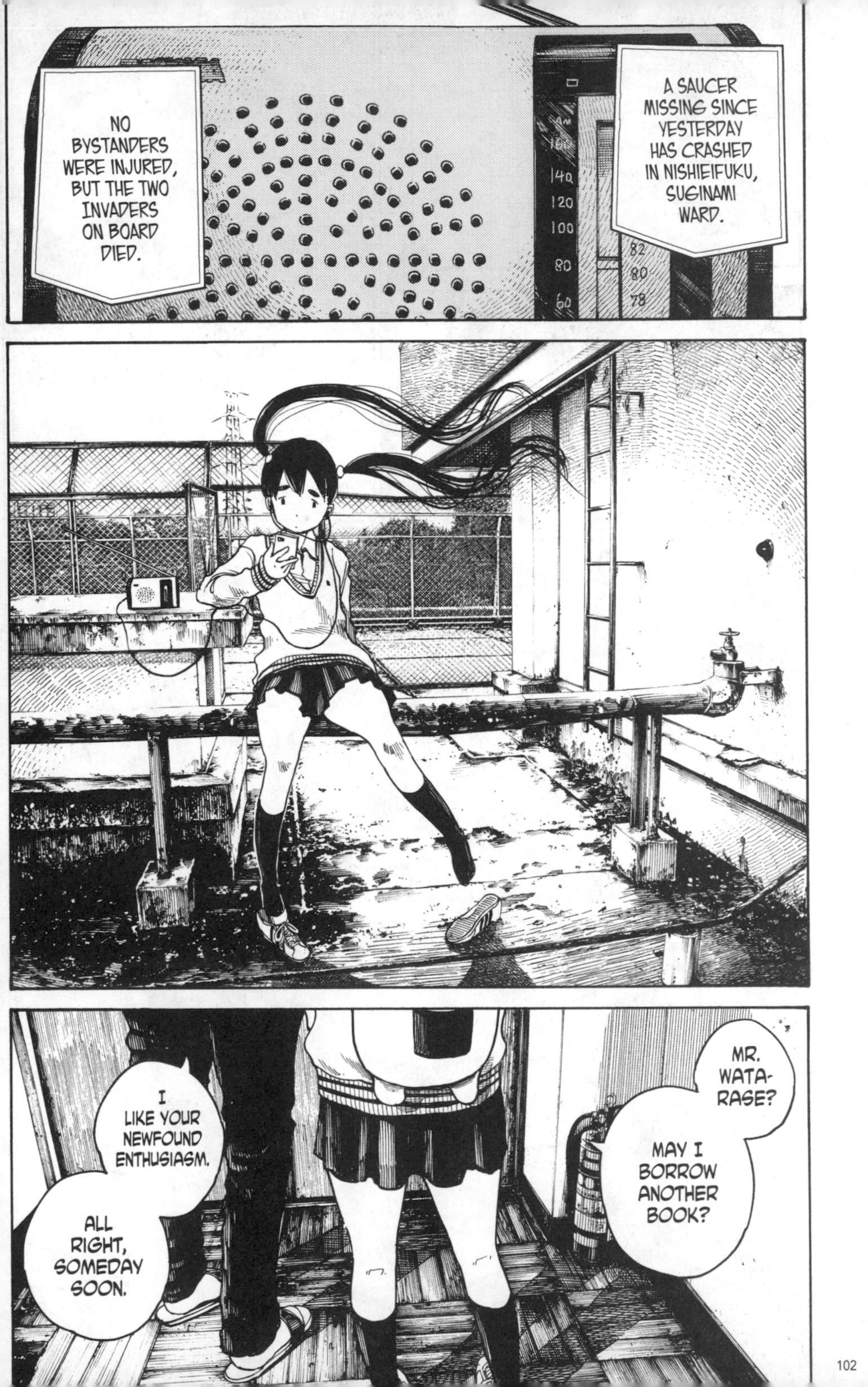
A SAUCER MISSING SINCE YESTERDAY HAS CRASHED IN NISHIEIFUKU, SUGINAMI WARD.
NO BYSTANDERS WERE INJURED, BUT THE TWO INVADERS ON BOARD DIED.
MR. WATA-RASE?
MAY I BORROW ANOTHER BOOK?
I LIKE YOUR NEWFOUND ENTHUSIASM.
ALL RIGHT, SOMEDAY SOON.

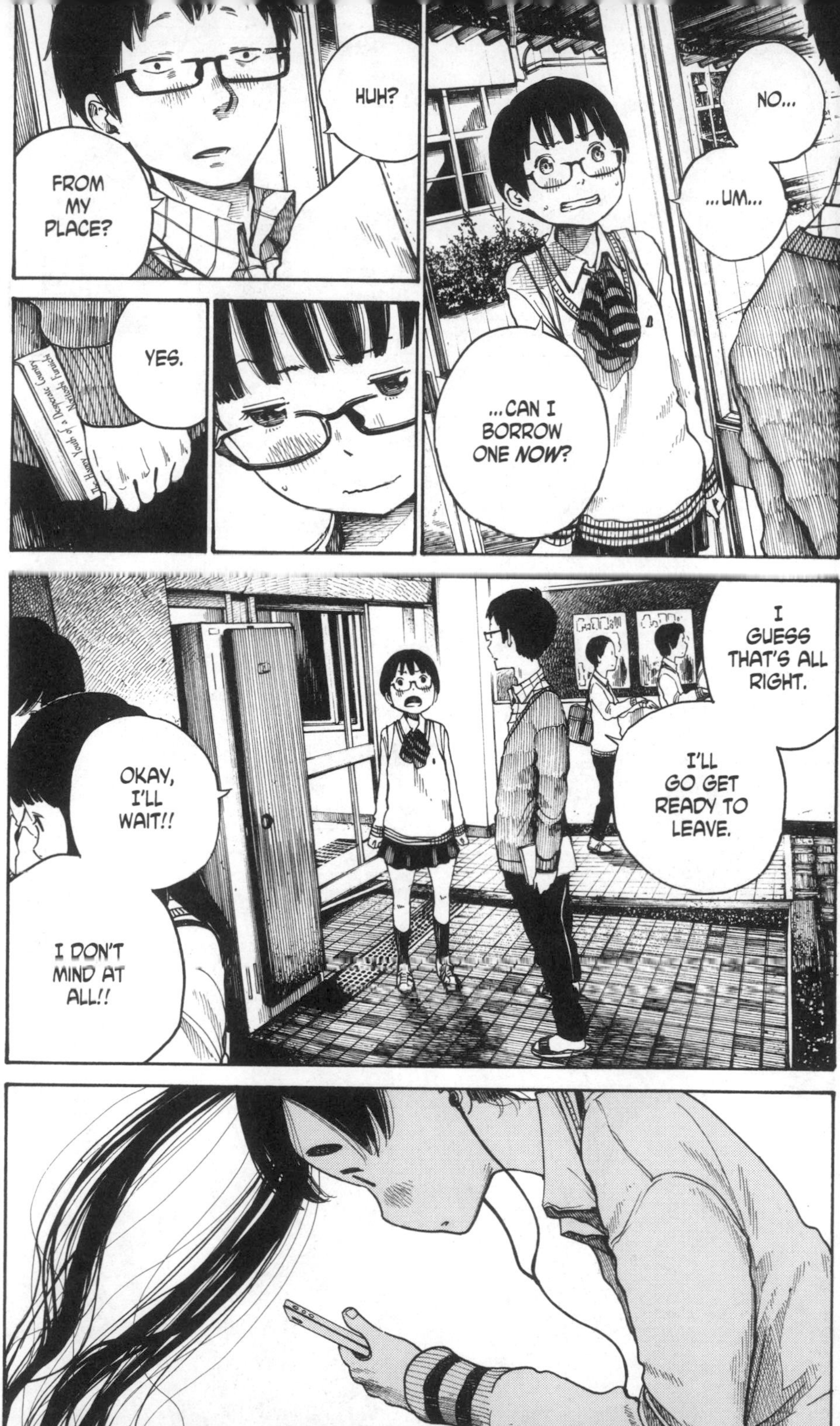
NO...
...UM...
...CAN I BORROW ONE NOW?
HUH?
FROM MY PLACE?
YES.
The Happy Youth of a Desperate Country
Noritoshi Furuichi
I GUESS THAT'S ALL RIGHT.
I'LL GO GET READY TO LEAVE.
OKAY, I'LL WAIT!!
I DON'T MIND AT ALL!!

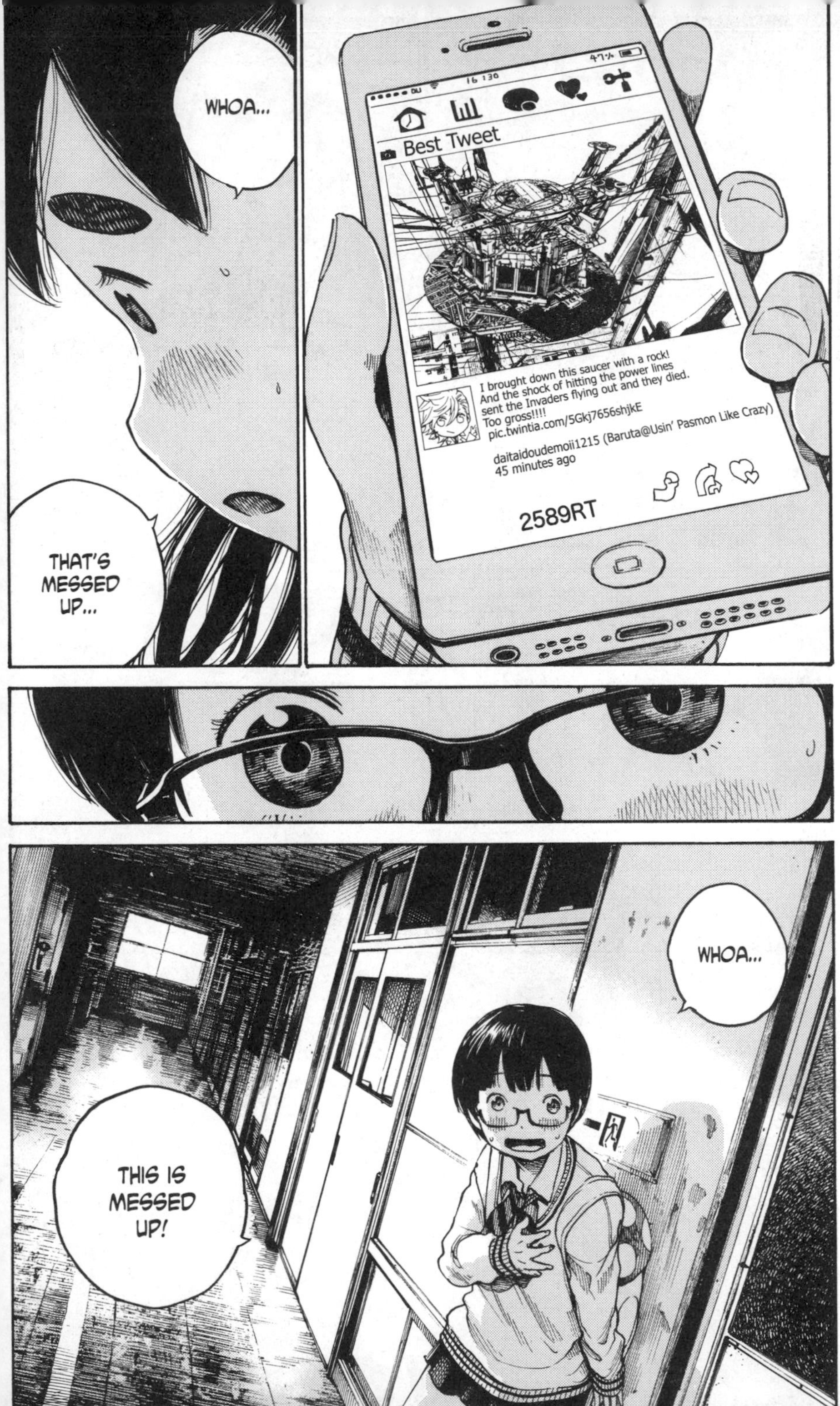
Best Tweet
I brought down this saucer with a rock!
And the shock of hitting the power lines
sent the Invaders flying out and they died.
Too gross!!!!
pic.twintia.com/5Gkj7656shjkE
daitaidoudemoii1215 (Baruta@Usin' Pasmon Like Crazy)
45 minutes ago
2589RT
WHOA...
THAT'S MESSED UP...
WHOA...
THIS IS MESSED UP!

CHAPTER 5

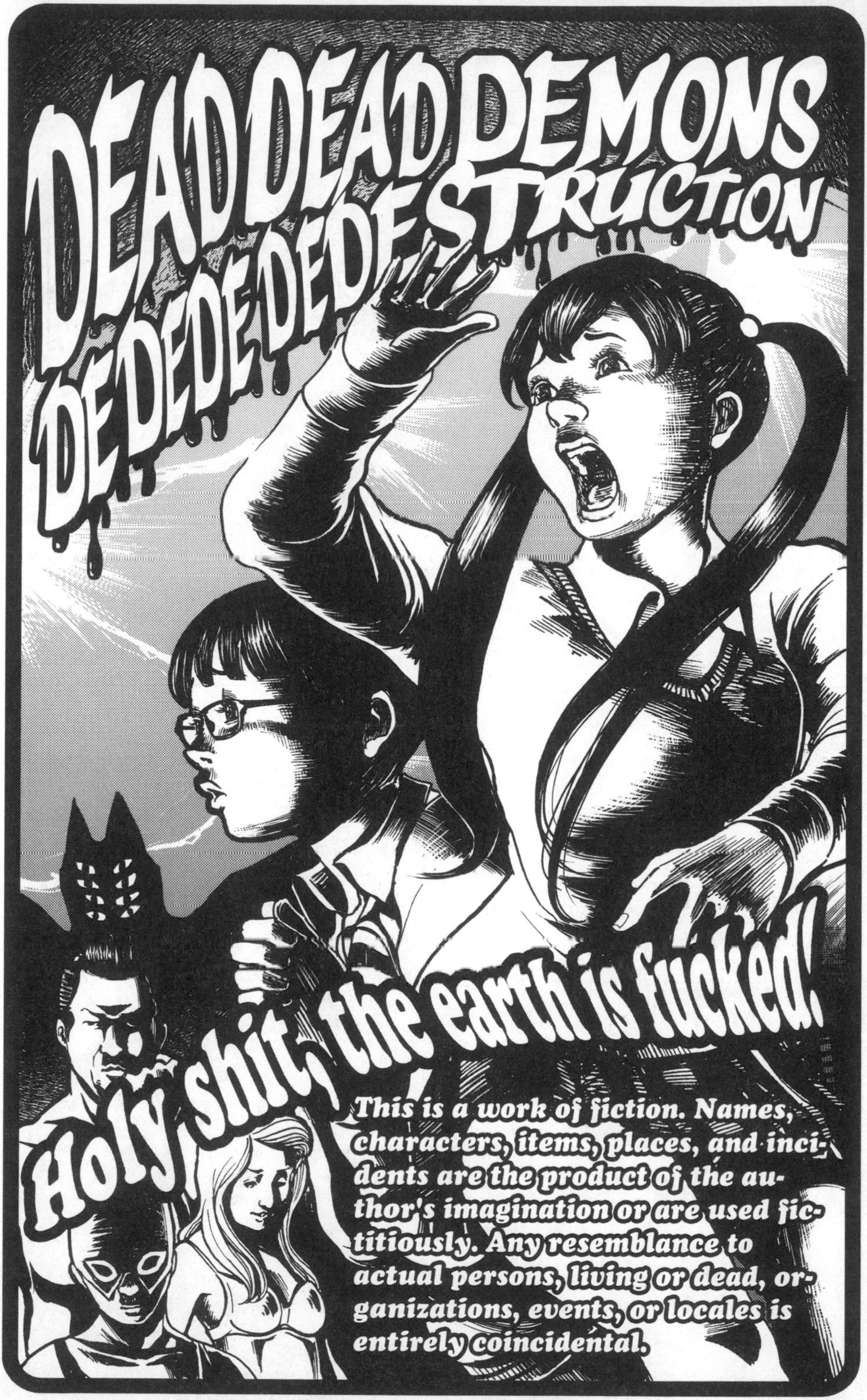
DEAD DEAD DEMONS
DE DE DE DE DESTRUCTION
Holy shit, the earth is fucked!
This is a work of fiction. Names, characters, items, places, and incidents are the product of the author's imagination or are used fictitiously. Any resemblance to actual persons, living or dead, organizations, events, or locales is entirely coincidental.

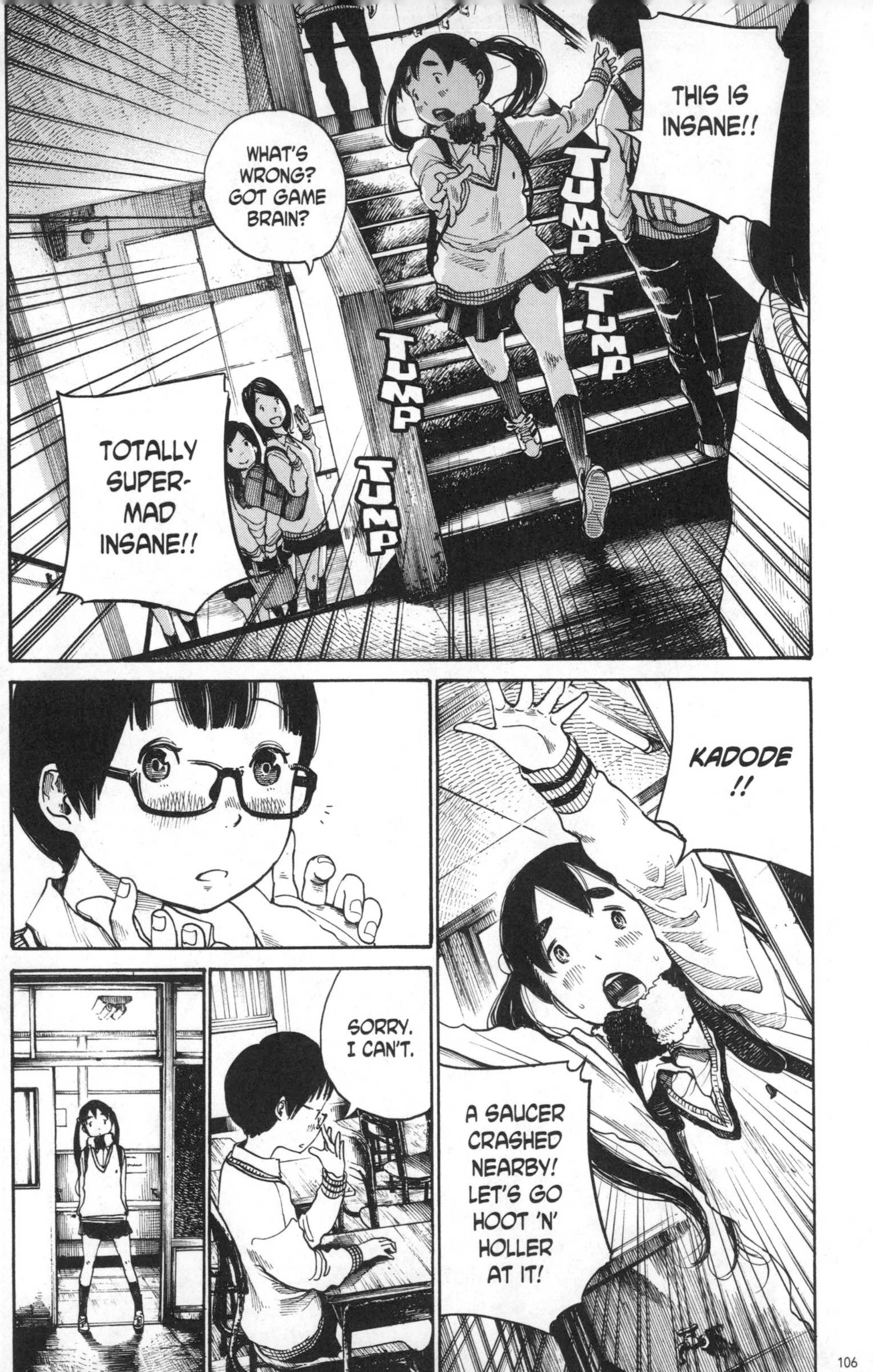
THIS IS INSANE!!
TUMP
WHAT'S WRONG? GOT GAME BRAIN?
TUMP
TUMP
TOTALLY SUPER-MAD INSANE!!
TUMP
KADODE !!
A SAUCER CRASHED NEARBY! LET'S GO HOOT 'N' HOLLER AT IT!
SORRY. I CAN'T.

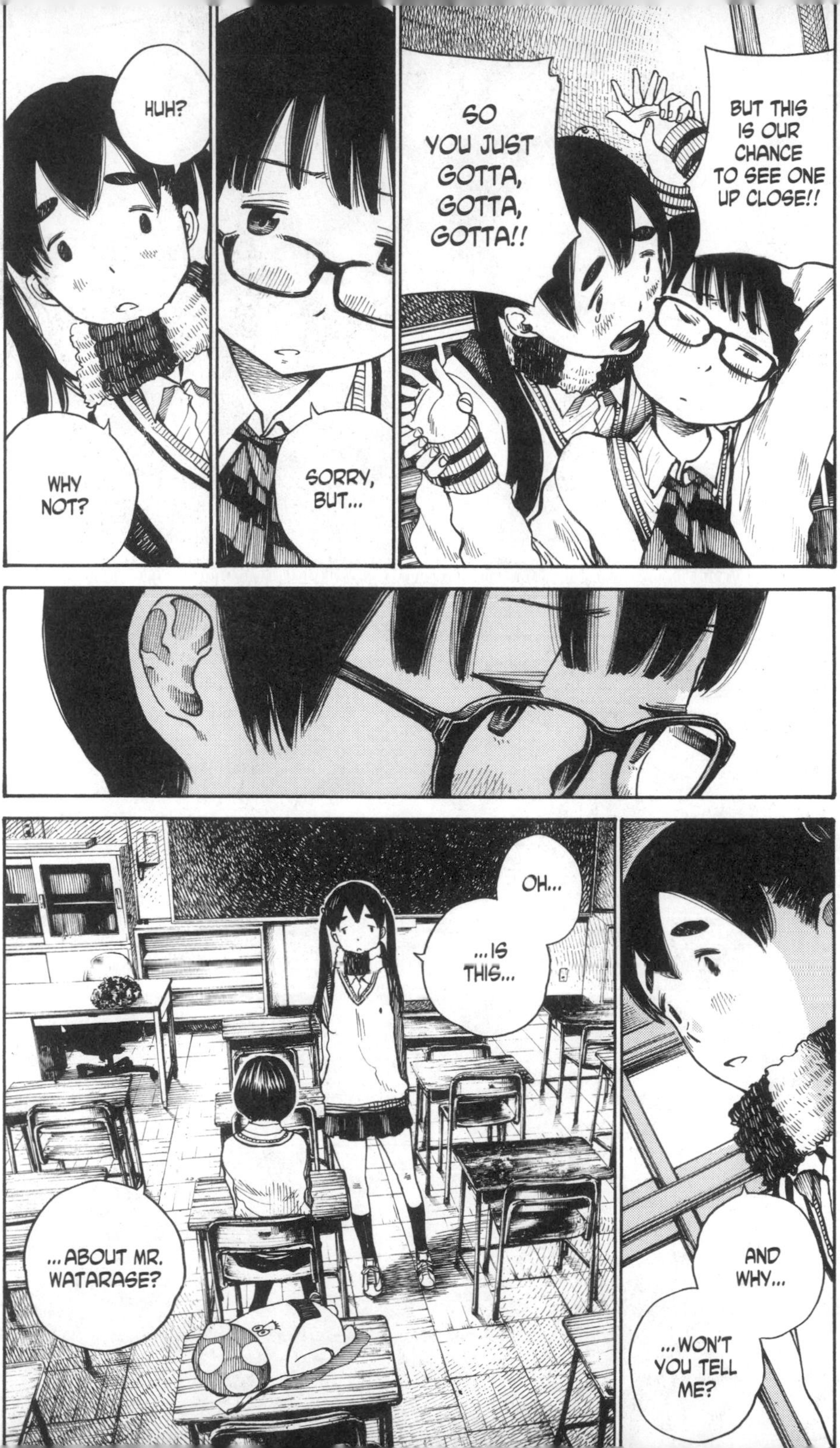
BUT THIS IS OUR CHANCE TO SEE ONE UP CLOSE!!
SO YOU JUST GOTTA, GOTTA, GOTTA!!
SORRY, BUT...
HUH?
WHY NOT?
AND WHY...
...WON'T YOU TELL ME?
OH...
...IS THIS...
...ABOUT MR. WATARASE?

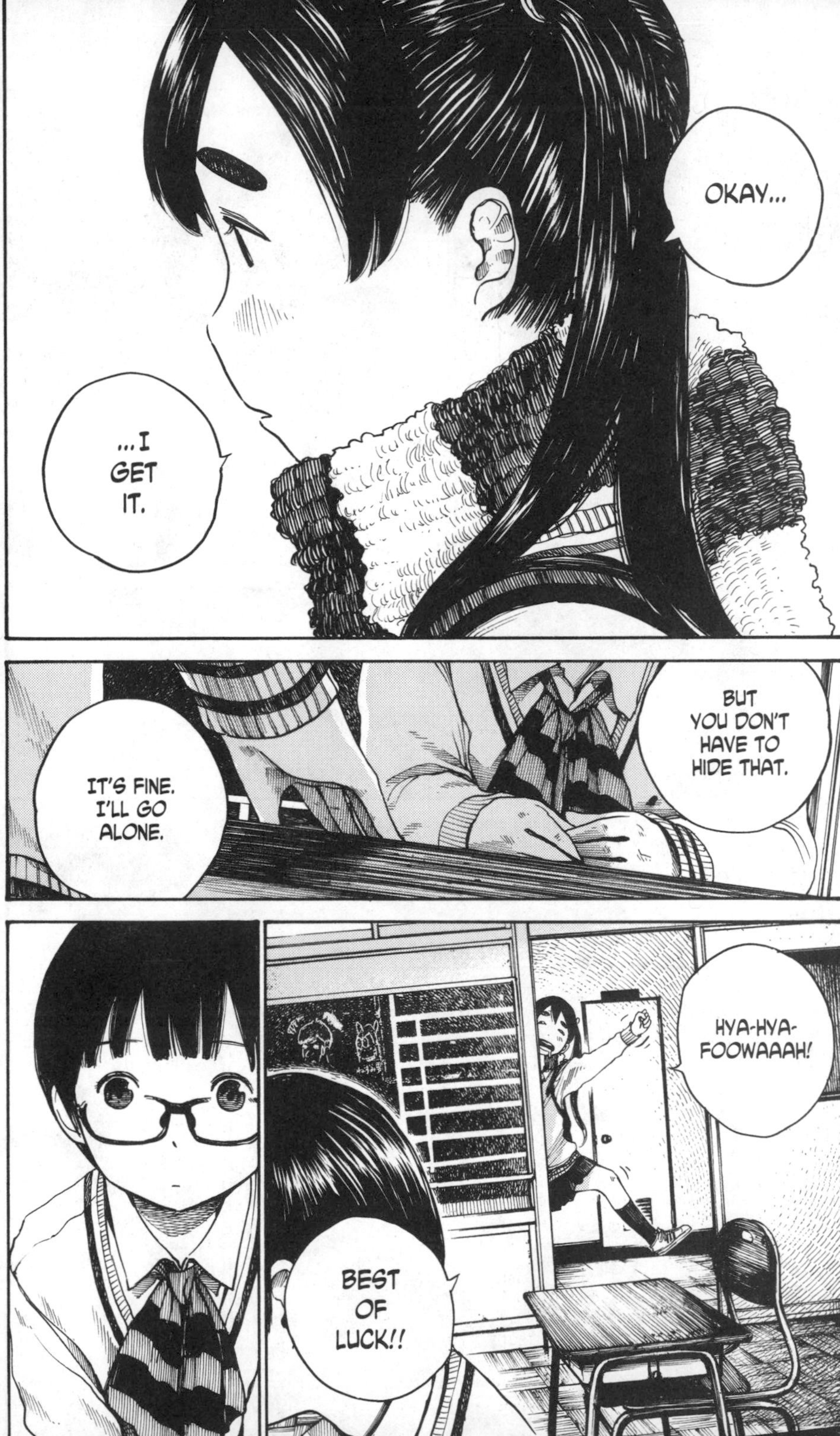
OKAY...
...I GET IT.
BUT YOU DON'T HAVE TO HIDE THAT.
IT'S FINE. I'LL GO ALONE.
HYA-HYA-FOOWAAAH!
BEST OF LUCK!!

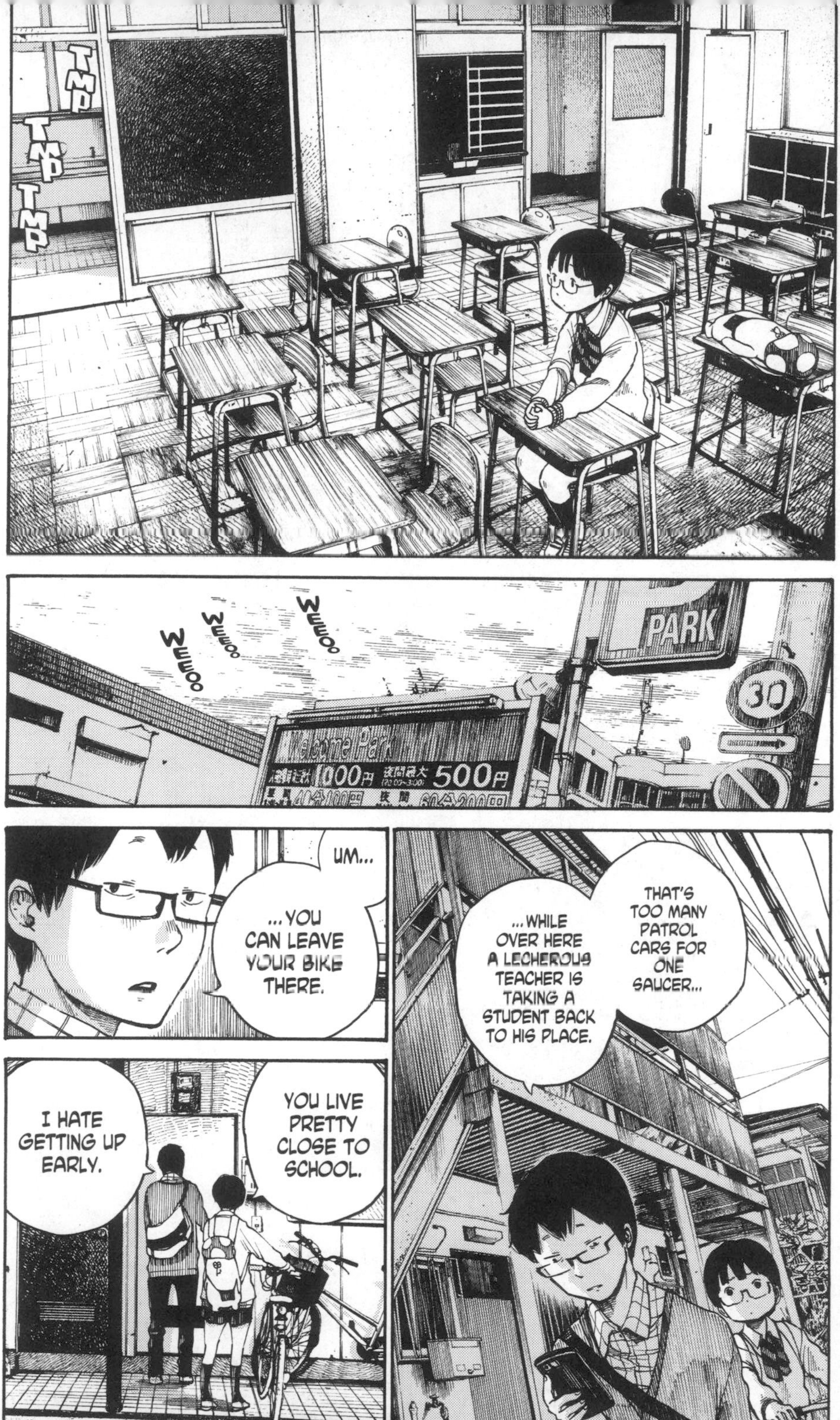
TMP
TMP
TMP
WEEOO
WEEOO
WEEOO
PARK
30
Welcome Park
1000円
500円
THAT'S TOO MANY PATROL CARS FOR ONE SAUCER...
...WHILE OVER HERE A LECHEROUS TEACHER IS TAKING A STUDENT BACK TO HIS PLACE.
UM...
...YOU CAN LEAVE YOUR BIKE THERE.
YOU LIVE PRETTY CLOSE TO SCHOOL.
I HATE GETTING UP EARLY.

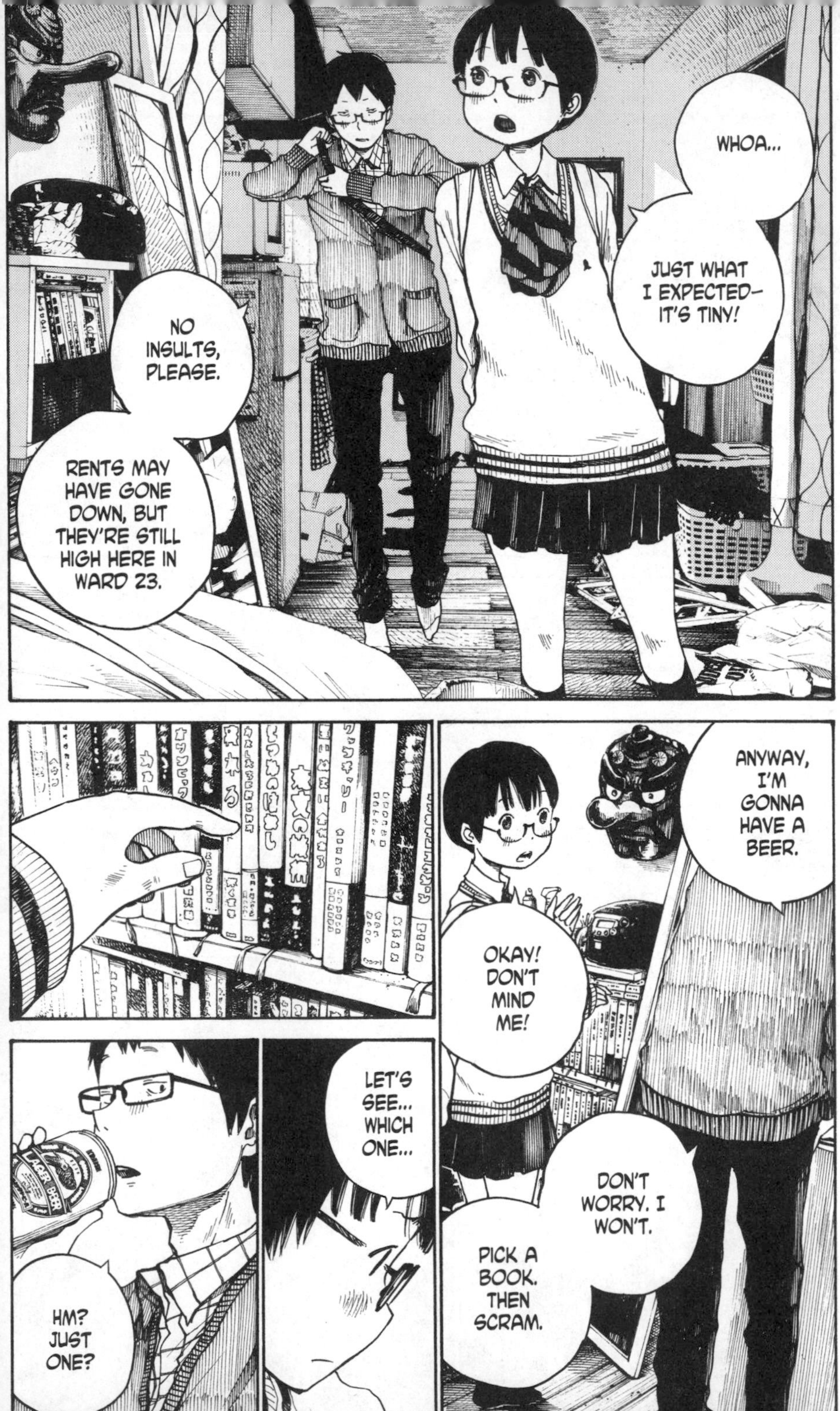
WHOA...
JUST WHAT I EXPECTED— IT'S TINY!
NO INSULTS, PLEASE.
RENTS MAY HAVE GONE DOWN, BUT THEY'RE STILL HIGH HERE IN WARD 23.
ANYWAY, I'M GONNA HAVE A BEER.
OKAY! DON'T MIND ME!
DON'T WORRY. I WON'T.
PICK A BOOK. THEN SCRAM.
LET'S SEE... WHICH ONE...
LAGER BEER
HM? JUST ONE?

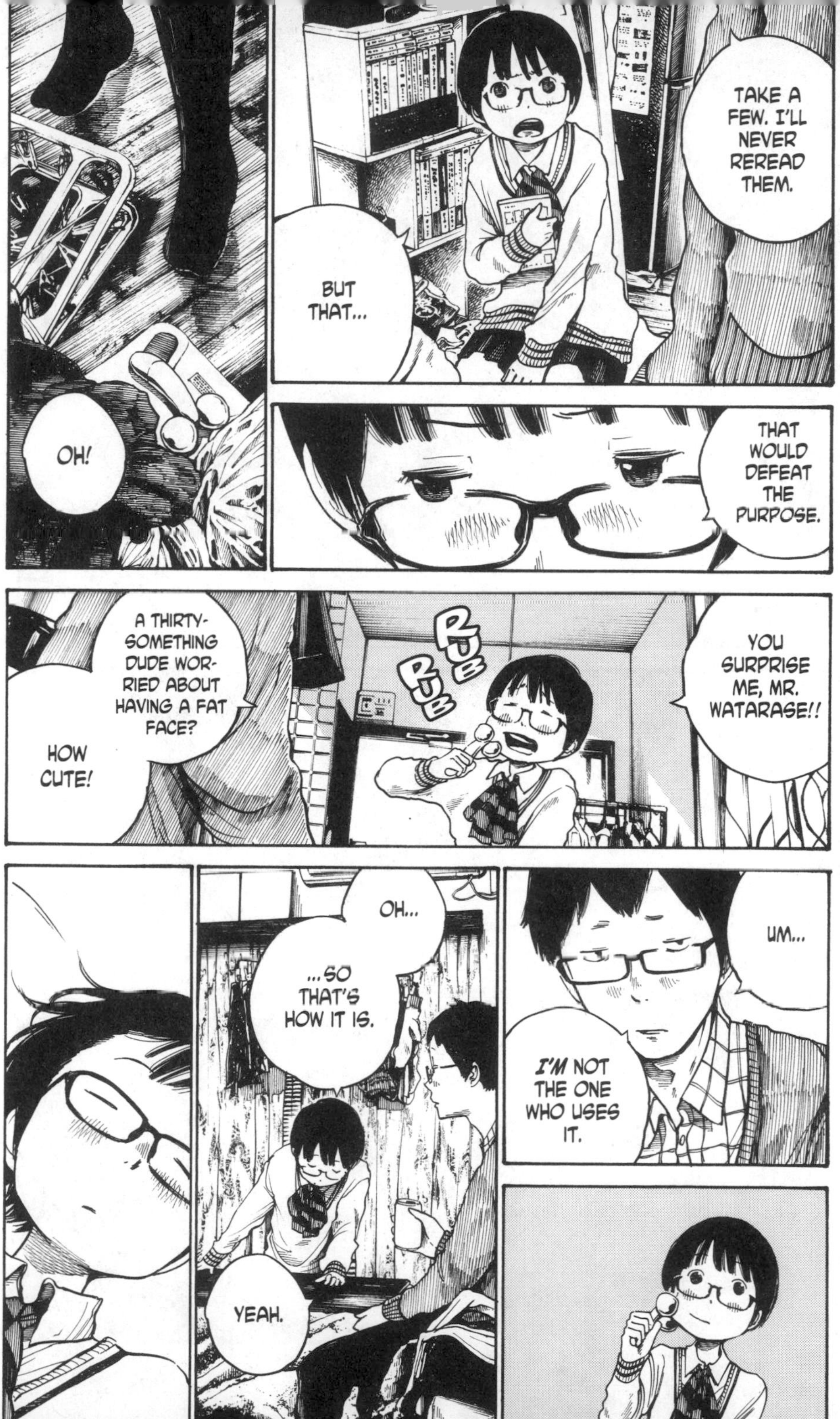
TAKE A FEW. I'LL NEVER REREAD THEM.
BUT THAT...
THAT WOULD DEFEAT THE PURPOSE.
OH!
YOU SURPRISE ME, MR. WATARASE!!
RUB RUB
A THIRTY-SOMETHING DUDE WORRIED ABOUT HAVING A FAT FACE?
HOW CUTE!
UM...
I'M NOT THE ONE WHO USES IT.
OH...
...SO THAT'S HOW IT IS.
YEAH.

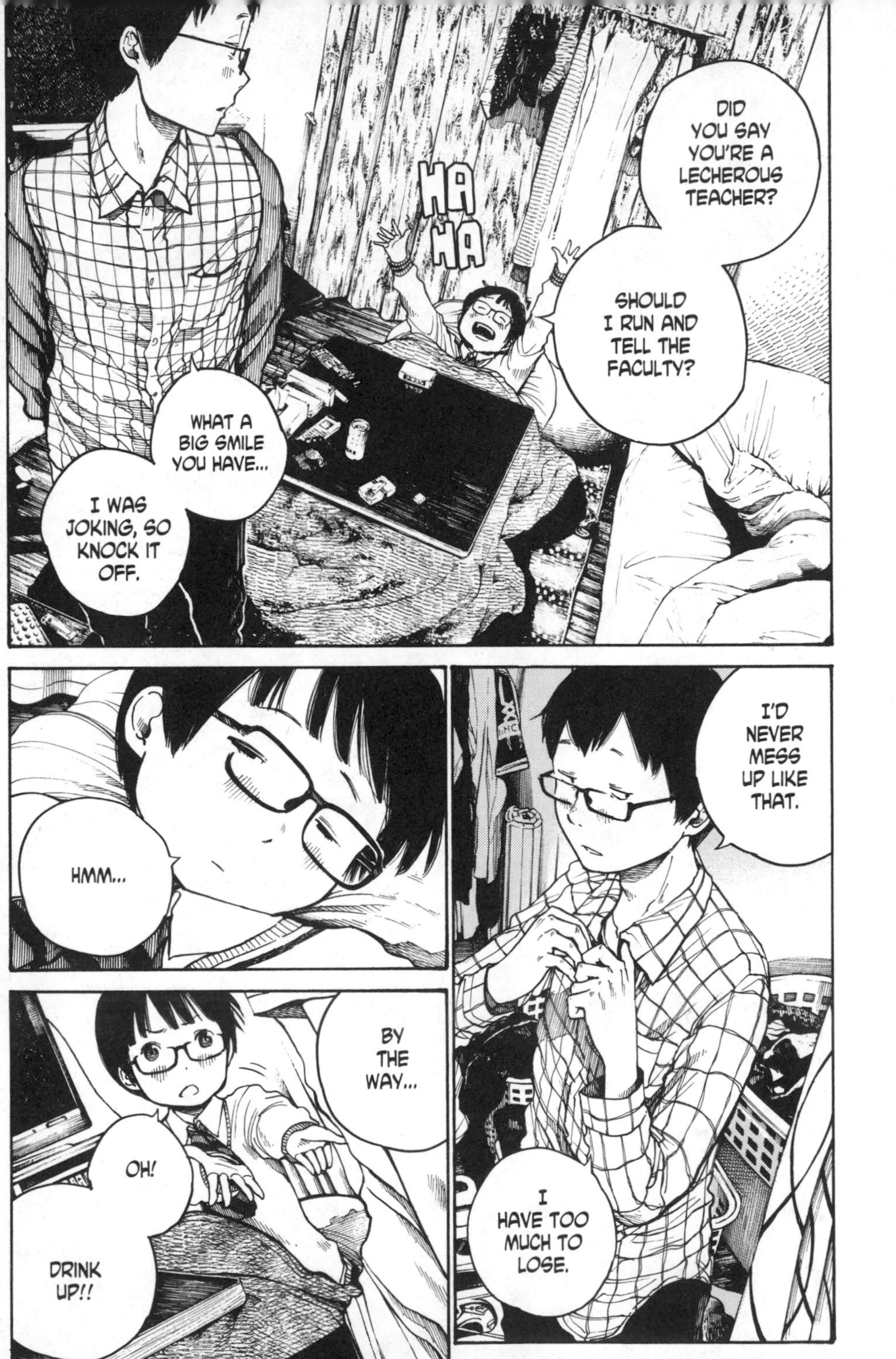
DID YOU SAY YOU'RE A LECHEROUS TEACHER?
HA HA
SHOULD I RUN AND TELL THE FACULTY?
WHAT A BIG SMILE YOU HAVE...
I WAS JOKING, SO KNOCK IT OFF.
I'D NEVER MESS UP LIKE THAT.
I HAVE TOO MUCH TO LOSE.
HMM...
BY THE WAY...
OH!
DRINK UP!!

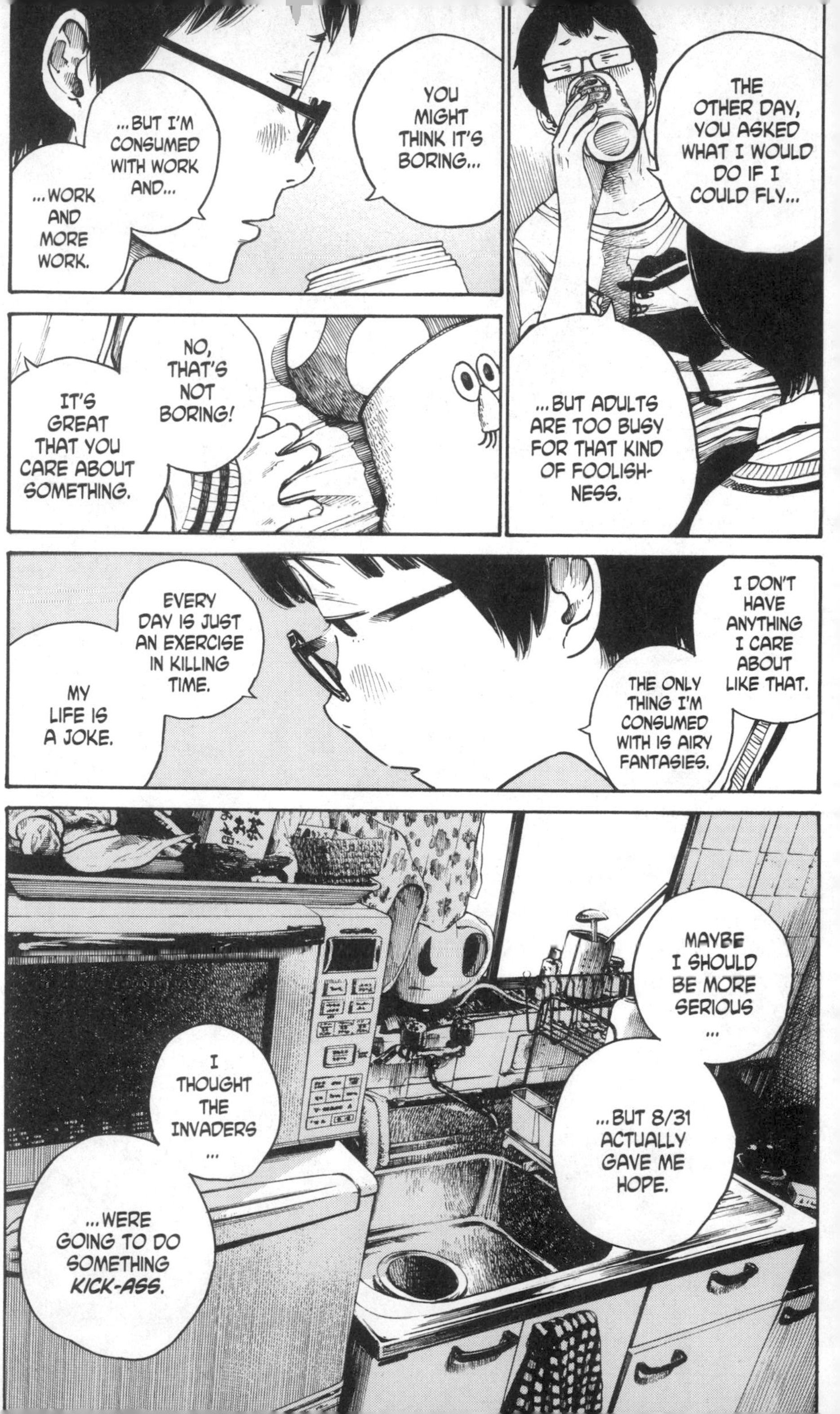
THE OTHER DAY, YOU ASKED WHAT I WOULD DO IF I COULD FLY...
...BUT ADULTS ARE TOO BUSY FOR THAT KIND OF FOOLISH-NESS.
YOU MIGHT THINK IT'S BORING...
...BUT I'M CONSUMED WITH WORK AND...
...WORK AND MORE WORK.
NO, THAT'S NOT BORING!
IT'S GREAT THAT YOU CARE ABOUT SOMETHING.
I DON'T HAVE ANYTHING I CARE ABOUT LIKE THAT.
THE ONLY THING I'M CONSUMED WITH IS AIRY FANTASIES.
EVERY DAY IS JUST AN EXERCISE IN KILLING TIME.
MY LIFE IS A JOKE.
MAYBE I SHOULD BE MORE SERIOUS...
...BUT 8/31 ACTUALLY GAVE ME HOPE.
I THOUGHT THE INVADERS...
...WERE GOING TO DO SOMETHING *KICK-ASS*.

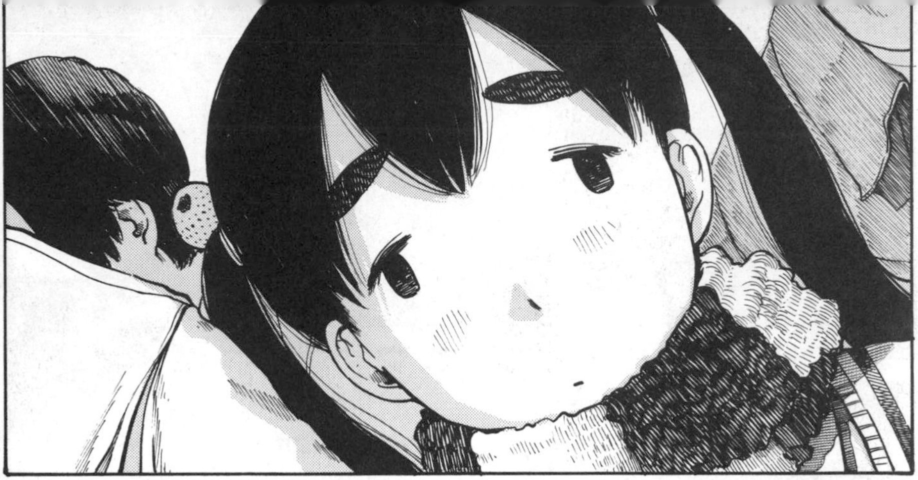

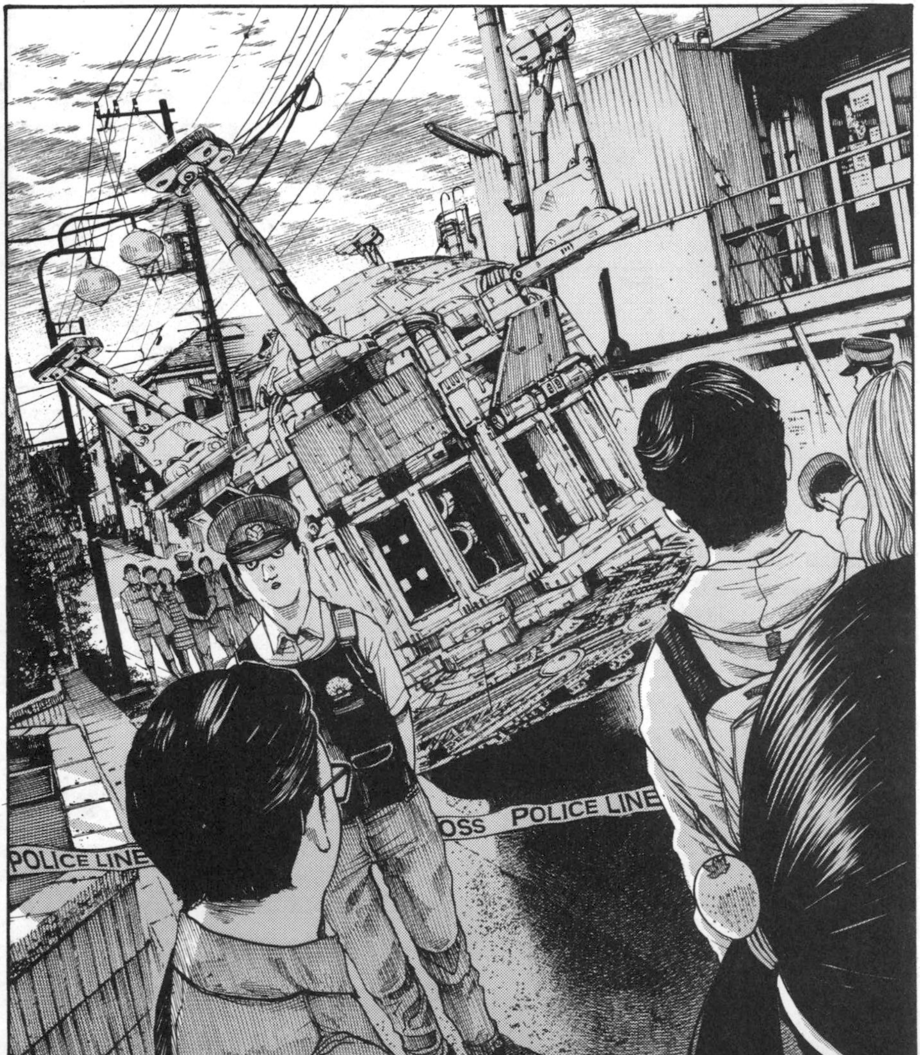
POLICE LINE
OSS
POLICE LINE

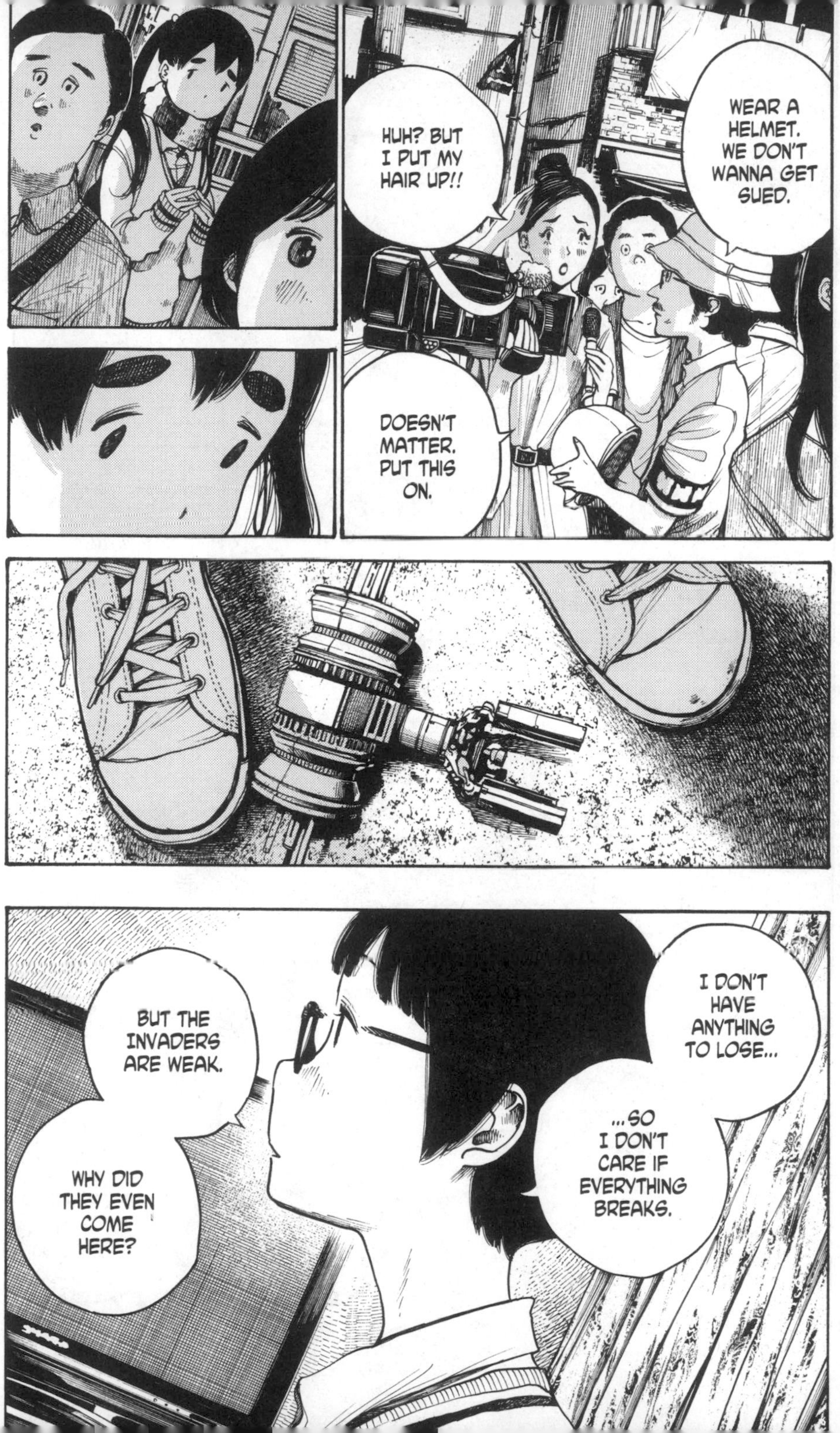
WEAR A HELMET. WE DON'T WANNA GET SUED.
HUH? BUT I PUT MY HAIR UP!!
DOESN'T MATTER. PUT THIS ON.
I DON'T HAVE ANYTHING TO LOSE...
...SO I DON'T CARE IF EVERYTHING BREAKS.
BUT THE INVADERS ARE WEAK.
WHY DID THEY EVEN COME HERE?

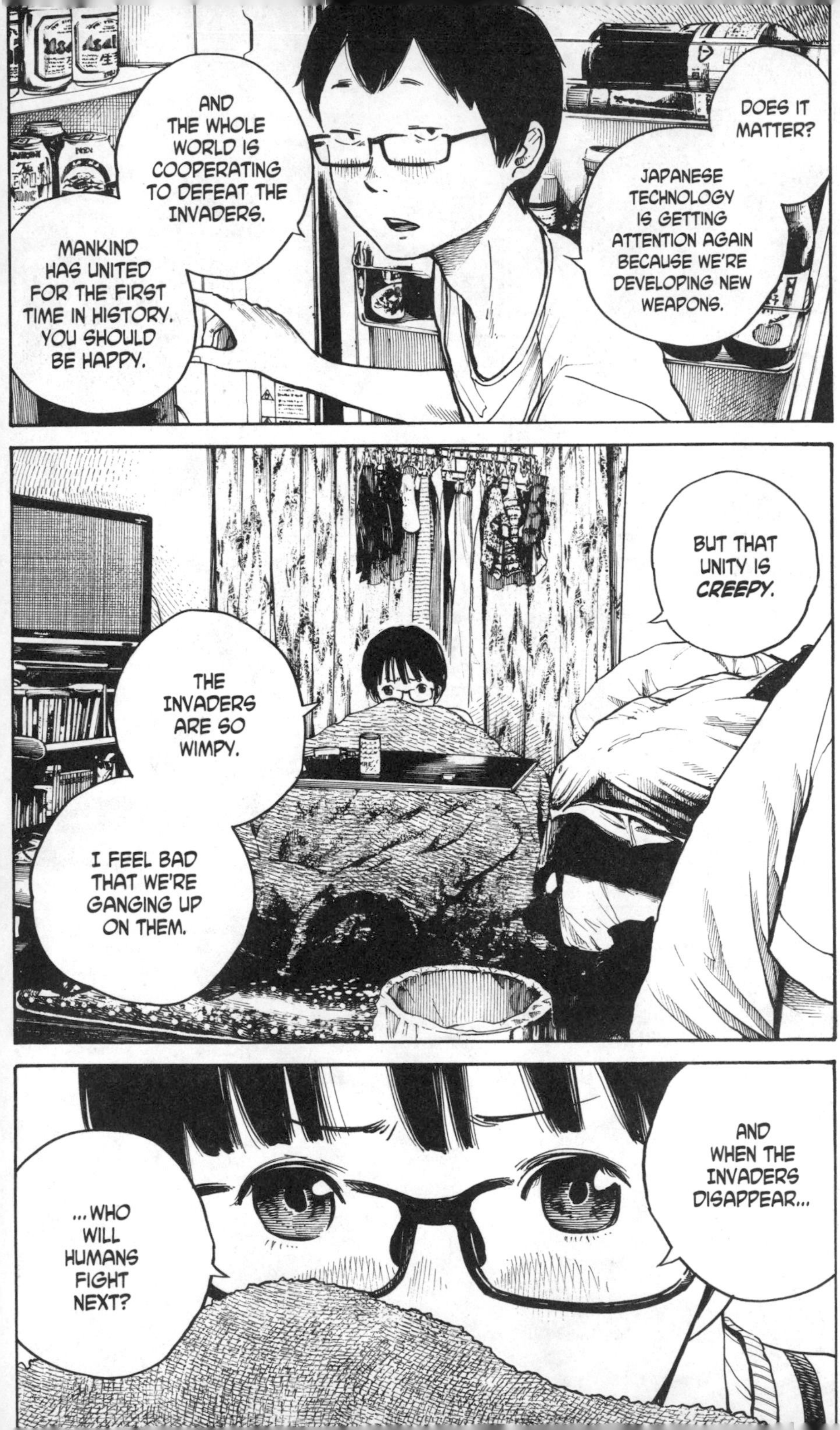
DOES IT MATTER?
JAPANESE TECHNOLOGY IS GETTING ATTENTION AGAIN BECAUSE WE'RE DEVELOPING NEW WEAPONS.
AND THE WHOLE WORLD IS COOPERATING TO DEFEAT THE INVADERS.
MANKIND HAS UNITED FOR THE FIRST TIME IN HISTORY. YOU SHOULD BE HAPPY.
BUT THAT UNITY IS *CREEPY*.
THE INVADERS ARE SO WIMPY.
I FEEL BAD THAT WE'RE GANGING UP ON THEM.
AND WHEN THE INVADERS DISAPPEAR...
...WHO WILL HUMANS FIGHT NEXT?

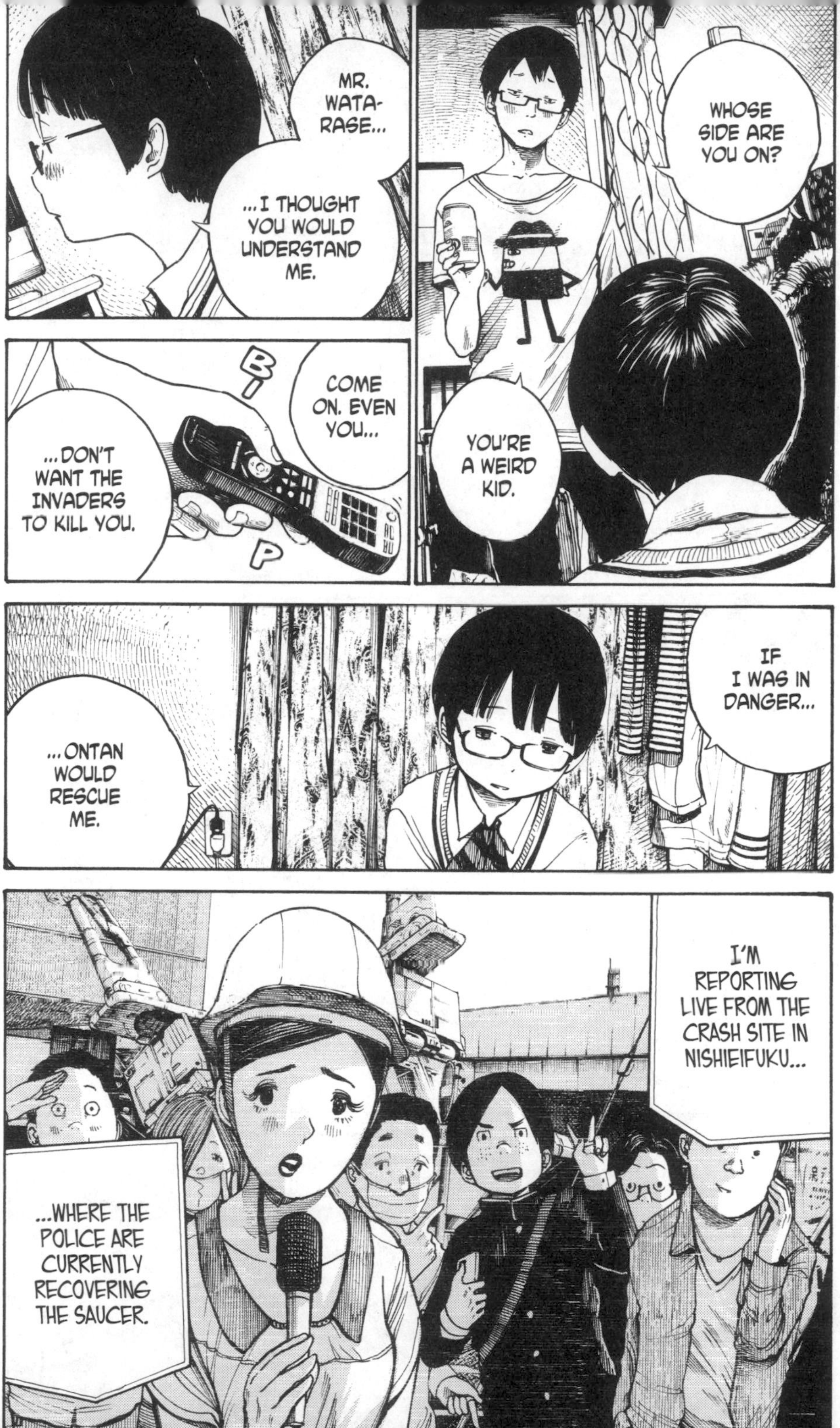

WHOSE SIDE ARE YOU ON?
YOU'RE A WEIRD KID.
MR. WATARASE...
...I THOUGHT YOU WOULD UNDERSTAND ME.
COME ON. EVEN YOU...
...DON'T WANT THE INVADERS TO KILL YOU.
BIP
IF I WAS IN DANGER...
...ONTAN WOULD RESCUE ME.
I'M REPORTING LIVE FROM THE CRASH SITE IN NISHIEIFUKU...
...WHERE THE POLICE ARE CURRENTLY RECOVERING THE SAUCER.

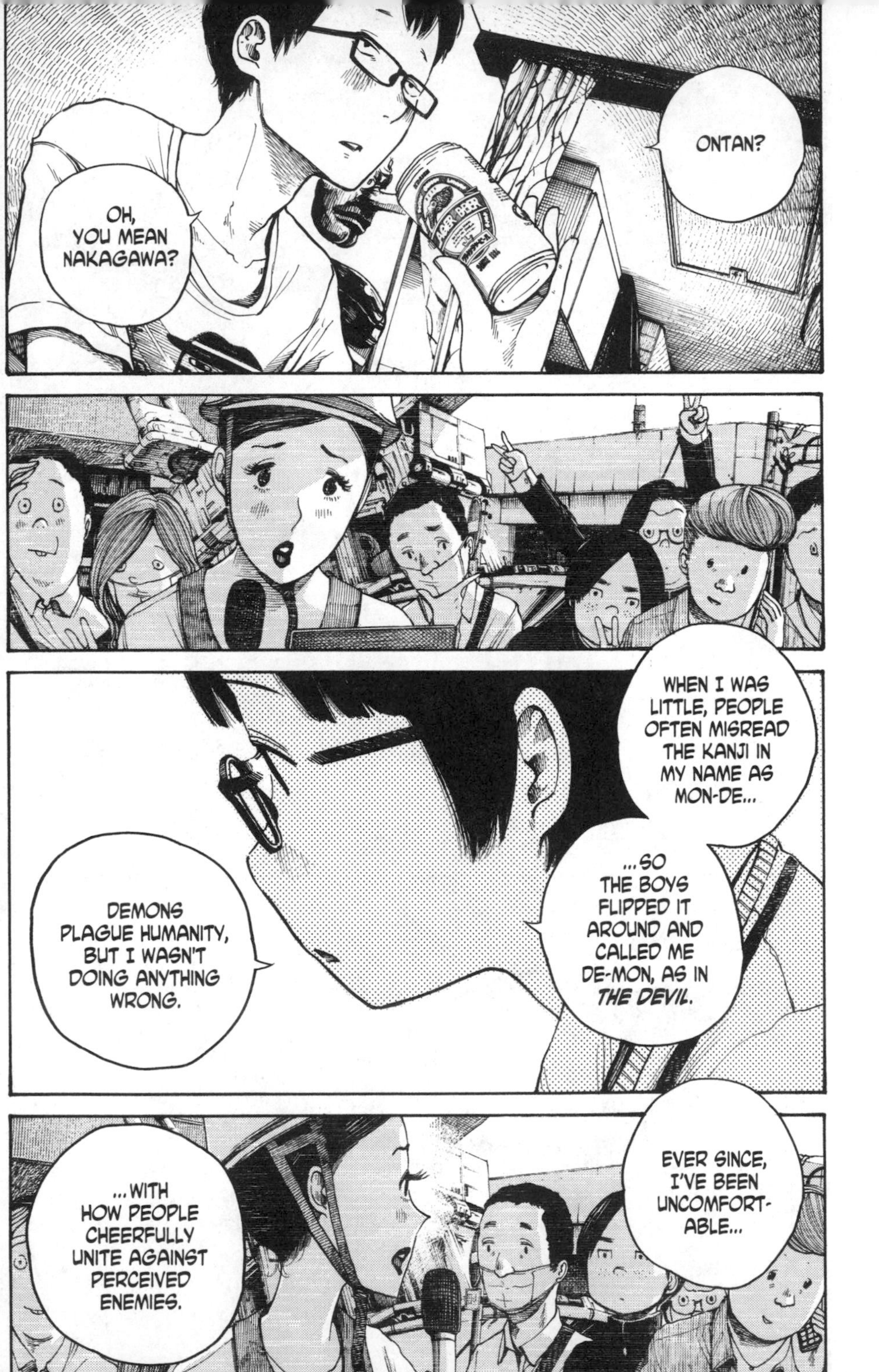
ONTAN?
OH, YOU MEAN NAKAGAWA?
WHEN I WAS LITTLE, PEOPLE OFTEN MISREAD THE KANJI IN MY NAME AS MON-DE...
...SO THE BOYS FLIPPED IT AROUND AND CALLED ME DE-MON, AS IN *THE DEVIL*.
DEMONS PLAGUE HUMANITY, BUT I WASN'T DOING ANYTHING WRONG.
EVER SINCE, I'VE BEEN UNCOMFORT-ABLE...
...WITH HOW PEOPLE CHEERFULLY UNITE AGAINST PERCEIVED ENEMIES.

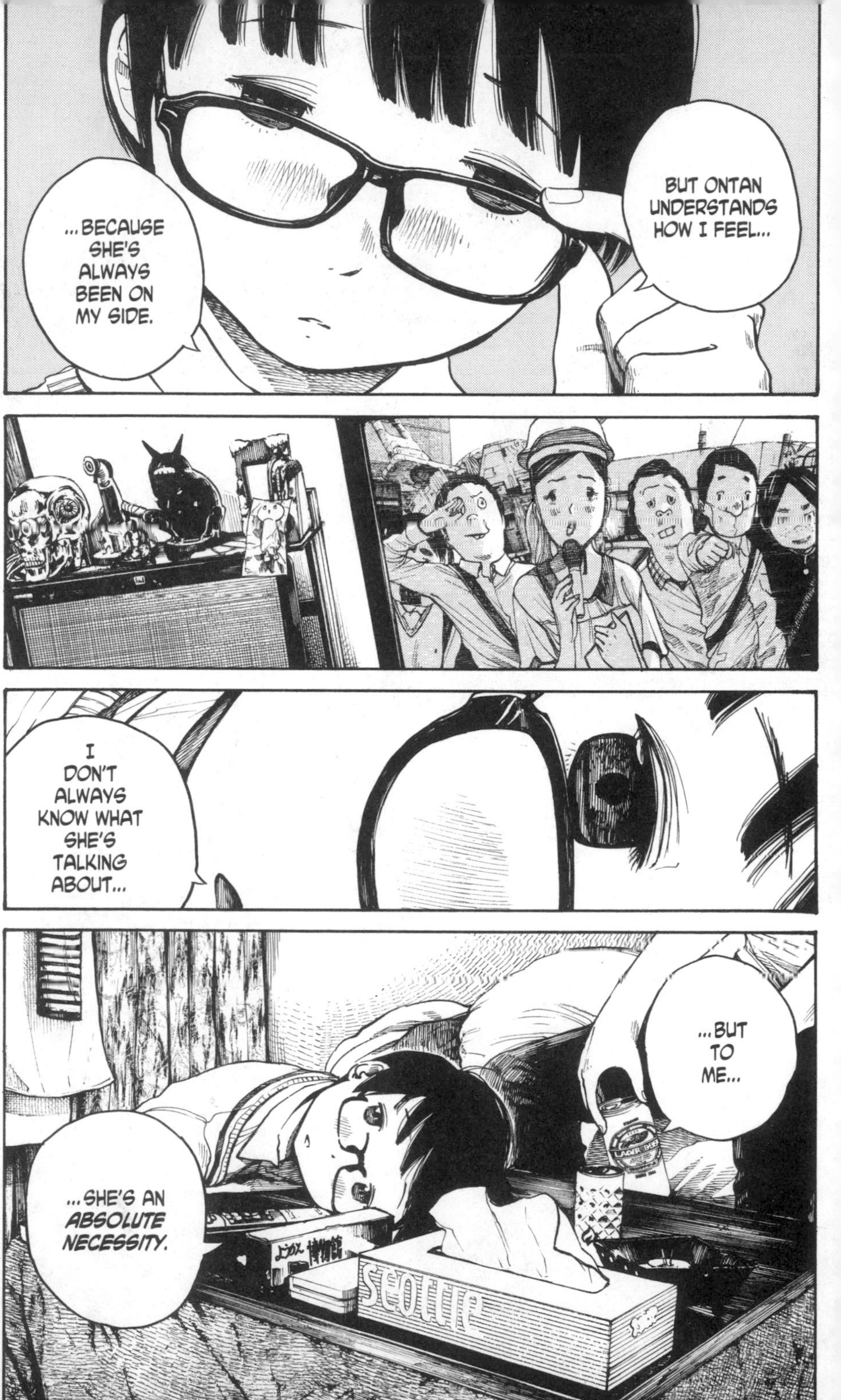
BUT ONTAN UNDERSTANDS HOW I FEEL...
...BECAUSE SHE'S ALWAYS BEEN ON MY SIDE.
I DON'T ALWAYS KNOW WHAT SHE'S TALKING ABOUT...
...BUT TO ME...
...SHE'S AN *ABSOLUTE NECESSITY.*

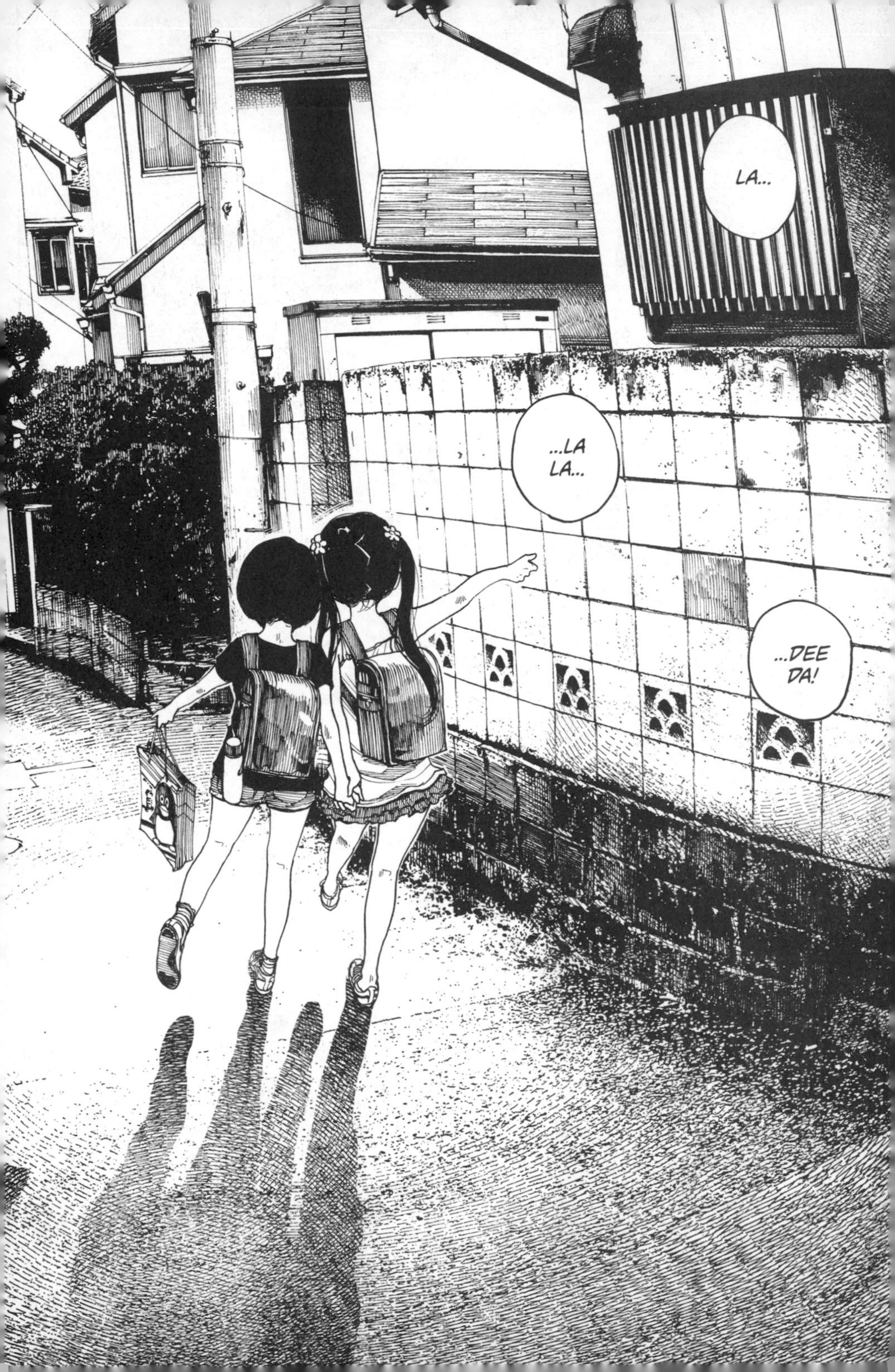
LA...
...LA LA...
...DEE DA!

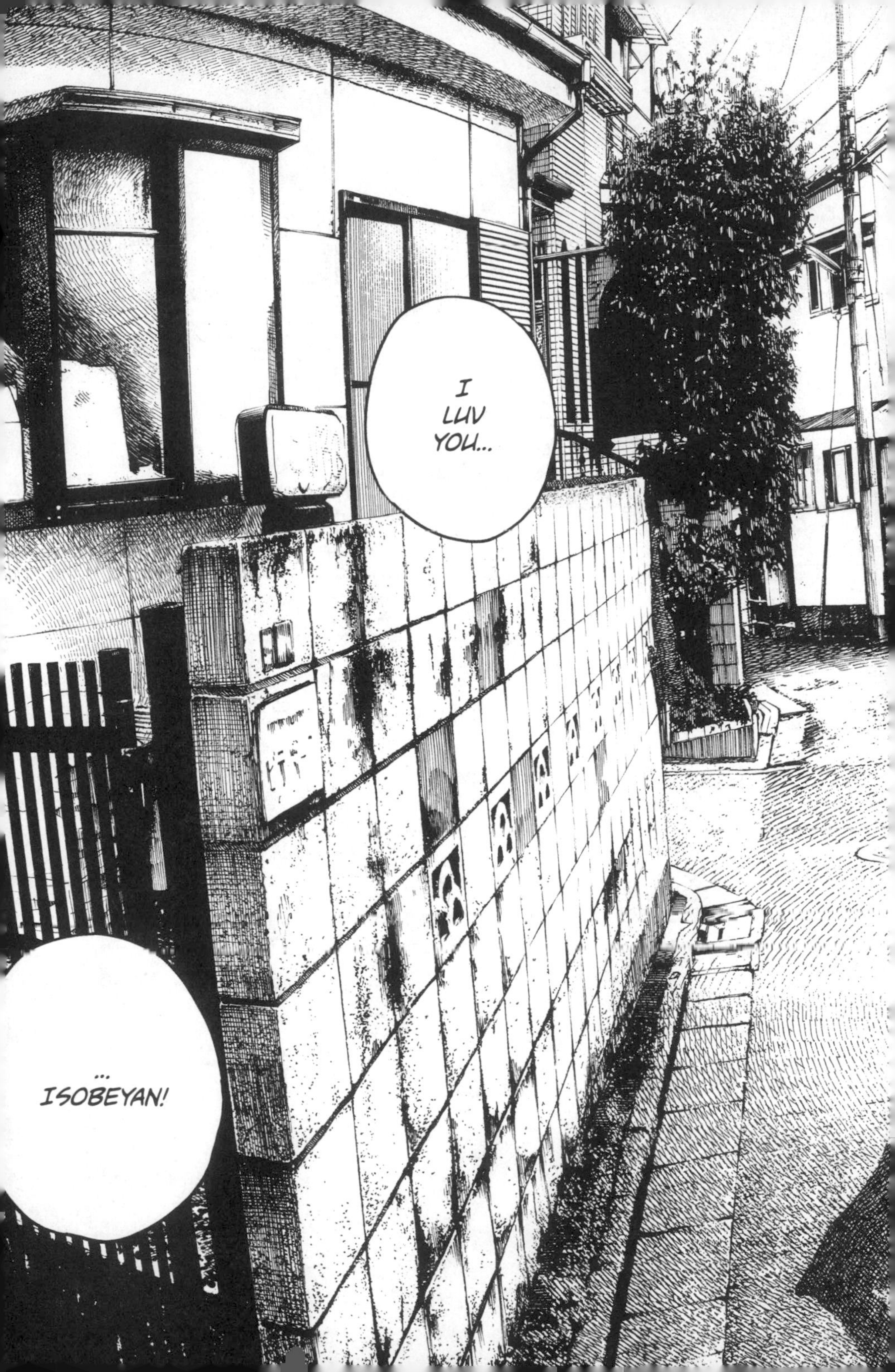
I LUV YOU...
... ISOBEYAN!

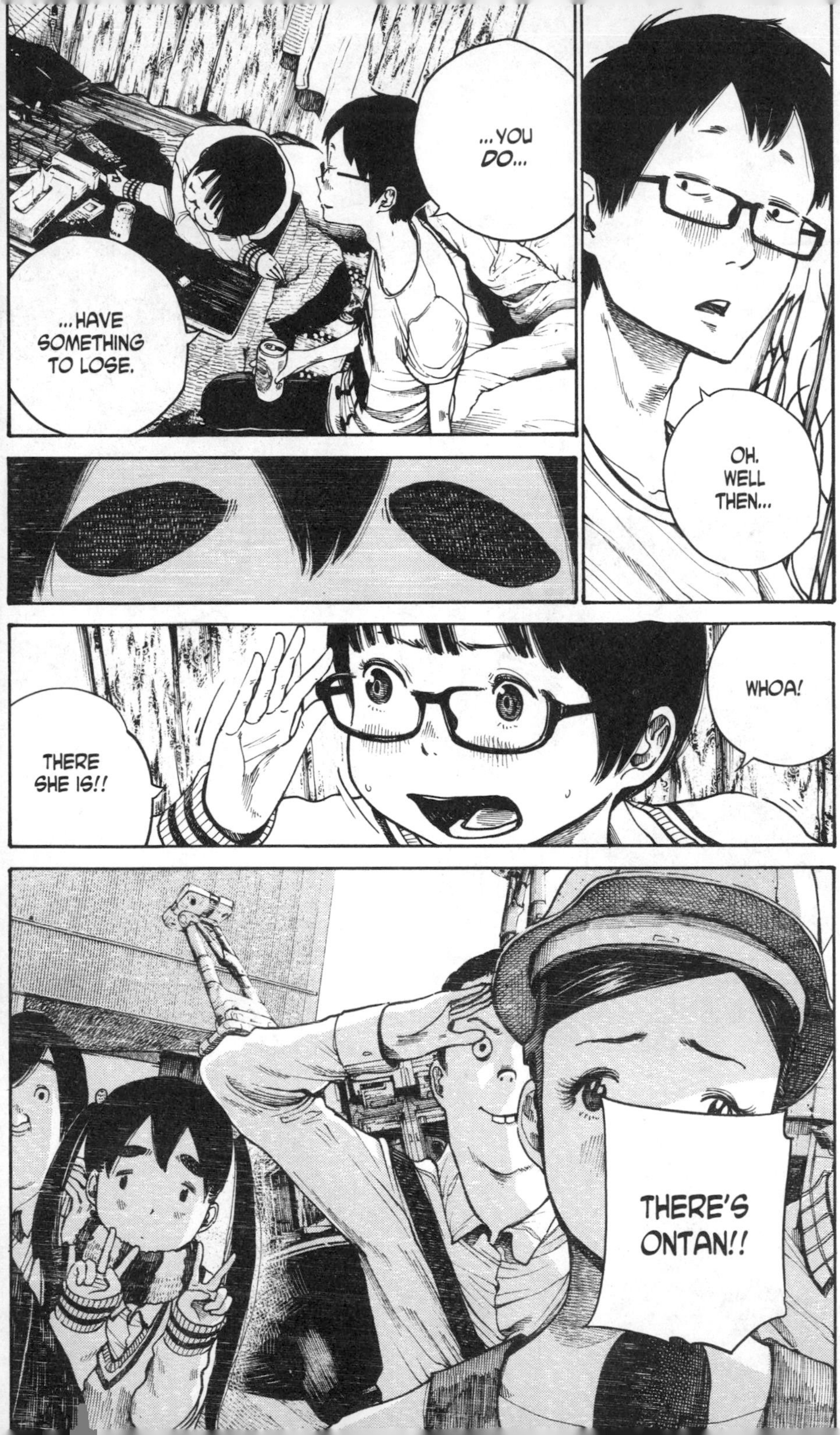
...YOU DO...
...HAVE SOMETHING TO LOSE.
OH. WELL THEN...
WHOA!
THERE SHE IS!!
THERE'S ONTAN!!

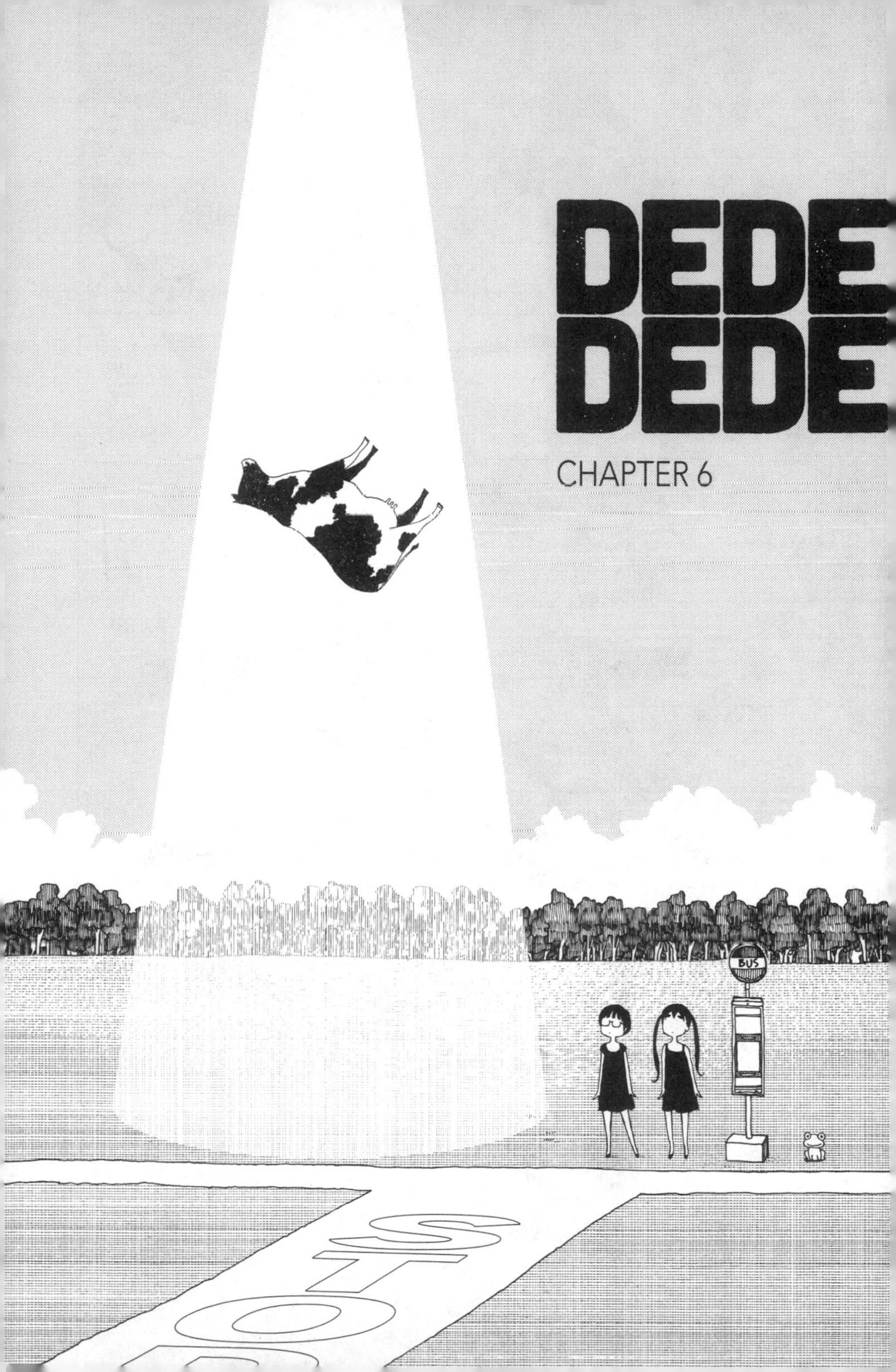
DEDE DEDE
CHAPTER 6
BUS

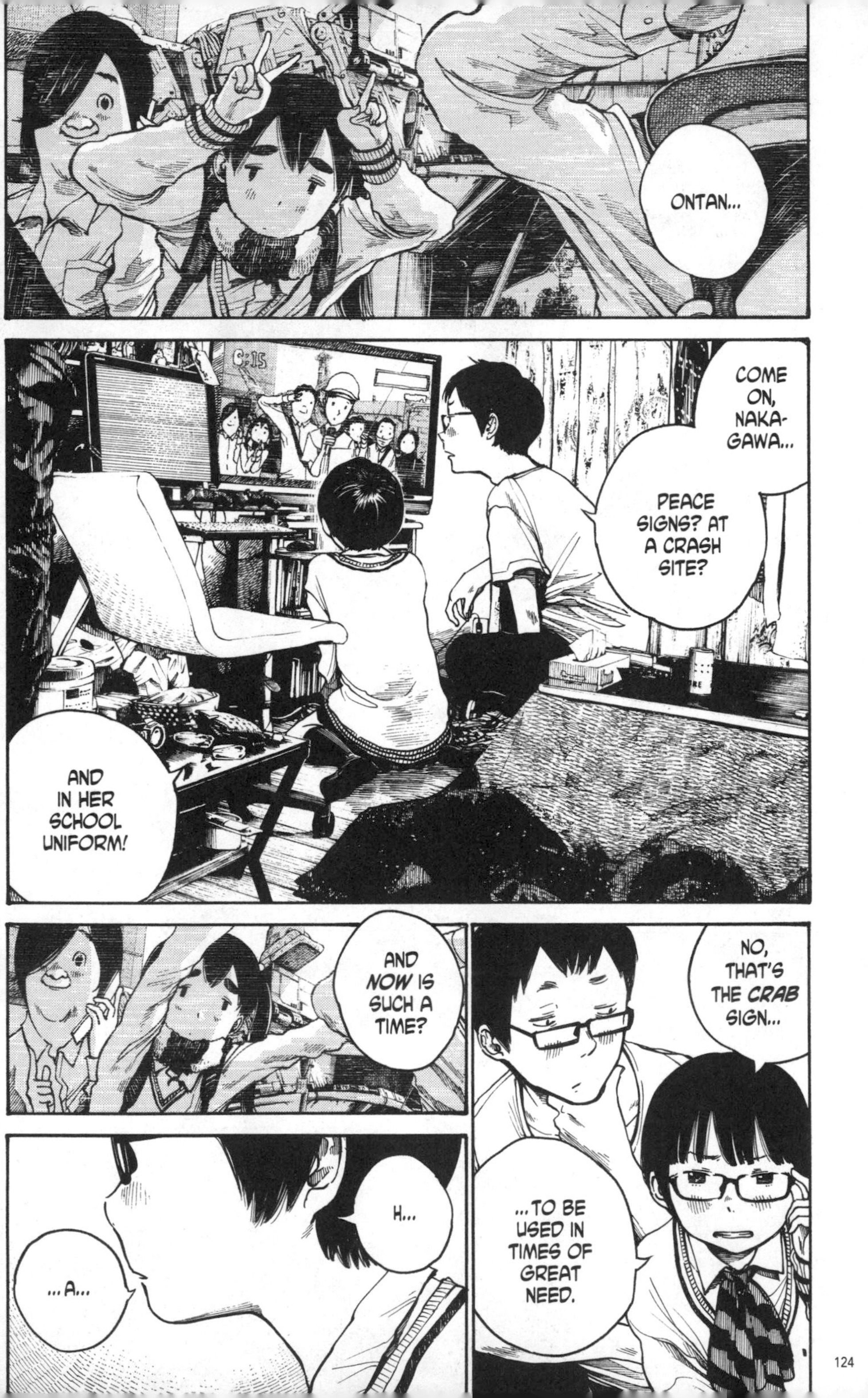
ONTAN...
COME ON, NAKAGAWA...
PEACE SIGNS? AT A CRASH SITE?
AND IN HER SCHOOL UNIFORM!
NO, THAT'S THE *CRAB* SIGN...
...TO BE USED IN TIMES OF GREAT NEED.
AND *NOW* IS SUCH A TIME?
H...
...A...

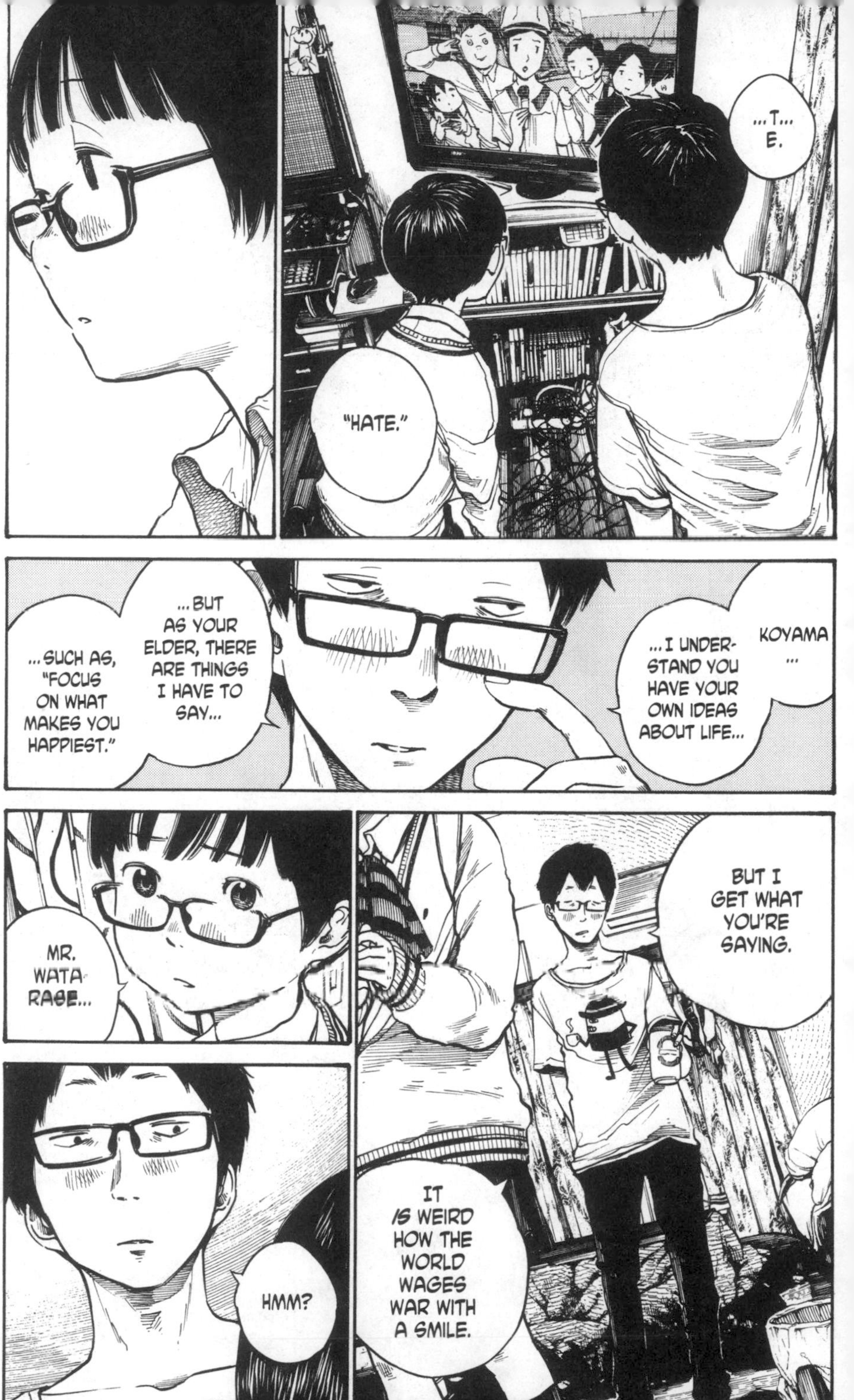
...T... E.
"HATE."
KOYAMA ...
...I UNDER-STAND YOU HAVE YOUR OWN IDEAS ABOUT LIFE...
...BUT AS YOUR ELDER, THERE ARE THINGS I HAVE TO SAY...
...SUCH AS, "FOCUS ON WHAT MAKES YOU HAPPIEST."
BUT I GET WHAT YOU'RE SAYING.
IT *IS* WEIRD HOW THE WORLD WAGES WAR WITH A SMILE.
MR. WATA-RASE...
HMM?

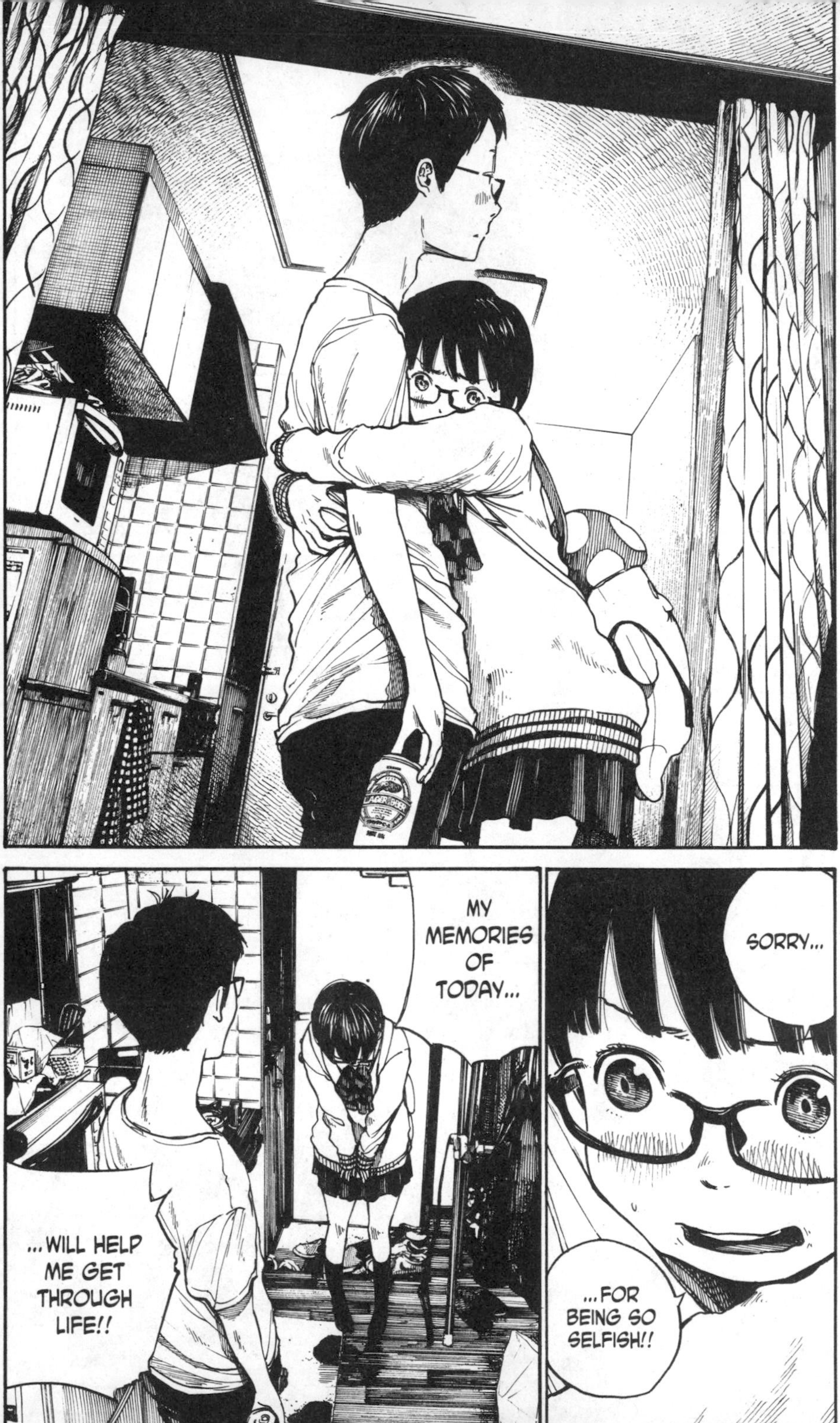
SORRY...
...FOR BEING SO SELFISH!!
MY MEMORIES OF TODAY...
...WILL HELP ME GET THROUGH LIFE!!

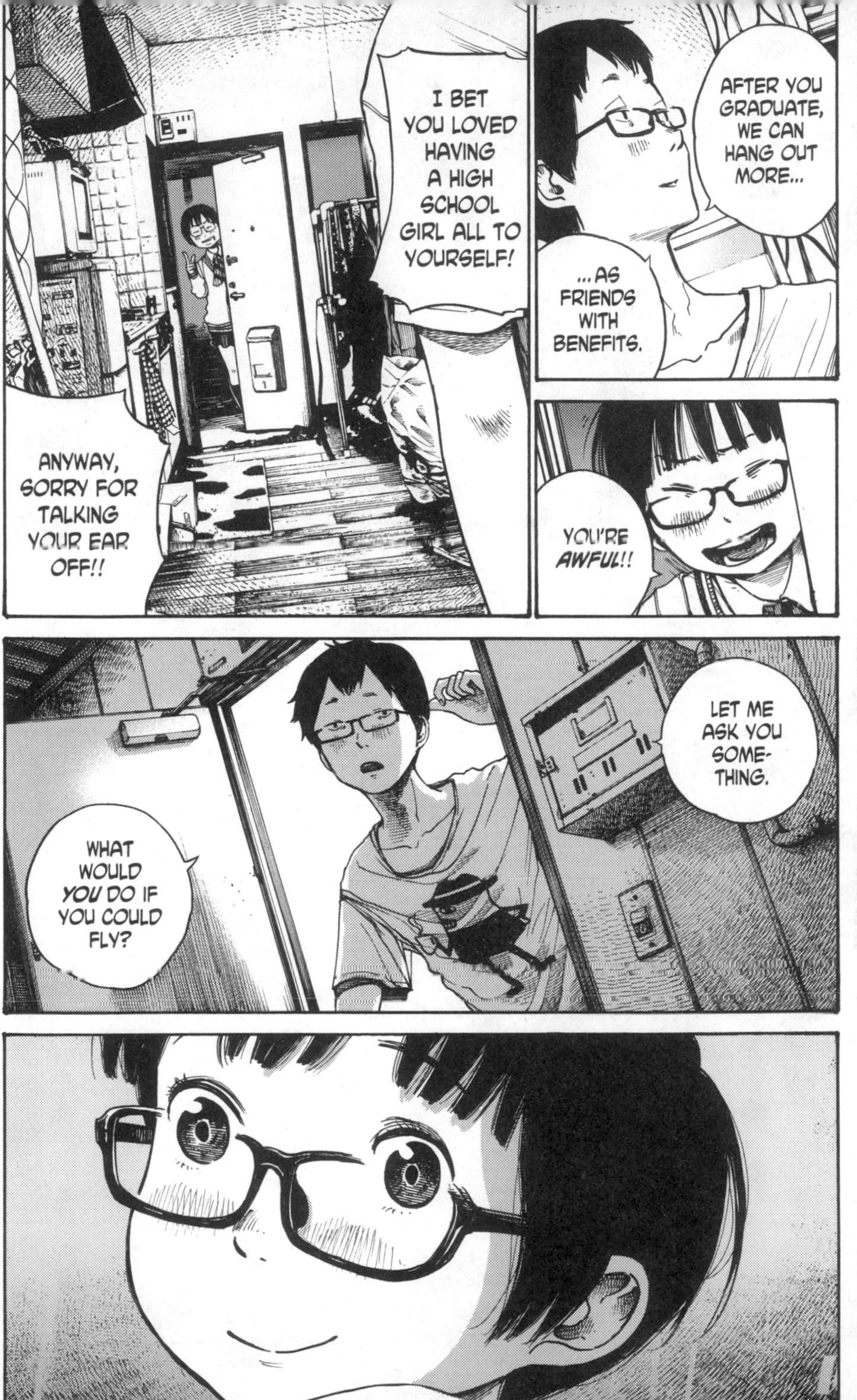
AFTER YOU GRADUATE, WE CAN HANG OUT MORE...
...AS FRIENDS WITH BENEFITS.
YOU'RE AWFUL!!
I BET YOU LOVED HAVING A HIGH SCHOOL GIRL ALL TO YOURSELF!
ANYWAY, SORRY FOR TALKING YOUR EAR OFF!!
LET ME ASK YOU SOMETHING.
WHAT WOULD YOU DO IF YOU COULD FLY?

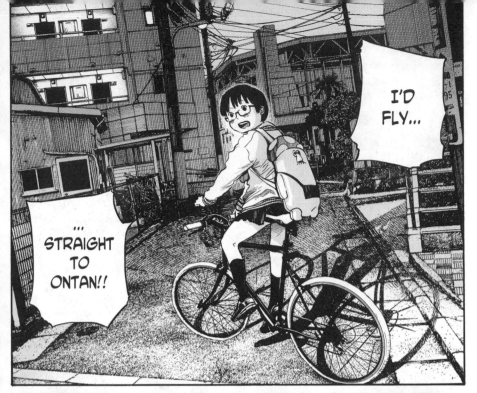

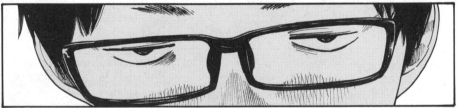

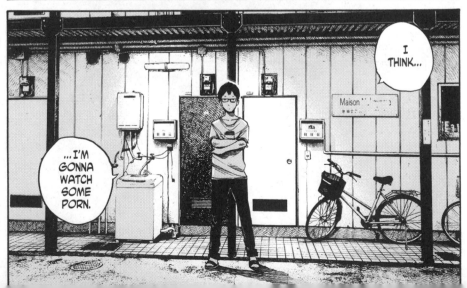

128

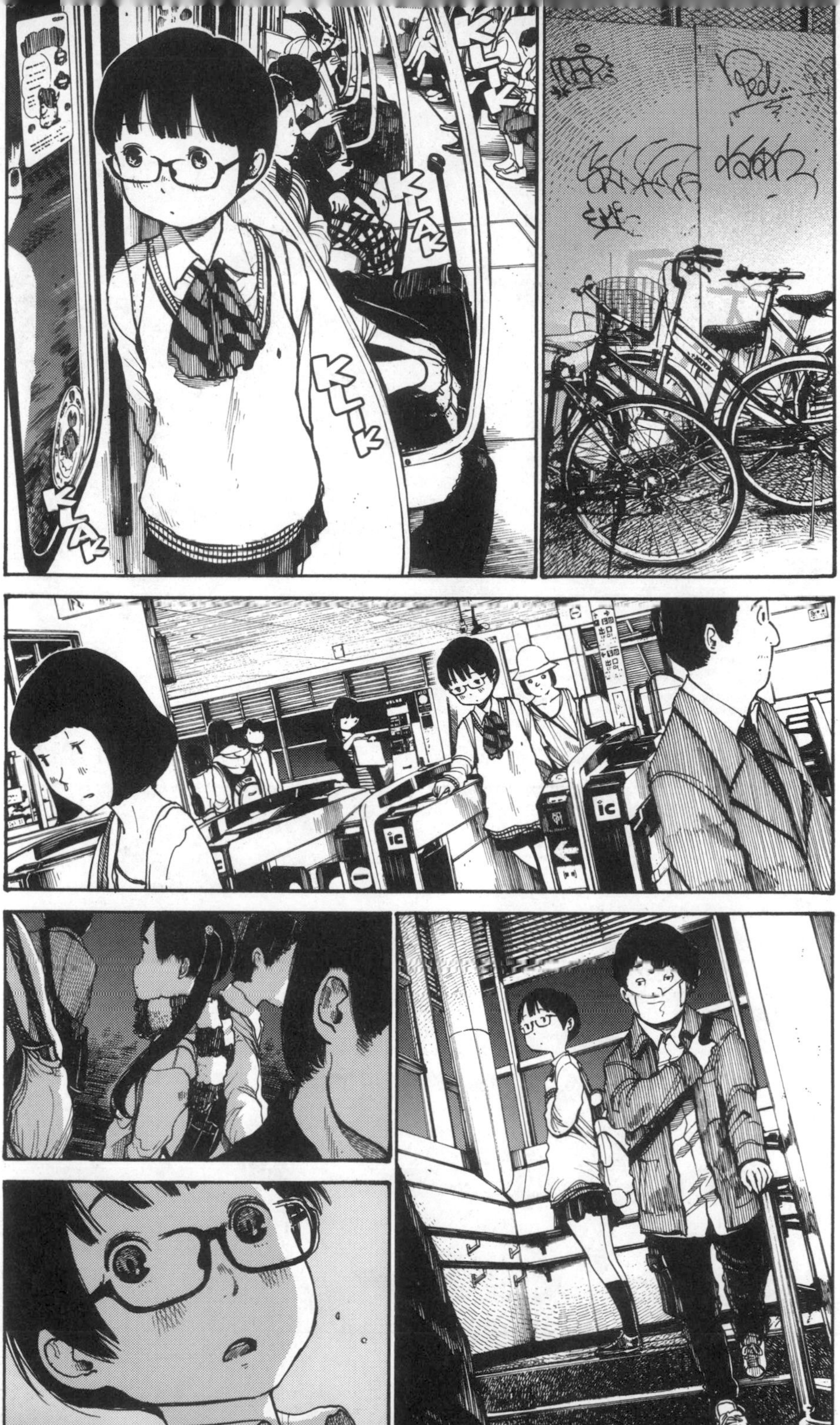
KLIK
KLAK
KLIK
KLAK

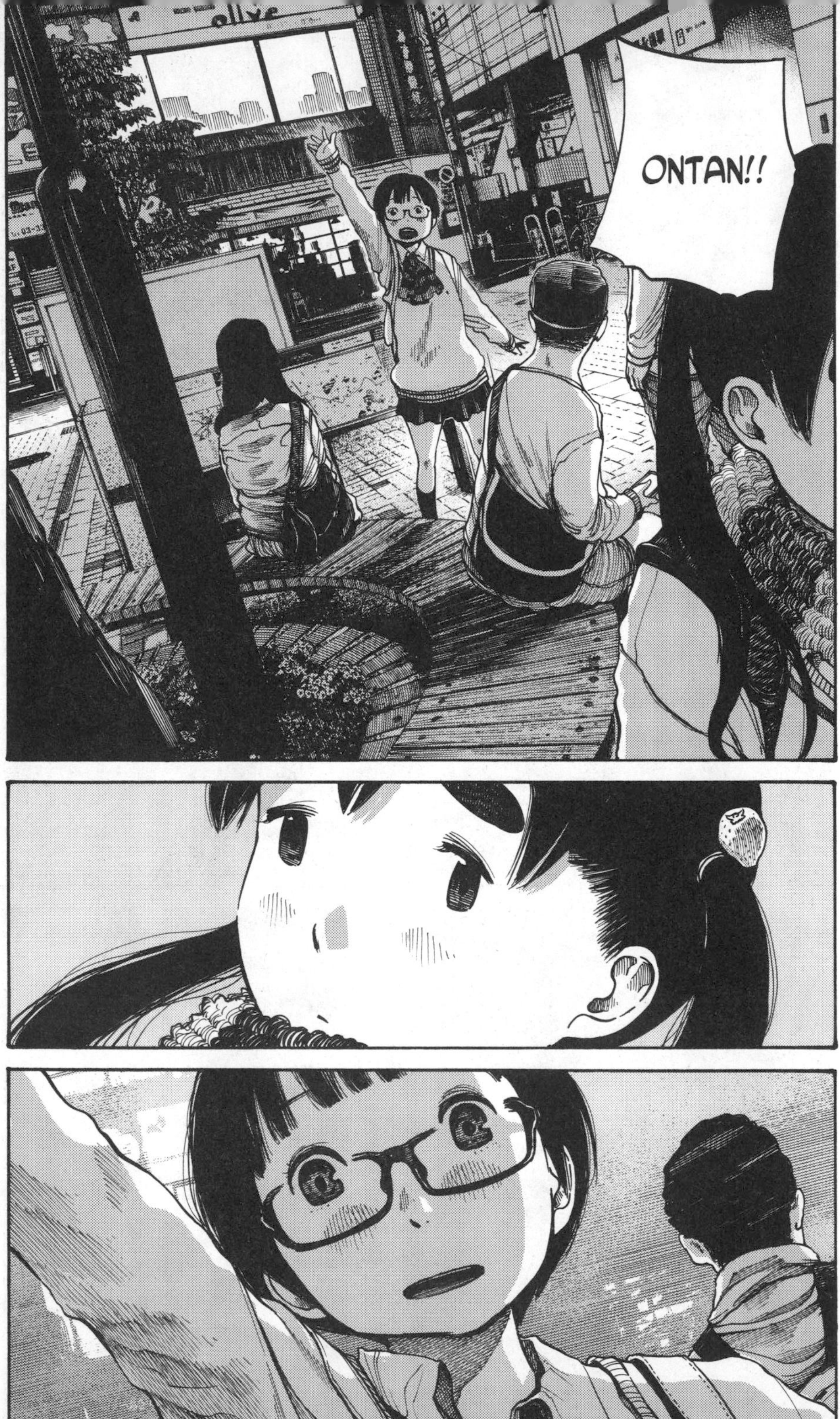
ONTAN!!

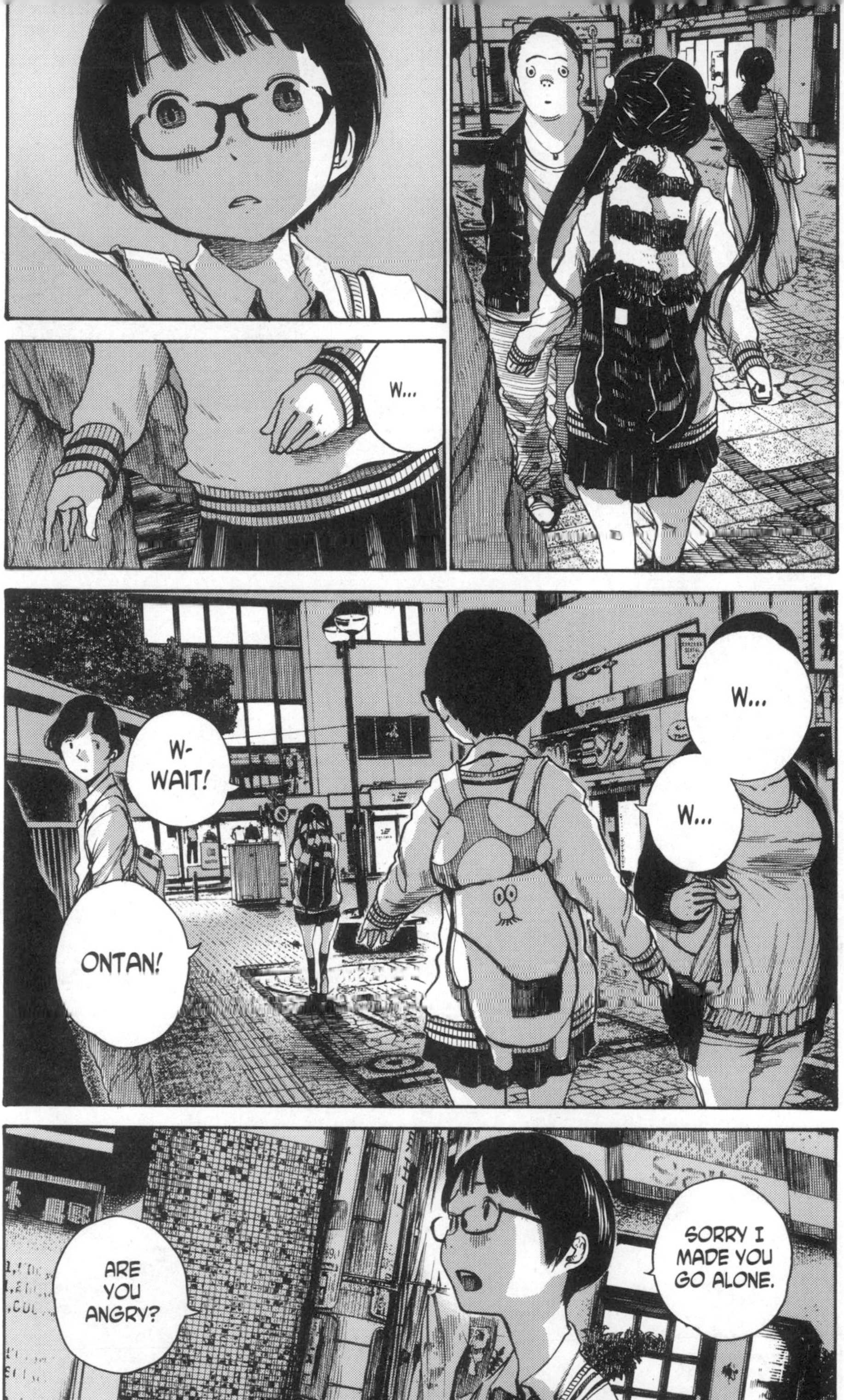
W...
W...
W...
W- WAIT!
ONTAN!
SORRY I MADE YOU GO ALONE.
ARE YOU ANGRY?

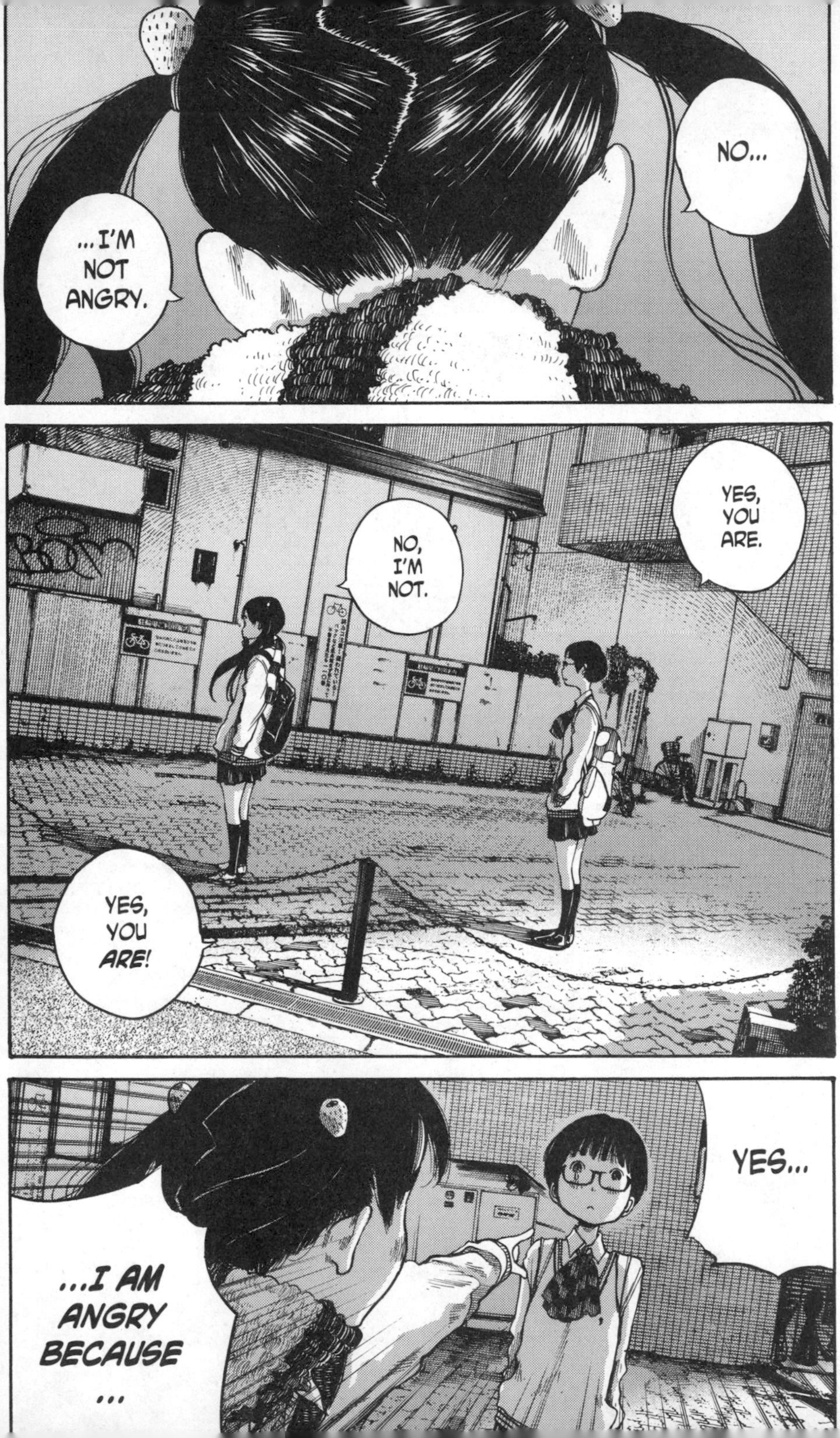
NO...
...I'M NOT ANGRY.
YES, YOU ARE.
NO, I'M NOT.
YES, YOU ARE!
YES...
...I AM ANGRY BECAUSE ...

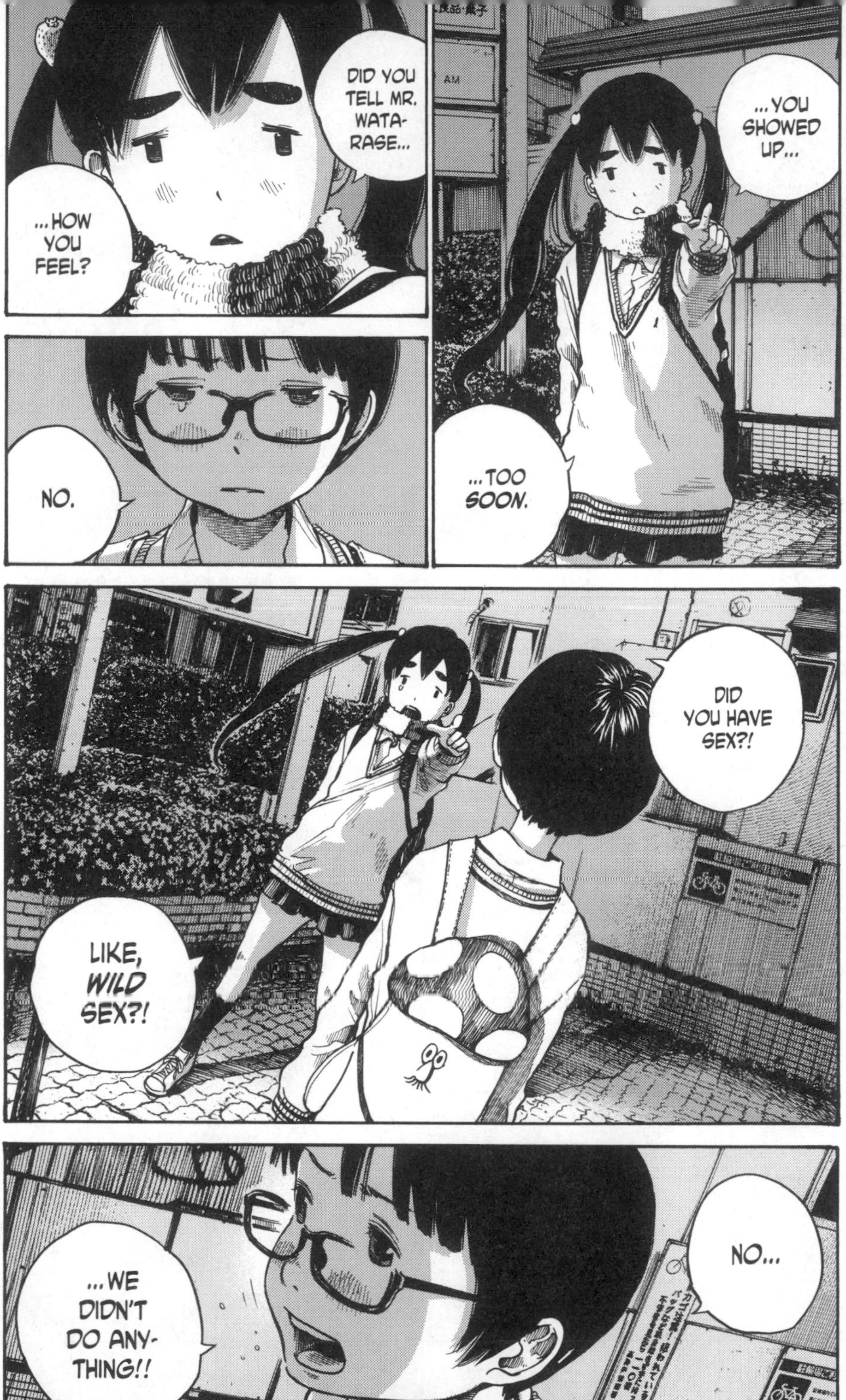
...YOU SHOWED UP...
...TOO SOON.
DID YOU TELL MR. WATA-RASE...
...HOW YOU FEEL?
NO.
DID YOU HAVE SEX?!
LIKE, WILD SEX?!
NO...
...WE DIDN'T DO ANY-THING!!

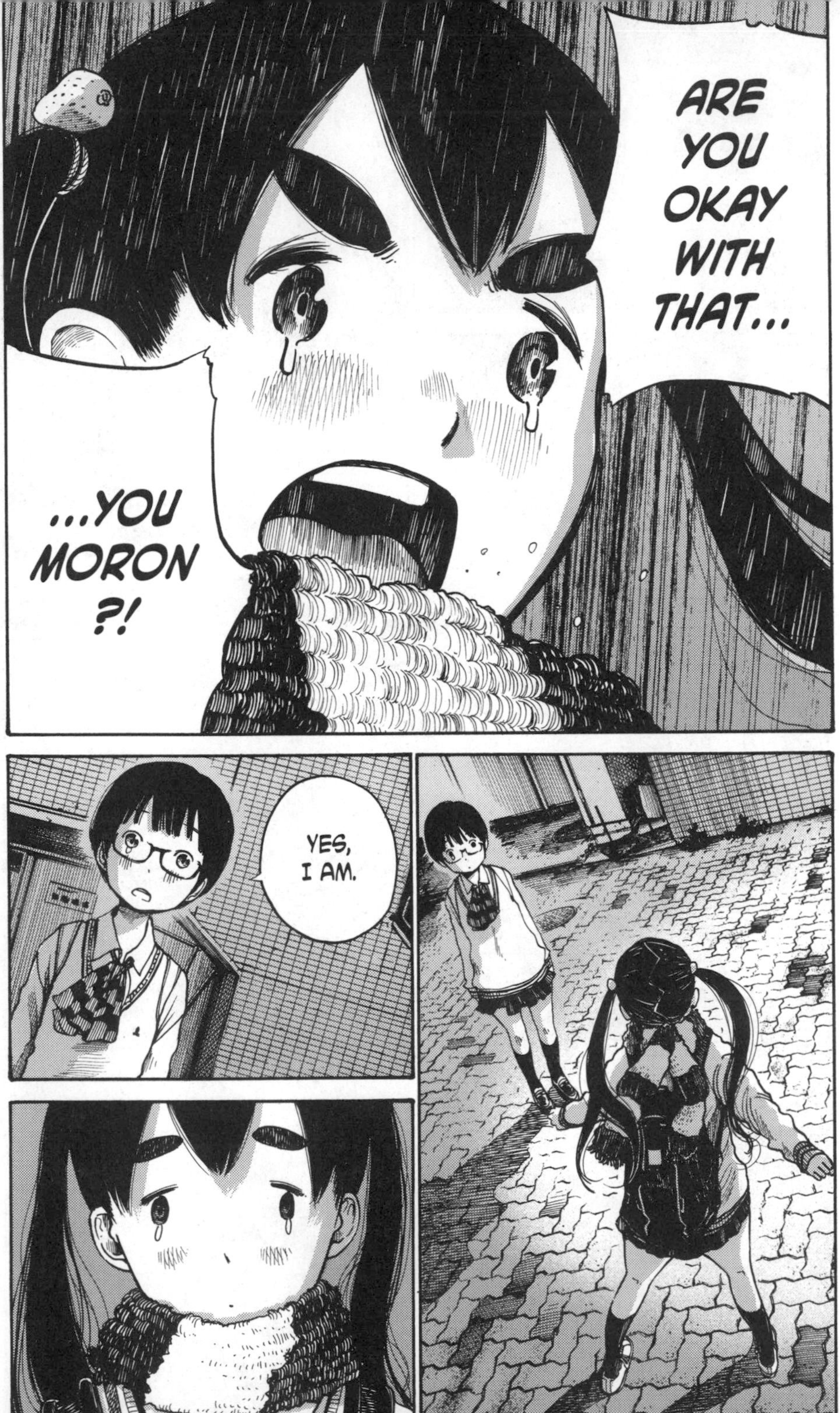
ARE YOU OKAY WITH THAT...
...YOU MORON ?!
YES, I AM.

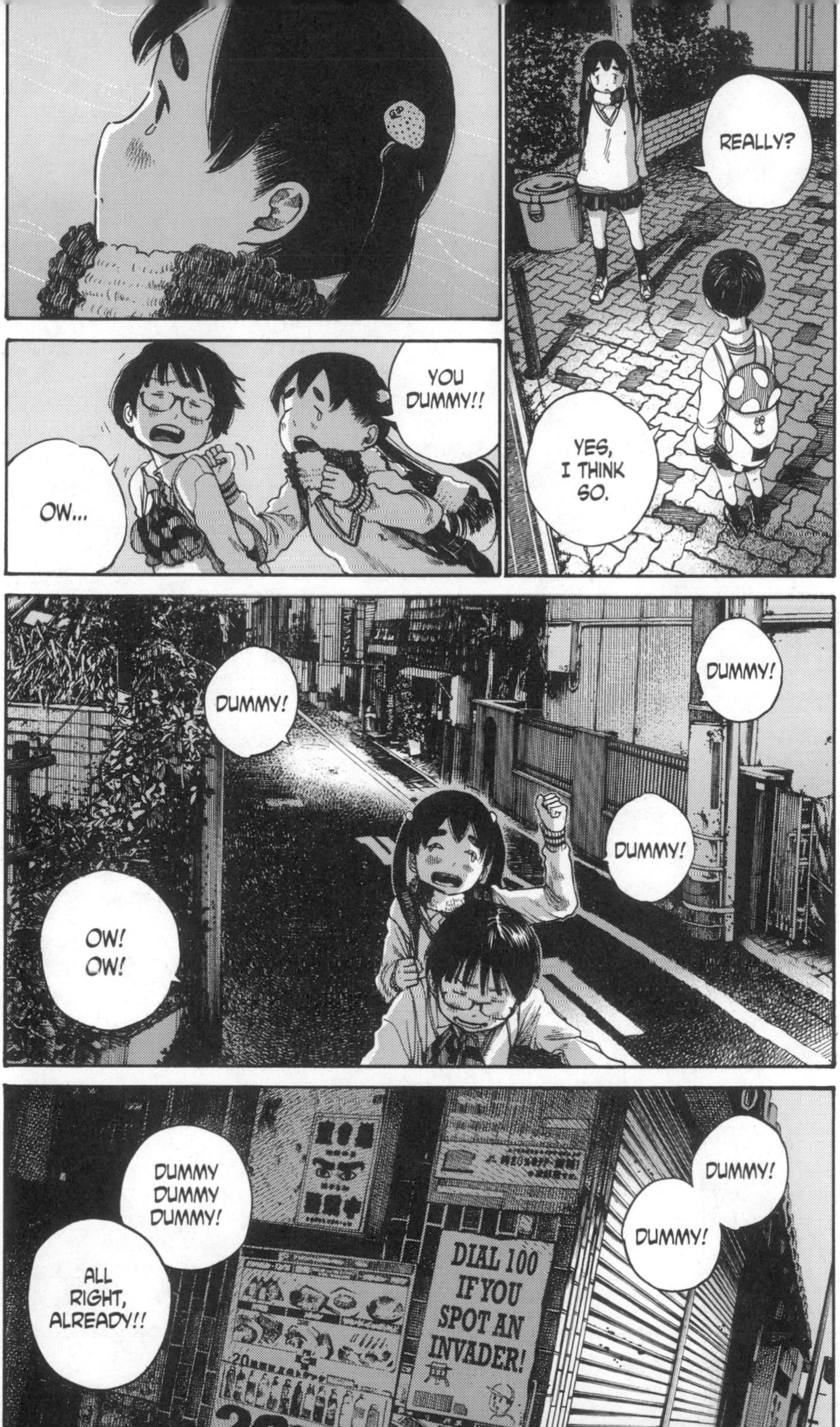
REALLY?
YES, I THINK SO.
YOU DUMMY!!
OW...
DUMMY!
DUMMY!
DUMMY!
OW! OW!
DUMMY!
DUMMY!
DUMMY DUMMY DUMMY!
ALL RIGHT, ALREADY!!
DIAL 100 IF YOU SPOT AN INVADER!

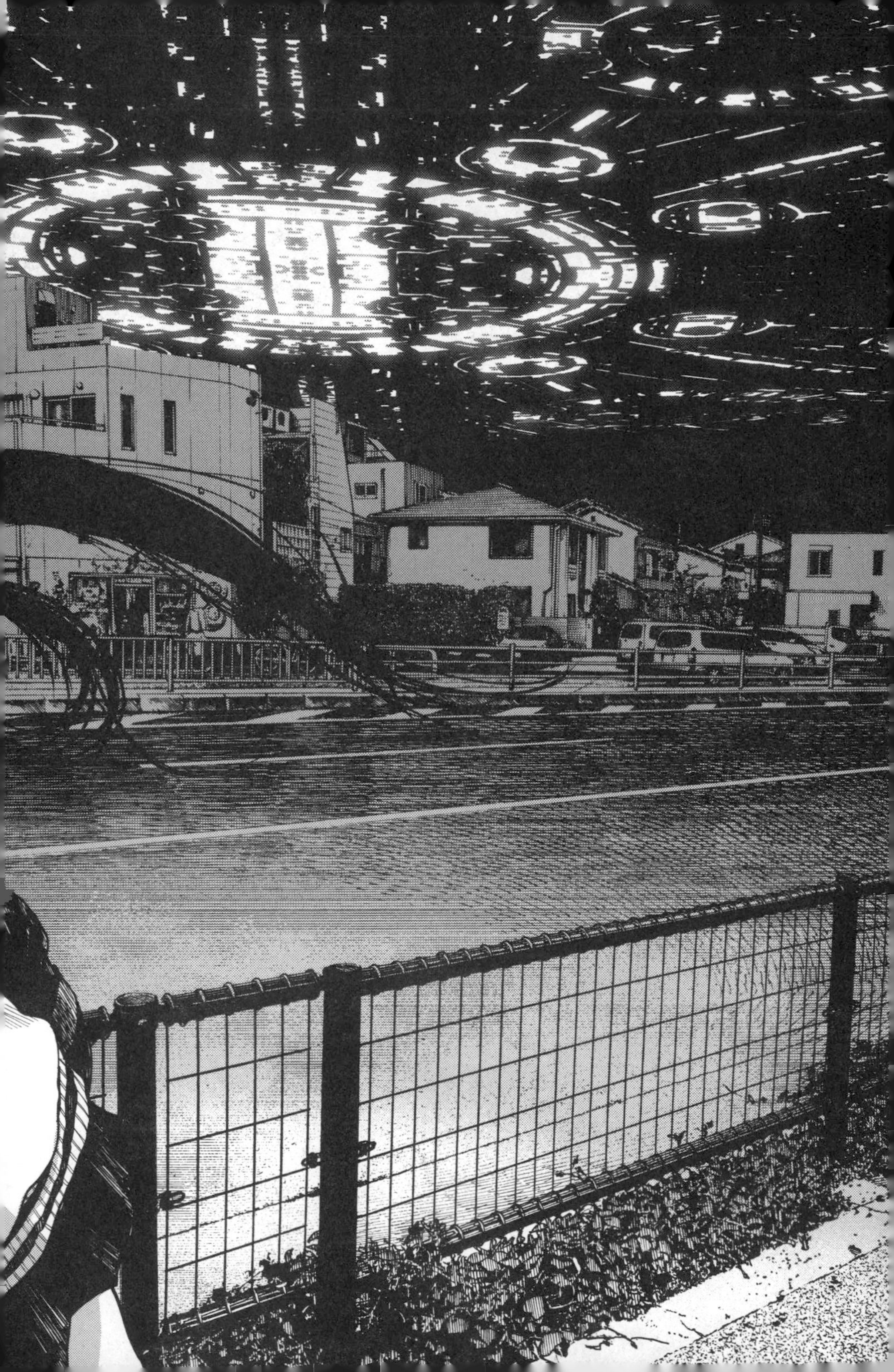

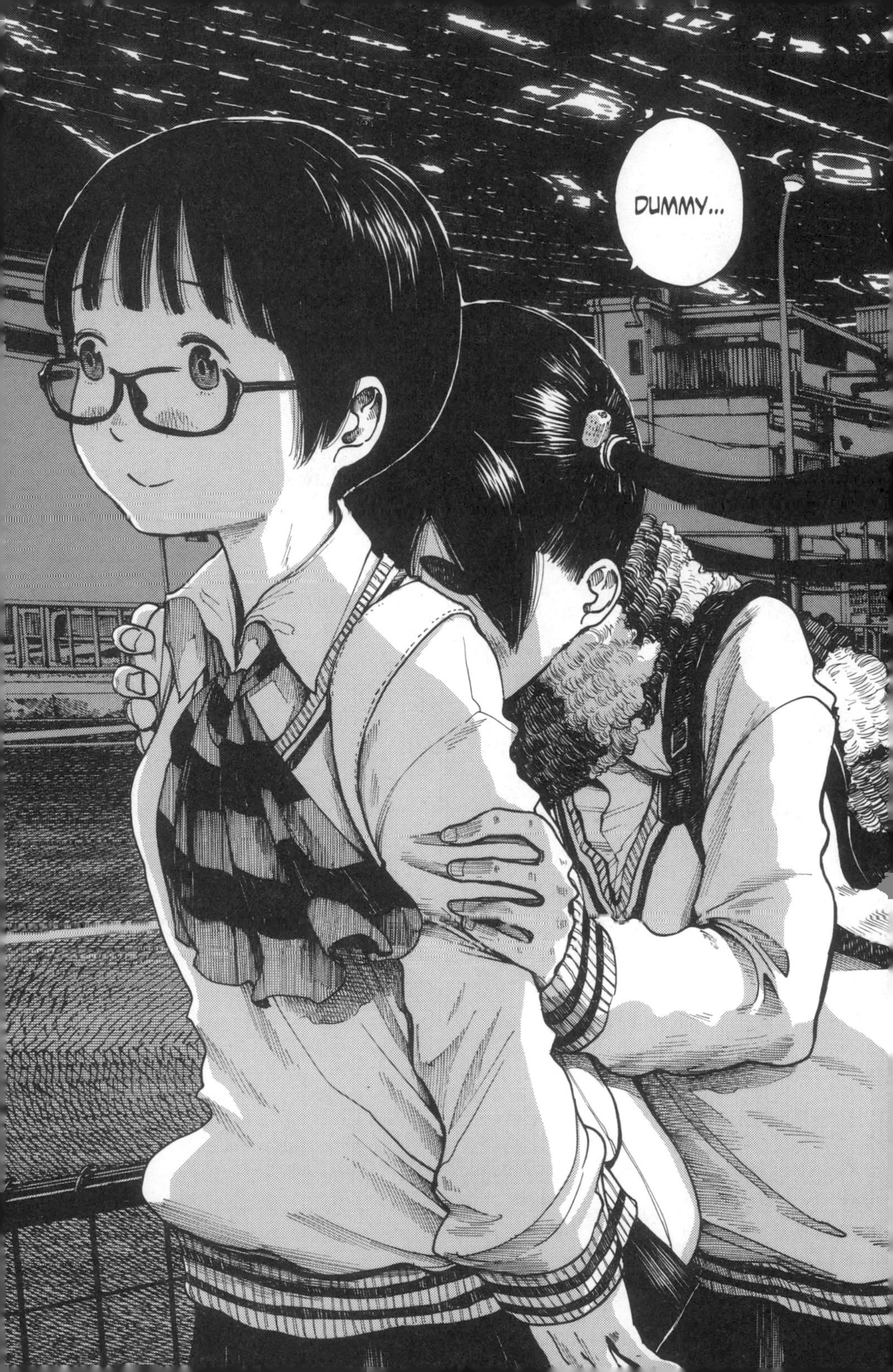
DUMMY...

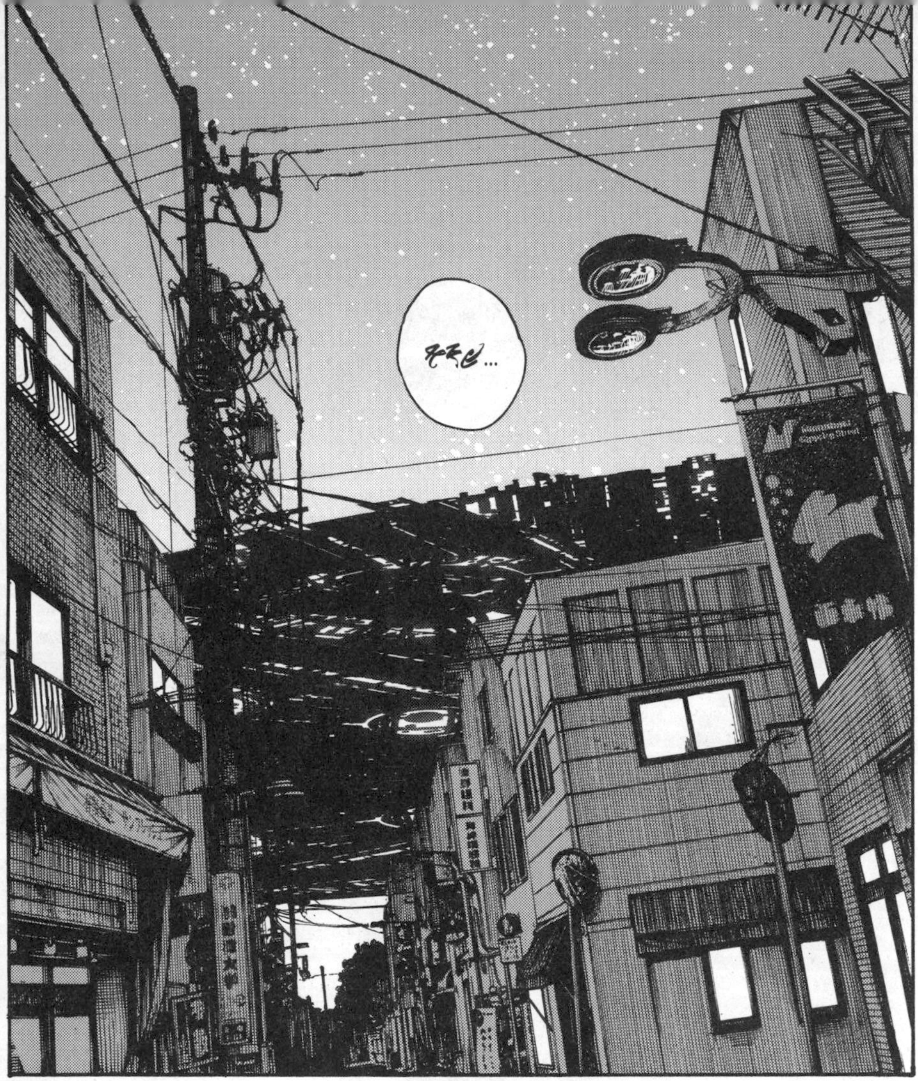

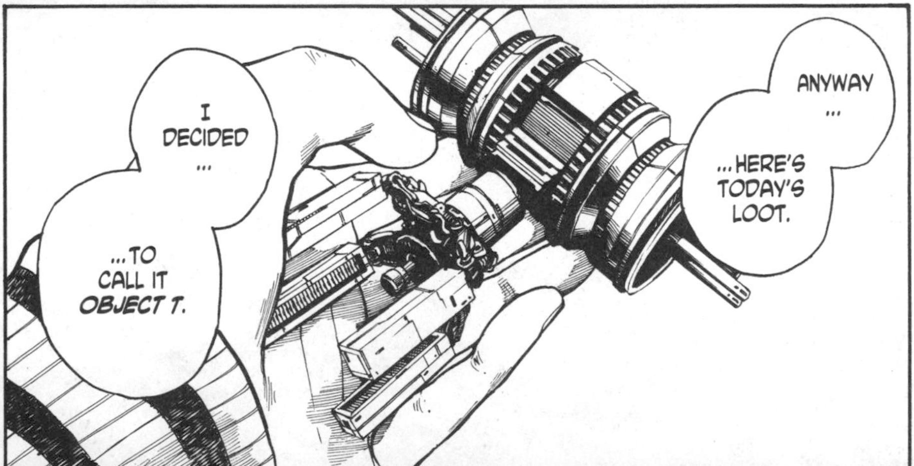

ANYWAY ...
...HERE'S TODAY'S LOOT.
I DECIDED ...
...TO CALL IT *OBJECT T.*

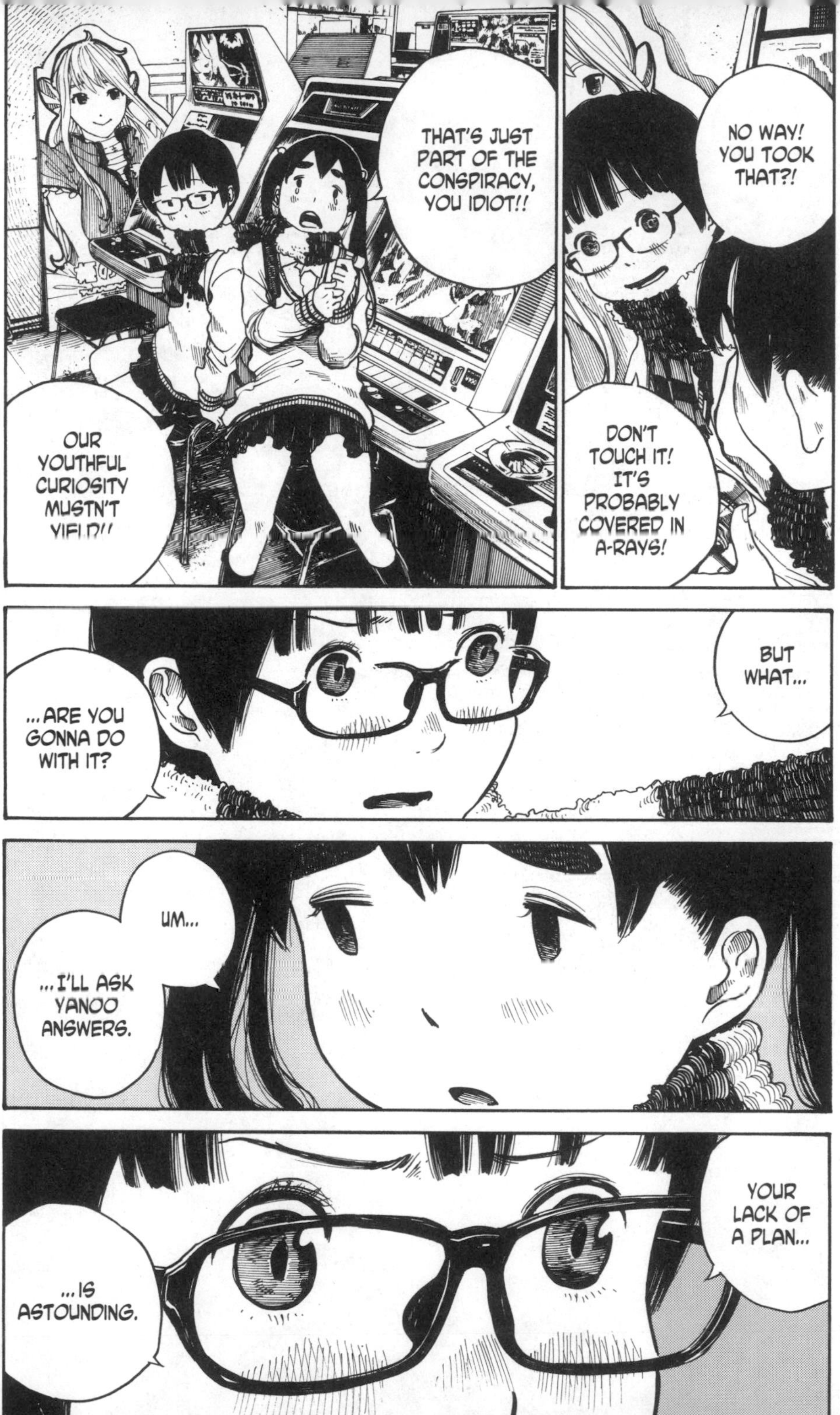
NO WAY! YOU TOOK THAT?!
DON'T TOUCH IT! IT'S PROBABLY COVERED IN A-RAYS!
THAT'S JUST PART OF THE CONSPIRACY, YOU IDIOT!!
OUR YOUTHFUL CURIOSITY MUSTN'T YIELD!!
BUT WHAT...
...ARE YOU GONNA DO WITH IT?
UM...
...I'LL ASK YANOO ANSWERS.
YOUR LACK OF A PLAN...
...IS ASTOUNDING.

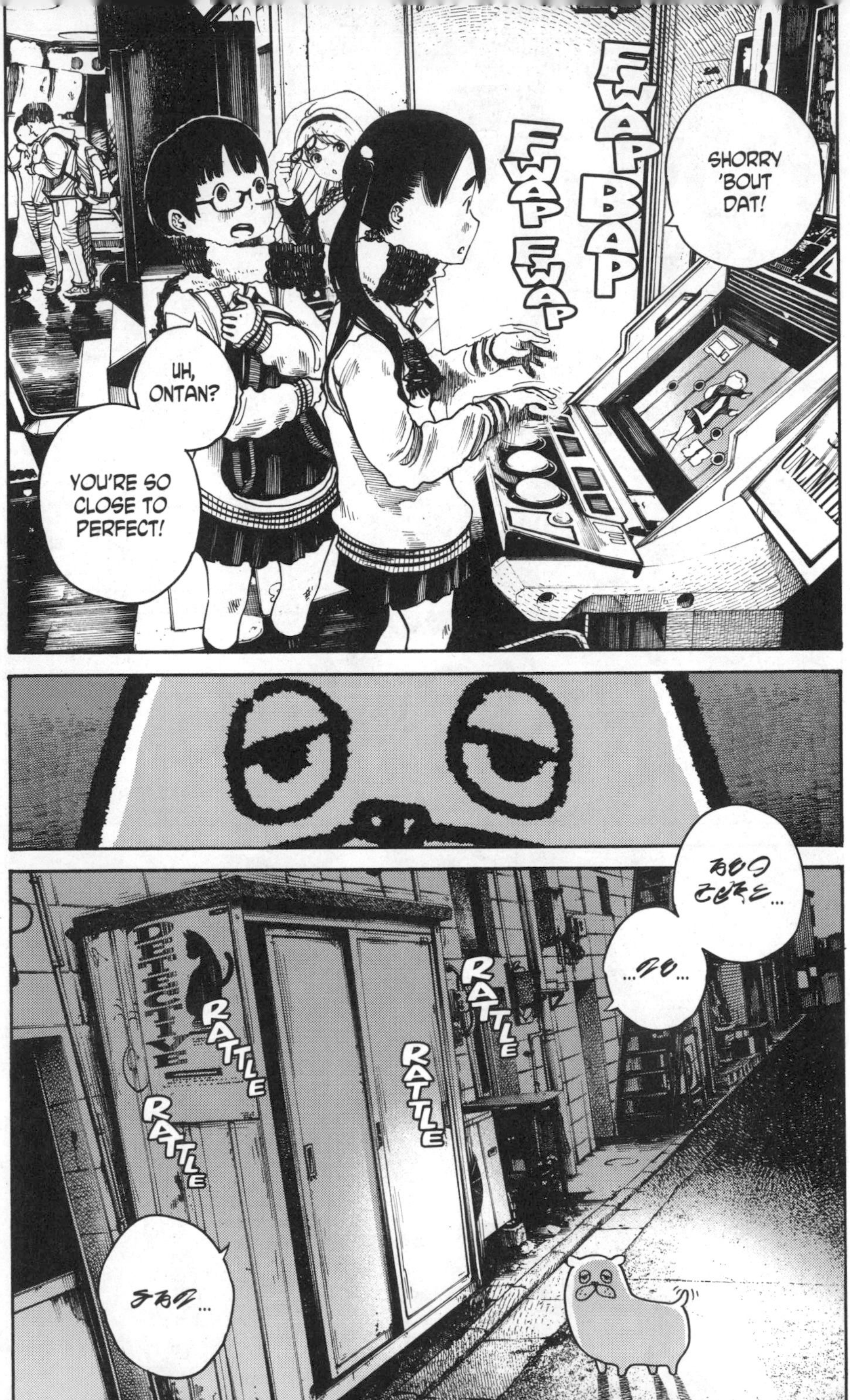
SHORRY 'BOUT DAT!
FWAP BAP
FWAP FWAP
UH, ONTAN?
YOU'RE SO CLOSE TO PERFECT!
RATTLE
RATTLE
DETECTIVE
RATTLE
RATTLE

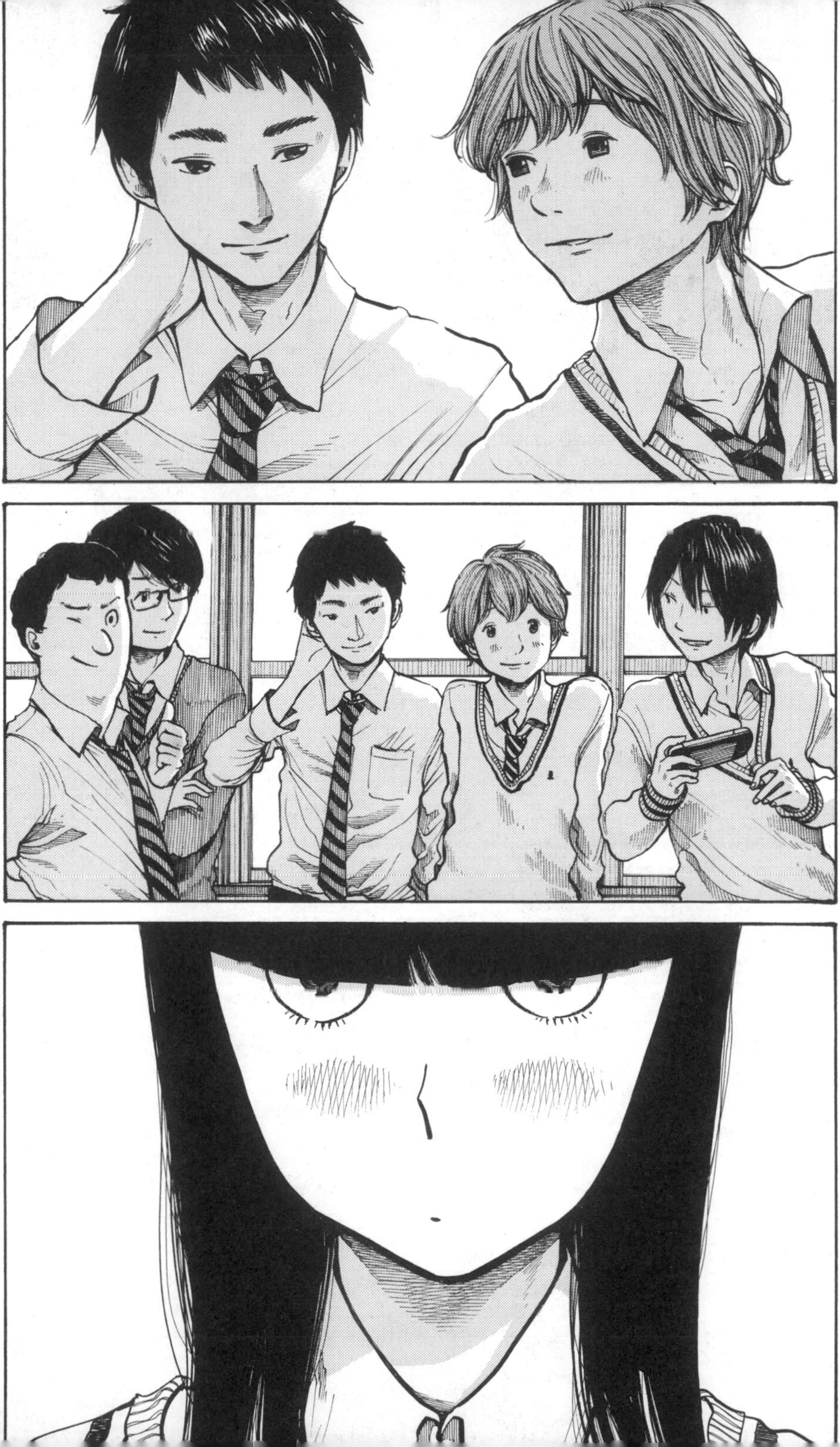

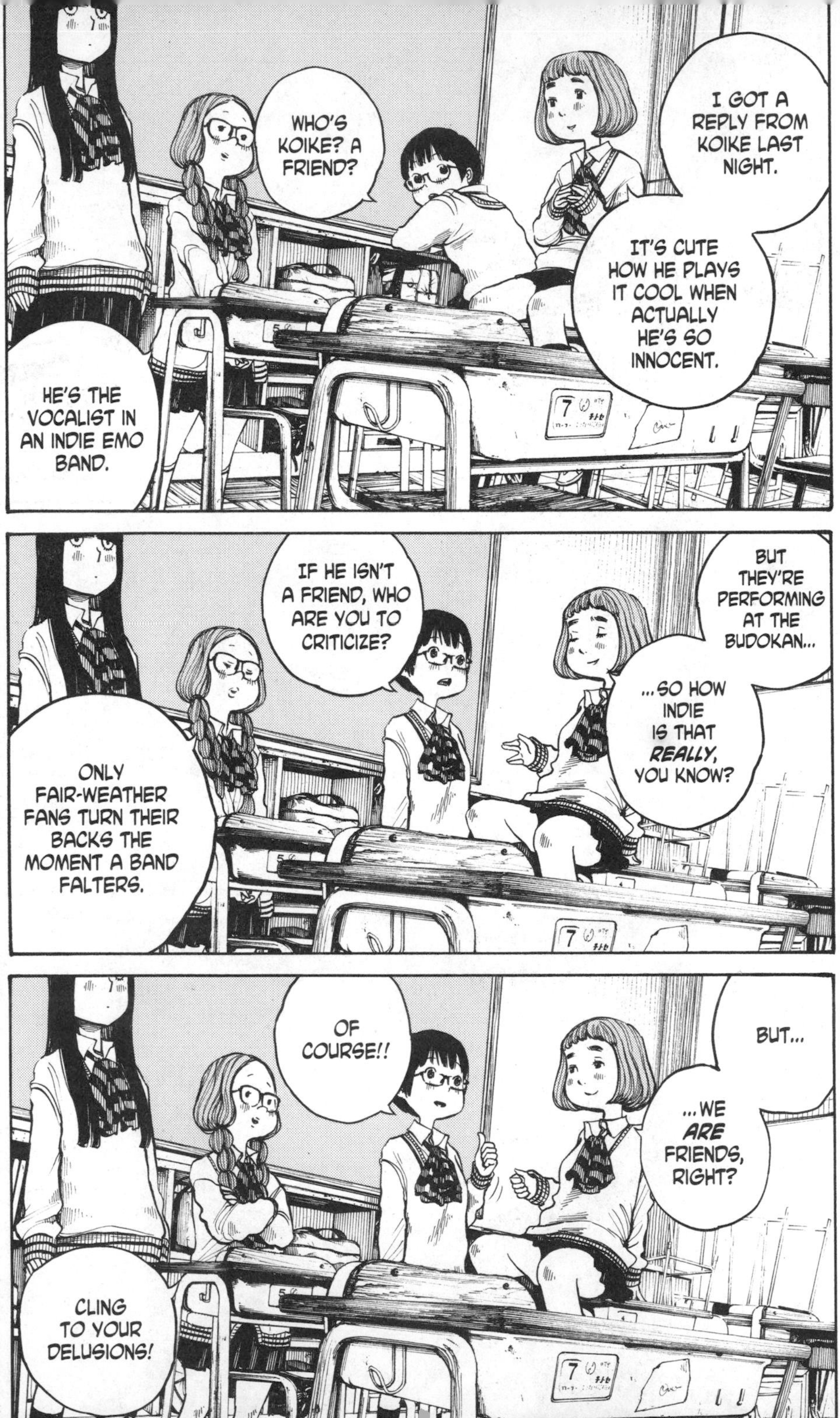
I GOT A REPLY FROM KOIKE LAST NIGHT.
IT'S CUTE HOW HE PLAYS IT COOL WHEN ACTUALLY HE'S SO INNOCENT.
WHO'S KOIKE? A FRIEND?
HE'S THE VOCALIST IN AN INDIE EMO BAND.
BUT THEY'RE PERFORMING AT THE BUDOKAN...
...SO HOW INDIE IS THAT *REALLY*, YOU KNOW?
IF HE ISN'T A FRIEND, WHO ARE YOU TO CRITICIZE?
ONLY FAIR-WEATHER FANS TURN THEIR BACKS THE MOMENT A BAND FALTERS.
BUT...
...WE *ARE* FRIENDS, RIGHT?
OF COURSE!!
CLING TO YOUR DELUSIONS!

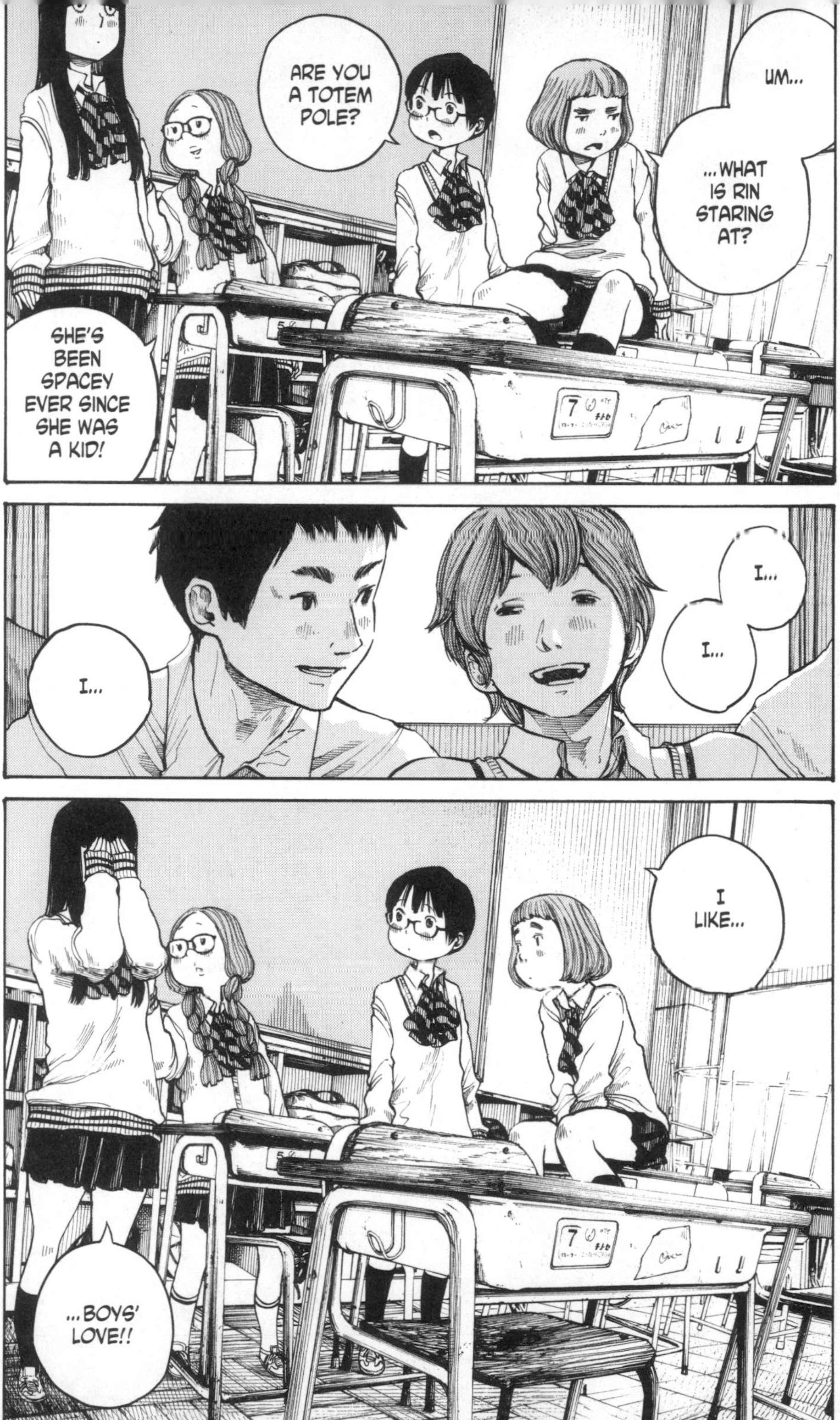
UM...
...WHAT IS RIN STARING AT?
ARE YOU A TOTEM POLE?
SHE'S BEEN SPACEY EVER SINCE SHE WAS A KID!
I...
I...
I...
I LIKE...
...BOYS' LOVE!!

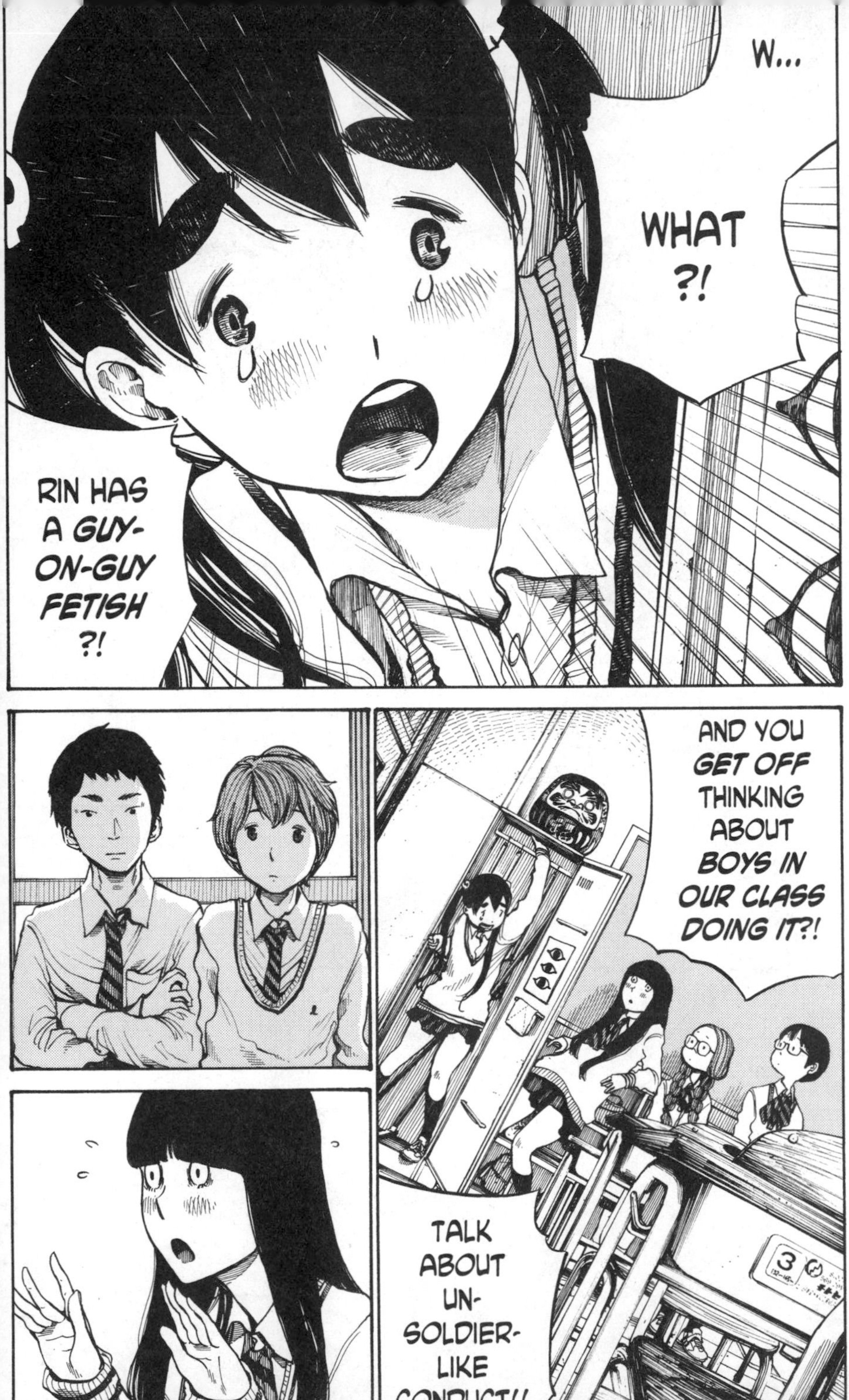
W...
WHAT ?!
RIN HAS A *GUY-ON-GUY FETISH* ?!
AND YOU *GET OFF* THINKING ABOUT *BOYS IN OUR CLASS DOING IT*?!
TALK ABOUT UN-SOLDIER-LIKE CONDUCT!!

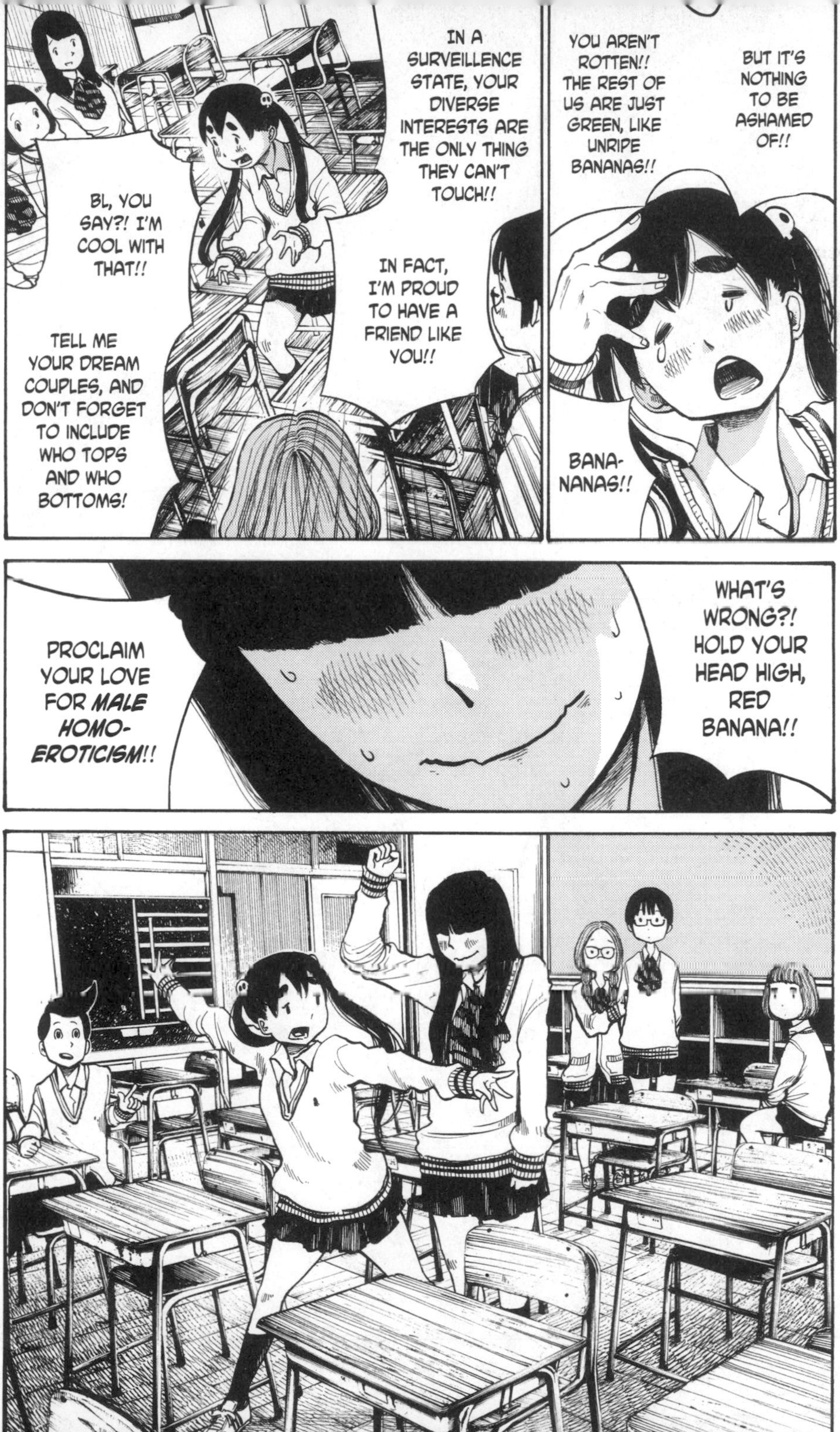
BUT IT'S NOTHING TO BE ASHAMED OF!!
YOU AREN'T ROTTEN!! THE REST OF US ARE JUST GREEN, LIKE UNRIPE BANANAS!!
BANA-NANAS!!
IN A SURVEILLANCE STATE, YOUR DIVERSE INTERESTS ARE THE ONLY THING THEY CAN'T TOUCH!!
IN FACT, I'M PROUD TO HAVE A FRIEND LIKE YOU!!
BL, YOU SAY?! I'M COOL WITH THAT!!
TELL ME YOUR DREAM COUPLES, AND DON'T FORGET TO INCLUDE WHO TOPS AND WHO BOTTOMS!
WHAT'S WRONG?! HOLD YOUR HEAD HIGH, RED BANANA!!
PROCLAIM YOUR LOVE FOR *MALE HOMO-EROTICISM*!!

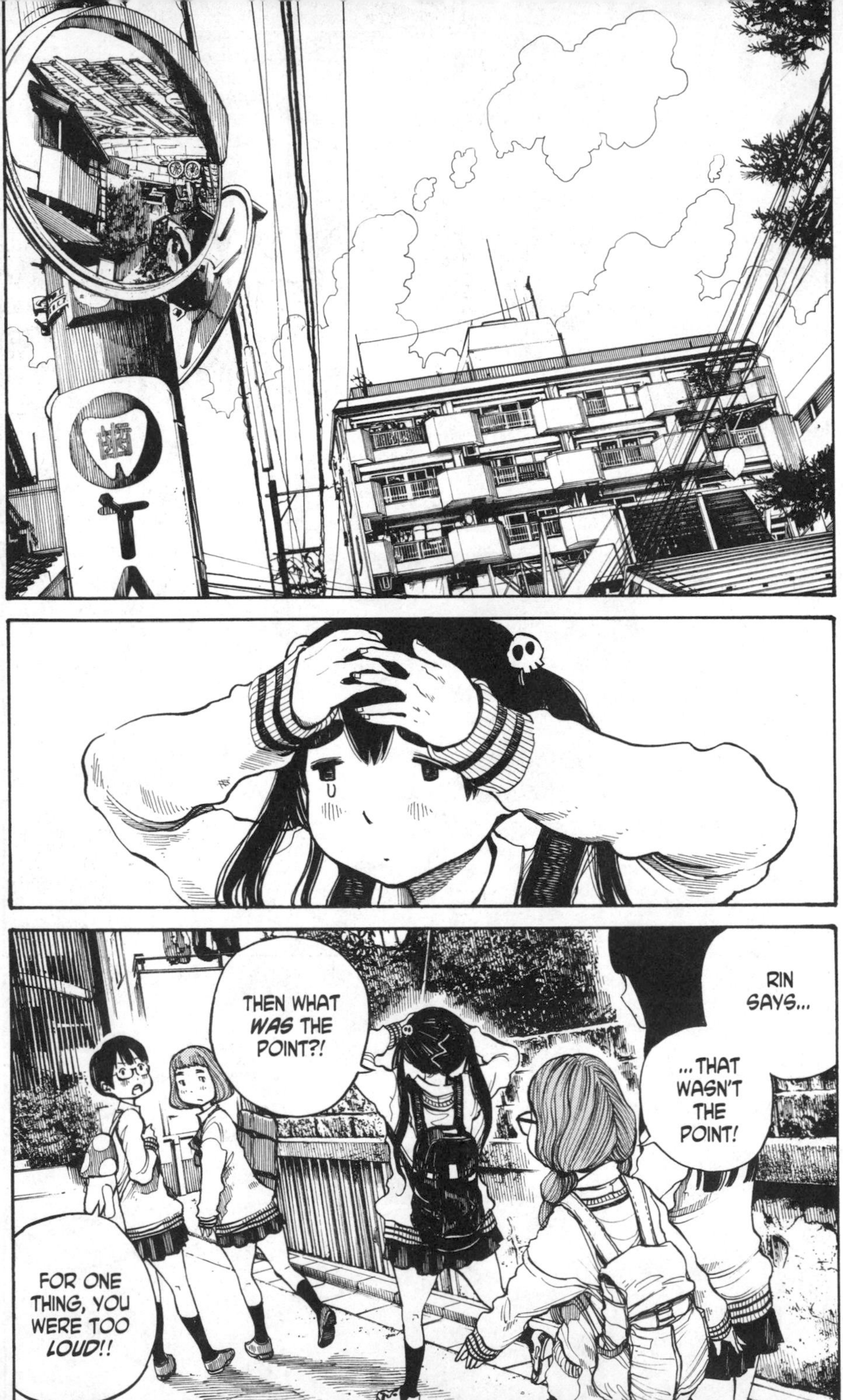
RIN SAYS...
...THAT WASN'T THE POINT!
THEN WHAT *WAS* THE POINT?!
FOR ONE THING, YOU WERE TOO *LOUD*!!

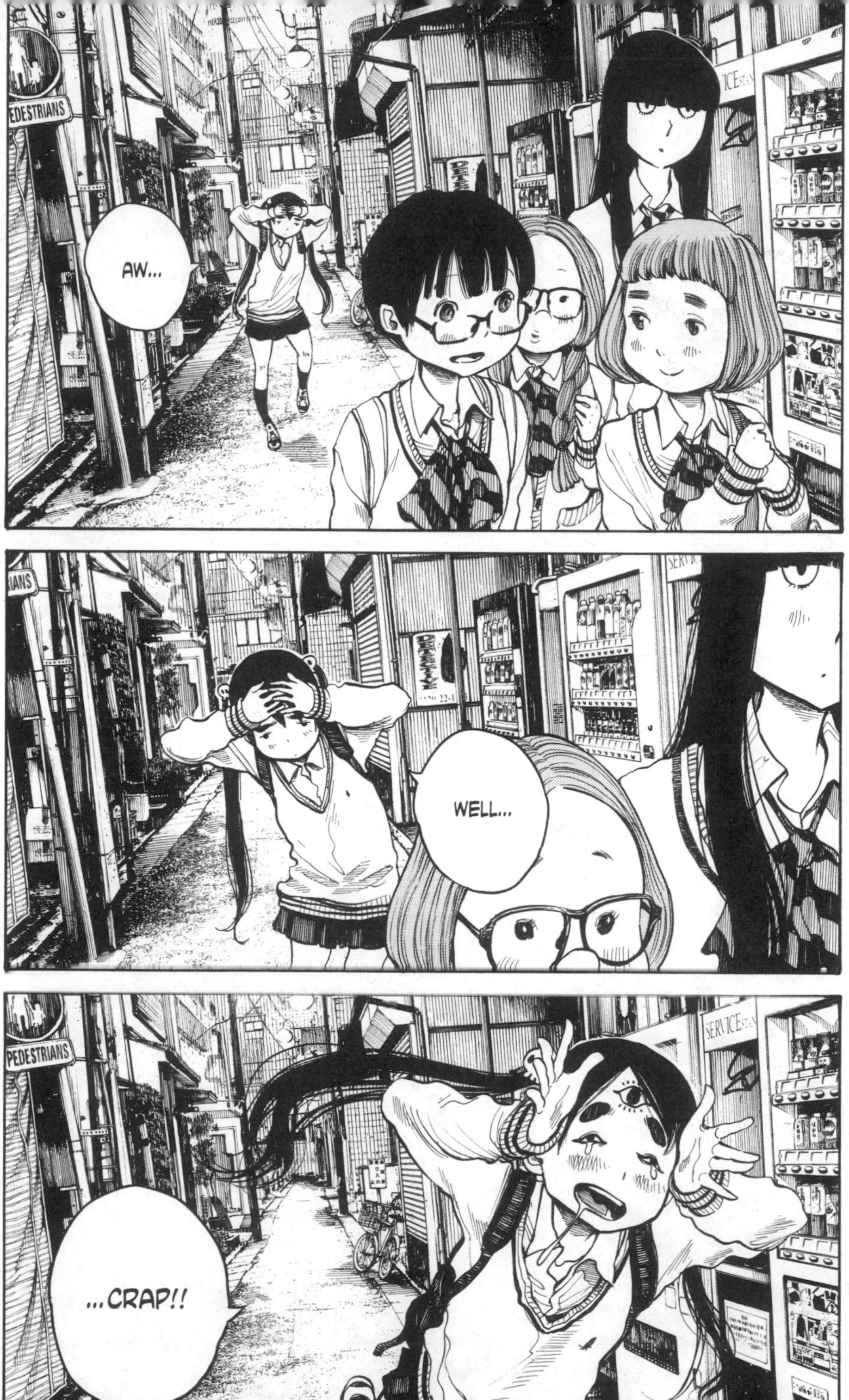
PEDESTRIANS
AW...
WELL...
...CRAP!!

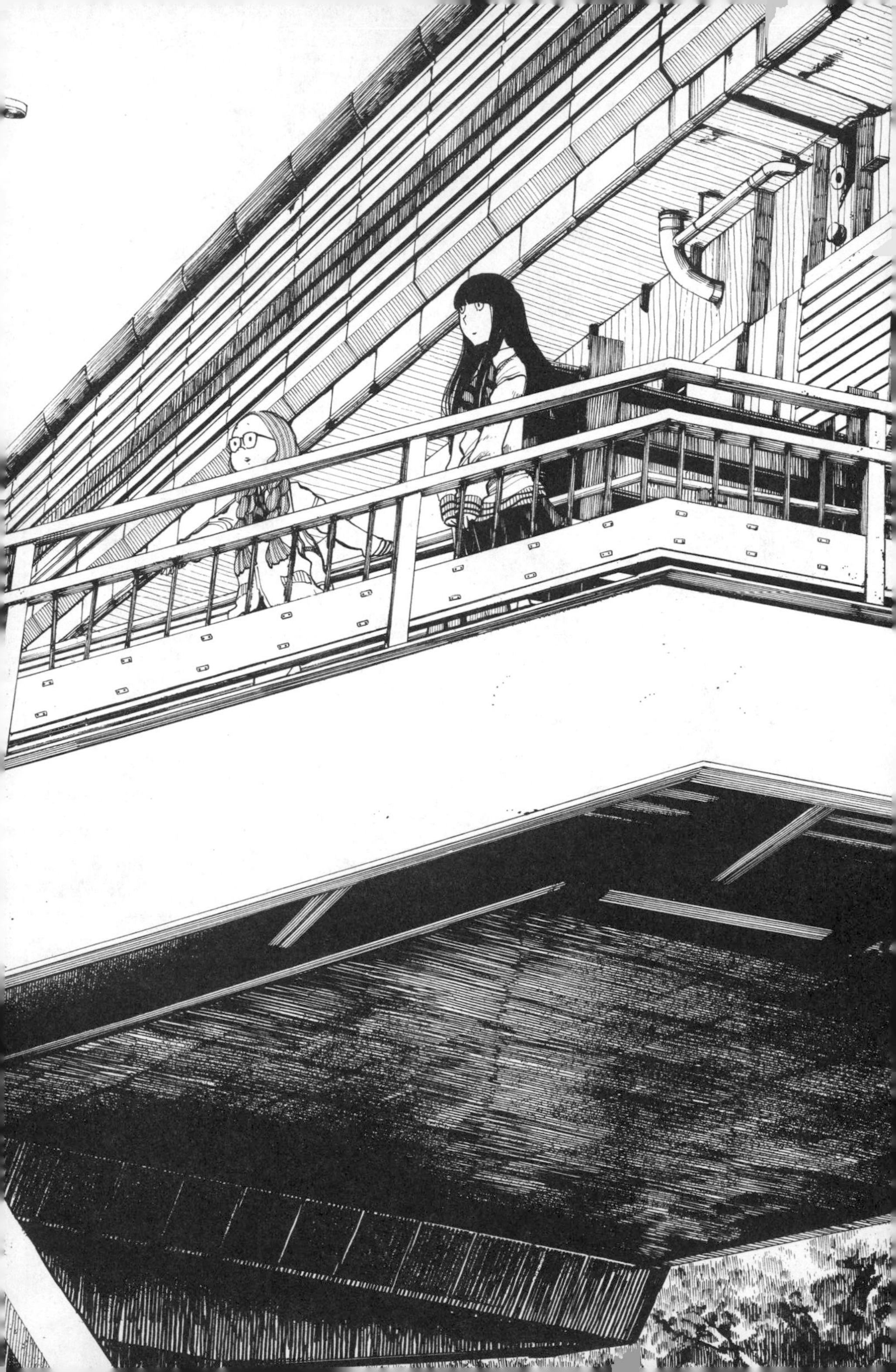

Dead Dead Demon's
Dededede Destruction
Volume 1
Inio Asano

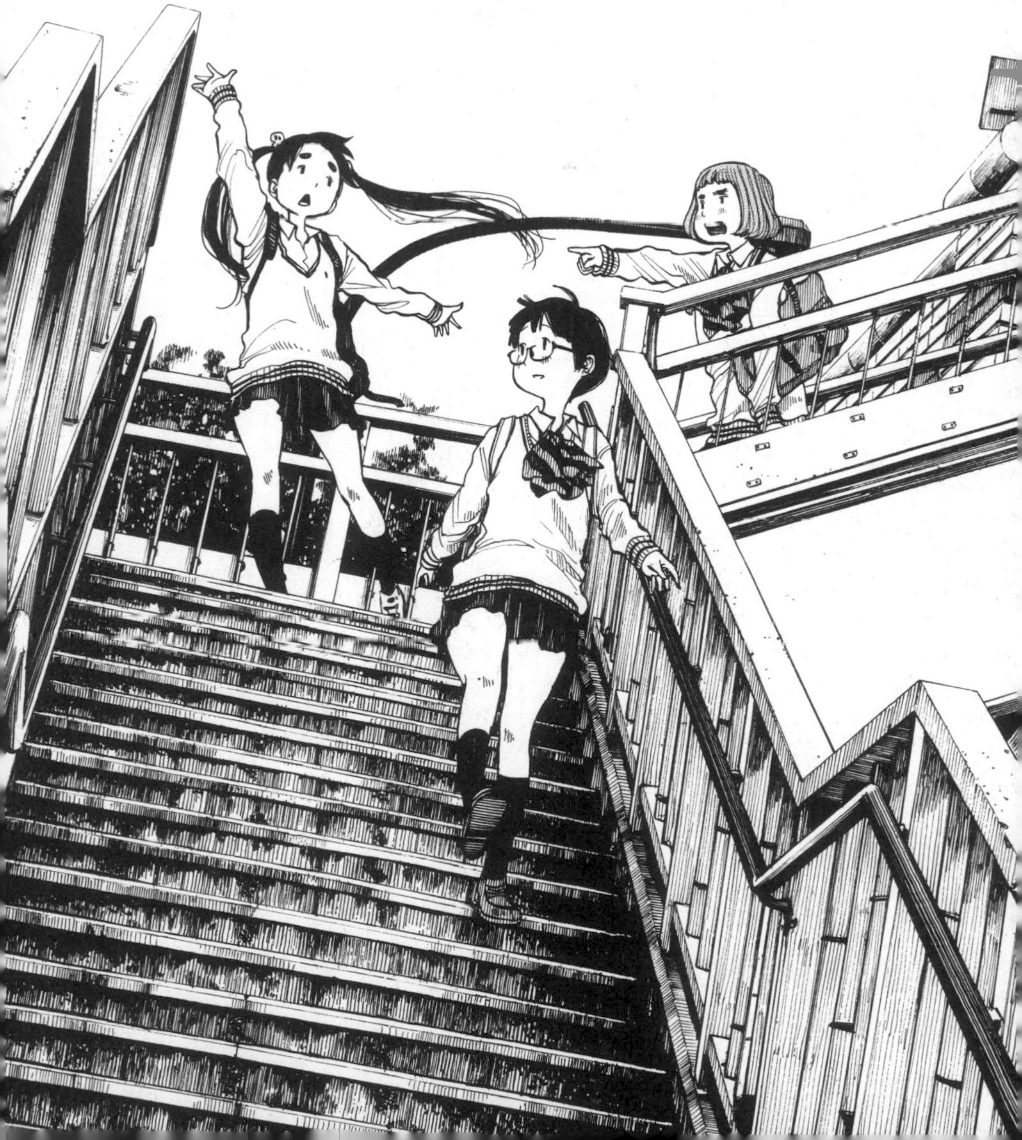

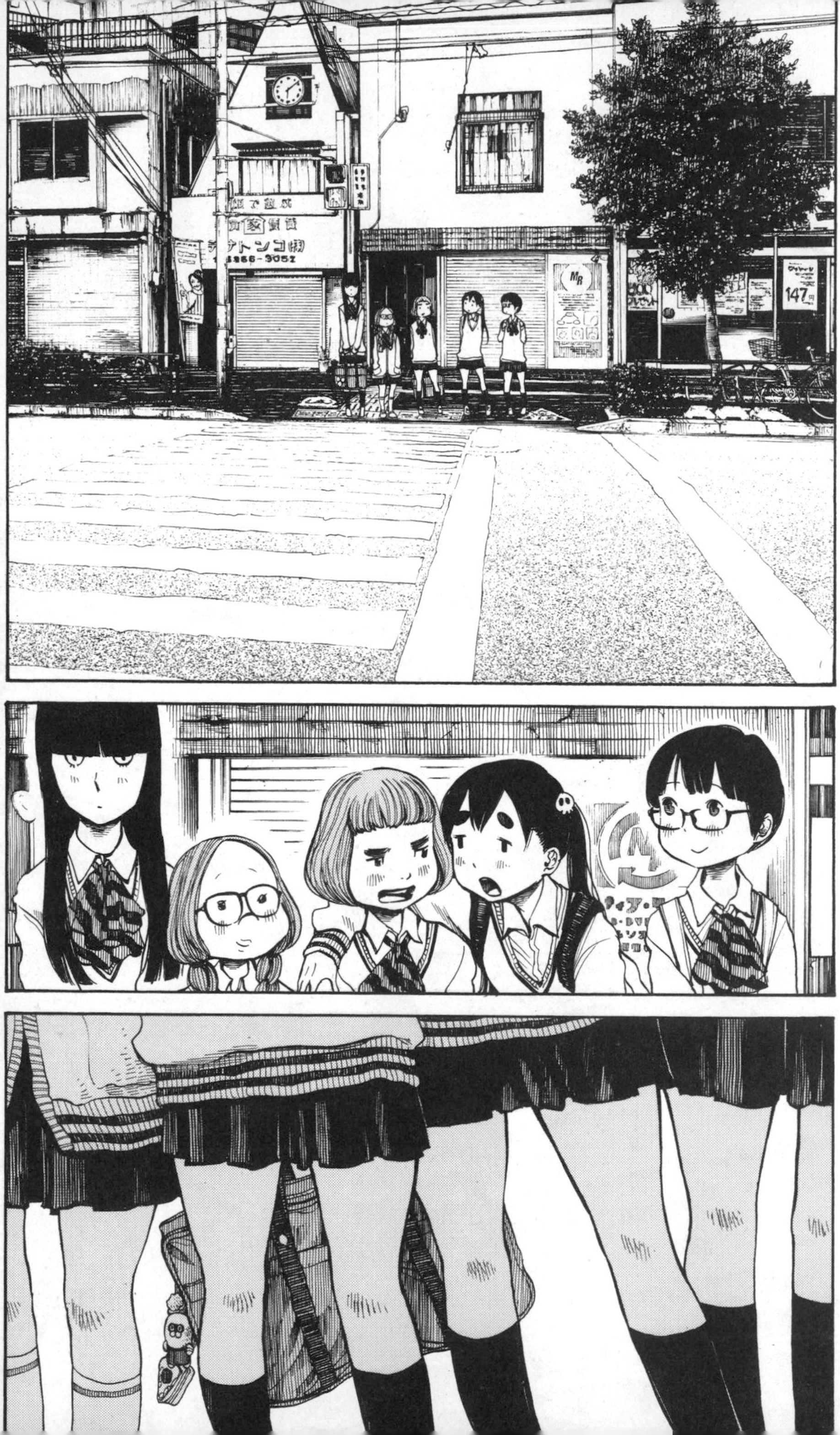
147円

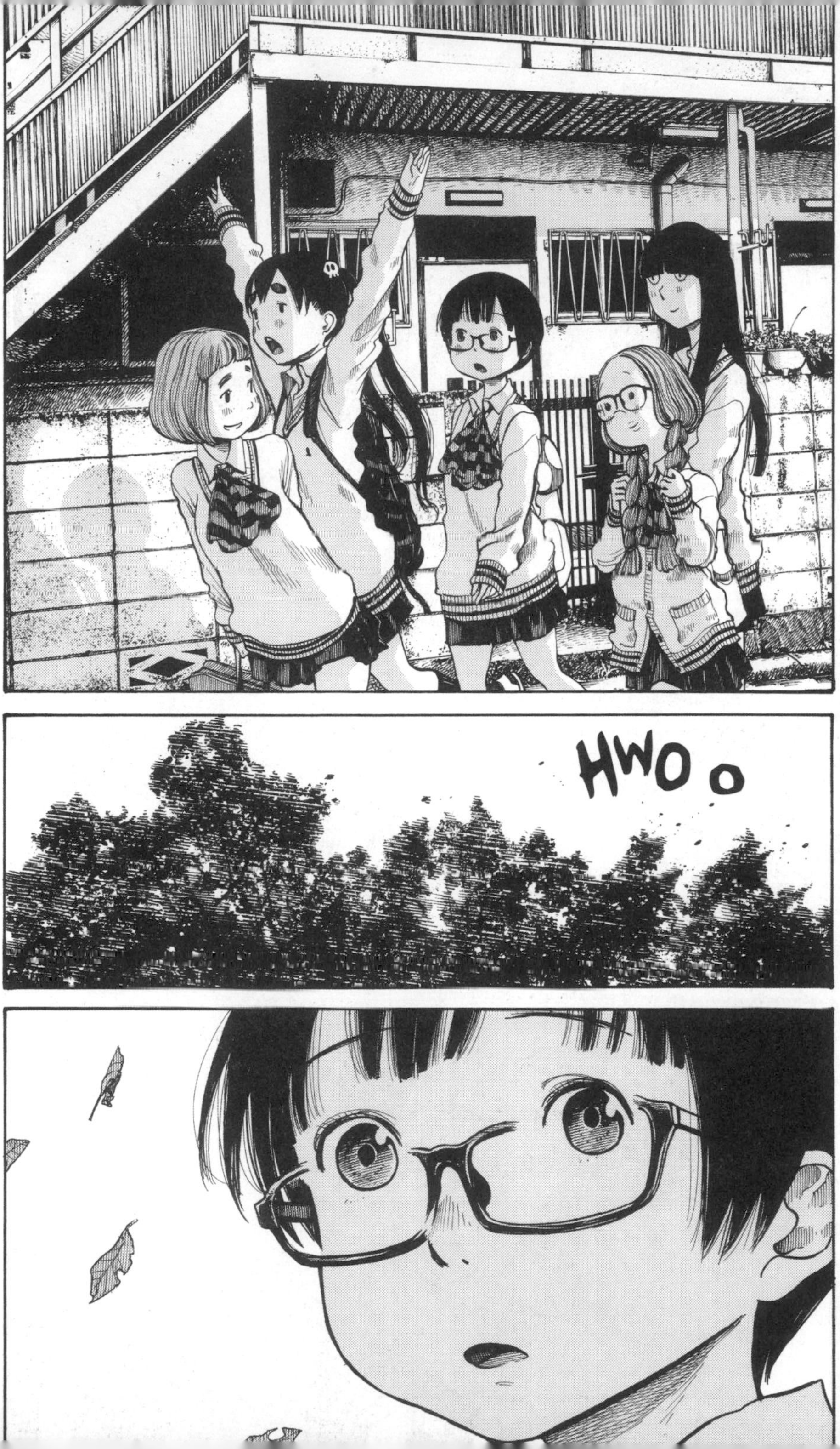
HWO O

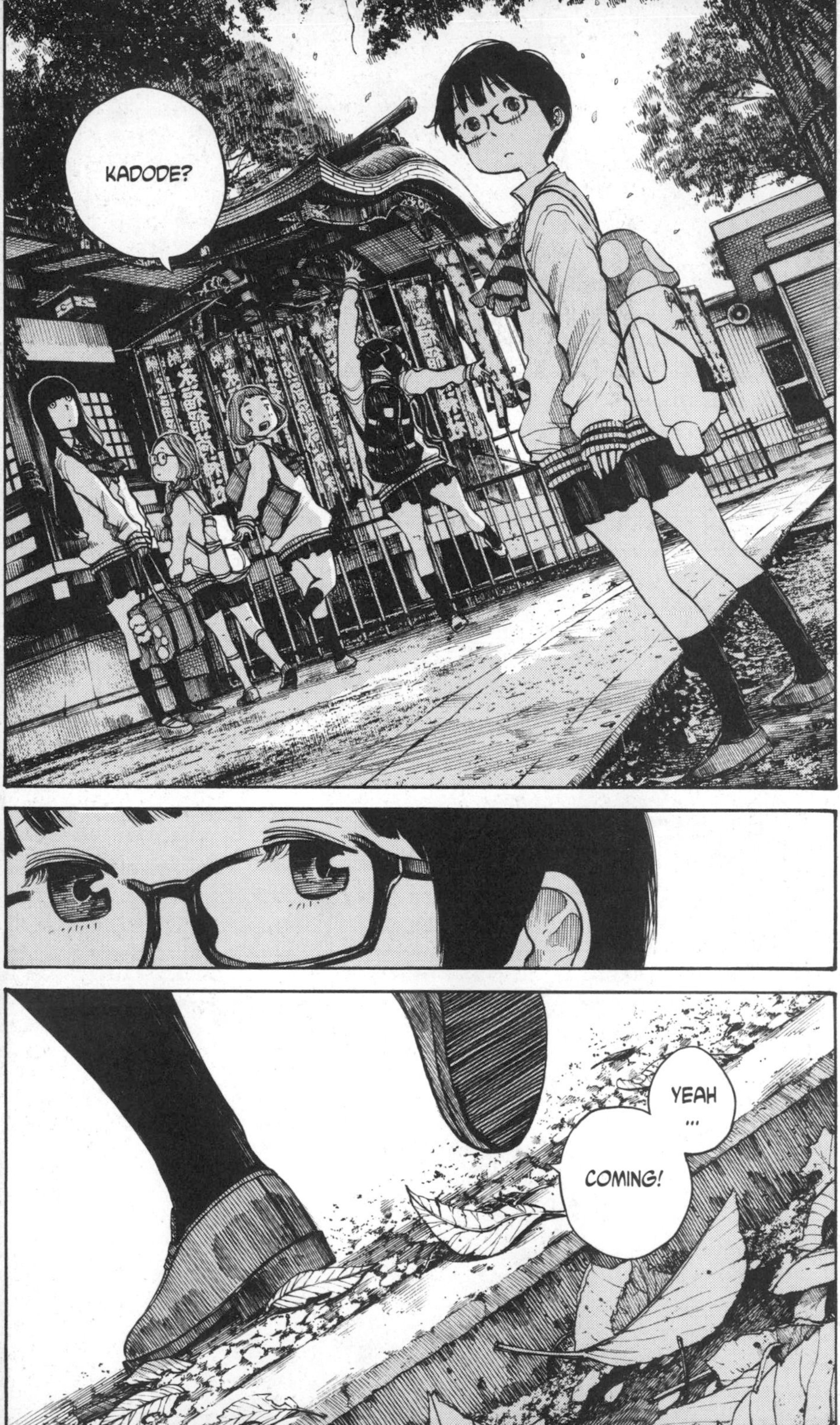
KADODE?
YEAH
...
COMING!

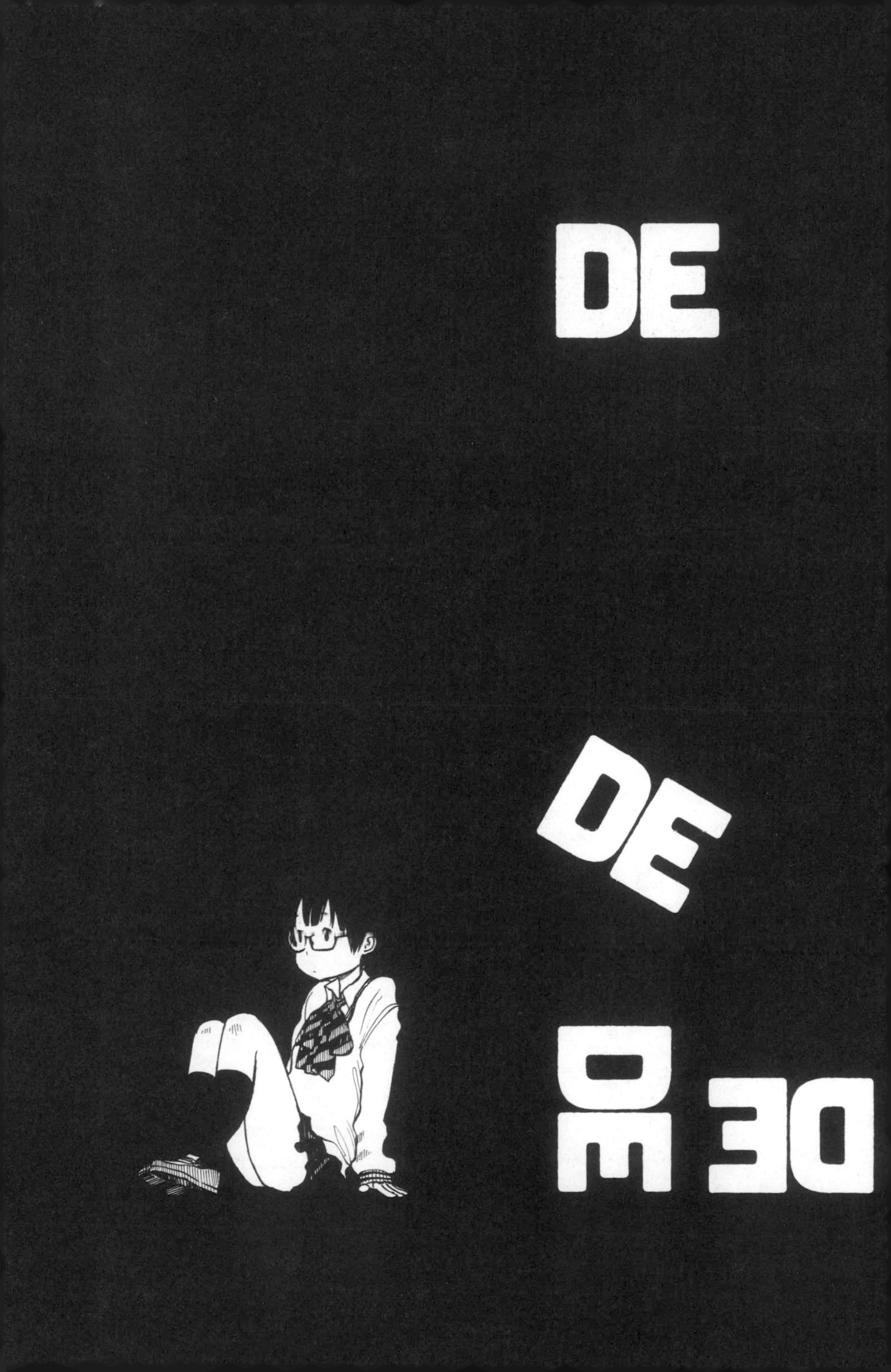
DE
DE

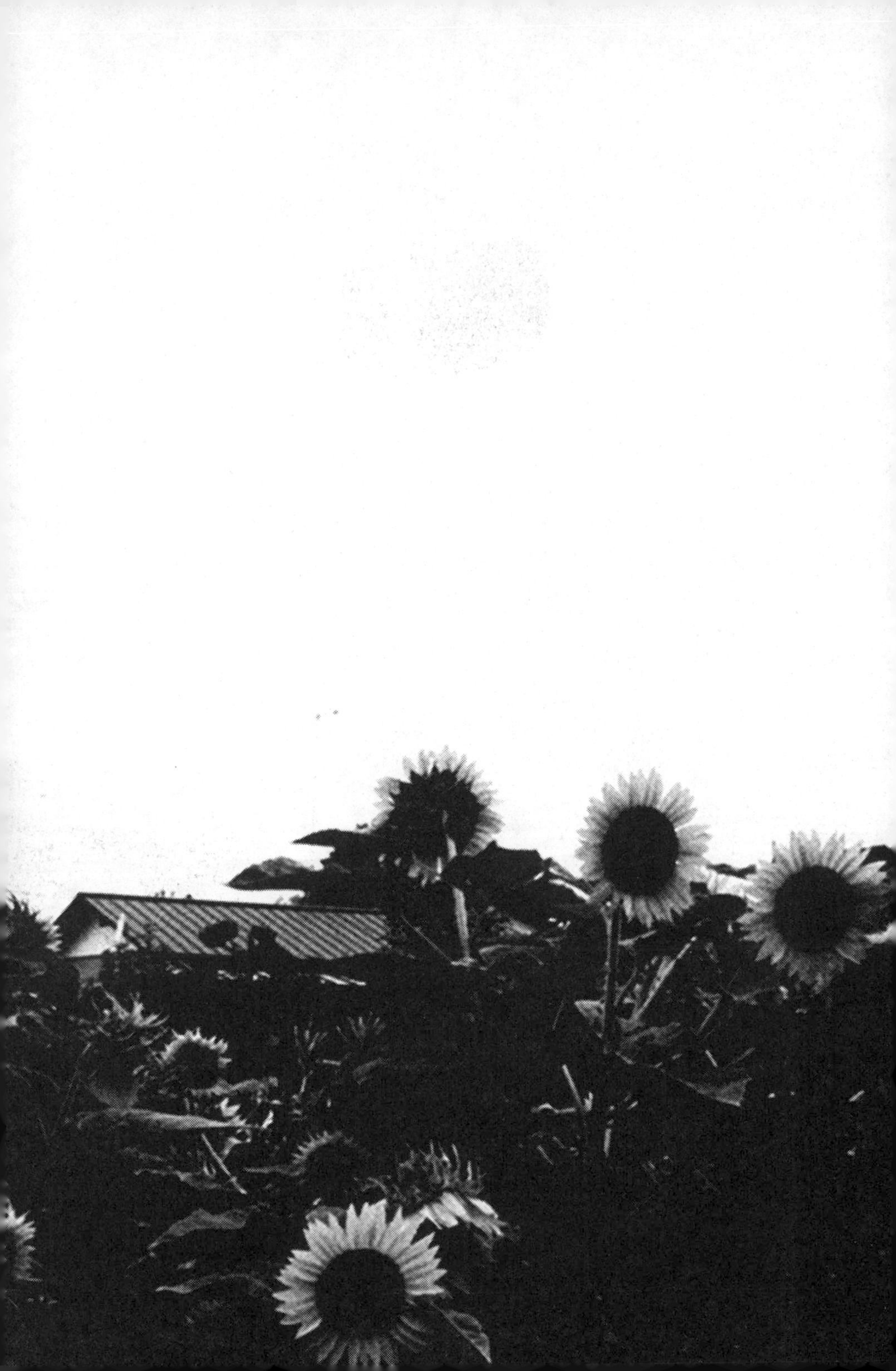

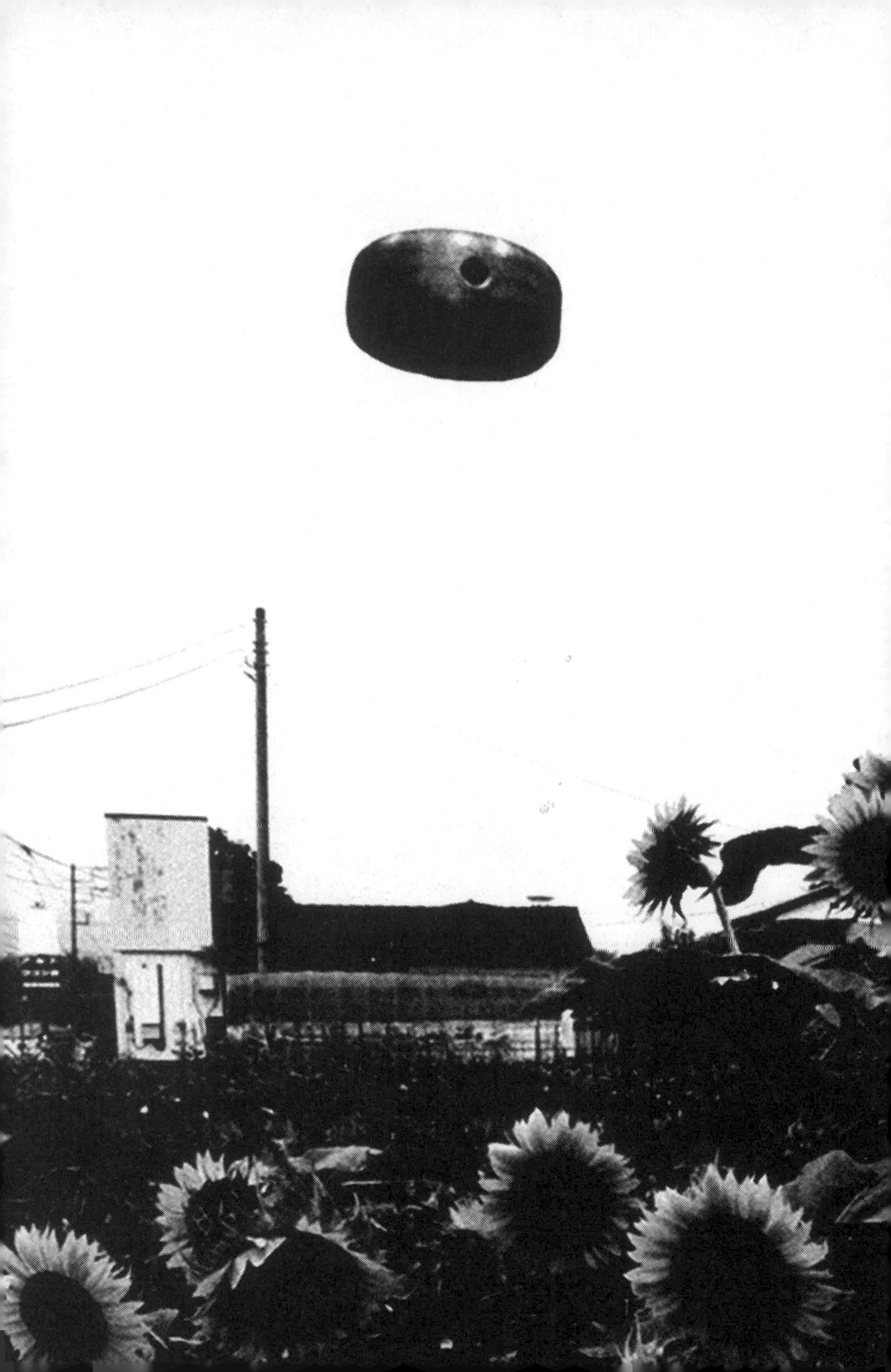

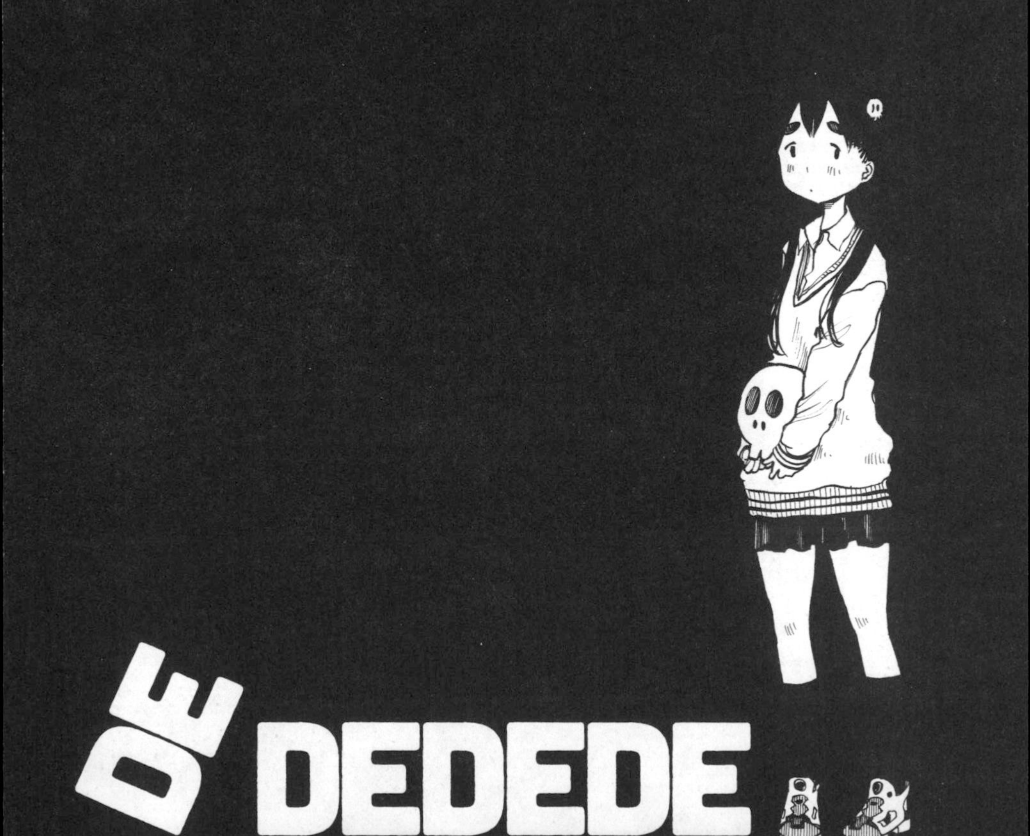
DE
DEDEDE

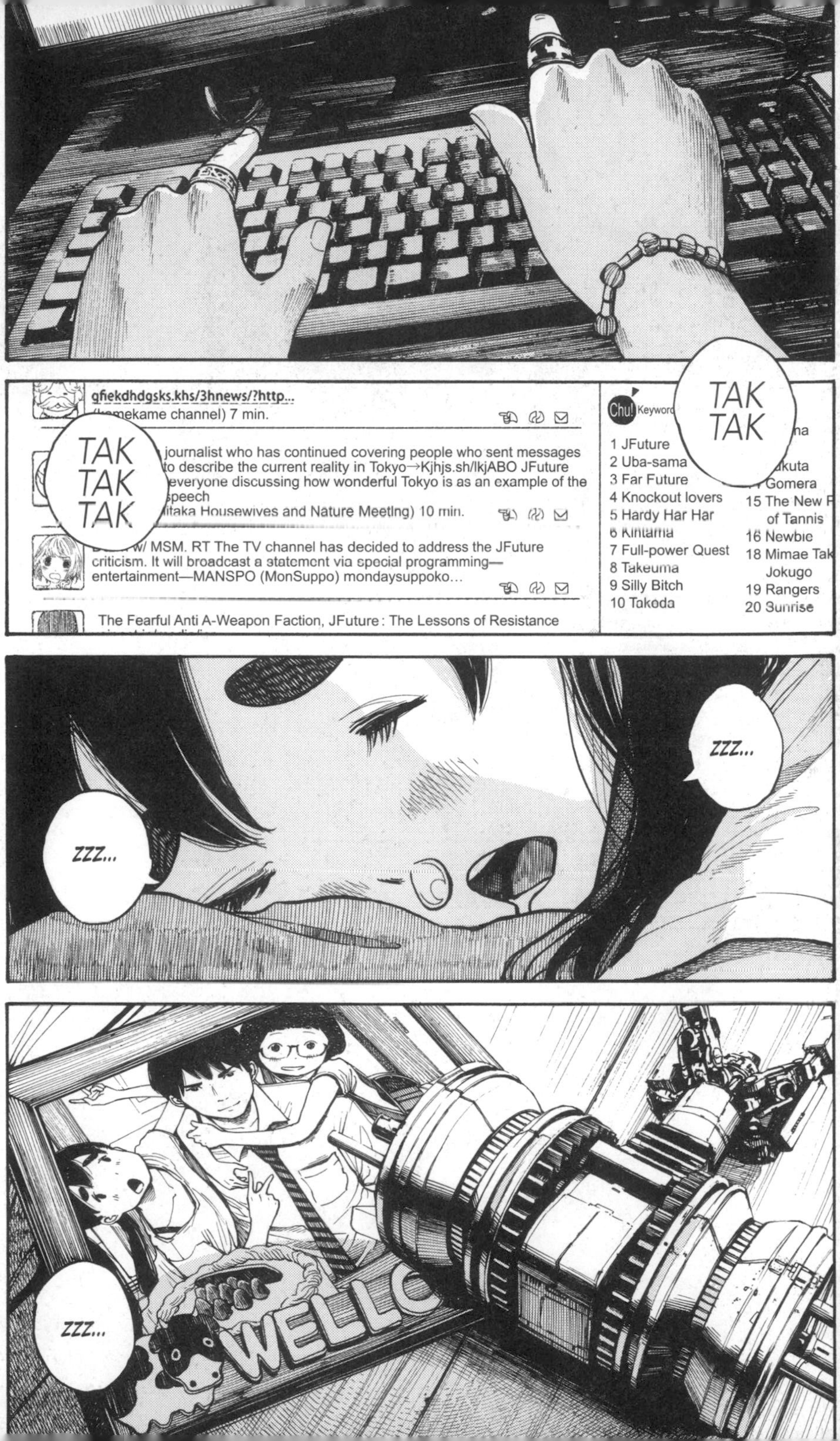
TAK TAK
TAK TAK TAK
qfiekdhdgsks.khs/3hnews/?http...
kamekame channel) 7 min.
journalist who has continued covering people who sent messages to describe the current reality in Tokyo→Kjhjs.sh/lkjABO JFuture everyone discussing how wonderful Tokyo is as an example of the speech
litaka Housewives and Nature Meeting) 10 min.
w/ MSM. RT The TV channel has decided to address the JFuture criticism. It will broadcast a statement via special programming—entertainment—MANSPO (MonSuppo) mondaysuppoko…
The Fearful Anti A-Weapon Faction, JFuture: The Lessons of Resistance
Chu! Keyword
1 JFuture
2 Uba-sama
3 Far Future
4 Knockout lovers
5 Hardy Har Har
6 Kintama
7 Full-power Quest
8 Takeuma
9 Silly Bitch
10 Takoda
Gomera
15 The New
of Tannis
16 Newbie
18 Mimae Tak
Jokugo
19 Rangers
20 Sunrise
ZZZ...
ZZZ...
ZZZ...
WELLC

CHAPTER 7

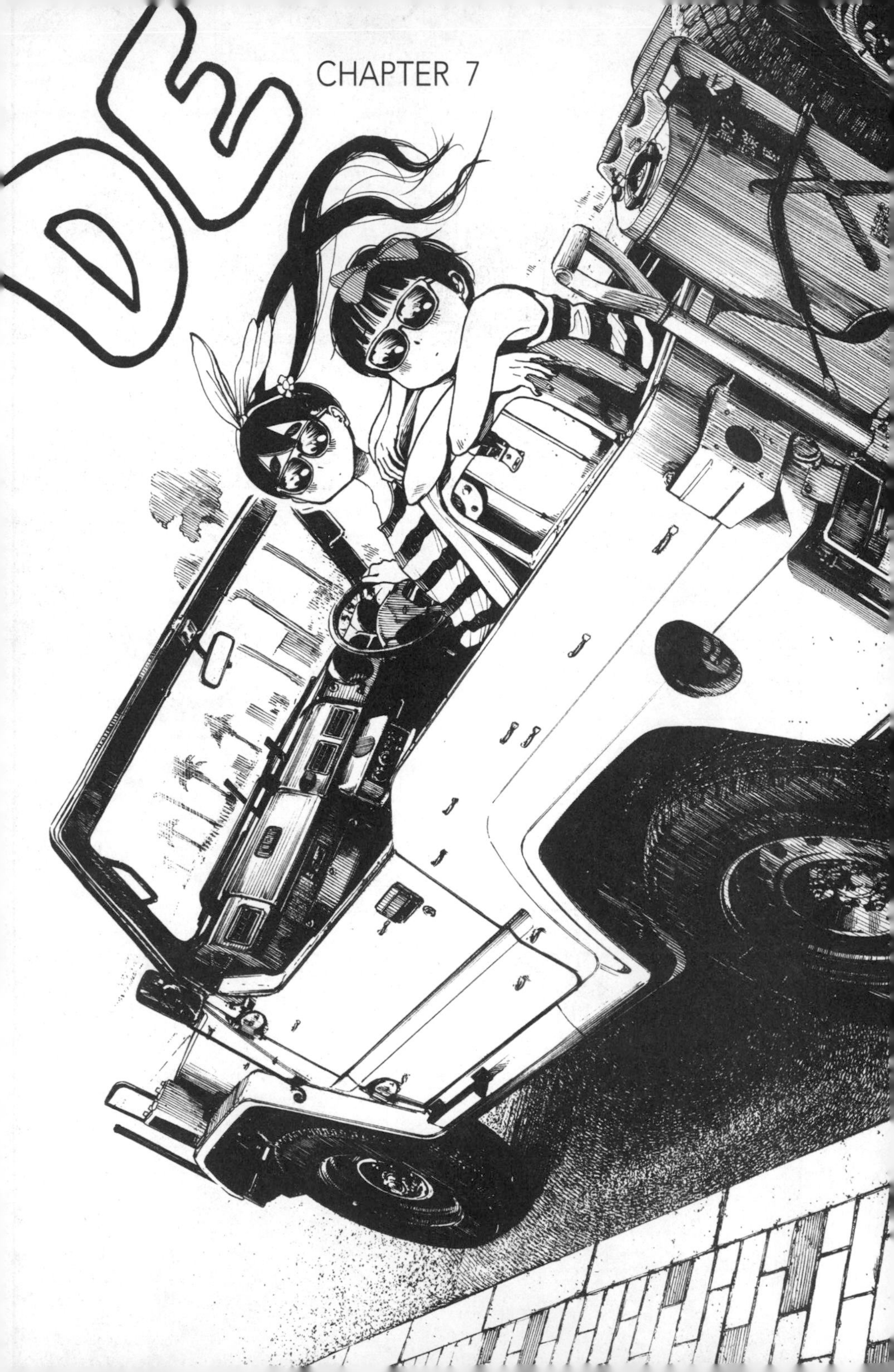

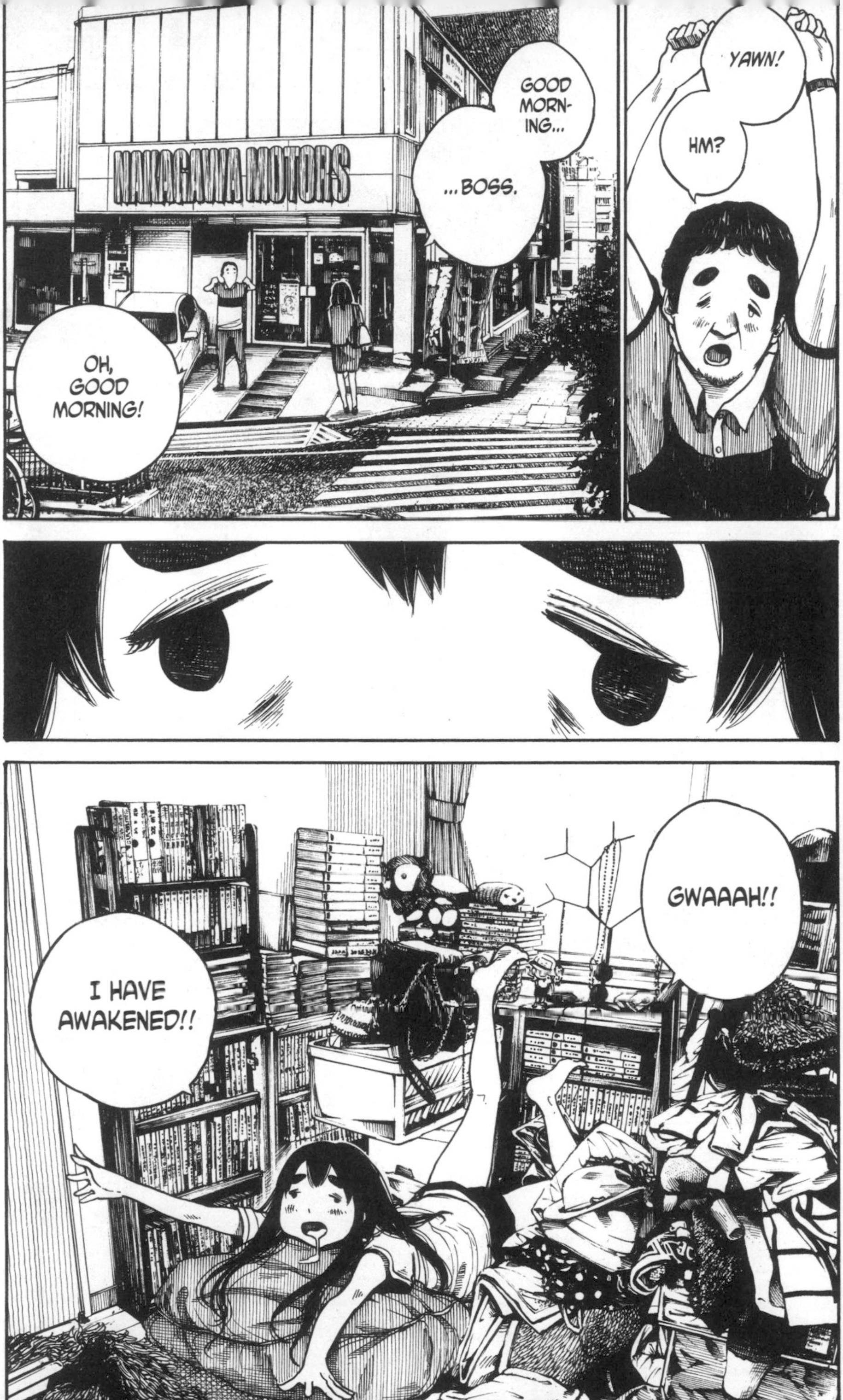
YAWN!
HM?
GOOD MORN-ING...
...BOSS.
NAKAGAWA MOTORS
OH, GOOD MORNING!
GWAAAH!!
I HAVE AWAKENED!!

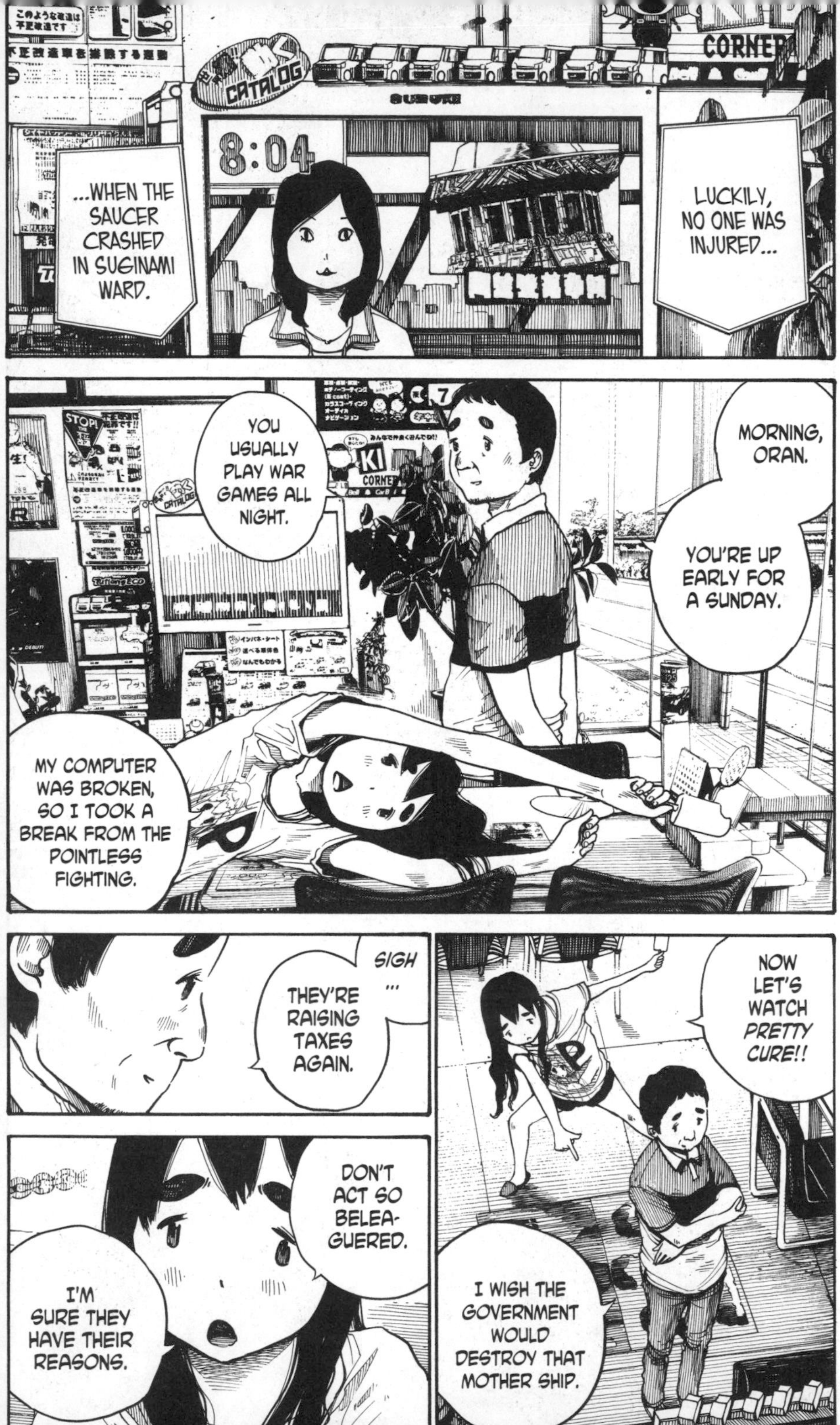
LUCKILY, NO ONE WAS INJURED...
...WHEN THE SAUCER CRASHED IN SUGINAMI WARD.
8:04
CATALOG
CORNER
MORNING, ORAN.
YOU'RE UP EARLY FOR A SUNDAY.
YOU USUALLY PLAY WAR GAMES ALL NIGHT.
MY COMPUTER WAS BROKEN, SO I TOOK A BREAK FROM THE POINTLESS FIGHTING.
NOW LET'S WATCH *PRETTY CURE!!*
I WISH THE GOVERNMENT WOULD DESTROY THAT MOTHER SHIP.
SIGH ...
THEY'RE RAISING TAXES AGAIN.
DON'T ACT SO BELEA-GUERED.
I'M SURE THEY HAVE THEIR REASONS.

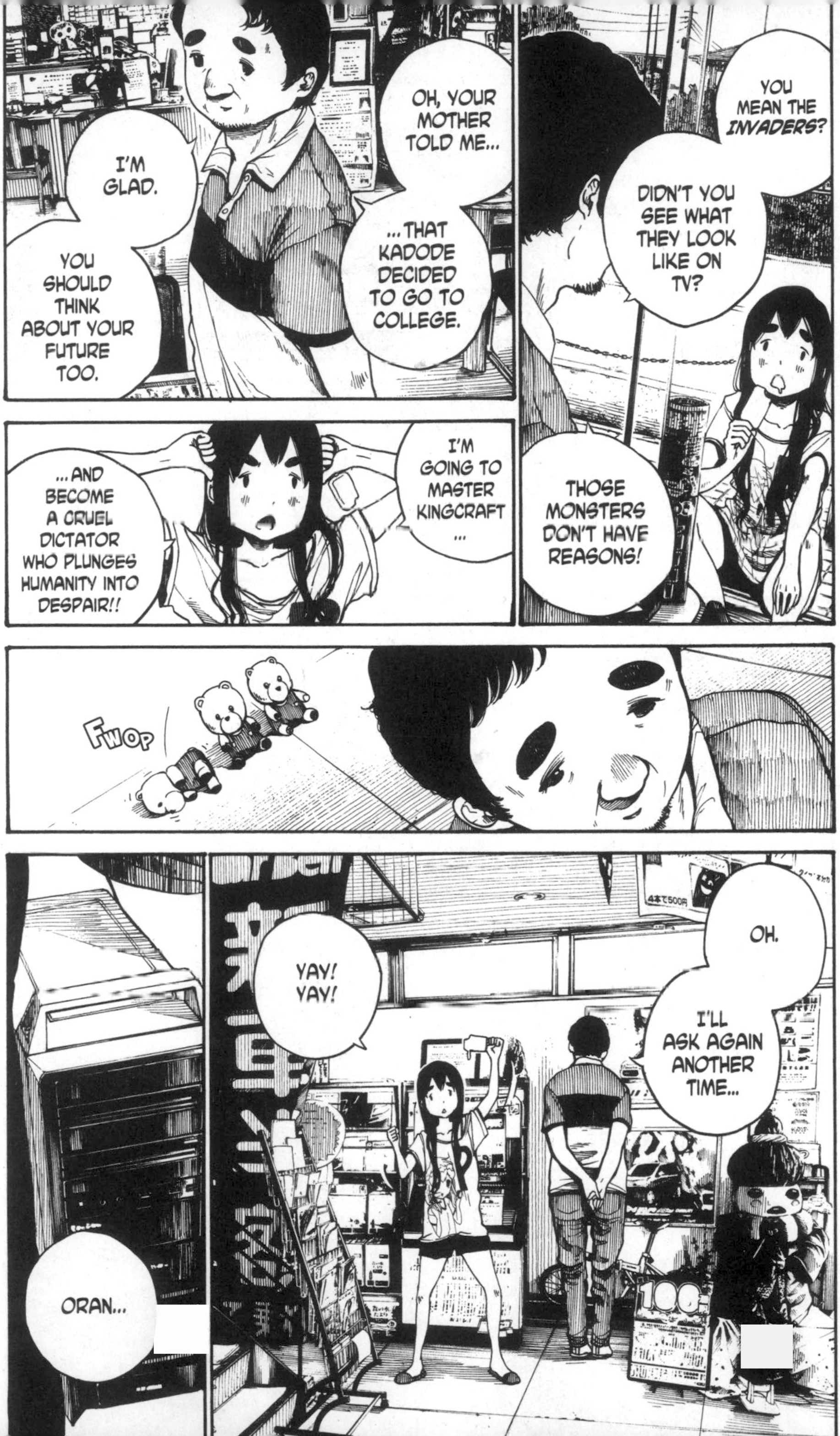
YOU MEAN THE INVADERS?
DIDN'T YOU SEE WHAT THEY LOOK LIKE ON TV?
THOSE MONSTERS DON'T HAVE REASONS!
OH, YOUR MOTHER TOLD ME...
...THAT KADODE DECIDED TO GO TO COLLEGE.
I'M GLAD.
YOU SHOULD THINK ABOUT YOUR FUTURE TOO.
I'M GOING TO MASTER KINGCRAFT...
...AND BECOME A CRUEL DICTATOR WHO PLUNGES HUMANITY INTO DESPAIR!!
FWOP
OH.
I'LL ASK AGAIN ANOTHER TIME...
YAY! YAY!
ORAN...

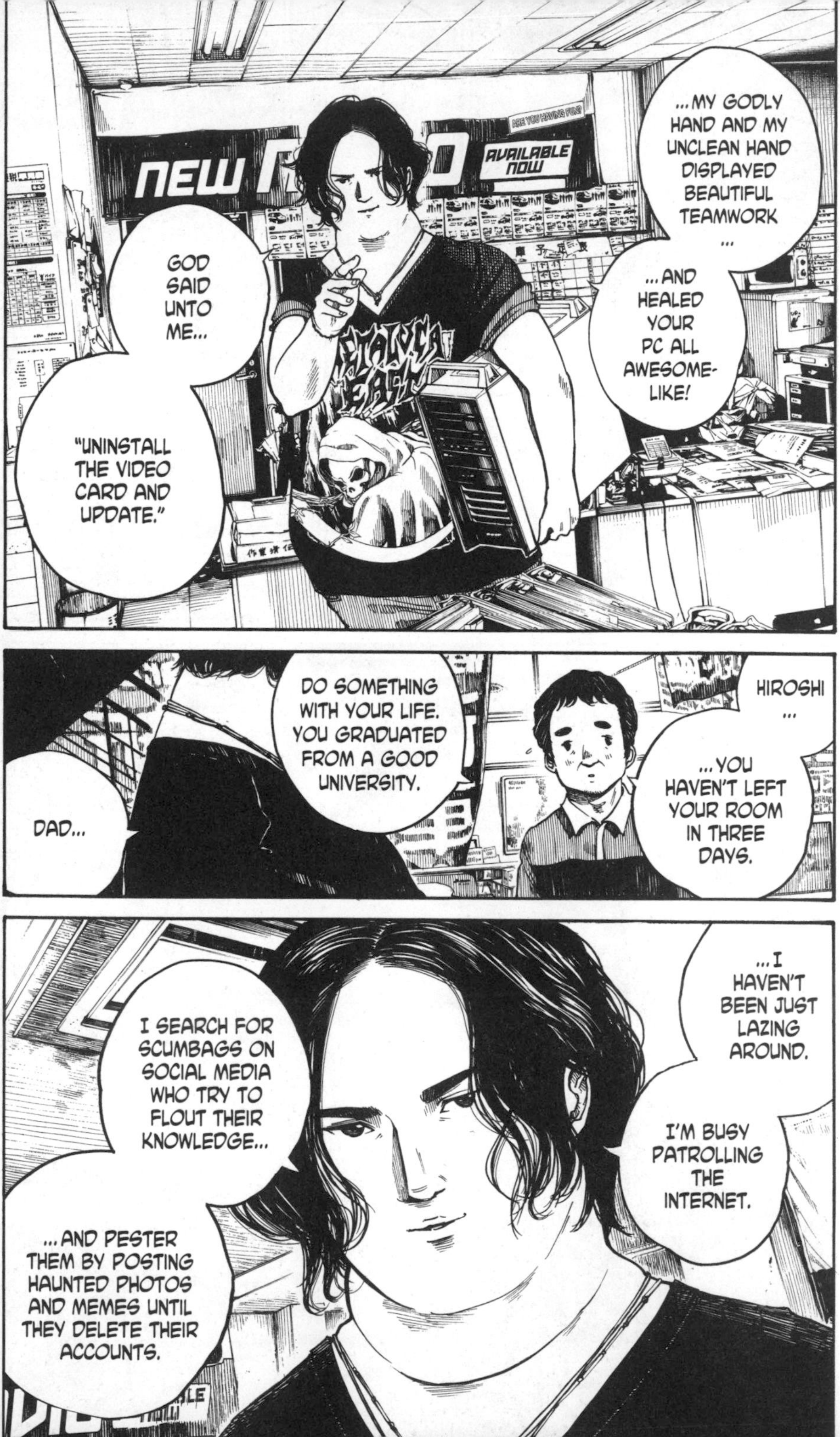

ARE YOU HAVING FUN?
AVAILABLE NOW
...MY GODLY HAND AND MY UNCLEAN HAND DISPLAYED BEAUTIFUL TEAMWORK ...
...AND HEALED YOUR PC ALL AWESOME-LIKE!
GOD SAID UNTO ME...
"UNINSTALL THE VIDEO CARD AND UPDATE."
HIROSHI ...
...YOU HAVEN'T LEFT YOUR ROOM IN THREE DAYS.
DO SOMETHING WITH YOUR LIFE. YOU GRADUATED FROM A GOOD UNIVERSITY.
DAD...
...I HAVEN'T BEEN JUST LAZING AROUND.
I'M BUSY PATROLLING THE INTERNET.
I SEARCH FOR SCUMBAGS ON SOCIAL MEDIA WHO TRY TO FLOUT THEIR KNOWLEDGE...
...AND PESTER THEM BY POSTING HAUNTED PHOTOS AND MEMES UNTIL THEY DELETE THEIR ACCOUNTS.

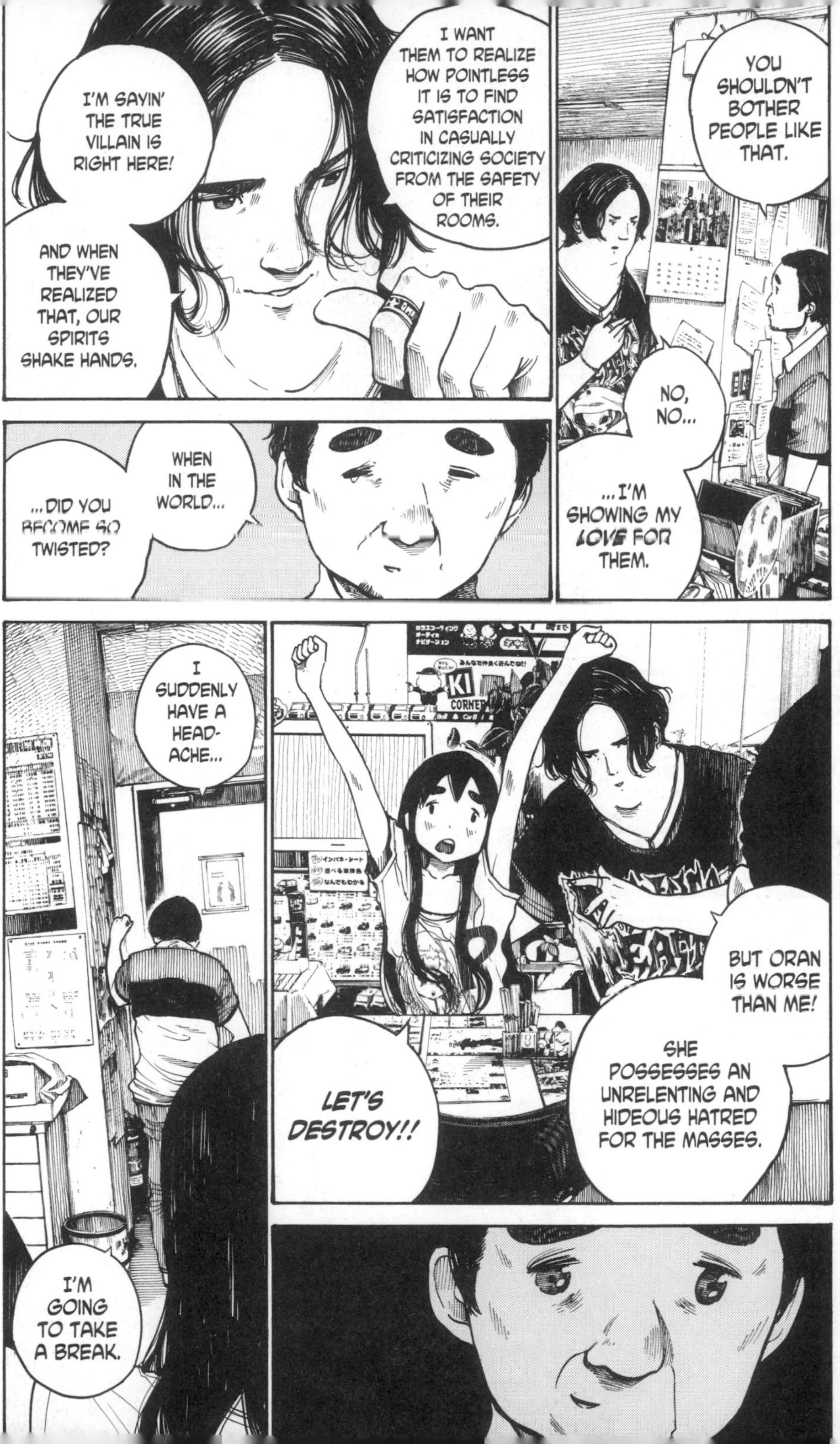
YOU SHOULDN'T BOTHER PEOPLE LIKE THAT.
NO, NO...
...I'M SHOWING MY *LOVE* FOR THEM.
I WANT THEM TO REALIZE HOW POINTLESS IT IS TO FIND SATISFACTION IN CASUALLY CRITICIZING SOCIETY FROM THE SAFETY OF THEIR ROOMS.
I'M SAYIN' THE TRUE VILLAIN IS RIGHT HERE!
AND WHEN THEY'VE REALIZED THAT, OUR SPIRITS SHAKE HANDS.
WHEN IN THE WORLD...
...DID YOU BECOME SO TWISTED?
BUT ORAN IS WORSE THAN ME!
SHE POSSESSES AN UNRELENTING AND HIDEOUS HATRED FOR THE MASSES.
LET'S DESTROY!!
I SUDDENLY HAVE A HEAD-ACHE...
I'M GOING TO TAKE A BREAK.

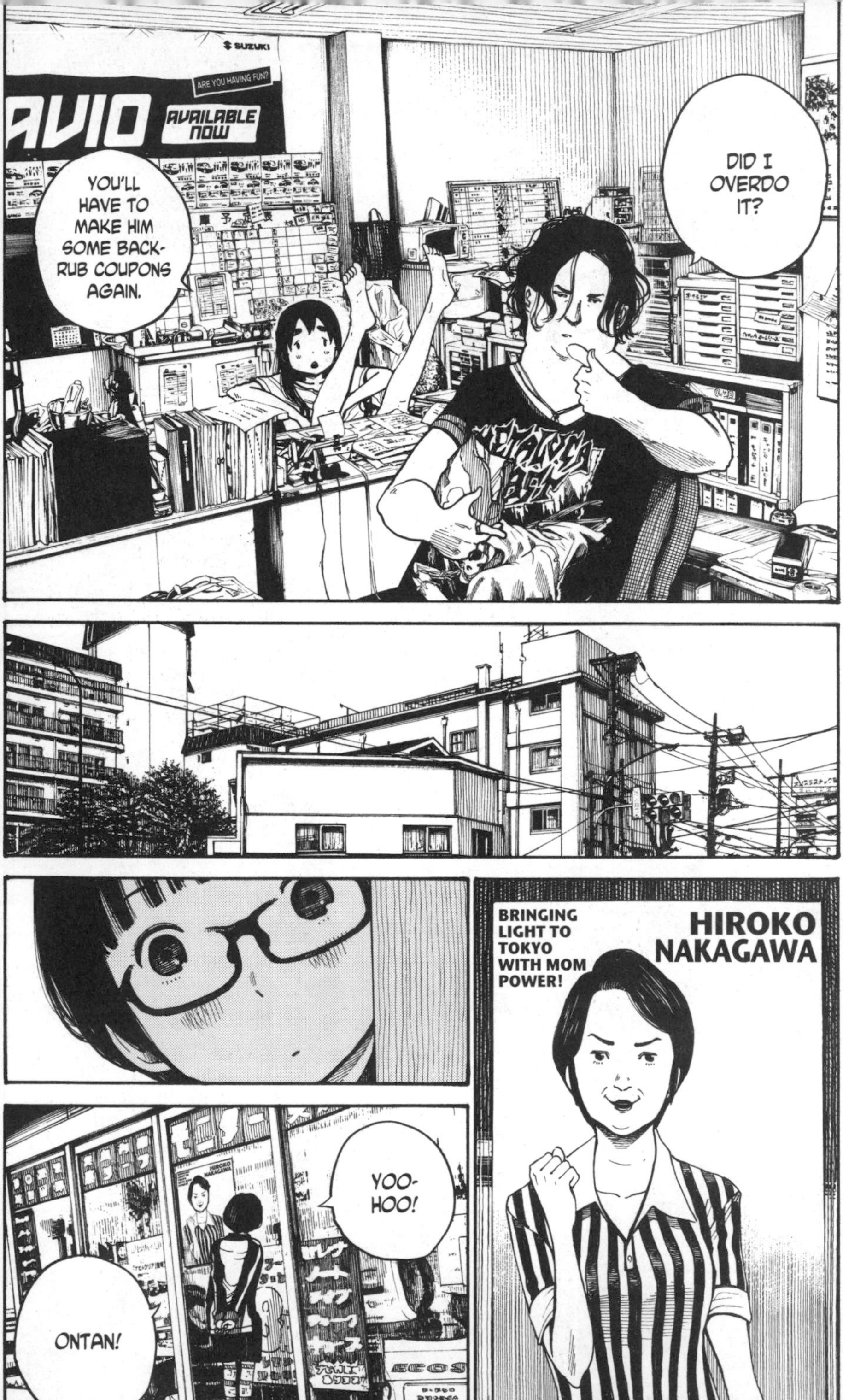
SUZUKI
ARE YOU HAVING FUN?
AVIO
AVAILABLE NOW
DID I OVERDO IT?
YOU'LL HAVE TO MAKE HIM SOME BACK-RUB COUPONS AGAIN.
HIROKO NAKAGAWA
BRINGING LIGHT TO TOKYO WITH MOM POWER!
HIROKO NAKAGAWA
YOO-HOO!
ONTAN!

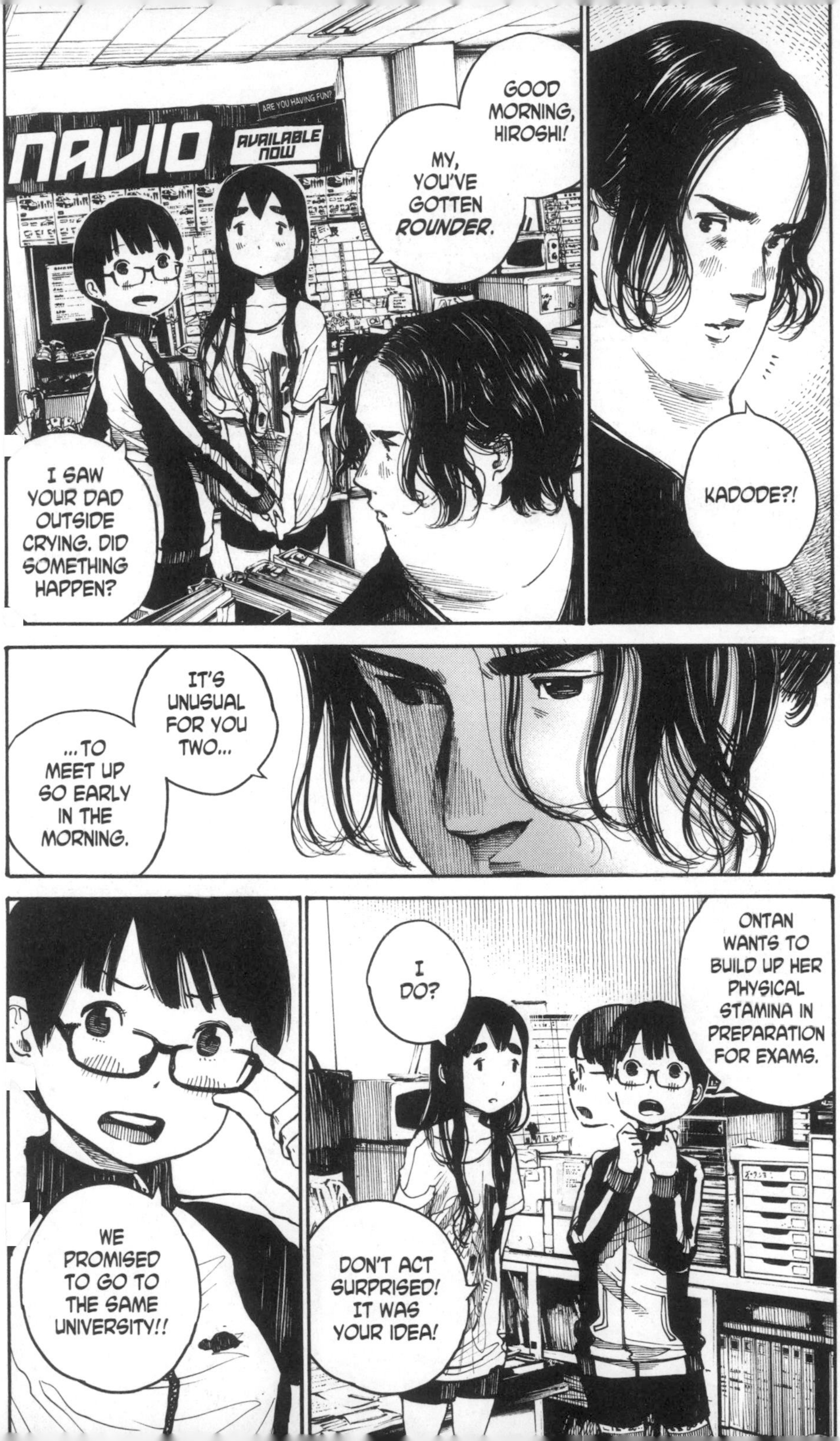
KADODE?!
GOOD MORNING, HIROSHI!
MY, YOU'VE GOTTEN *ROUNDER*.
ARE YOU HAVING FUN?
NAVIO
AVAILABLE NOW
I SAW YOUR DAD OUTSIDE CRYING. DID SOMETHING HAPPEN?
IT'S UNUSUAL FOR YOU TWO...
...TO MEET UP SO EARLY IN THE MORNING.
ONTAN WANTS TO BUILD UP HER PHYSICAL STAMINA IN PREPARATION FOR EXAMS.
I DO?
DON'T ACT SURPRISED! IT WAS YOUR IDEA!
WE PROMISED TO GO TO THE SAME UNIVERSITY!!

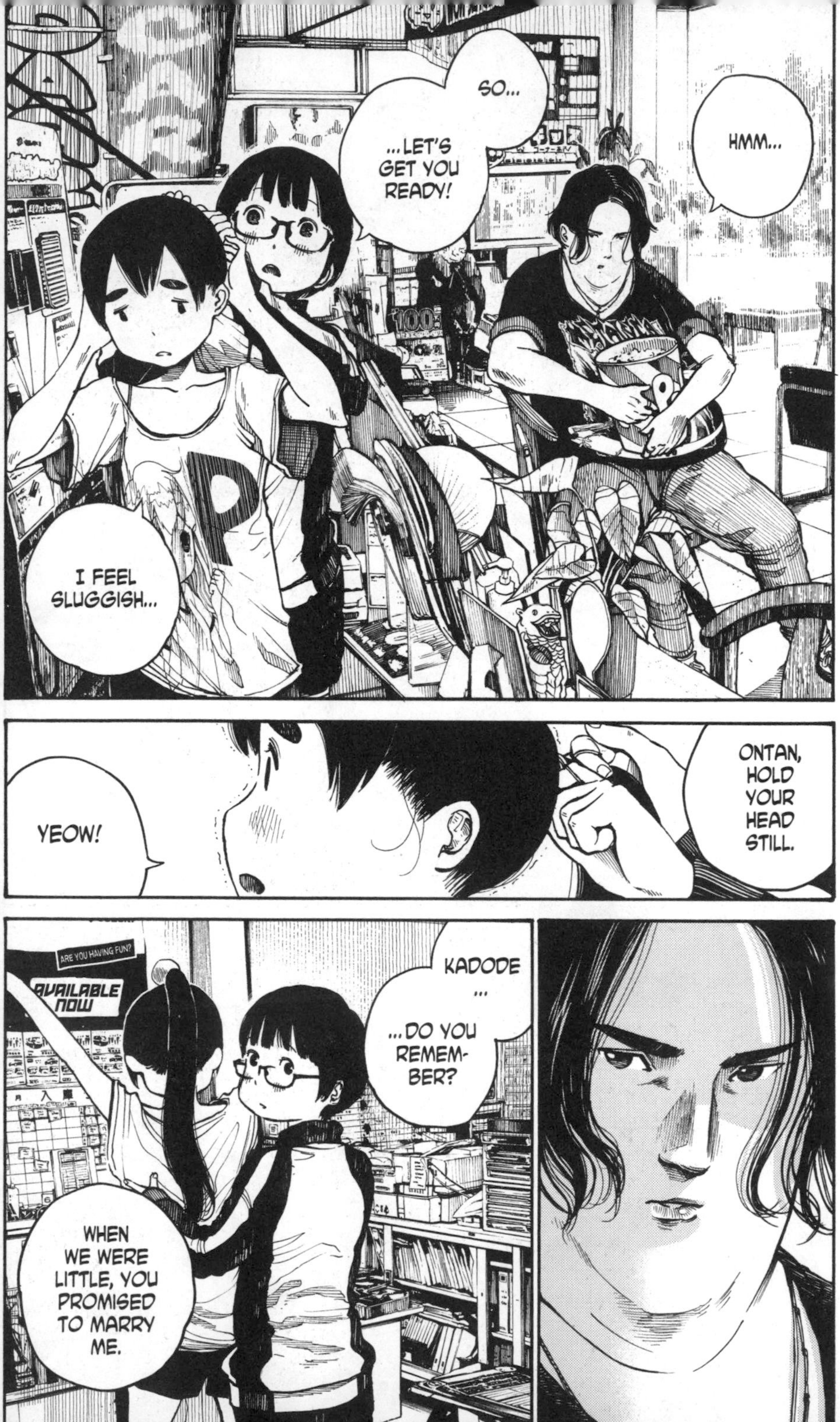
HMM...
SO... ...LET'S GET YOU READY!
I FEEL SLUGGISH...
ONTAN, HOLD YOUR HEAD STILL.
YEOW!
KADODE ... ...DO YOU REMEM- BER?
ARE YOU HAVING FUN?
AVAILABLE NOW
WHEN WE WERE LITTLE, YOU PROMISED TO MARRY ME.

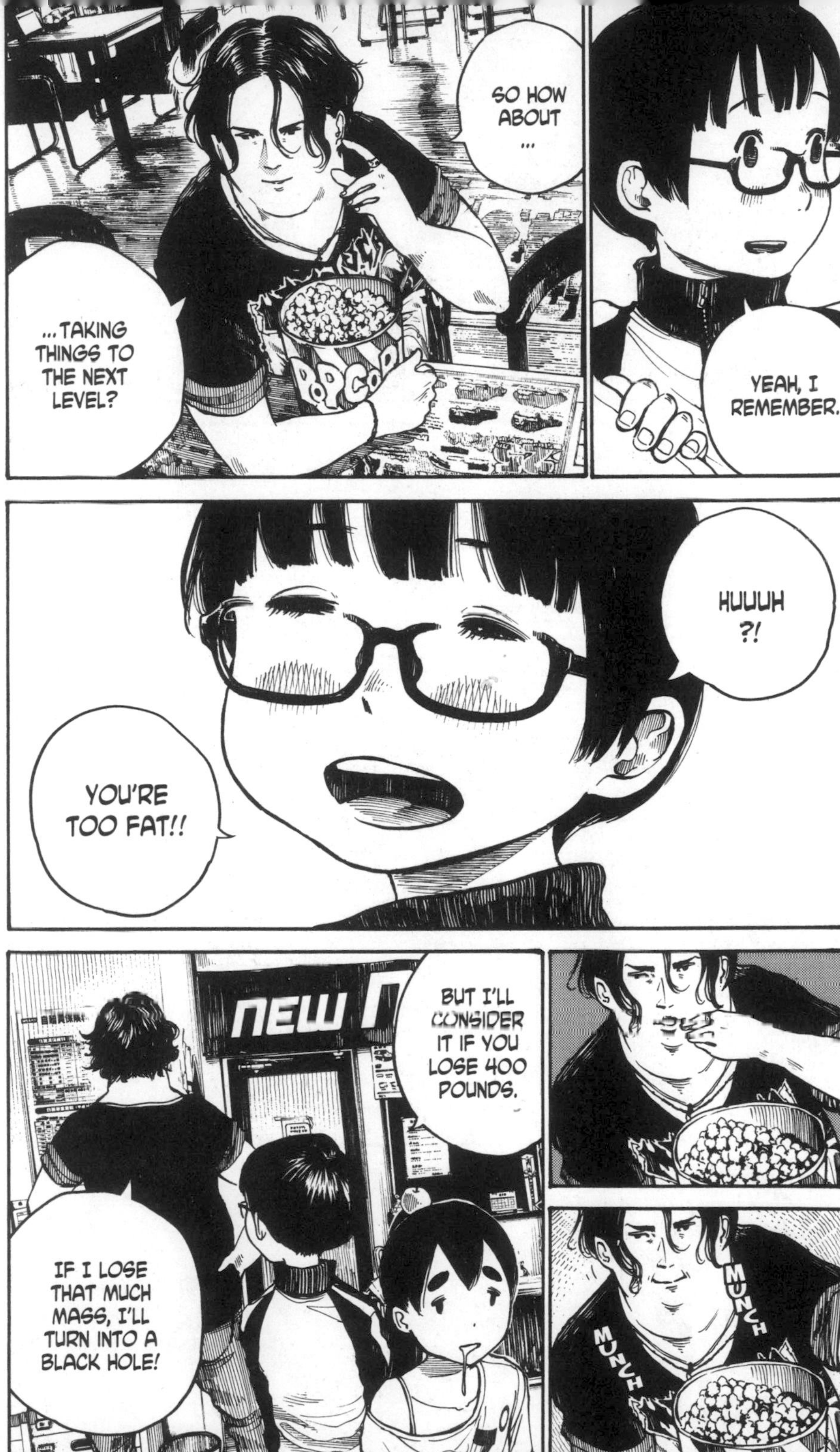
YEAH, I REMEMBER.
SO HOW ABOUT ...
...TAKING THINGS TO THE NEXT LEVEL?
HUUUH ?!
YOU'RE TOO FAT!!
MUNCH
MUNCH
BUT I'LL CONSIDER IT IF YOU LOSE 400 POUNDS.
IF I LOSE THAT MUCH MASS, I'LL TURN INTO A BLACK HOLE!
NEW

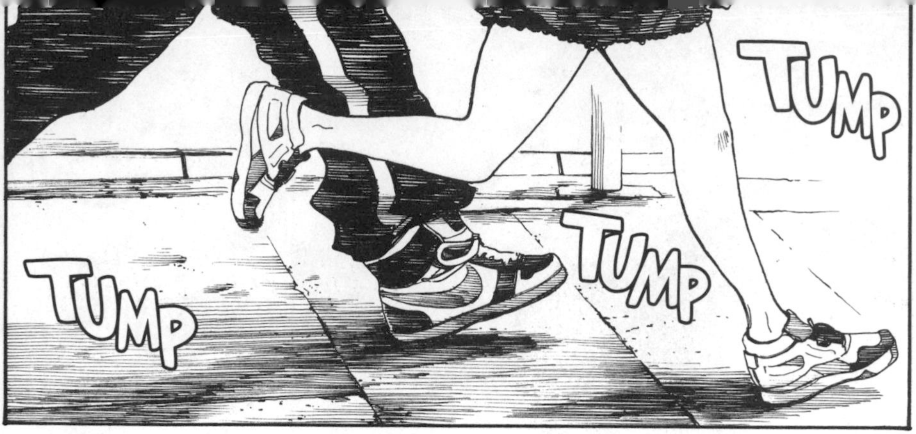
TUMP
TUMP
TUMP

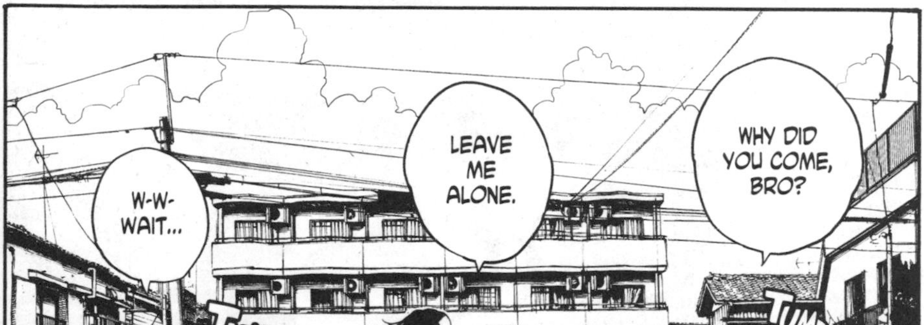
WHY DID YOU COME, BRO?
TUMP
LEAVE ME ALONE.
TUMP
W-W-WAIT...
TUMP

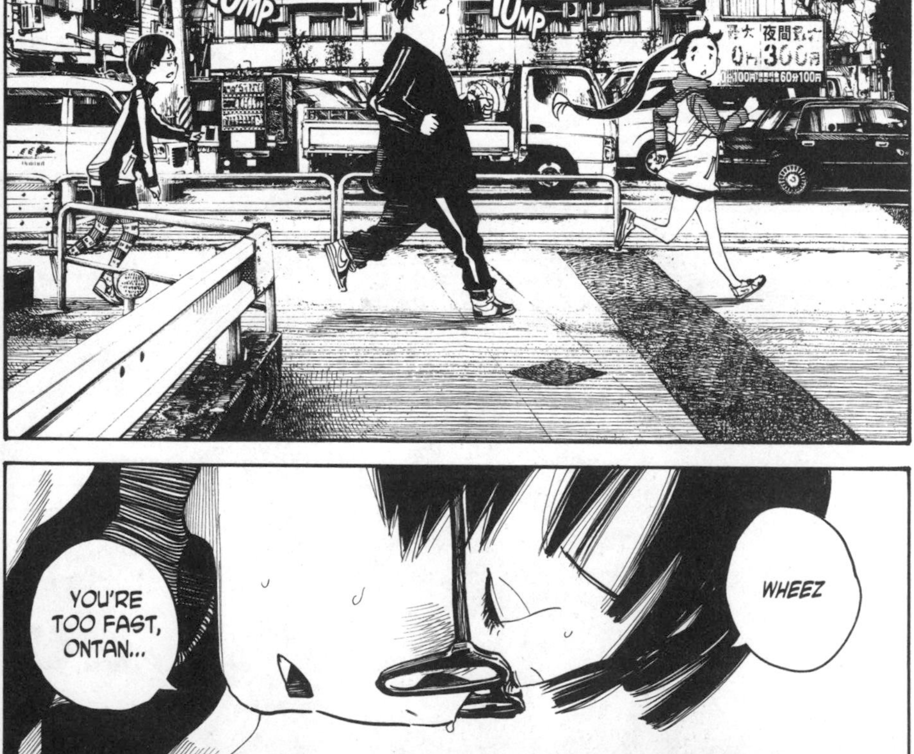
WHEEZ
YOU'RE TOO FAST, ONTAN...

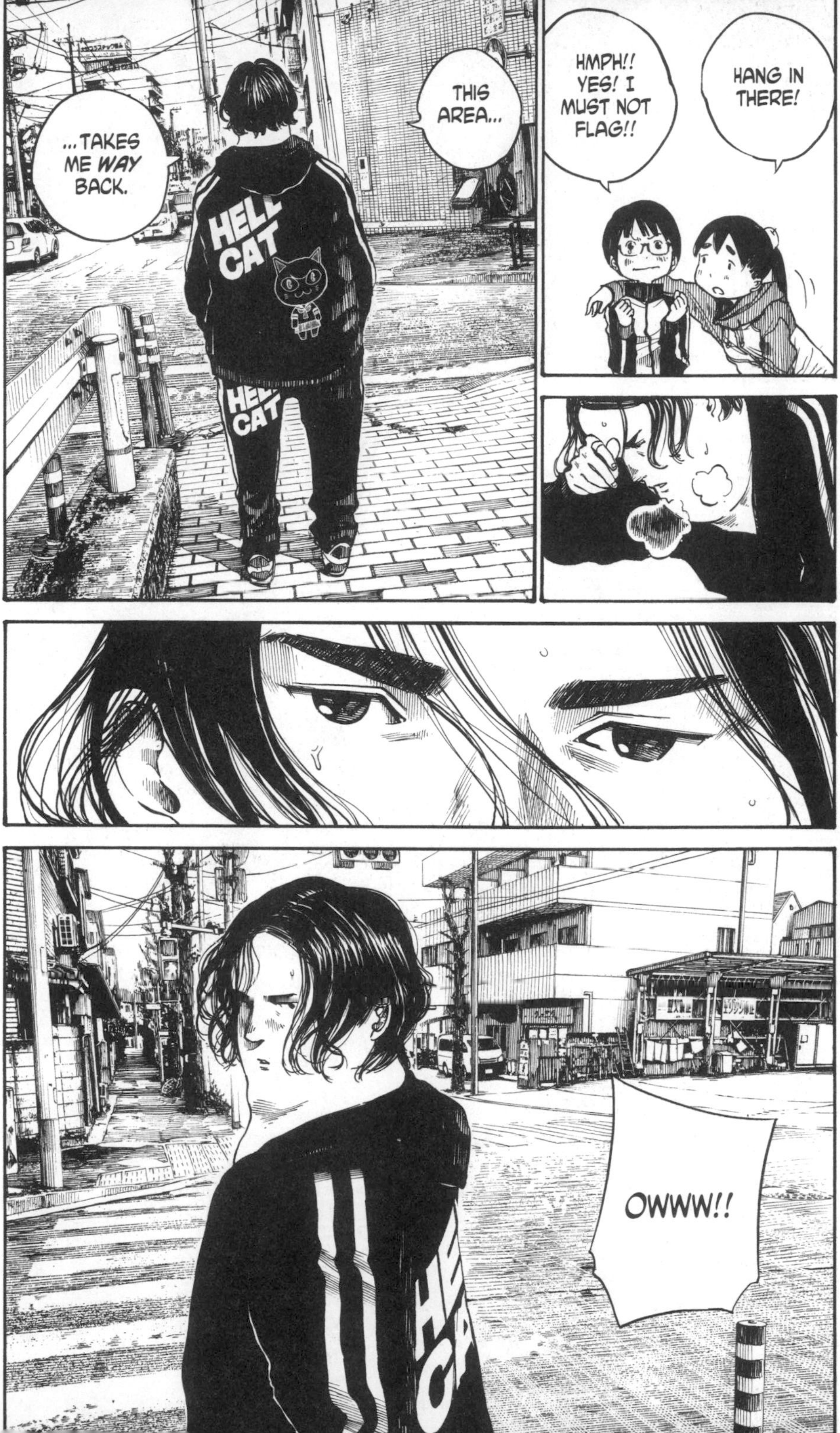
HANG IN THERE!
HMPH!! YES! I MUST NOT FLAG!!
THIS AREA...
...TAKES ME WAY BACK.
OWWW!!

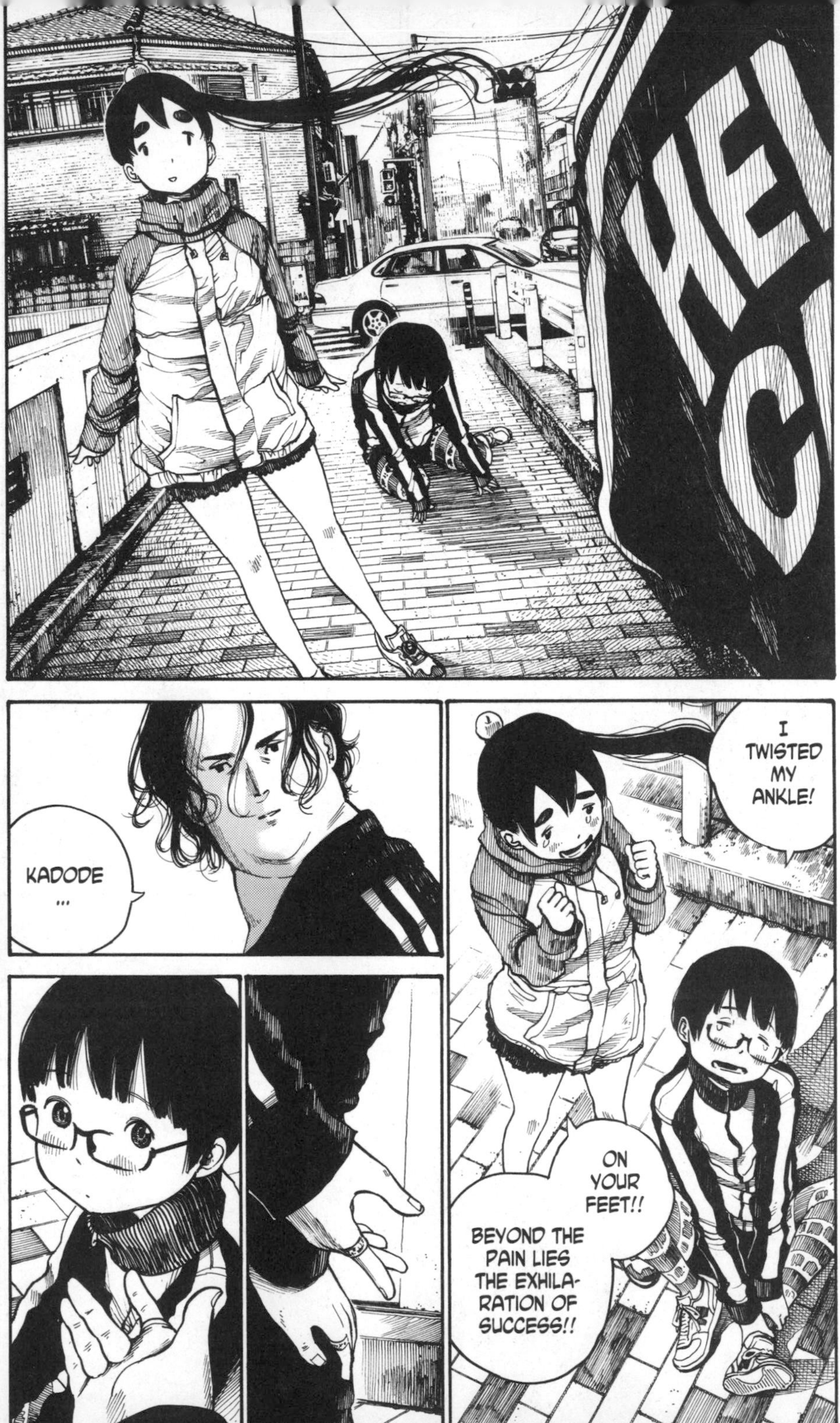
I TWISTED MY ANKLE!
ON YOUR FEET!!
BEYOND THE PAIN LIES THE EXHILA-RATION OF SUCCESS!!
KADODE ...

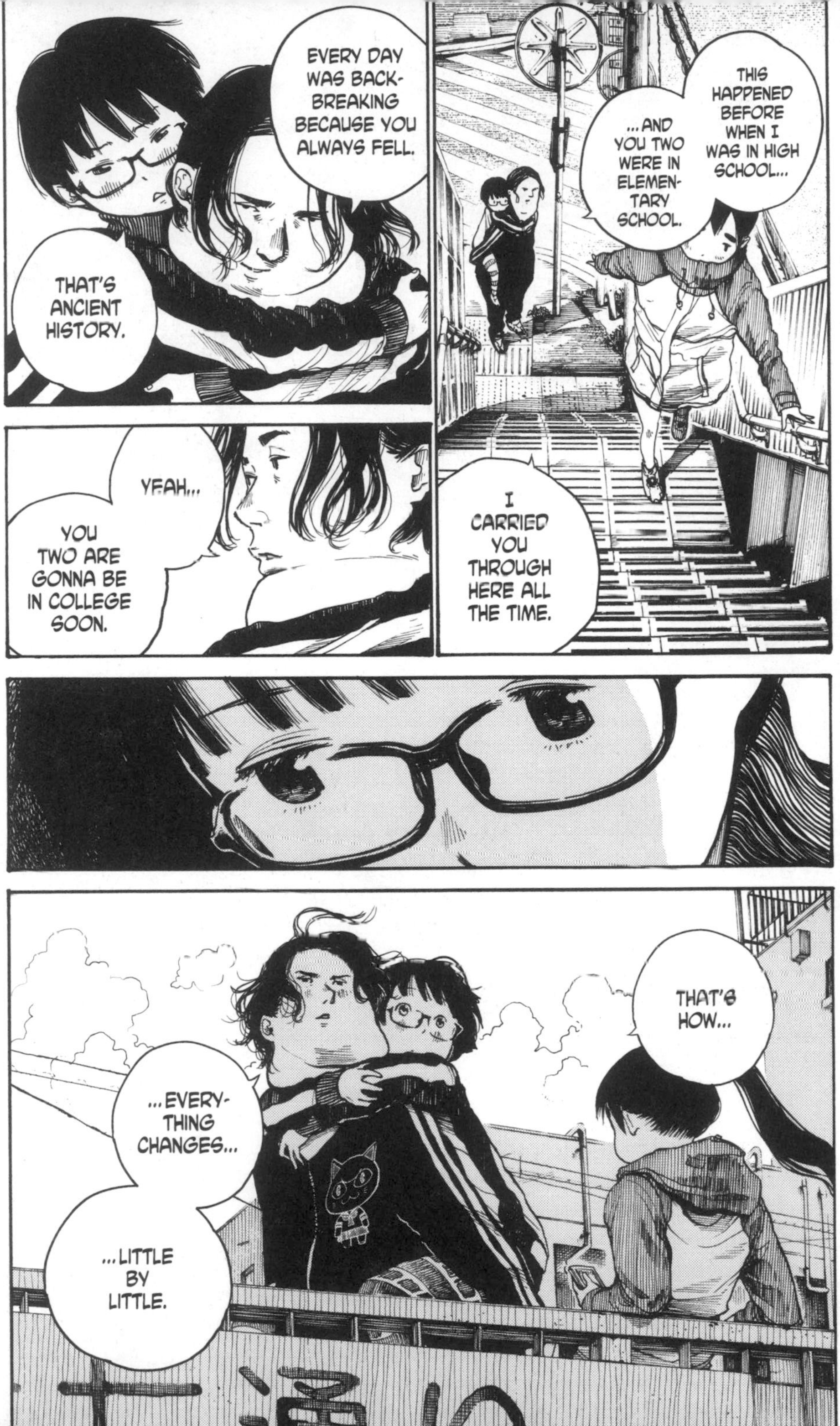
THIS HAPPENED BEFORE WHEN I WAS IN HIGH SCHOOL...
...AND YOU TWO WERE IN ELEMENTARY SCHOOL.
I CARRIED YOU THROUGH HERE ALL THE TIME.
EVERY DAY WAS BACK-BREAKING BECAUSE YOU ALWAYS FELL.
THAT'S ANCIENT HISTORY.
YEAH...
YOU TWO ARE GONNA BE IN COLLEGE SOON.
THAT'S HOW...
...EVERYTHING CHANGES...
...LITTLE BY LITTLE.

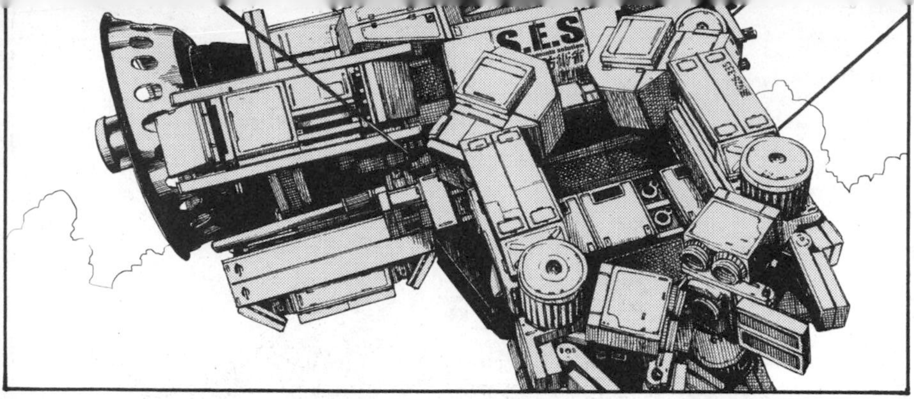
S.E.S

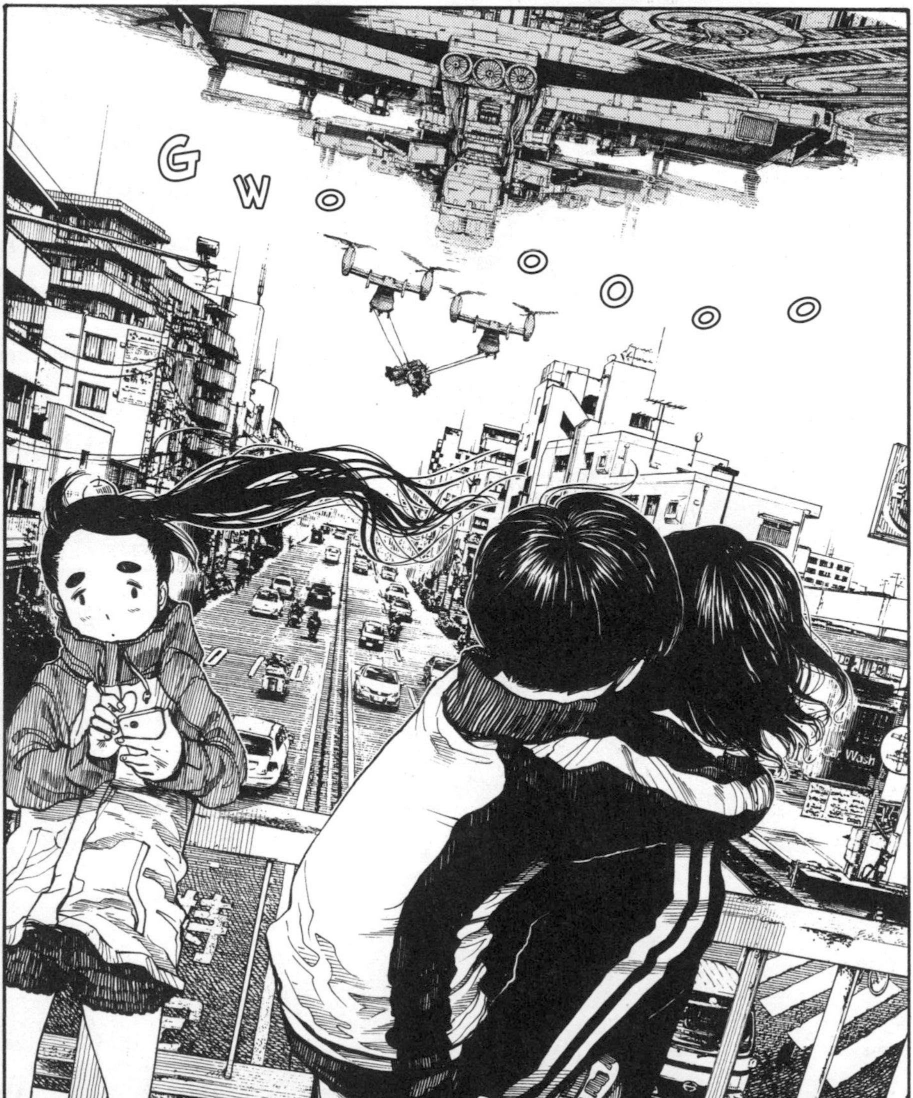
GWOOOOO
Wash

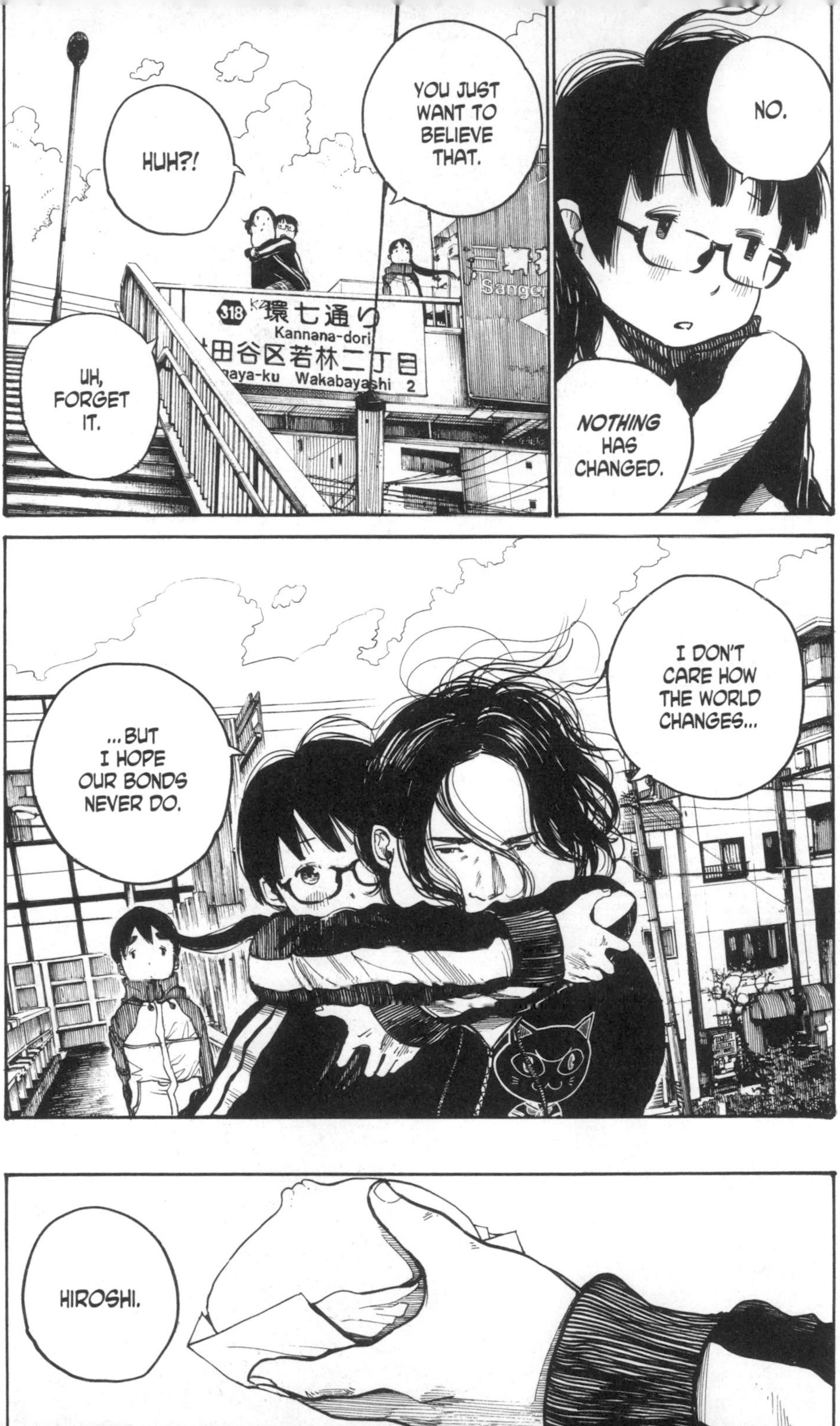
NO.
NOTHING HAS CHANGED.
YOU JUST WANT TO BELIEVE THAT.
HUH?!
Kannana-dori
Wakabayashi 2
UH, FORGET IT.
I DON'T CARE HOW THE WORLD CHANGES...
...BUT I HOPE OUR BONDS NEVER DO.
HIROSHI.

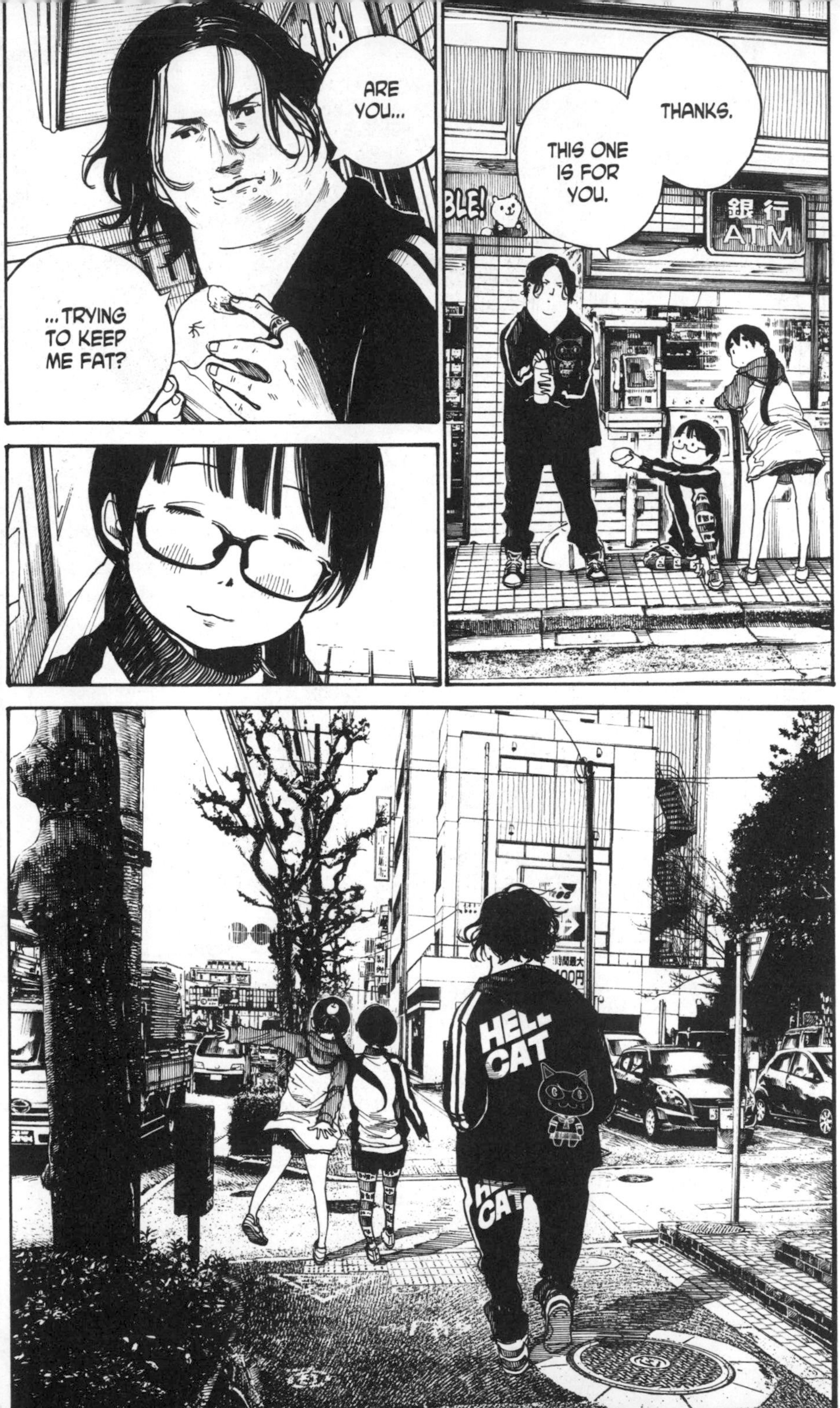
THANKS.
THIS ONE IS FOR YOU.
BLE!
銀行 ATM
ARE YOU...
...TRYING TO KEEP ME FAT?
HELL CAT

CHAPTER 8

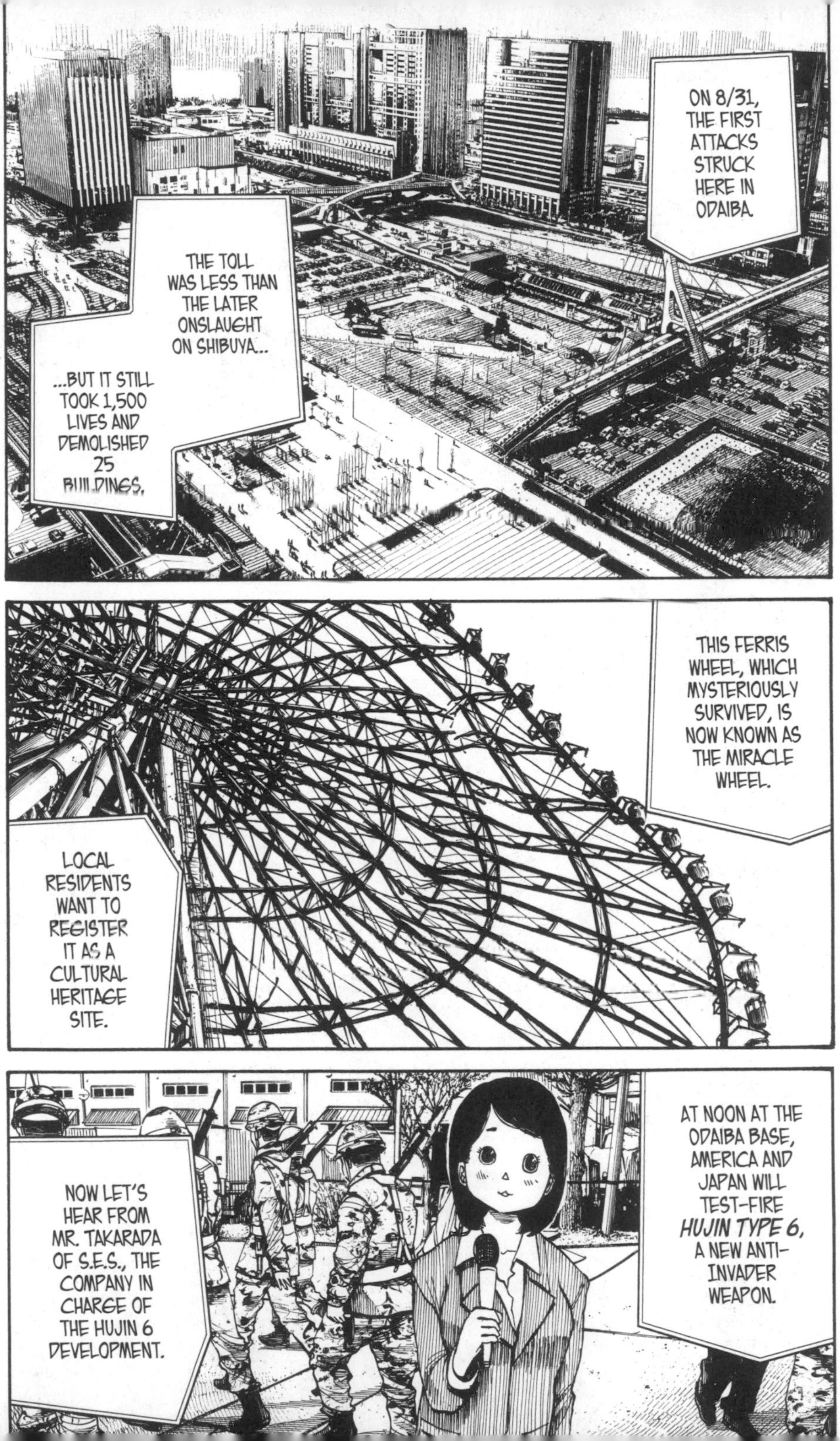
ON 8/31, THE FIRST ATTACKS STRUCK HERE IN ODAIBA.
THE TOLL WAS LESS THAN THE LATER ONSLAUGHT ON SHIBUYA...
...BUT IT STILL TOOK 1,500 LIVES AND DEMOLISHED 25 BUILDINGS.
THIS FERRIS WHEEL, WHICH MYSTERIOUSLY SURVIVED, IS NOW KNOWN AS THE MIRACLE WHEEL.
LOCAL RESIDENTS WANT TO REGISTER IT AS A CULTURAL HERITAGE SITE.
AT NOON AT THE ODAIBA BASE, AMERICA AND JAPAN WILL TEST-FIRE *HUJIN TYPE 6*, A NEW ANTI-INVADER WEAPON.
NOW LET'S HEAR FROM MR. TAKARADA OF S.E.S., THE COMPANY IN CHARGE OF THE HUJIN 6 DEVELOPMENT.

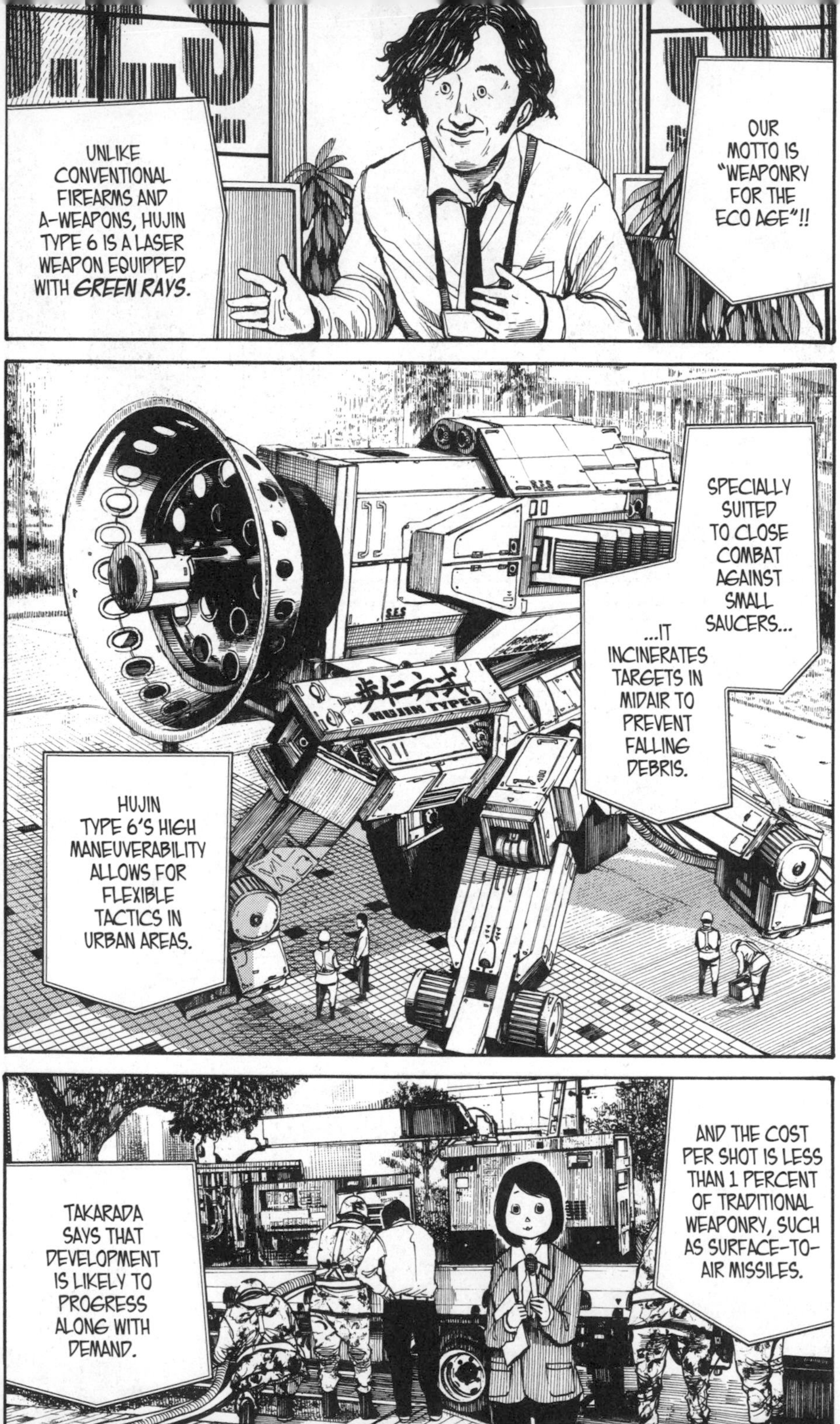
OUR MOTTO IS "WEAPONRY FOR THE ECO AGE"!!
UNLIKE CONVENTIONAL FIREARMS AND A-WEAPONS, HUJIN TYPE 6 IS A LASER WEAPON EQUIPPED WITH *GREEN RAYS*.
SPECIALLY SUITED TO CLOSE COMBAT AGAINST SMALL SAUCERS...
...IT INCINERATES TARGETS IN MIDAIR TO PREVENT FALLING DEBRIS.
HUJIN TYPE 6'S HIGH MANEUVERABILITY ALLOWS FOR FLEXIBLE TACTICS IN URBAN AREAS.
AND THE COST PER SHOT IS LESS THAN 1 PERCENT OF TRADITIONAL WEAPONRY, SUCH AS SURFACE-TO-AIR MISSILES.
TAKARADA SAYS THAT DEVELOPMENT IS LIKELY TO PROGRESS ALONG WITH DEMAND.

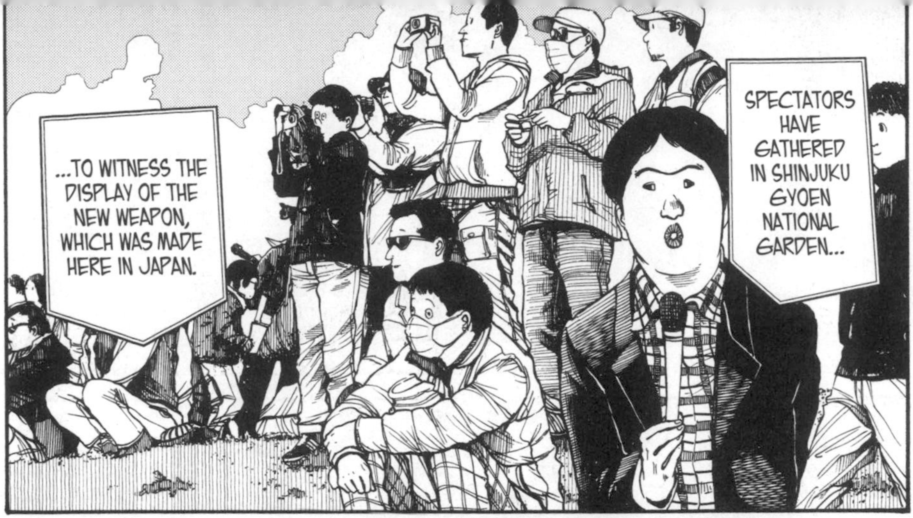
SPECTATORS HAVE GATHERED IN SHINJUKU GYOEN NATIONAL GARDEN...
...TO WITNESS THE DISPLAY OF THE NEW WEAPON, WHICH WAS MADE HERE IN JAPAN.

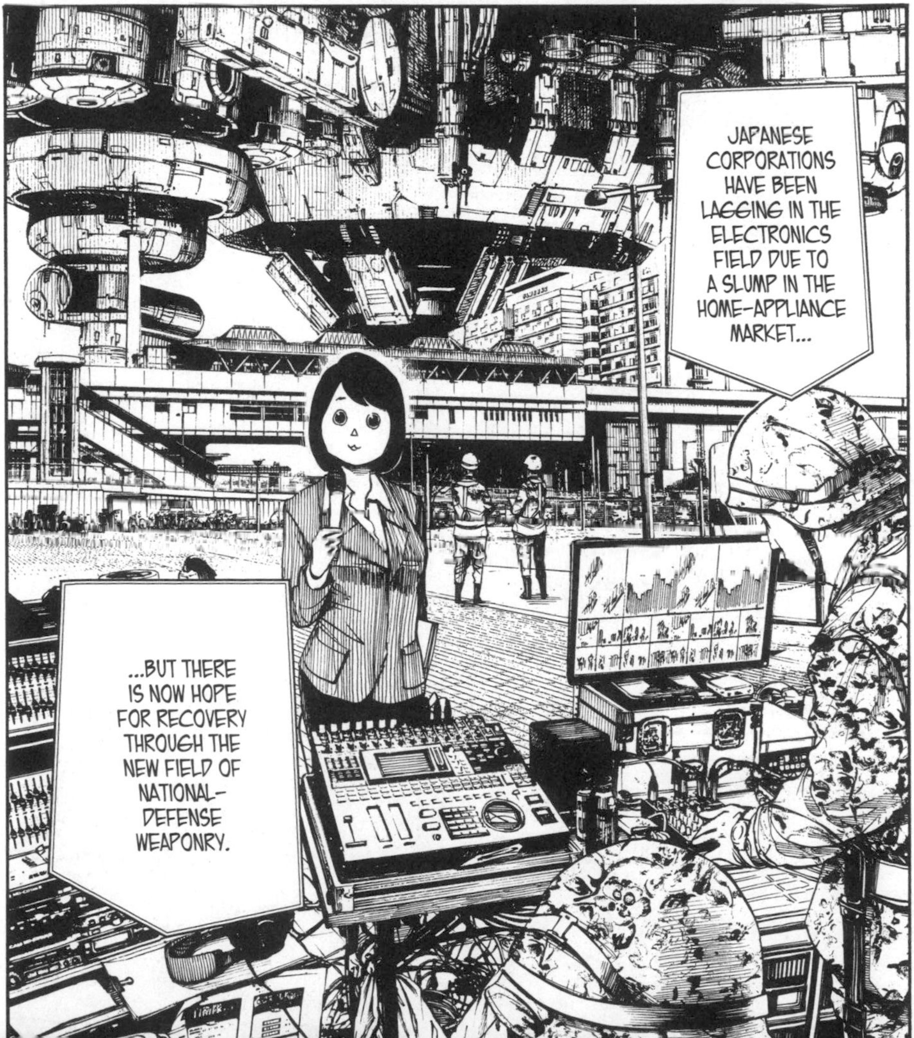
JAPANESE CORPORATIONS HAVE BEEN LAGGING IN THE ELECTRONICS FIELD DUE TO A SLUMP IN THE HOME-APPLIANCE MARKET...
...BUT THERE IS NOW HOPE FOR RECOVERY THROUGH THE NEW FIELD OF NATIONAL-DEFENSE WEAPONRY.

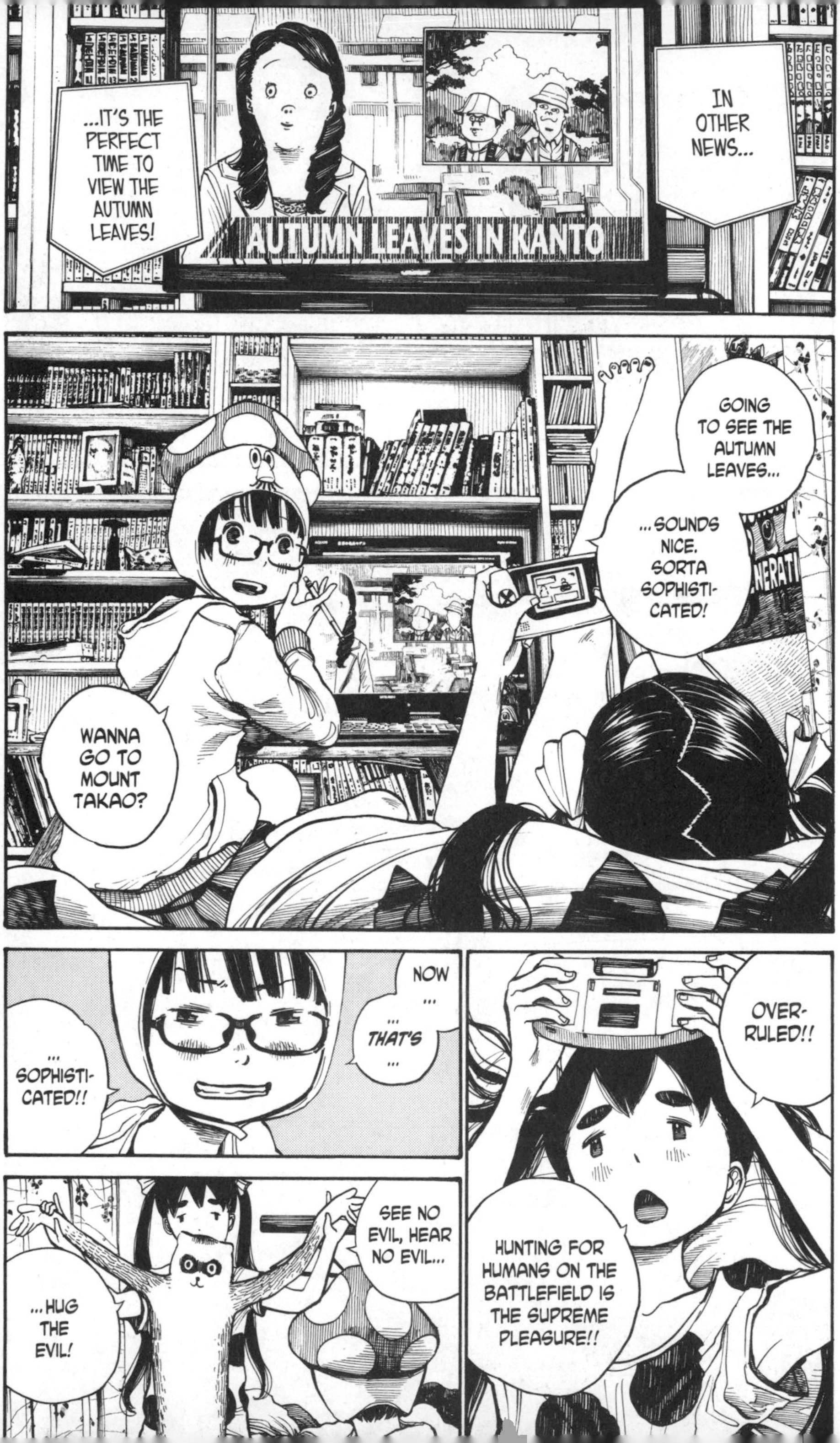
IN OTHER NEWS...
...IT'S THE PERFECT TIME TO VIEW THE AUTUMN LEAVES!
AUTUMN LEAVES IN KANTO
GOING TO SEE THE AUTUMN LEAVES...
...SOUNDS NICE. SORTA SOPHISTI-CATED!
WANNA GO TO MOUNT TAKAO?
OVER-RULED!!
HUNTING FOR HUMANS ON THE BATTLEFIELD IS THE SUPREME PLEASURE!!
NOW ...
... THAT'S ...
... SOPHISTI-CATED!!
SEE NO EVIL, HEAR NO EVIL...
...HUG THE EVIL!

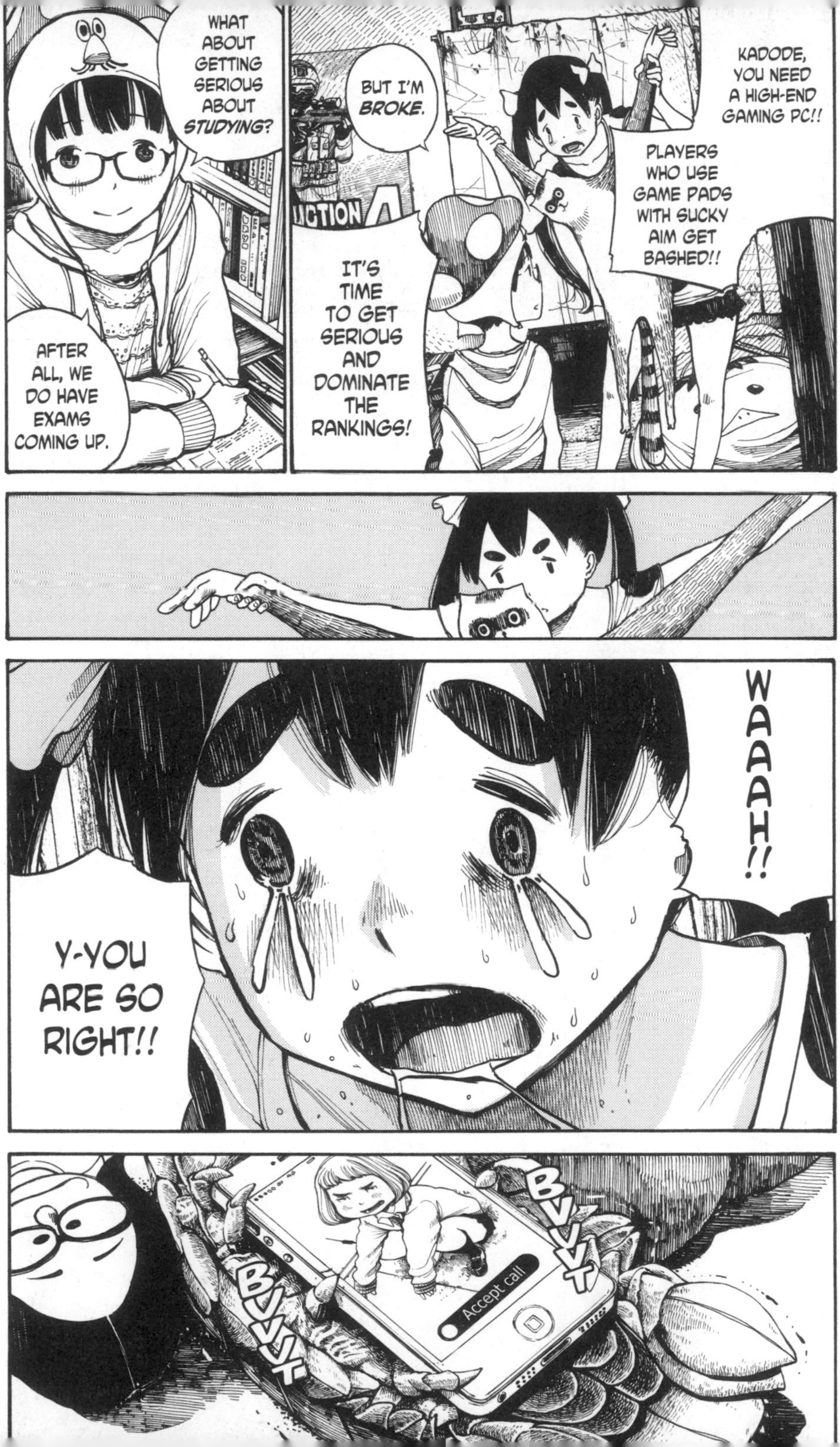
KADODE, YOU NEED A HIGH-END GAMING PC!!
PLAYERS WHO USE GAME PADS WITH SUCKY AIM GET BASHED!!
BUT I'M *BROKE*.
IT'S TIME TO GET SERIOUS AND DOMINATE THE RANKINGS!
WHAT ABOUT GETTING SERIOUS ABOUT *STUDYING*?
AFTER ALL, WE DO HAVE EXAMS COMING UP.
WAAAAH!!
Y-YOU ARE SO RIGHT!!
BVVVT
Accept call
BVVVT
BVVVT

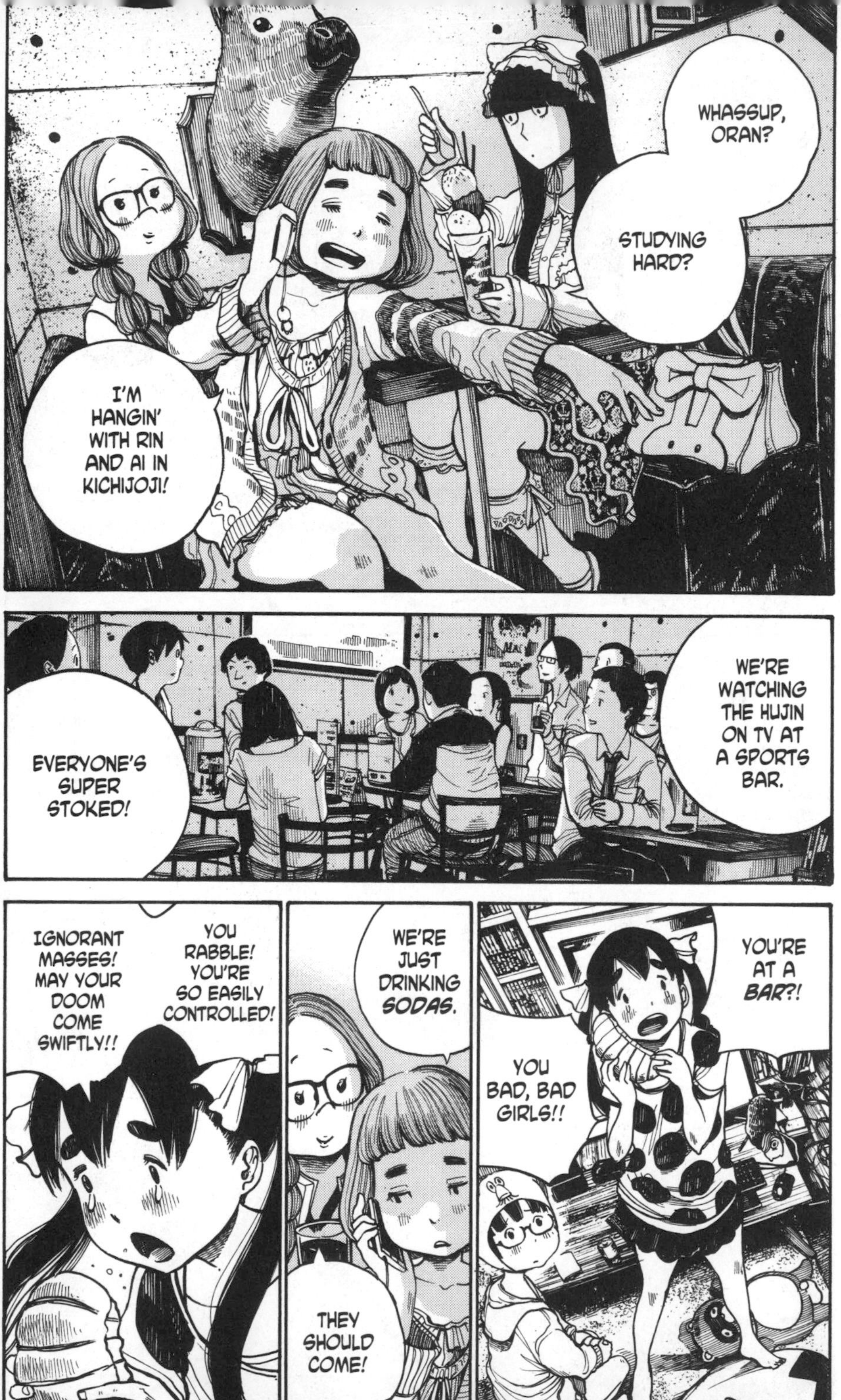
WHASSUP, ORAN?
STUDYING HARD?
I'M HANGIN' WITH RIN AND AI IN KICHIJOJI!
WE'RE WATCHING THE HUJIN ON TV AT A SPORTS BAR.
EVERYONE'S SUPER STOKED!
YOU'RE AT A *BAR*?!
YOU BAD, BAD GIRLS!!
WE'RE JUST DRINKING *SODAS*.
THEY SHOULD COME!
YOU RABBLE! YOU'RE SO EASILY CONTROLLED!
IGNORANT MASSES! MAY YOUR DOOM COME SWIFTLY!!

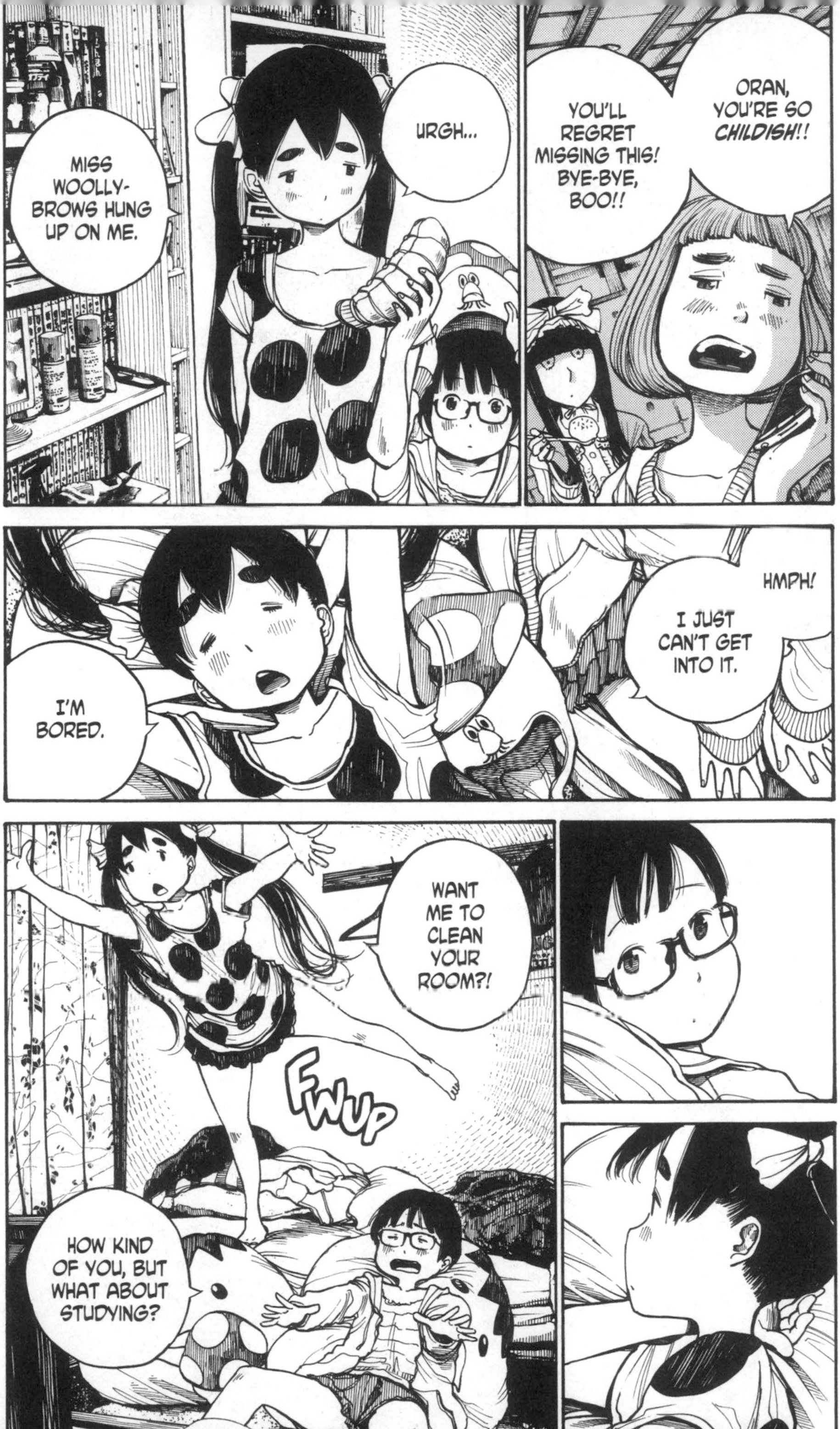
ORAN, YOU'RE SO CHILDISH!!
YOU'LL REGRET MISSING THIS! BYE-BYE, BOO!!
URGH...
MISS WOOLLY-BROWS HUNG UP ON ME.
HMPH!
I JUST CAN'T GET INTO IT.
I'M BORED.
WANT ME TO CLEAN YOUR ROOM?!
FWUP
HOW KIND OF YOU, BUT WHAT ABOUT STUDYING?

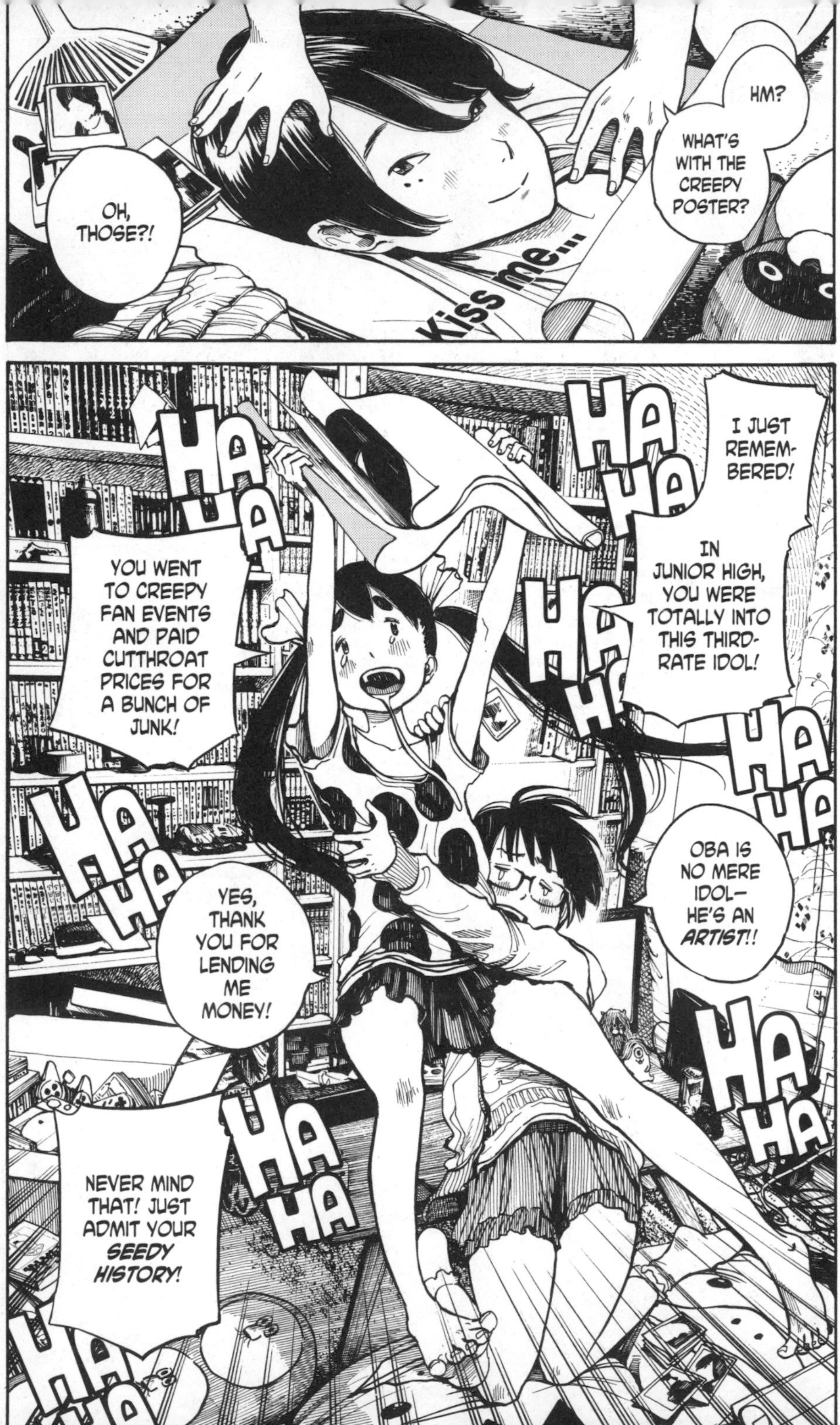
HM?
WHAT'S WITH THE CREEPY POSTER?
Kiss me...
OH, THOSE?!
HA HA HA
I JUST REMEMBERED!
IN JUNIOR HIGH, YOU WERE TOTALLY INTO THIS THIRD-RATE IDOL!
HA HA HA
HA HA HA
YOU WENT TO CREEPY FAN EVENTS AND PAID CUTTHROAT PRICES FOR A BUNCH OF JUNK!
OBA IS NO MERE IDOL— HE'S AN *ARTIST*!!
YES, THANK YOU FOR LENDING ME MONEY!
HA HA HA
HA HA HA
HA HA
NEVER MIND THAT! JUST ADMIT YOUR *SEEDY HISTORY*!
HA HA

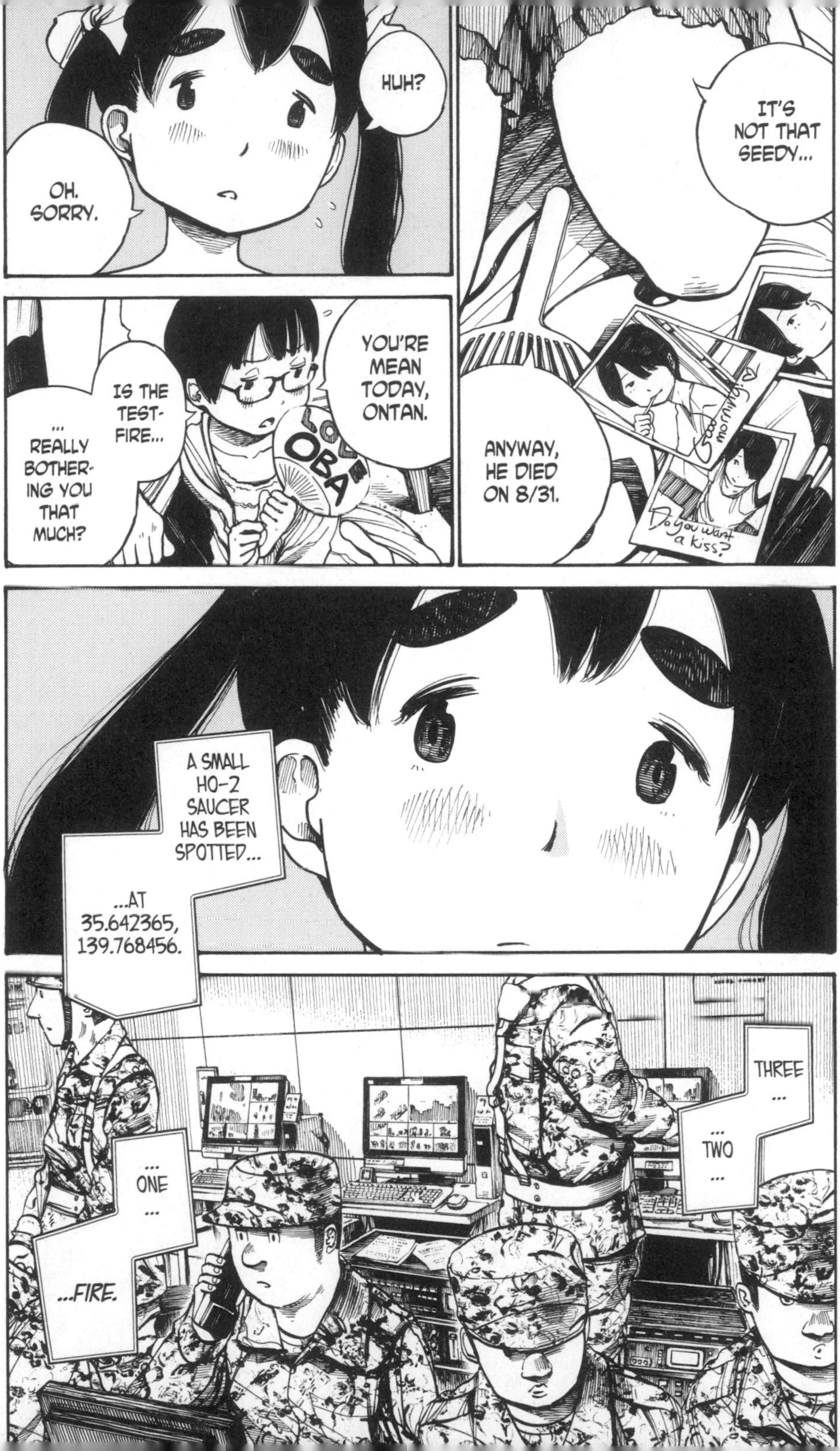
IT'S NOT THAT SEEDY...
Good morning
Do you want a kiss?
ANYWAY, HE DIED ON 8/31.
HUH?
OH. SORRY.
YOU'RE MEAN TODAY, ONTAN.
IS THE TEST-FIRE...
...REALLY BOTHERING YOU THAT MUCH?
OBA
A SMALL HO-2 SAUCER HAS BEEN SPOTTED...
...AT 35.642365, 139.768456.
THREE...
...TWO...
...ONE...
...FIRE.

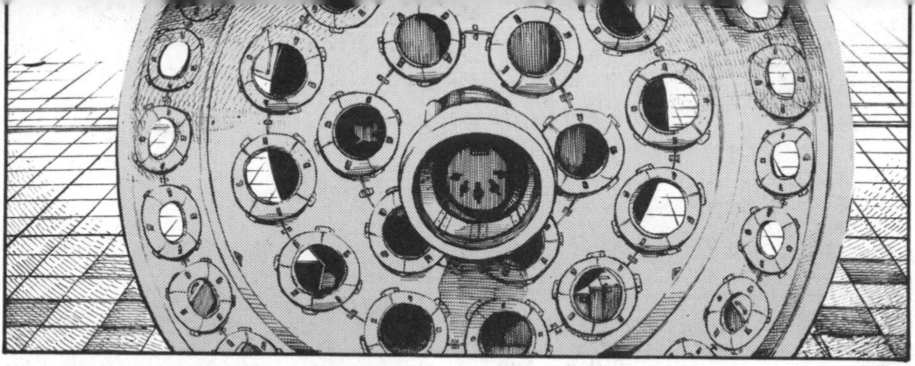

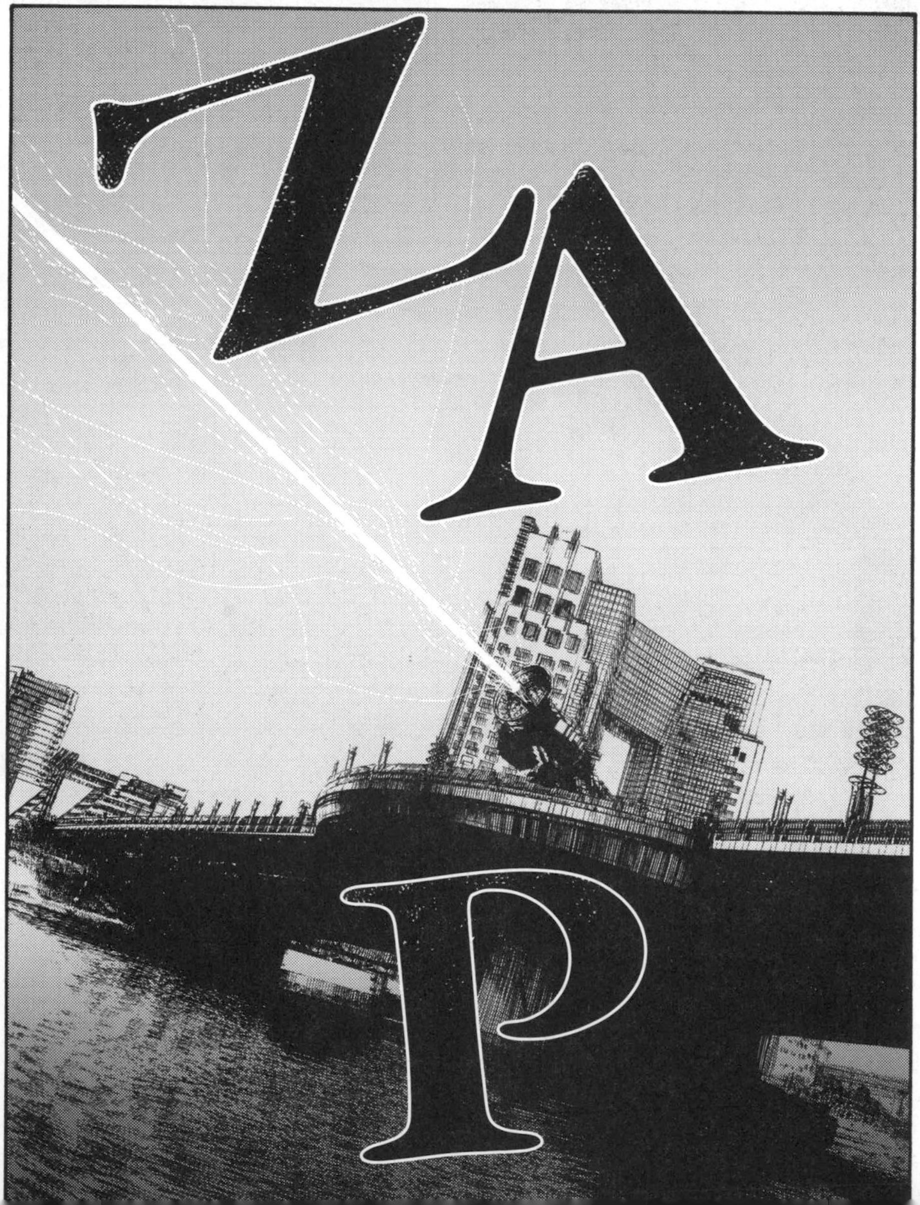
ZAP

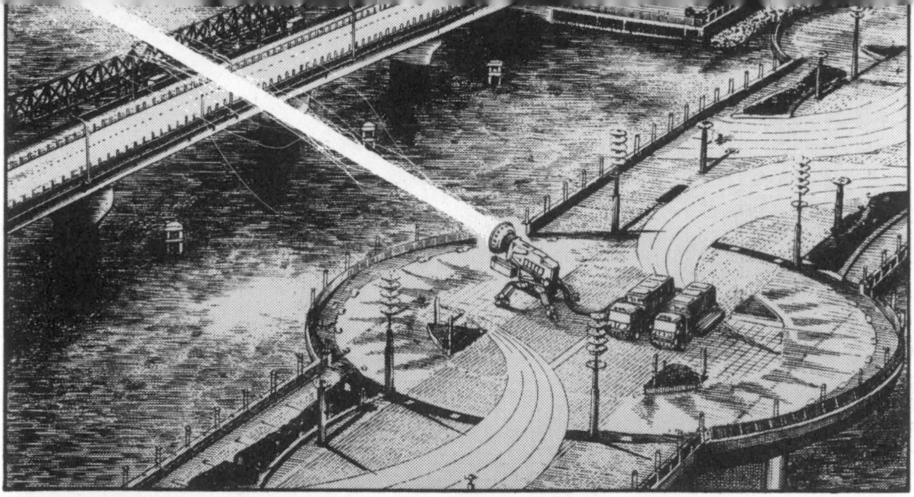
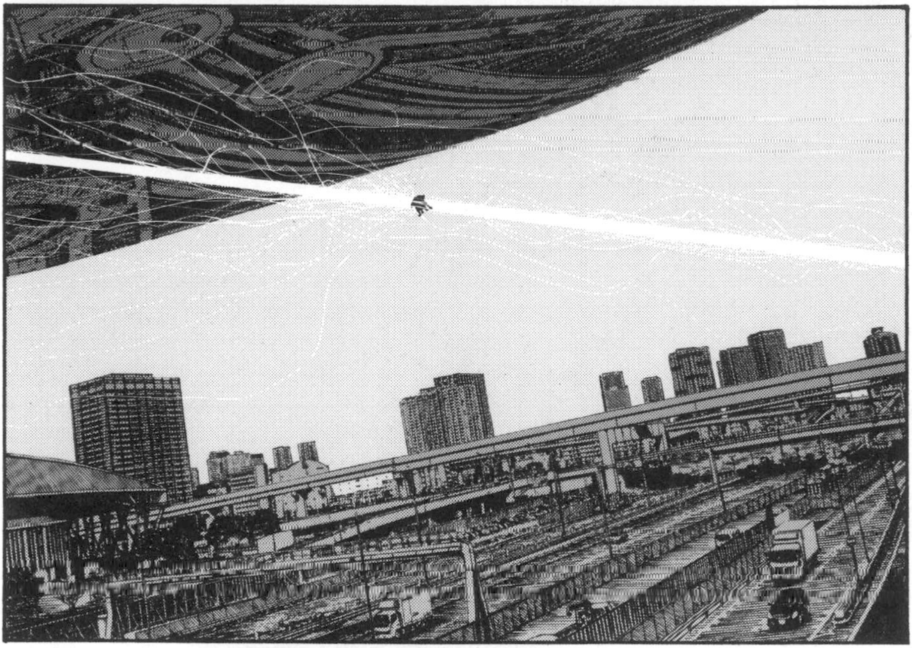
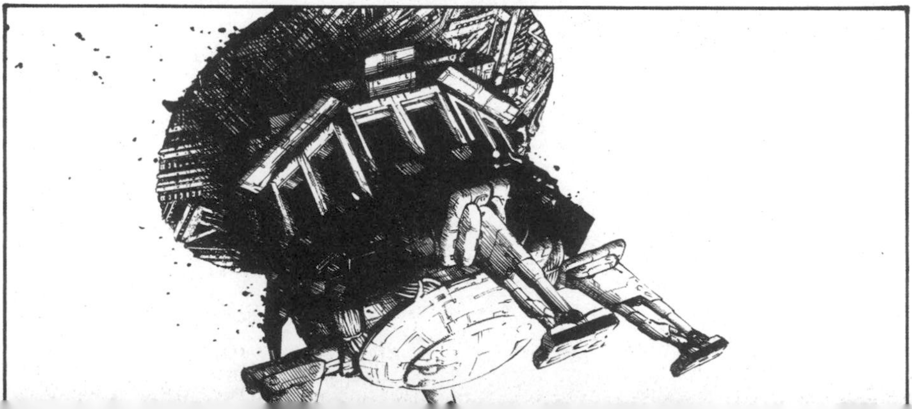

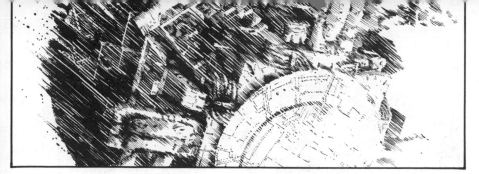

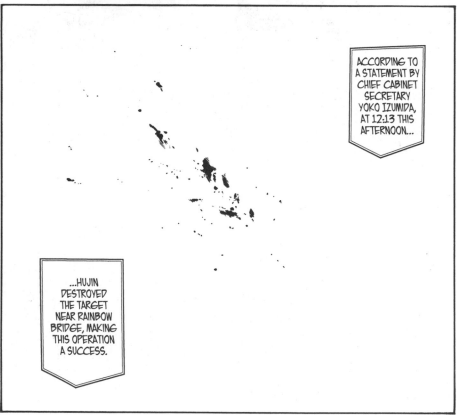

ACCORDING TO A STATEMENT BY CHIEF CABINET SECRETARY YOKO IZUMIDA, AT 12:13 THIS AFTERNOON...
...HUJIN DESTROYED THE TARGET NEAR RAINBOW BRIDGE, MAKING THIS OPERATION A SUCCESS.
JAPAN'S CLEAN WEAPON FOR URBAN WARFARE IS RECEIVING PRAISE AT HOME AND ABROAD.
A ROWDY CROWD OF YOUNG PEOPLE CELEBRATING AROUND SHINJUKU STATION IS REQUIRING POLICE TO...

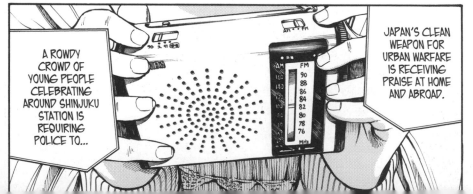

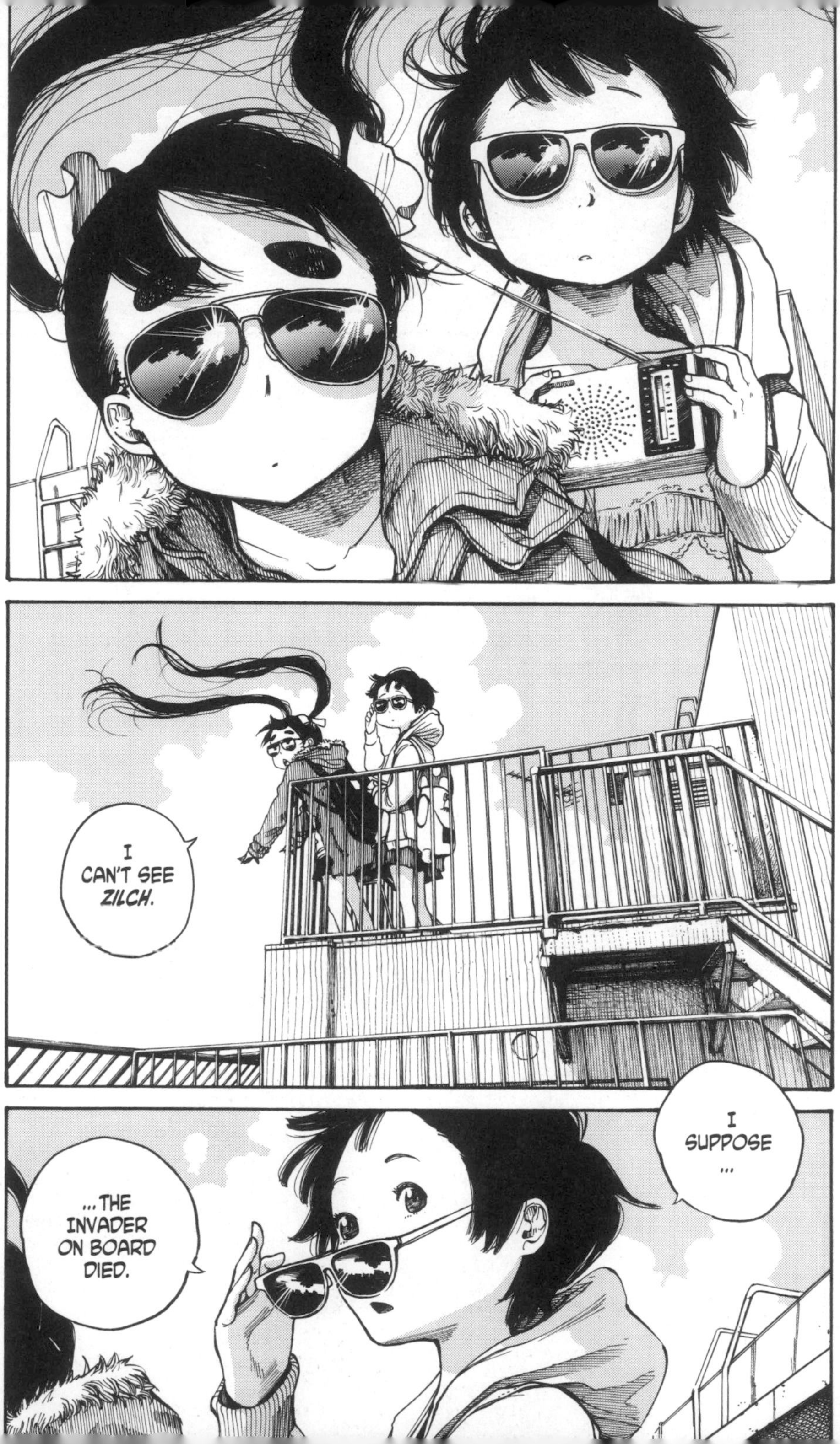

I CAN'T SEE ZILCH.
I SUPPOSE ...
...THE INVADER ON BOARD DIED.

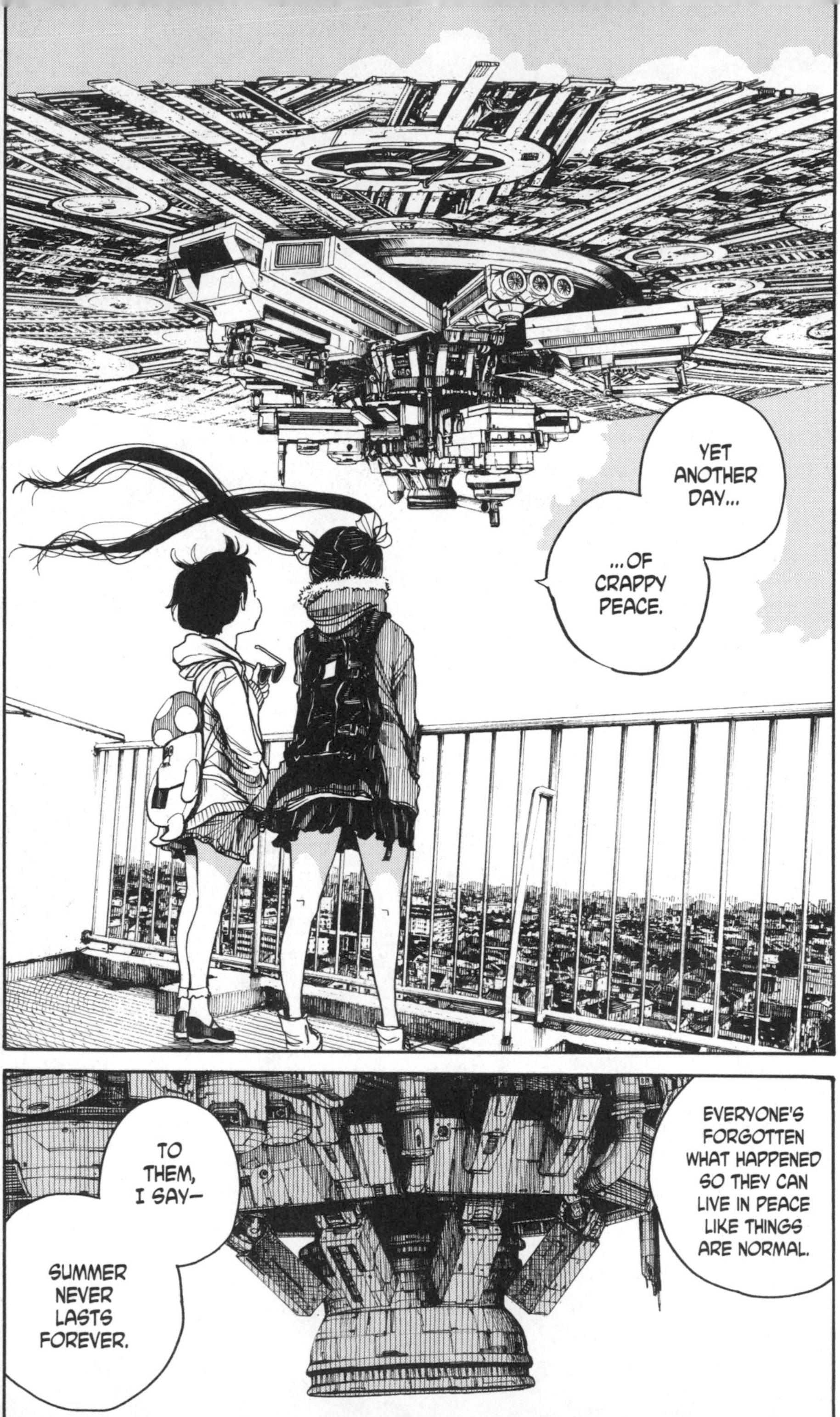
YET ANOTHER DAY...
...OF CRAPPY PEACE.
EVERYONE'S FORGOTTEN WHAT HAPPENED SO THEY CAN LIVE IN PEACE LIKE THINGS ARE NORMAL.
TO THEM, I SAY—
SUMMER NEVER LASTS FOREVER.

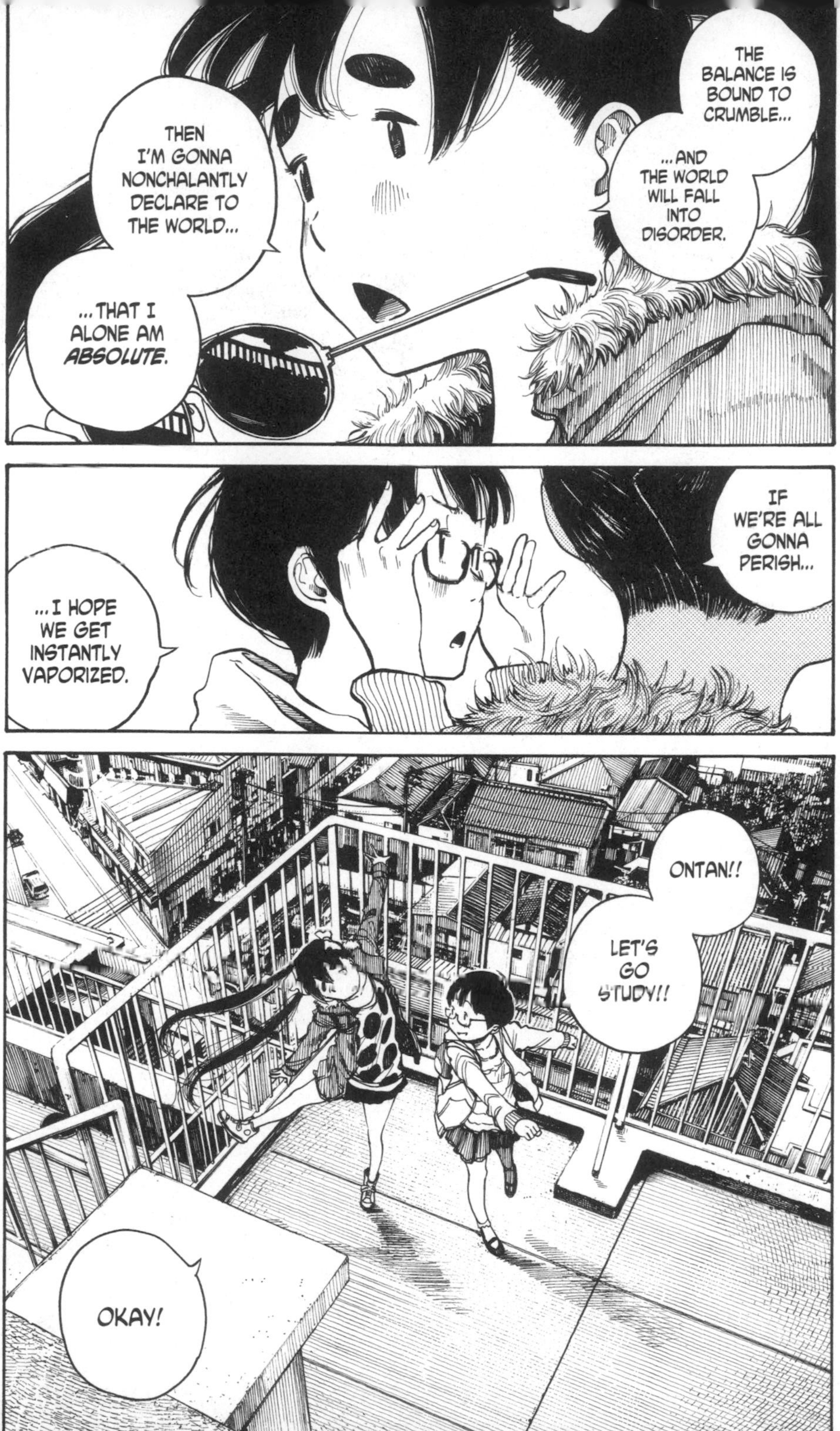
THE BALANCE IS BOUND TO CRUMBLE...
...AND THE WORLD WILL FALL INTO DISORDER.
THEN I'M GONNA NONCHALANTLY DECLARE TO THE WORLD...
...THAT I ALONE AM *ABSOLUTE*.
IF WE'RE ALL GONNA PERISH...
...I HOPE WE GET INSTANTLY VAPORIZED.
ONTAN!!
LET'S GO STUDY!!
OKAY!

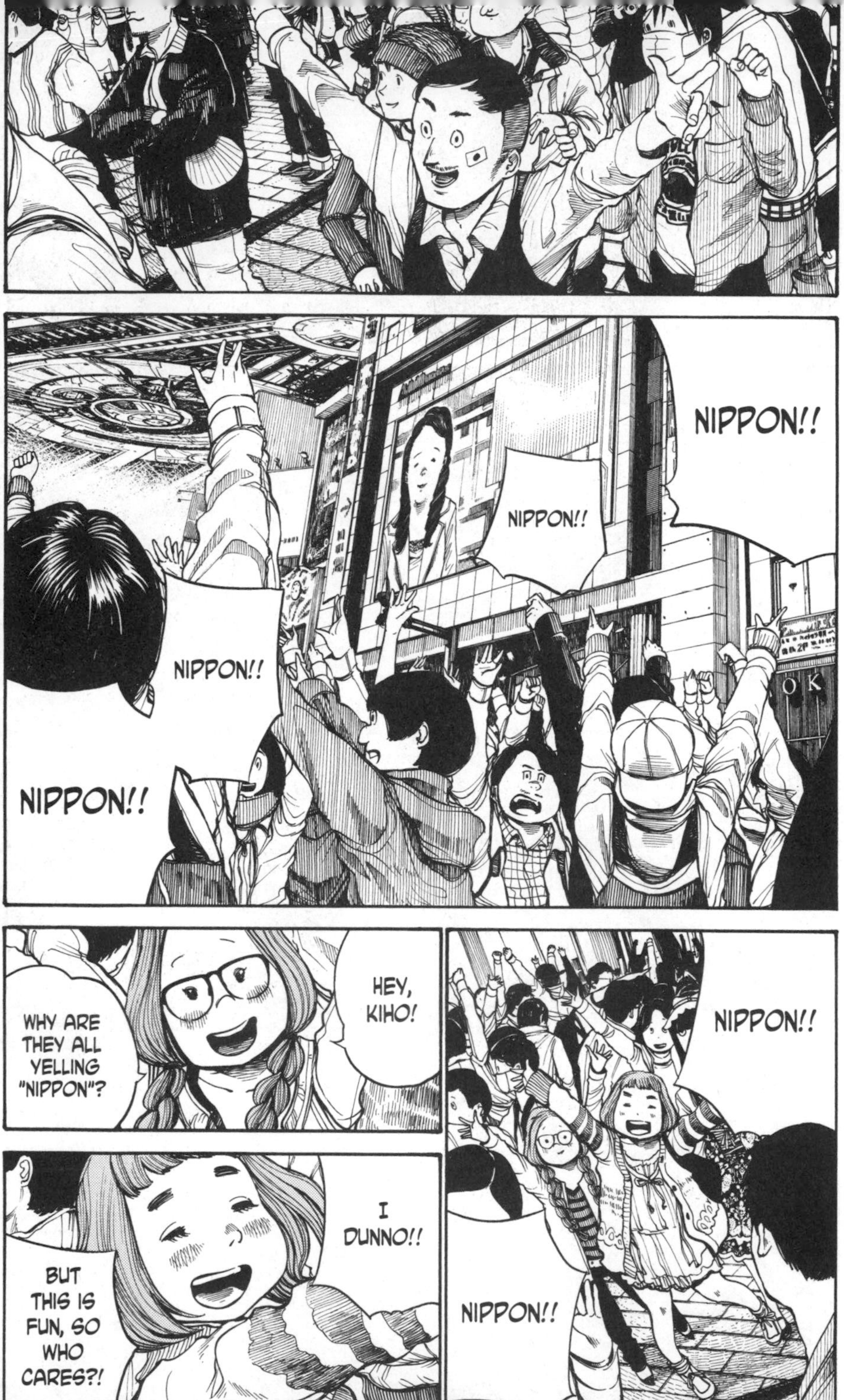
NIPPON!!
NIPPON!!
NIPPON!!
NIPPON!!
NIPPON!!
NIPPON!!
HEY, KIHO!
WHY ARE THEY ALL YELLING "NIPPON"?
I DUNNO!!
BUT THIS IS FUN, SO WHO CARES?!

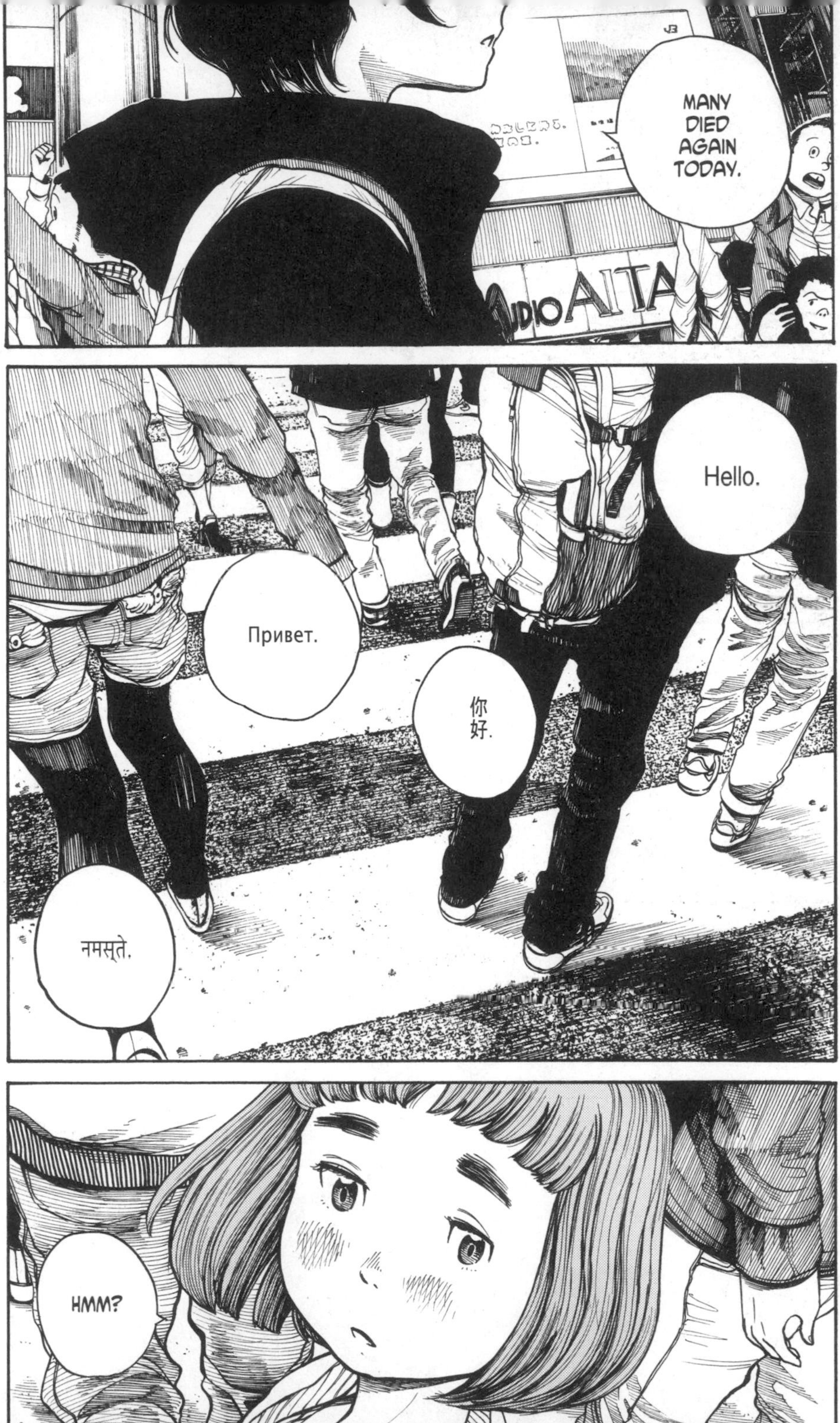
MANY DIED AGAIN TODAY.
AUDIO AITA
Hello.
Привет.
你好.
नमस्ते.
HMM?

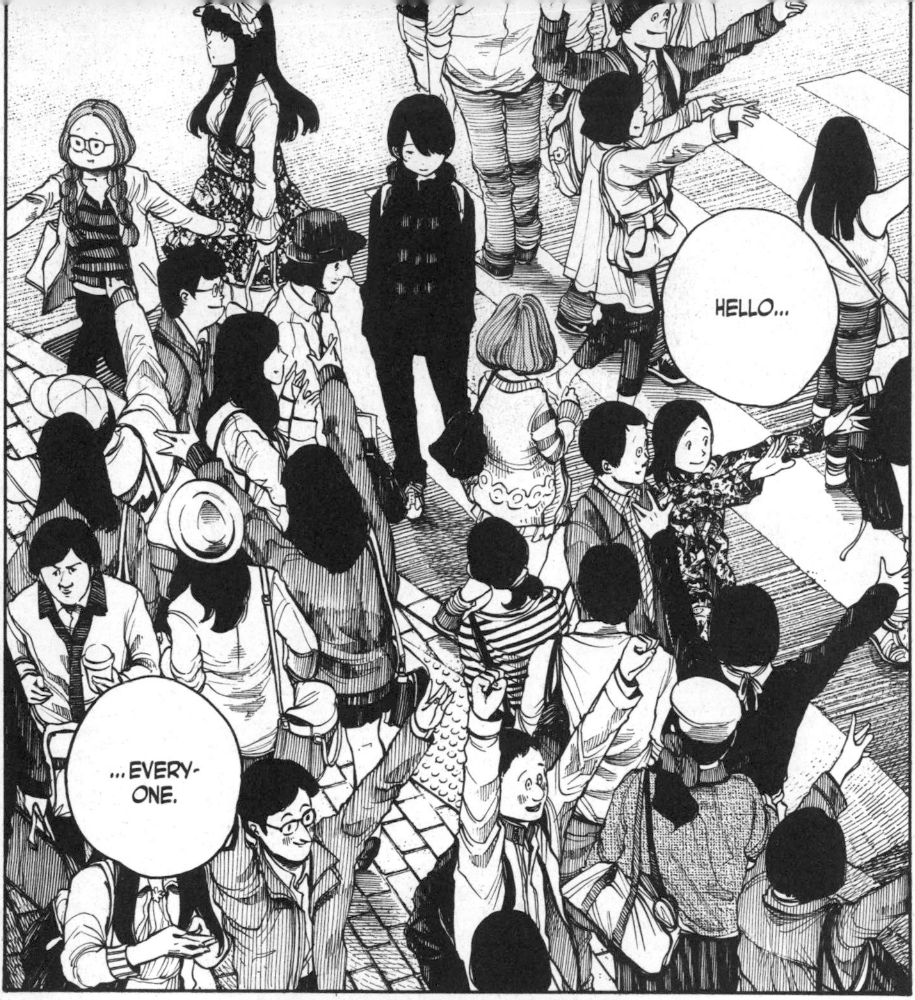
HELLO...
...EVERY-ONE.

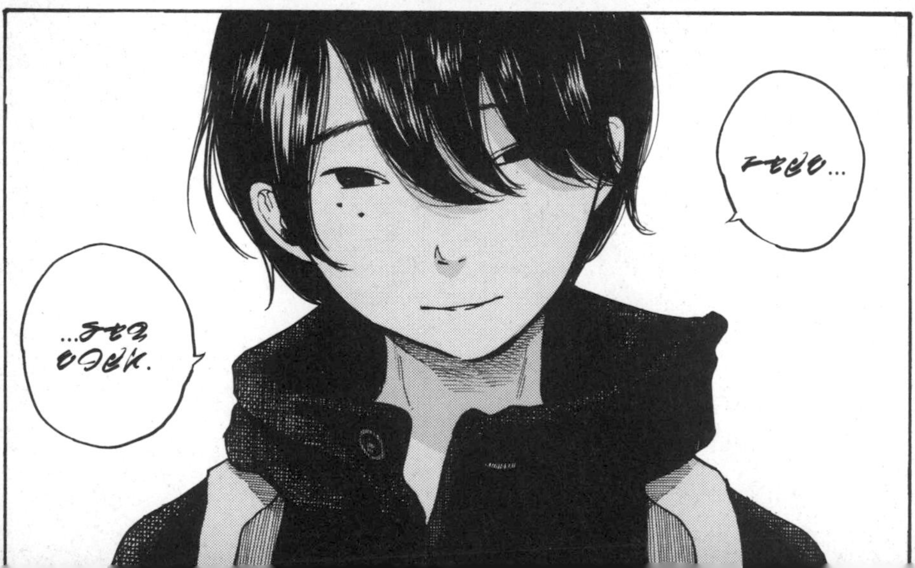

Dead Dead Demon's Dededede Destruction 1 - The End

Dead Dead Demon's
Dededede Destruction Volume 1
Inio Asano

Background Assistants: Satsuki Sato
                           Ran Atsumori
                           Buuko

DE

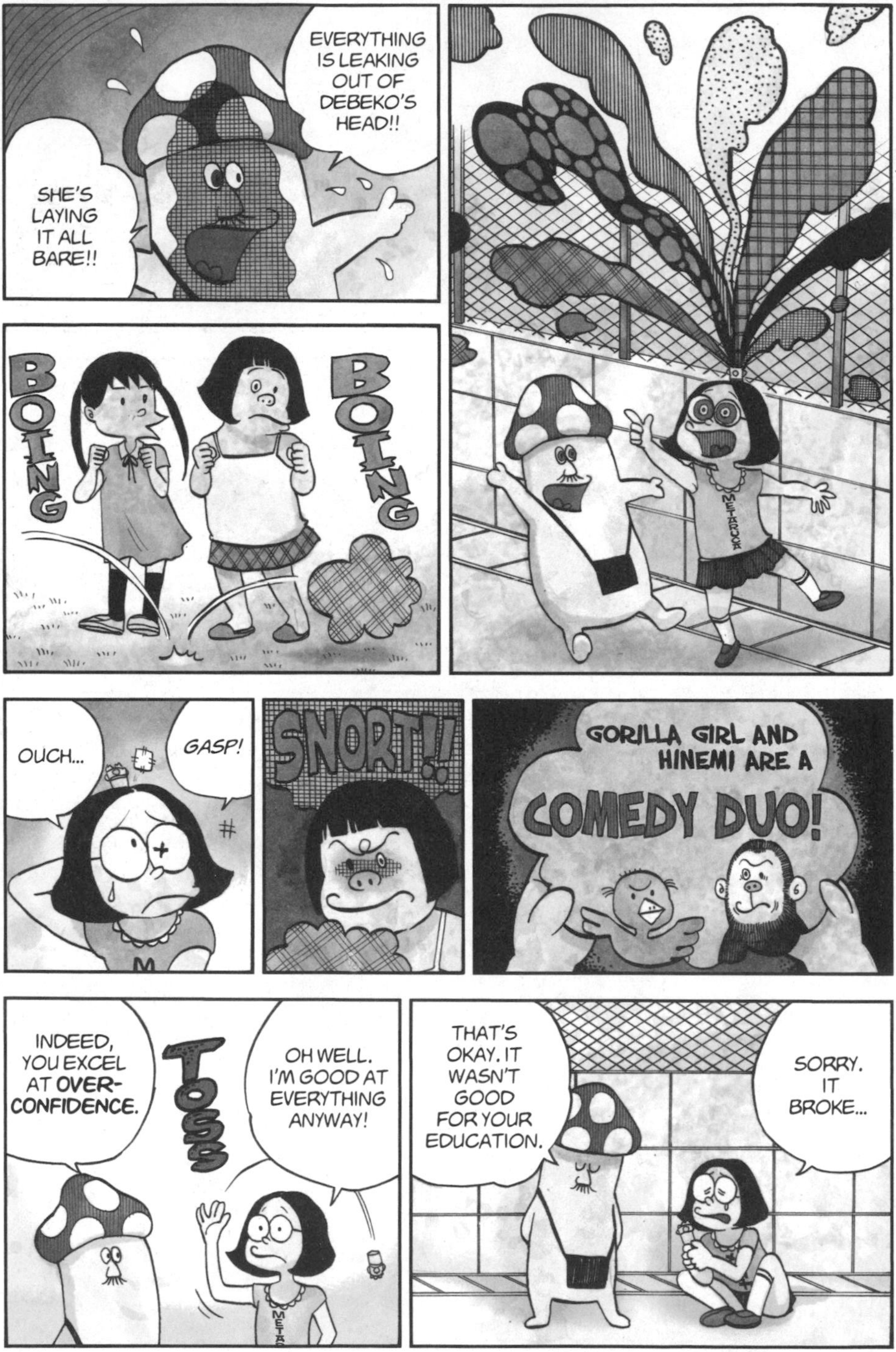
EVERYTHING IS LEAKING OUT OF DEBEKO'S HEAD!!
SHE'S LAYING IT ALL BARE!!
BOING
BOING
GORILLA GIRL AND HINEMI ARE A COMEDY DUO!
SNORT!!
GASP!
OUCH...
SORRY. IT BROKE...
THAT'S OKAY. IT WASN'T GOOD FOR YOUR EDUCATION.
OH WELL. I'M GOOD AT EVERYTHING ANYWAY!
TOSS
INDEED, YOU EXCEL AT **OVER-CONFIDENCE**.

☆ Volume 2 goes on sale July 2018! Look for it!

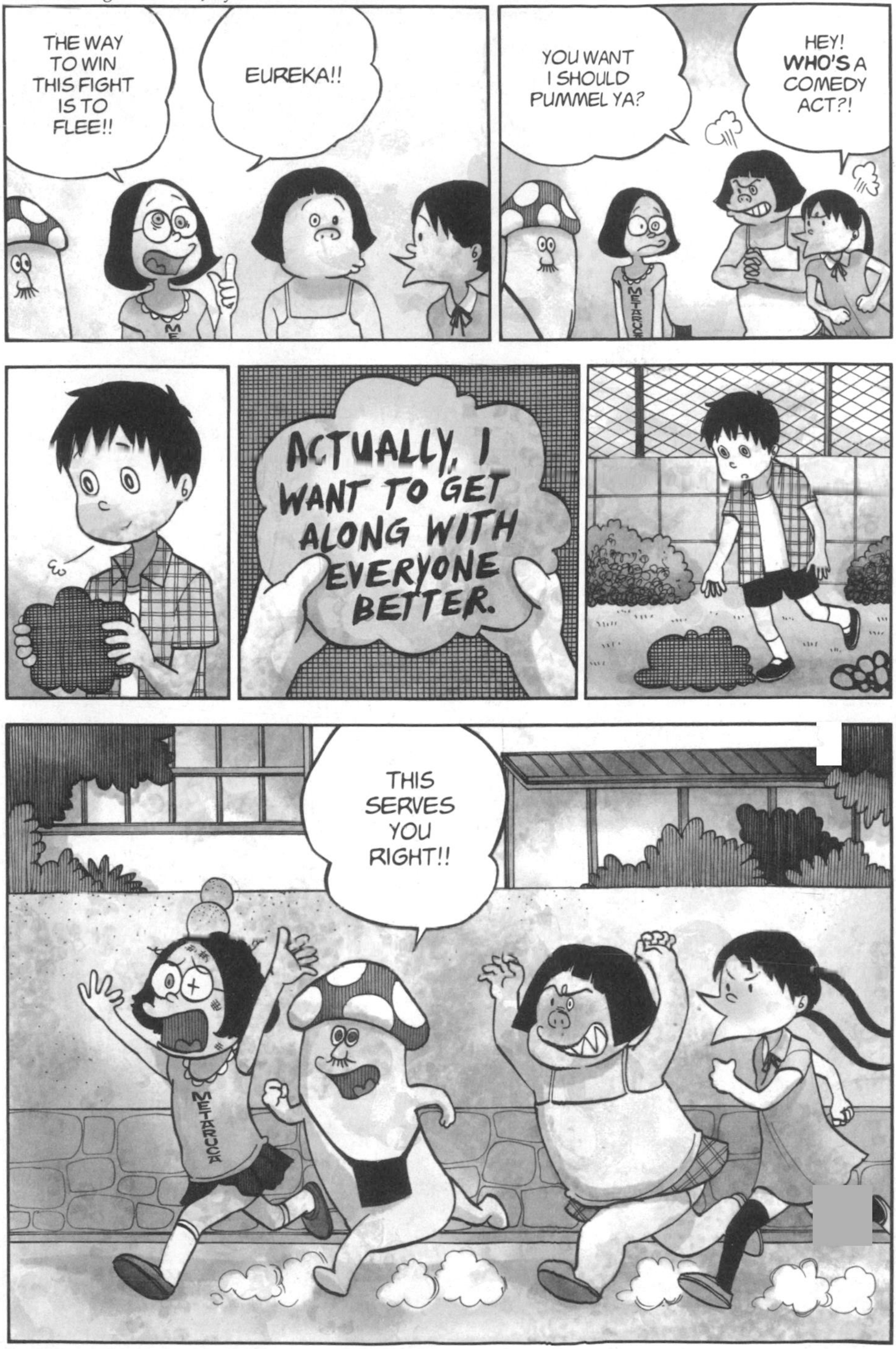
THE WAY TO WIN THIS FIGHT IS TO FLEE!!
EUREKA!!
YOU WANT I SHOULD PUMMEL YA?
HEY! **WHO'S** A COMEDY ACT?!
ACTUALLY, I WANT TO GET ALONG WITH EVERYONE BETTER.
THIS SERVES YOU RIGHT!!

DEAD DEAD DEMON'S DEDEDEDE DESTRUCTION

Volume 1
VIZ Signature Edition

Story and Art by **Inio Asano**

Translation **John Werry**
Touch-Up Art & Lettering **Annaliese Christman**
Design **Shawn Carrico**
Editor **Pancha Diaz**

DEAD DEAD DEMON'S DEDEDEDE DESTRUCTION Vol. 1
by Inio ASANO
© 2014 Inio ASANO
All rights reserved.
Original Japanese edition published by SHOGAKUKAN.
English translation rights in the United States of America,
Canada, the United Kingdom, Ireland, Australia and
New Zealand arranged with SHOGAKUKAN.

Original Cover Design **Kaoru KUROKI+Bay Bridge Studio**

Printed in Canada

Published by VIZ Media, LLC
P.O. Box 77010
San Francisco, CA 94107

10 9 8 7 6 5 4 3 2 1
First printing, April 2018

viz.com

vizsignature.com